# THE ILLUSTRATED ENCYCLOPEDIA OF

# WHALES
## AND DOLPHINS

# THE ILLUSTRATED ENCYCLOPEDIA OF

# WHALES

## AND DOLPHINS

Dr. Anthony R. Martin

and an international team of experts

PORTLAND HOUSE
New York

# A SALAMANDER BOOK

© 1990 Salamander Books Ltd., 129-137 York Way, London N7 9LG, United Kingdom.

This 1990 edition published by Portland House, a division of dilithium Press, Ltd., distributed by Crown Publishers, Inc., 225 Park Avenue South, New York, New York 10003.

Printed and bound in Singapore

ISBN 0-517-02564-7

hgfedcba

**Credits**
Scientific editor: Dr. Anthony R. Martin
In-house editor: Geoffrey Rogers
Designer: Jill Coote
Artwork design for Part One: Stuart Watkinson
Illustrators: Peter Bull, Rod Ferring, Bruce Pearson, David Thompson
Colour reproductions: Scantrans Pte. Ltd.
Filmset: SX Composing Ltd.

*Half-title page: A male humpback whale singing off Hawaii.*
*Title page: A killer whale startles a group of southern sea lions.*
*This page: Spinner dolphins travelling at speed.*
*Opposite contents page: A gray whale off Vancouver Island, Canada.*

# THE AUTHORS

**Anthony R. Martin B.Sc., Ph.D.**
Tony Martin moved to Cambridge in 1978 to join the Sea Mammal Research Unit of the UK Natural Environment Research Council, where he is currently a Senior Scientific Officer. His research interests include population dynamics, feeding, migration, stock assessment and the use of satellite-linked radio transmitters in whale and dolphin studies. Tony has carried out marine mammal research from the Arctic to the tropics, and frequently broadcasts on many cetacean-related topics. He has been a UK delegate to the Scientific Committee of the International Whaling Commission since 1979 and gained his doctorate in 1986 with a thesis on the biology of large whales.

**Gregory P. Donovan B.Sc.**
Greg Donovan has worked for the International Whaling Commission since 1977, as the editor of its scientific publications, after studying zoology and, somewhat surprisingly, specializing in ultrasound production in rodents. He is a member of the International Whaling Commission Scientific Committee and has undertaken research fieldwork in Peru, Hawaii, Alaska, Iceland, Greenland and Spain. Much of his work has centred on population biology and estimation, mainly by shipboard and aerial surveys but also using photo-identification studies.

**Stephen Leatherwood B.A.**
Stephen Leatherwood is a marine biologist, specializing in the biology and conservation of marine mammals. Increasingly, his work has focused on the effects of human activities on marine mammals, especially in developing nations, and on measures to control or mitigate these effects. He has written and broadcast extensively, and has served as scientific adviser to over a dozen scientific and conservation organizations. At present, he is based in Nairobi with the UN, performing the duties of secretary to the Marine Mammal Action Plan, a global effort to ensure the conservation of marine mammals worldwide.

**Philip S. Hammond B.A., D.Phil.**
Having completed his studies at the University of York in the UK, Phil Hammond began working for the Inter-American Tropical Tuna Commission (IATTC) in San Diego, California in 1979 and became Head of the Tuna-Dolphin Investigation at the IATTC in 1982. He returned to the UK in 1984, joining the Sea Mammal Research Unit in Cambridge, UK, where his work includes the use of photographs of natural markings and capture-recapture statistical models as the basis of estimates of cetacean population parameters. His practical research work has included the initiation of a study of bottlenose dolphins in Scotland. He is Vice-Chairman of the Scientific Committee of the International Whaling Commission.

**Graham J.B. Ross B.Sc., Ph.D.**
Graham Ross majored in zoology and botany at the University of Witwatersrand, Johannesburg, graduating in 1967. He joined the Port Elizabeth Museum as a marine biologist, concentrating on the little-known marine mammal fauna of the southwestern Indian Ocean. His results, based on strandings, incidental captures and at-sea observations, formed the basis of his doctoral thesis. His special interests include the classification of beaked whales and the enigmatic bottlenose dolphin, the food and feeding interrelationships of marine mammals, and the influence of short- and long-term changes in the environment on populations of these animals.

**James G. Mead M.A, Ph.D.**
James Mead obtained his Ph.D. in evolutionary biology and, following two seasons as a biological technician at a shore whaling station in Newfoundland, he joined the Smithsonian Institution as Curator of Marine Mammals in the National Museum of Natural History in July of 1972. He has studied the natural history of whales and dolphins by examining carcasses of animals that have died during strandings. He is particularly interested in the beaked whales and has carried out field work in Newfoundland, Argentina, Peru, Japan and the eastern coast of the United States. He was the second President of the Society for Marine Mammalogy.

**Randall R. Reeves B.A.**
Randy Reeves was born and raised in Nebraska. With a degree in history, he went on to graduate school at Princeton University, where he became interested in conservation issues. Eventually he became a successful itinerant marine mammalogist, with home bases at various times at the Smithsonian Institution in Washington, D.C., Hubbs Marine Research Institute in San Diego, California, and the Arctic Biological Station in Quebec. He is an active field biologist, travelling widely, and has co-authored a number of internationally acclaimed books on cetacean subjects.

**Aleta A. Hohn M.S., Ph.D.**
Aleta began studying marine mammal biology in 1976 as a volunteer at the Smithsonian Institution, completing her Master's degree there in 1980. She has since worked as a biologist for the US Fish and Wildlife Service, Marine Mammal Section, and the US National Marine Fisheries Service in La Jolla, California. Her studies there have included research on dolphin, porpoise, and manatee life history, surveys of marine mammals in the eastern Pacific and coordination of the Marine Mammal Salvage Program. She has served on the Board of Governors of the Society for Marine Mammalogy and received her Ph.D. from UCLA in 1989.

**Christina H. Lockyer B.Sc., D.Sc.**
Christina Lockyer is a Principal Scientific Officer with the UK Natural Environment Research Council, at their Sea Mammal Research Unit in Cambridge. She holds a doctorate from the University of East Anglia and has researched the cetacean field for more than 20 years. Her work has taken her worldwide and has focused on the population biology and ecology of both whales and dolphins. She has been providing advice to the Scientific Committee of the International Whaling Commission since 1972 and currently holds the position of President of the Society for Marine Mammalogy.

**Thomas A. Jefferson M.Sc.**
Tom Jefferson is Senior Research Technician at the Marine Mammal Research Program at Texas A & M University, Galveston. His field experience has involved Dall's porpoises, vaquitas, spinner and bottlenose dolphins, and killer, humpback and gray whales.

**Marc A. Webber M.A.**
Marc Webber is a Field Associate at the California Academy of Sciences, San Francisco. As Curator of Mammals at the California Marine Mammal Center, he was responsible for the capture, transport and rehabilitation of stranded pinnipeds and cetaceans, and the ongoing research and coordination of a marine mammal stranding network covering 800km of the northern California coast.

# THE ARTISTS

**Bruce Pearson** has prepared the ten paintings of whales and dolphins in their habitat. He travels a great deal to observe and paint the natural world, including a number of visits to the Antarctic, where he had close experience of a wide range of different whale species.

**David Thompson**, a biologist at the Sea Mammal Research Unit in Cambridge, has used his experience with cetaceans in the Atlantic, Pacific and Antarctic to prepare the scale outlines plus paintings of little-known species for which photographs are not available.

# CONTENTS

# PART ONE

From the very beginning of this project, our aims have been clear; to provide an up-to-date, authoritative and comprehensive reference work on these fascinating animals, yet one that is easily readable and understandable by students and professional biologists alike. At the same time, the format and style of the book provides an exciting opportunity to publish a profusion of high-quality photographs to ensure that the text does not become divorced from the visual reality of the subject. No single author can have personal experience of all species of whales, dolphins and porpoises (collectively known as cetaceans), so the decision was made at an early stage to invite a number of respected scientists from around the world to provide accounts of species with which they are personally familiar. This has resulted in a more thorough and comprehensive work than I could have achieved alone.

In Part One of the book we explore what cetaceans are, consider their origins, how they live, and examine their physical and sensual capabilities. We look at some of the ways in which cetaceans and man interact, how and where to go about seeing them in the flesh, why strandings occur (and how to cope if you come across one), and what type of research is now being carried out worldwide to increase our knowledge of these extraordinary creatures.

Public interest in cetaceans has increased dramatically in recent years. Captive displays of dolphins, the many excellent television documentaries, and the extensive media coverage of such topics as 'scientific' whaling and the entrapped gray whales off Alaska all play their part. The destruction of many whale stocks for oil and meat over the past two centuries and the recent fight to end whaling have become symbols of man's ability to cause environmental problems, and then to stop himself just before it's too late. Luckily, and it was certainly due more to luck than judgment, man has not yet extinguished any species of cetacean, although three are in a perilous state and many others are threatened.

Much of the incentive for producing this kind of book has come from my personal experience of researching, lecturing and broadcasting on cetaceans for well over a decade. Part of the duties of working in a publicly funded laboratory is to respond to questions and queries from a great variety of people, ranging from ten-year-old schoolchildren to university professors. This book contains the answers to most of the questions that are asked, and care has been taken to remain objective; to avoid the anthropomorphic and romantic perspective that still pervades so many books on these creatures. Even when stripped of the fantasies and embellishments that have accumulated over the centuries, the truth about whales, dolphins and porpoises is quite astonishing enough and often still hard to believe. We hope you agree.

*Tony Martin*

*Right: The unmistakable shape of a male killer whale, photographed here at Peninsula Valdés, Argentina. This animal hunts sea lions by snatching them off the beach, then reversing into the sea.*

# WHAT ARE WHALES?

Everyone knows what a whale is and what a dolphin looks like. Or do they? Why will some readers of this book identify the television star, Flipper, as a porpoise and others as a dolphin?

For various reasons, our perception of these sea animals is rather confused. When the cry 'Save the whale' went up in the 1970s, few people responded 'Which whale?', although they might well have queried which of the 40 or so different types of animal known as whales in the English language were in need of saving. It seems likely that an appeal to 'Save the bird' would have been met with a few more questions!

## What's in a name?
All whales, dolphins and porpoises are known collectively as 'cetaceans', from the Latin 'cetus' (a large sea animal) and the Greek 'ketos' (a sea monster). Like man, they are warm-blooded, air-breathing mammals that mate, give birth to live young and suckle their young on milk over a period of many months. Unlike man – and unlike all other mammals, except a small group called the Sirenia, or sea cows – cetaceans have evolved to carry out all the normal mammalian functions entirely in water. With insignificant exceptions, they never venture onto land. Nevertheless, they are not fish, do not lay eggs and do not have gills.

We know that at least 78 different types, or species, of cetacean currently exist on this planet. Even in the twentieth century, species new to man are being discovered and more are almost certainly

*Below: All cetaceans, from the large whales, such as this humpback,* *to the smallest dolphin and porpoise share one basic body shape.*

yet to be found. During the last few years, whale enthusiasts have become very excited by reports of sightings in the eastern Pacific of what must be a species of beaked whale new to science. We have been sharing our planet with this large creature for hundreds of thousands of years without ever realizing it!

The known cetaceans range in size from the enormous blue whale, which can reach a weight of 150 tonnes and is the largest creature ever to have existed on earth, to the diminutive franciscana and vaquita, which rarely exceed 50kg. With a maximum body length of about 31m, the blue whale is 18 times the maximum length and an amazing 3,000 times the weight of the smallest species. Between these two extremes, cetaceans abound in a variety of sizes.

The terms 'whale', 'dolphin' and 'porpoise' refer in broad terms to cetaceans of different size classes. Thus, species with a body length of 3m or more are usually called whales, and species smaller than this are called dolphins. The exceptions are six closely related species, none exceeding 2.2m, which are known as porpoises (the family Phocoenidae).

Unfortunately, the situation is not quite as simple as it sounds and overlaps do exist. For example, the smallest whale, the dwarf sperm whale, is smaller than the largest dolphin, the bottlenose. Similarly, the largest porpoise, the spectacled, is considerably larger than many animals called dolphins. This strict demarcation by size breaks down because the terms are applied to taxonomic groups of species and these usually contain animals of varying size. Thus, the three sperm whales are considered to be more closely related to each

other than to any other cetacean, yet the largest species has a body weight 200 times that of the smallest. The name 'dolphin' is used for members of two groups: the river dolphins and the mainly oceanic dolphins of the family Delphinidae, the latter including the bottlenose, which is the dolphin most commonly seen in captive displays around the world.

Further confusion surrounds the name 'porpoise'. In the United States, it is sometimes applied to every cetacean that is not a whale, but it seems that the terminology used elsewhere is becoming increasingly accepted.

Every type of cetacean is likely to be known by many different local names in several different languages. To prevent confusion, each species is given an internationally recognized two-part scientific name that serves to distinguish it from all other creatures. The first part is the genus, the second defines the species.

## Cetaceans and other marine mammals
Of the mammals that took to the sea millions of years ago, three major groups survive today. The first, the order Sirenia (sea cows, represented by the manatees and dugong), consists of only three living species. The second is the order Cetacea (whales, dolphins and porpoises). The third group, the Pinnipedia (seals, sea lions, fur seals and walrus), is a suborder of the order Carnivora, the meat eaters. A fourth group, the order Desmotilia, became extinct during the Miocene epoch less than 15 million years ago, and is known today only from fossils.

Sirenians, or sea cows, are purely aquatic herbivores, spending their time in shallow coastal waters or rivers, grazing the abundant vegetation. This is the group that gave rise to mariners' fables of mermaids. During the past three centuries, two species have become extinct. One of these, the Steller's sea cow, was the largest species, measuring about 8m in length. The survivors – two manatees and the dugong – are superficially similar to cetaceans. They have a horizontal tail, no external hind limbs and a rounded, fairly dolphinlike shape. However, there are differences that distinguish them from other animals; for example, sirenians have only six neck vertebrae (not seven as in nearly all other mammals), continuous tooth replacement along the tooth row and mammary nipples in the 'armpits' behind the forelimbs.

Cetaceans – the whales, dolphins and porpoises that are the subject of this book – are the other completely aquatic group of modern mammals. Seventy-eight

## Basic anatomy of a typical dolphin

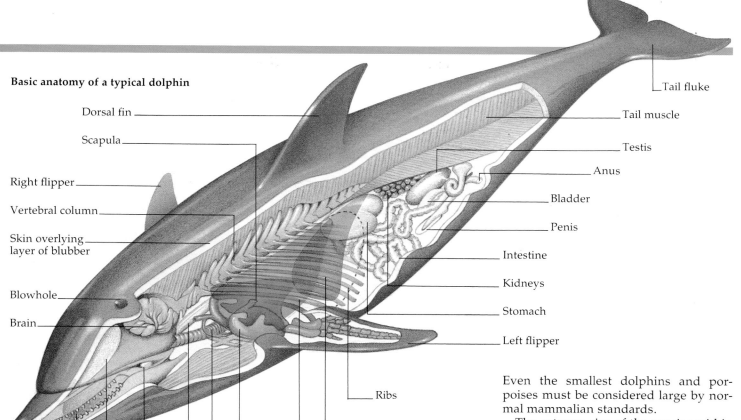

Dorsal fin

Scapula

Right flipper

Vertebral column

Skin overlying
layer of blubber

Blowhole

Brain

Teeth

Tongue

Melon (fatty tissue
on rostrum)

Position of eye

Oesophagus

Trachea

Heart

Ribs

Liver

Right lung (left lung
shown by dotted outline)

Tail fluke

Tail muscle

Testis

Anus

Bladder

Penis

Intestine

Kidneys

Stomach

Left flipper

different species are generally recognized but opinions differ slightly on exactly how many species really exist. Furthermore, it is expected that one or more new species, seen at sea but not yet closely examined, will soon be added to the list.

Although all cetaceans are grouped together in one taxonomic order, two quite distinct groupings are immediately recognizable. These are characterized by the type of feeding equipment in the mouth and reflect two quite different ways of life. The first group – the suborder Mysticeti – comprises all 11 species of filter-feeding baleen whales. The second – the suborder Odontoceti – embraces the remaining 67 species, all of which have teeth and are therefore known as the toothed whales. All the dolphins and porpoises are included in this group. These species catch their prey – usually squid or fish – one at a time using a variety of techniques.

The third major group of sea mammals – the suborder Pinnipedia – consists of 34

species of seals and their allies. All pinnipeds are amphibious, spending part of their life in water and part on land. Most are covered in dense hair that protects the skin from abrasion on rocks, as well as providing thermal insulation. They have short, flattened tails and webbed limbs with claws at the end of all five digits. Unlike modern cetaceans and sirenians, but in common with the other carnivores to which they are related, they also have several different types of teeth for cutting and chewing.

A few other sea mammals are worthy of mention here. The polar bear spends most of its life in the sea or on sea ice, but it is a member of the bear family, Ursidae, which is essentially land based. Some otters, particularly the sea otter, make their living at least partly in a marine habitat and are clearly well adapted to hunting in water. Otters are the only amphibious members of the family Mustelidae which, like that of the bears and seals, is in the order Carnivora.

### Body size and shape
The chief characteristic that everyone associates with whales is their size. Included in the cetaceans are many of the largest animals ever to have lived on earth, and the blue whale is the largest.

Even the smallest dolphins and porpoises must be considered large by normal mammalian standards.

The extreme size of the species within the order as a whole is no accident. Historically, cetaceans have not always been so large, but some families, mostly of baleen whales, must have evolved in this direction for the simple reason that bigger was better. Generally speaking, larger offspring must have survived and reproduced more effectively than their smaller siblings. Large size can also be an advantage on land, but here an increase in weight entails an additional burden for the supporting limbs and a potential loss of mobility. However, in the sea, where the body is supported by the upthrust of water and an animal is effectively almost weightless, these disadvantages do not apply. It would be fascinating to return to earth in a few million years time to see if the blue whale had reached its optimum size or was still evolving towards an even larger body.

Despite the great range of size, coloration and habits within the cetacean group, a basic external body shape is common to all. True, some have a large fin on the back – the dorsal fin – while others have none at all. Some have narrow 'beaks' and others a blunt forehead. Some have a small mouth and others have a mouth large enough to consume a family-sized car. Nevertheless, all have a body that is basically rounded, larger at the front than at the back and smooth to the touch. They have nostrils on top of the head, no external hind limbs and a large, flat, horizontal blade at the end of the tail to provide forward motion. These features are all characteristic of a well-adapted, water-dwelling mammal.

# THE EVOLUTION OF WHALES

There are still large gaps in our knowledge of the evolutionary pathways that led to the extraordinary variety of whales, dolphins and porpoises we see today. Nevertheless, work on the fossil record by palaeontologists over many decades and, more recently, by geneticists and molecular biologists on living animals, has provided a reasonable picture of the process. Sadly, we evolved too late to see the majority of cetacean species; they had developed and disappeared long before man appeared.

Most authorities agree that modern-day cetaceans have developed from land-based animals that colonized brackish estuaries about 55 million years ago. Current evidence points towards a shared ancestry with even-toed ungulates, the hoofed mammals that today include cows and deer.

The transition to an aquatic life seems to have occurred around the ancient Tethys Sea, in the region of what is now the Mediterranean Sea and the Asian subcontinent. Fossil evidence suggests that the ancestors of today's whales and dolphins, called Archaeoceti (the first sub-order of cetaceans), probably existed here along the margins of the sea, perhaps in estuaries. The fossils indicate that they became progressively adapted to an ever more aquatic way of life but probably retained four recognizable limbs for millions of years.

## Adapting to life in water

As in all other life forms, evolution in cetaceans is brought about by adaptation to the environment in which they live. In their mammalian predecessors, the process of moving from a terrestrial to an aquatic existence clearly demanded a great deal of adaptation. Principally, it meant developing a new mode of locomotion (from walking to swimming), a physiology to cope with a dense medium (water rather than air), new methods of detecting and catching prey, and a means of breathing efficiently at the sea surface.

This adaptation was achieved by changing every part of the body, particularly the head. The nostrils moved progressively from the front, as in a dog or horse, to the top of the skull; the upper jaw (the rostrum) became broad or elongate, according to the type of prey taken; the teeth evolved from those of a carnivore, which has different kinds of teeth (heterodonty) into one of several different, very characteristic types of homodonty (in which all the teeth are the same). The physical signs of improved acoustic senses in the toothed whales included the development of a melon (a fatty tissue structure on the rostrum that probably focuses sound) and specialized bones within the inner ear. The head thus contains the greatest amount of information about the state of evolution reached by any particular cetacean.

As well as changes to the head, adaptation to an aquatic way of life brought about fundamental alterations in the rest of the body. Perhaps the most obvious one is the streamlined body shape. It is no coincidence that dolphins and large fish – sharks, for example – share a very similar, torpedolike body shape, since this is the easiest to push through the dense fluid medium of water. Another adaptation shared with fish is the means of propulsion. A broad, flat blade is a much more efficient means of providing the power for movement in water than the normal limbs of a terrestrial mammal. Cetaceans gradually evolved a paddle at the end of the tail and underwent changes in the vertebral column to support the great slab of muscle with which to move it. At the same time, the forelimbs developed into blades for twisting and turning, and the hind limbs regressed into non-functional pieces of relic bone and cartilage that in today's whales and dolphins are buried in the abdominal blubber and muscle. Again, as in fish, most lineages developed a dorsal fin for stability, but in some it was later lost; in others it served a second purpose, that of temperature regulation. A further external adaptation was the loss of body hair; thermal insulation was subsequently provided by a layer of thick blubber.

Once these fundamental changes had been achieved, further modifications to the body form allowed particular branches of the cetacean 'tree' to specialize still further. Thus, one branch – the baleen whales – developed the means to exploit the vast swarms of plankton that flourish in productive seas; their teeth were gradually replaced by sievelike baleen and they became filter feeders. Various dolphins adapted to live in the fresh water of rivers and lakes, often with poor visibility but good stocks of fish. Some of these, like the river dolphins that exist today, developed a highly advanced acoustic sense with which to find and chase fish and long, thin jaws armed with many sharp pointed teeth in order to grab them. The sense of sight was ineffectual in muddy rivers and was slowly lost, an evolutionary process that has resulted in two present-day species – the Indus and Ganges River dolphins (*Platanista*) – having no lens in the eye at all.

## The emergence of cetaceans

The archaeocetes possessed features that distinguished them as primitive cetaceans, albeit far less adapted to an aquatic environment than today's whales and dolphins. At that stage, they may even have hauled themselves out onto land to breed in the same way as modern seals. The most primitive representatives of the Archaeoceti, called protocetids, have been found as fossils in what are now Asia, North Africa and North America. They had the heterodont (i.e. varied) dentition of meat-eaters, with teeth for grasping and cutting. We infer that they included fish in their diet and it may have been selection for more efficient fish-catching that brought about their move to an increasingly aquatic habit. During the later part of the Eocene epoch (55-38 million years ago), archaeocetes are thought to have spread from the Tethys to many other parts of the world's oceans, becoming more effectively adapted as time passed. More advanced archaeocetes developed, taking on an external appearance that we would recognize as similar to modern cetaceans. One of the most significant examples is the Basilosauridae family, animals of considerable size – estimated at up to 21m in length – mostly known from fossils discovered in the southeastern United States. *Basilosaurus* was whalelike in form, but had a small head in comparison with modern cetaceans. It retained a heterodont dentition and a flexible neck. Like other advanced archaeocetes, it also had tail flukes, paddlelike pectoral fins and atrophied hind limbs.

## The first toothed and baleen whales

Archaeocetes dominated the Eocene epoch, having probably taken over the niche occupied by large marine reptilian predators, such as *Ichthyosaurus*, which mysteriously died out with the other dinosaurs at the end of the Cretaceous period (about 65 million years ago). Towards the end of the Eocene, archaeocetes themselves were becoming less abundant and they essentially disappeared from the fossil record about 38 million years ago. One family may have survived into the Oligocene epoch (38-25 million years ago) but, by this time, representatives of the two current sub-orders of cetaceans, Odontoceti (toothed whales) and Mysticeti (baleen whales) were dominant. The reasons for the relatively sudden demise of archaeocete whales are unknown, and it is even possible that gaps in the fossil record give a misleading impression of that period. If they did indeed suddenly die out, then global mass-extinction for some unknown reason and out-competition by the emergent 'modern' cetaceans are considered possible causes.

Early mysticetes still retained teeth, but in some these slowly became adapted for sieving rather than grasping prey; the teeth developed an irregular profile and the upper and lower teeth intermeshed when the mouth was closed. Baleen itself is not composed of tooth material, but is similar to the skinlike tissue forming the ridges of the palate in many modern mammals. Therefore, baleen replaced teeth in the mouth of mysticetes rather than evolving from them. Remarkably, the foetuses of today's baleen whales still retain tooth buds below the gumline, clearly indicating ancestry from toothed whale stock. However, these never develop and are replaced by baleen in the juvenile animal.

## Modern toothed whales and dolphins

By about 25 million years ago – the end of the Oligocene epoch – a wide variety of odontocetes ranged across the world's oceans. None were the same as any of today's species, but their general body form, way of life and dentition were unmistakably similar to modern toothed whales and dolphins. Some of these – the shark-toothed dolphins (Squalodontidae) for example – may have had a lifestyle similar to the modern killer whale (*Orcinus orca*). Others, such as the sperm whales (Physeteridae), now represented by the familiar sperm whale (*Physeter macrocephalus*), survive to the present day. Further modern families, including the beaked whales (Ziphiidae) and the river dolphins (Platanistoidea), evolved later during the Miocene, 25-5 million years ago. (There is still doubt over whether the river dolphins form a single family or should be classed in as many as

four with similarities caused by convergent evolution rather than recent ancestry.) By the end of the Miocene epoch, some 5 million years ago, most, or perhaps all, modern families had become established. We cannot be completely sure that all had evolved by then because of gaps in the fossil record, but we certainly know of the existence of the oceanic dolphins (Delphinidae) – the most successful and diverse existing family of cetaceans, with 26 surviving species – and of the closely related pilot and killer whales (Globicephalidae).

The origins of the porpoises (Phocoenidae) and the beluga/narwhal group (Monodontidae) are unclear. Fossil records of both first appear in the late Miocene, about 10 million years ago. The earliest known monodontids are from California and Mexico, indicating that adaptation to the current, purely Arctic distribution of two of the three existing species must have occurred relatively recently. Porpoises seem to have originated in the temperate regions of the North and South Pacific and possibly radiated from here to other parts of the world during the Pliocene (5-2 million years ago).

## Modern baleen whales

The origins of the four surviving families of baleen whales are considered to be quite different from one another, there being such a variety of form and function within the suborder. A fifth family, the Cetotheriidae, now extinct, was probably the immediate ancestor of the Balaenopteridae, which today includes the humpback whale, blue whale and other similarly shaped rorquals. The cetotheriids seem to have finally disappeared only about 3 million years ago, but by then recognizable balaenopterids had been coexisting with them for about 7 or 8 million years. At its peak in the Miocene epoch, the cetotheriid family was very

successful, encompassing more than 50 species of small and medium-sized whales. Its evolution demonstrated the physical changes required to adapt to feeding with a sievelike apparatus, changes that continued even after the balaenopterids had become abundant. The adaptions included the 'telescoping' of the skull to provide strength and a suitable platform from which the baleen could hang, the development of a soft-tissue connector between the skull and lower jaws to permit a wide gape, and the general increase in size of the head and feeding apparatus.

The right whales (Balaenidae & Neobalaenidae) appeared as a distinct group much earlier than the rorquals, and their origin is unclear. Balaenids from the early Miocene (25 million years ago) have been found in Patagonia, for example, and by then the family was already significantly different from contemporary cetotheriids.

The fourth mysticete family – Eschrichtiidae – is represented by only one modern species, the gray whale, *Eschrichtius robustus*. Known fossils only take us back 100,000 years or so, and none are distinguishable from the current animal. It is interesting that sub-fossils (remains that have become calcified but not turned to stone) reveal an ancient distribution of this family on both sides of the North Atlantic, in addition to its current range in the North Pacific Ocean. Gray whales did not finally become extinct in the Atlantic until the seventeenth or early eighteenth century. *Eschrichtius* is so different from all other whales that, despite a lack of hard evidence to prove this, we must assume that it has developed along a separate evolutionary branch for many millions of years. Certain similarities between *Eschrichtius* and some cetotheriids have led to speculation that gray whales were directly derived from the latter, but recent studies have discredited this idea.

**An artist's reconstruction of *Zygorhiza kochii*, a Durodontid archaeocete**

*This animal, probably an ancestor of modern cetaceans, was about 5-6m long and lived between 36 and 46 million years ago.*

# SWIMMING AND DIVING

Dolphins are renowned for their speed and the apparent effortless grace with which they achieve such rapid movement. Burst speeds of up to 55 kilometres per hour (kph) have been recorded for small cetaceans, although prolonged cruising is normally at the rate of about 6-15kph. Baleen whales are thought to migrate at average speeds of 4-15kph, but can outrun a catcher boat, achieving a speed of 30kph for short periods.

Early calculations and experiments based on rigid models of a dolphin's body suggested that the swimming performance of these animals was theoretically beyond the capacity of their muscles. Clearly, a real dolphin must outperform the model, but exactly how it does so was not understood until quite recently.

## How whales and dolphins swim

Two vital elements account for a whale or dolphin's phenomenal swimming ability. The first concerns the physical movements of the body and how these make the best use of the water's physical properties. The second is the extremely efficient form and function of the body, which permits a great amount of forward propulsion for each unit of energy spent in swimming.

Propulsion is provided by the broad, flat tail flukes as they are moved up and down. These are boneless and composed of an extremely tough, fairly rigid fibrous material, perhaps comparable with dense rubber. The end of the spine extends into the flukes, providing a robust area of attachment, but the vertebrae here are tiny and circular in shape. The flukes are thicker at the front than the back and are a perfect hydrofoil in shape, i.e. they have a cross-section very much like that of an aircraft wing. This familiar shape is the most resistant to drag, both in air and water. The tips of the flukes are able to flex upwards but not downwards. This is linked to the fact that forward propulsion is principally developed during the upstroke. As the flukes move upwards and displace water over their trailing edges, the area of low pressure created beneath them draws water from around the body further forward, literally 'pulling' the animal into the space created ahead. On the downward 'recovery' stroke, water spills over the edges of the flukes as the tips flex. Thus, the downstroke does not counteract the propulsion produced by the upstroke.

The forceful upward movement of the flukes is provided by a pair of large muscle bundles positioned above the midline on either side of the spine. They are attached to, and supported by, the pronounced blades of bone, or 'processes', that typically extend outwards and upwards from each individual vertebra along most of the spine. The downward stroke is brought about by smaller muscles that run below the midline in the rearmost part of the abdomen.

The action of swimming involves movement of the whole animal, not just of the tail flukes. In fact, not only the flukes but the rearmost third of the animal constitutes the tail. This section of the body is very flexible and, with every complete stroke, is swept through an arc of many tens of degrees relative to the rest of the body. Because of this, the part of the tail just in front of the flukes – the caudal peduncle – is laterally flattened to provide less drag.

The second part of the formula for rapid movement is the low degree of resistance to forward motion provided by the cetacean body as a whole. If you touch the skin of a live dolphin, you will notice how silky smooth it feels. It is slippery, but not slimy like that of a fish. It feels firm but not hard and, once again, can best be compared to rubber with a smooth finish. It is the structure of the skin and the tissue just below it that holds the secret of why a live dolphin outperforms a man-made model of itself in a swim-tank.

A solid object moving through a fluid medium, such as air or water, continuously displaces some of the medium in front of it and an equal amount of that medium fills the 'space' vacated immediately behind. The minimum resistance to movement occurs when the

*Right: Many species of large whale, such as this blue whale, raise their tail flukes into the air after taking their final breath before beginning a prolonged dive, indicating a steep descent into the sea.*

*Below left: A lively common dolphin bursts through the water surface to snatch a breath. Unlike seals, which exhale before they dive, all cetaceans dive with their lungs completely full of air.*

displaced medium flows perfectly smoothly from the front of the object to the rear, each successive 'layer' moving less with increasing distance from the object. This is known as laminar flow, and is the ideal to which fish, sea mammals and birds, as well as ship and aircraft designers, aspire.

Laminar flow is only possible over a smooth, rounded shape. Any sharp protuberance or cavity, or a rough surface, will set up irregularities in the flow, causing turbulence and increased drag. We have already seen how the basic cetacean body shape serves to minimize drag, but the skin may also actively combat turbulence by absorbing the energy it creates. This could be achieved by the structure of the skin itself, but it is also possible that fast-swimming dolphins can develop temporary areas of ridged skin that damp out incipient turbulence before it becomes a problem, thereby maintaining a high degree of swimming efficiency.

Some scientists believe that the skin performs another role in combating turbulence. Cetacean skin is known to shed cells rapidly; studies of a dolphin revealed that the outermost layer of skin was shed 12 times a day. The skin cells also exuded the tiny droplets of oil they contained. Either or both of these features may act as a lubricant to reduce friction through the water even further.

### Bow riding

Ocean travellers are often entertained by schools of dolphins that dash around the ship, vying for a favoured spot just in front of the bow. Here, they can often keep pace with a speeding ship, apparently without having to move a muscle. How can they do this? Once again, the answer involves a brief explanation of some principles of hydrodynamics.

A ship moving through water creates a wave immediately in front and to the sides of its bow. This wave is formed of water displaced by the ship and remains stationary in relation to the vessel. Within the wave is a pressure field and in a small region near the leading edge of the wave the pressure field exerts sufficient forward force to allow a dolphin to be pushed along against the flow of water. It is this region that the dolphins are seeking out and testing as they flit from side to side within 2m of the bow. If a dolphin finds a suitable spot, the animal must stop swimming at just the right moment, otherwise it will pop out of the pressure field again. Having found the spot, it can rest almost motionless, being pushed along until it gets tired of the game or the pressure field breaks down as the ship slows or as the bow is thrust out of the water. Small cetaceans sometimes bow ride around the head of a large whale, and youngsters often get a 'ride' from their mother's own pressure field in a similar way.

### Diving and respiration

These topics are inextricably linked, in terms of each species' behaviour and physiology. Clearly, a species that cannot hold its breath for long periods will be unable to dive to a great depth and, conversely, one that routinely feeds on deep ocean squid must have a physiology that allows it to survive for long periods without breathing.

All whales, dolphins and porpoises are able to remain submerged for longer periods of time than man, who becomes acutely distressed after three minutes, even when trained, and normally breathes about 15 times in each minute when resting. In contrast, some cetaceans can remain submerged for more than an hour, and none exhale and inhale more than about four times a minute

when at rest. Incredulous observers have followed an adult male sperm whale during a 92-minute feeding dive off the Azores Islands, listening to his echolocation 'clicks' via a hydrophone. Only very recently has it been discovered that elephant seals can dive for similarly amazing periods of time.

The ability to function underwater with infrequent breaths varies greatly between cetacean species and very much reflects their mode of feeding and preferred prey. Unlike members of the seal family, which exhale immediately before a dive, cetaceans inhale and dive with a lungful of air. Ironically, those species that dive the longest generally have the smallest lung capacity proportionate to their body size. In fact, air in the lungs plays a very minor role in long dives, for two reasons. Firstly, the amount of oxygen carried in even the largest lungs would be exhausted after a small proportion of the dive. Secondly, water pressure increases dramatically with depth, so that any gas in the lungs becomes rapidly compressed and reduces to almost nothing long before the deeper divers have reached anywhere near their target depth. In fact, the lungs collapse completely below about 100m depth.

Unable to store oxygen in their lungs, cetaceans have adapted to store it where it is most needed – in the muscle and in the blood. They have a proportionately large blood volume and their blood is very high in haemoglobin, which carries dissolved oxygen around the body and, importantly, to the brain. The muscle is rich in myoglobin, a protein that attracts oxygen from the blood and stores it for metabolism by the muscle during a dive. It has been estimated that 50 percent of oxygen capacity is stored in this way. The myoglobin gives muscle a characteristically dark coloration and, indeed, the longest divers, such as sperm whales, have muscle that looks almost black.

Deep-diving whales have other physiological features that allow them to extend the period between surfacings. These include the ability to 'shunt' blood to essential organs at the expense of less important parts of the body when oxygen levels become low; the dramatic slowing of the heart – bradycardia – to 10-50 percent of the rate at the water surface; and an anaerobic (oxygen-less) metabolism, whereby the tissues build up an 'oxygen debt', which is 'paid back' during the first few inhalations at the end of the dive.

### Breathing

The basic pattern of breathing is the same in all types of cetacean. The blowhole(s) open, an explosive exhalation is followed immediately by an inhalation, and the blowhole(s) close tight again. The whole sequence of events can take much less than half a second in dolphins and porpoises, which surface frequently for very short periods of time, but it may last a second or two in larger species, such as humpback and sperm whales, which have a more leisurely surfacing technique. In fact, the diving behaviour of the sperm whale is unique in many respects, not least because it usually remains almost motionless at the surface after a long dive, a male breathing perhaps 40 or 50 times before resubmerging. The normal cetacean behaviour is to exhale and inhale only once during each brief surfacing and to continue moving during each complete respiration sequence. Thus, the action of surfacing and breathing hardly impedes progress at all.

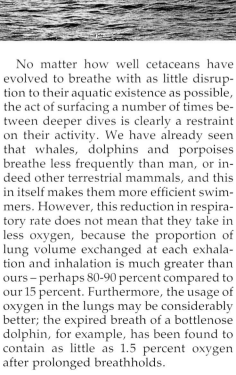

*Below: Like all toothed whales, dolphins and porpoises, this beluga has a single blowhole, whereas baleen whales have two blowholes, side by side.*

*Right: Blue whales have the tallest blow of all whales. It is composed mainly of condensed water vapour, but may also contain oil droplets.*

No matter how well cetaceans have evolved to breathe with as little disruption to their aquatic existence as possible, the act of surfacing a number of times between deeper dives is clearly a restraint on their activity. We have already seen that whales, dolphins and porpoises breathe less frequently than man, or indeed other terrestrial mammals, and this in itself makes them more efficient swimmers. However, this reduction in respiratory rate does not mean that they take in less oxygen, because the proportion of lung volume exchanged at each exhalation and inhalation is much greater than ours – perhaps 80-90 percent compared to our 15 percent. Furthermore, the usage of oxygen in the lungs may be considerably better; the expired breath of a bottlenose dolphin, for example, has been found to contain as little as 1.5 percent oxygen after prolonged breathholds.

## The blow

The blow is an intriguing characteristic of cetaceans, varying in size, shape and visibility between species. For example, the blow of a blue whale, most clearly seen in cold air, rises instantly to 9m as a tall, thin cone of smokelike vapour. In contrast, the blow of dolphins and porpoises is low and brief and, especially in warm air, not visible to the human eye. It is the blow, often combined with a brief glimpse of the animal's back, that enables an experienced observer to distinguish one species of whale from another, even at distances of many kilometres. Blue and fin whales have a single, very tall thin blow, the humpback a lower, slightly more bushy blow, and right whales two separate bushy blows that diverge on either side of the head. The sperm whale, like all odontocetes, has a single blowhole, in this case situated asymmetrically at the extreme front lefthand side of the top of the head. Its blow is low, bushy and thrust forward and to the left.

There is still some doubt about what exactly makes the blow so visible. It must include water vapour, which condenses in cold air, and probably a small amount of sea water that happens to be trapped in the blowhole. But there is speculation that it might also contain tiny droplets of oil or fat. These are produced by the respiratory system and may play a part in avoiding harmful conditions normally associated with diving in man, such as the 'bends'. (This decompression sickness is caused by the formation of tiny gas bubbles [mainly nitrogen] in the blood during too rapid an ascent following a dive with air tanks.)

## The physiology of diving

The ability to dive differs from family to family and from species to species. The deepest divers – those able to hold their breath for the longest period of time – are probably the sperm whale and some of the beaked whales. Very few accurate records exist showing the depths to which these species can descend, but sperm whales are known to dive to at least 1,100m and we think they may reach more than 3,000m on occasion. Evidence for this has been derived principally from the recovery of animals entrapped in submarine cables and others killed in water of known depth with fresh bottom-living fish in their stomachs. However, most feeding dives reach lesser depths than this and recent evidence from the Galapagos Islands indicates that female and immature sperm whales usually forage for about 40 minutes at less than 500m.

Baleen whales normally do not venture below about 100m, since they usually find their food in the upper sections of the water column and, particularly in the evenings, very often within a few metres of the surface. The normal surfacing pattern reflects this, with a typical sequence

**Cross-section through a sperm whale head**

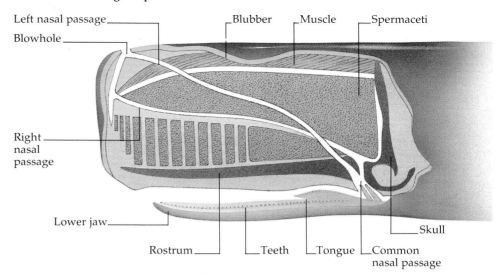

being, perhaps, 10-15 blows at 15-second intervals, followed by eight minutes below the surface. Dives in excess of 30 minutes have been recorded, but rarely.

Most species of dolphin and porpoise also spend nearly all their time within 100m of the surface. Clearly, the river dolphins rarely encounter water of any real depth, and most of the others feed mainly on small shoaling fish within a few tens of metres of the surface. Some medium-sized cetaceans, such as the pilot whales, beluga and narwhal, are known to dive many hundreds of metres if they need to, and evidence of stomach sampling in these species shows that they often forage deeply, taking midwater squid or bottom-dwelling fish.

Of the physiological adaptations that permit deep diving, lung collapse is almost unavoidable. It is worth seeing how cetacean anatomy has allowed for this phenomenon, and even taken advantage of it. When any whale or dolphin dives deeply, the lungs collapse for the simple reason that, being full of gas, they are compressible, whereas the body, being mostly water, is not. The cetacean diaphragm is set obliquely and the lungs are positioned in such a way that, with increasing depth, the abdominal organs press against the diaphragm and indirectly squash the lungs against the upper chest wall. There is no damage to the rib cage because, unlike ours, it is extremely flexible, with many fewer rigid attachments of ribs to the breastbone and spine, and with some 'floating' ribs. As the lungs are compressed, so the gas left in them, now mostly nitrogen, is pushed into the relatively incompressible and tough trachea, where gaseous exchange with the tissue is very limited. Therefore lung collapse limits the amount of nitrogen being absorbed into the blood during a dive, and prevents air embolism and decompression sickness. In this context, cetaceans possess a unique capillary network of blood vessels, called the *retia mirabilia*, meaning 'wonderful nets'. As

blood passes to the brain, it is thought that the retia mirabilia filter out any gas bubbles that form during long dives.

Any discussion of diving must mention one further anatomical feature – the head of the sperm whale, which is very large and complex, and different from that of any other animal. It consists mostly of a great mass of wax called spermaceti, which is liquid at normal body temperature, but becomes solid and shrinks slightly when cooled. The function – or functions – of this structure, which may weigh several tonnes, has intrigued biologists and whalers for centuries. An acoustic function has been proposed (see page 31), but in 1978 the British marine biologist Malcolm Clarke published an ingenious alternative.

Clarke calculated that the change in density brought about by cooling or warming the spermaceti would be enough to change the overall buoyancy of the whole animal, from slightly positive to slightly negative or vice versa. Thus, if the whale could control the temperature of the wax, it could control its tendency to sink, float or remain at the same depth (i.e. become neutrally buoyant). This ability would have major energy-saving benefits for an animal that spends much of its life either swimming down or up through deep oceanic waters. Dr. Clarke carefully examined the internal structure of the sperm whale head, particularly the relationship, size and structure of the air passages and wax-containing regions. He showed that sufficient cooling and warming could be achieved if the whale drew cold sea water into the right nasal passage, which passes close to the wax, before or during a dive and expelled it before the ascent. There is currently no direct evidence to prove that this is what sperm whales actually do, and it must be said that some scientists are sceptical of the theory. Nevertheless, it is an elegant hypothesis and somehow appropriate for such an enigmatic creature as the sperm whale.

# SENSES AND INTELLIGENCE

Cetaceans live in an environment very different to our own. Light is rapidly filtered out by the water in which they live, so vision is generally of less use to them as a sense than it is to most terrestrial animals. An extreme illustration of this is the way in which the eyes of two species of dolphins that live in the muddy waters of rivers in the Indian subcontinent have regressed to the extent that they now lack even a lens and can probably sense only crude changes in the intensity of light and perhaps its direction.

Nevertheless, cetaceans have developed great acuity in other senses that appear to have more than compensated for the lack of long-distance vision. Water is much denser than air, so sound travels faster and further. As a result, all species have highly developed hearing abilities and most, if not all, actually create sound in order to increase the amount of acoustic feedback they receive. There is also a growing amount of evidence that cetaceans make use of an invisible source of 'information', the earth's magnetic field,

in order to find their way around in the vast oceans. Touch and taste have been retained from the terrestrial ancestry of all cetaceans, and have evolved to fit the needs of a now totally aquatic animal. The sense of smell, however, has been lost by the toothed whales, dolphins and porpoises. Here, we consider these senses in turn and how they have become specialized in a wide range of cetaceans.

## Sight
The intensity of sunlight rapidly diminishes with depth in water, to the extent that it hardly penetrates below 400m, even in clear seas, and much less in turbid or highly productive water. Sunlight simply never reaches the depths at which sperm whales and some beaked whales are known to forage. Although luminous animals, such as some squid species, probably give off sufficient light to indicate their own presence, it seems likely that cetaceans searching for food below depths of 500m in the oceans must rely on their echolocational abilities.

Where sunlight is available, in the upper portion of the water column, almost all whales, dolphins and porpoises are able to take advantage of it. The cetacean eye has adapted to function both in air and water by gaining great elasticity of the lens. Vision is undoubtedly used for foraging, the maintenance of contact with other animals in the group and for examining the immediate environment, including obstacles and unusual objects such as boats and predators. Some species, such as the pilot and killer whales, make use of their ability to see in air by 'spy hopping' to get a clear view of any activity above the waves. There is evidence from studies of captive animals that at least some species of dolphins can discriminate colours, although sea water acts as such an efficient filter that everything below a few metres must appear as blue or green.

The position of the eyes, usually near the widest part of the head and far back from the tip of the jaws, has implications for the degree of stereoscopic vision available. Species with pointed 'beaks' usually have a good binocular view forward and downward, but others with blunt heads, of which the sperm whale is an extreme example, are not able to see immediately in front of their jaws at all and have monocular vision throughout most of their visual range.

## Hearing
You might be forgiven for thinking that cetaceans have no ears at all, for the demands of a streamlined body shape have long since dispensed with external ears, and the channel leading to the inner ear can only be seen as a small hole in the skin, a little way behind the eye. The inner elements of the ear are also radically different from those of a land mammal, particularly in that the cochlea, the essential organ of hearing, is acoustically isolated from the skull by foam-filled air spaces. Without this acoustical insulation, whales and dolphins would be unable to discern the direction of any sound they detect. This is because sound travels straight through a mammalian head in water but is mostly reflected off it in air. Thus, in air, the cochlea on the side of the head furthest from a sound source receives less signal strength than the one on the near side, whereas under water the signal strength is very similar.

This is why humans are unable to determine the direction of a sound source, a motorboat, say, when we put our heads under water. The foam surrounding the cetacean cochlea retains its

*Bottom left: Floating vertically, this spy hopping humpback whale raises its head to gain a better view of the photographer's boat.*

*Above: As in all whale species, the eyes of this gray whale calf are adapted so that it can see both in the air and under water.*

ability to reflect sound even under a pressure of 100 atmospheres (equivalent to a water depth of 1,000m). Thus, a whale is able to tell the direction of a sound even at the bottom of a deep dive.

Despite a great deal of experimental work carried out over the past few decades, there remains considerable disagreement about the path by which sound is received by the internal ear. It may pass through the water-filled channel, called the auditory meatus, between the outside of the head and the ear structure. However, many scientists point to the unique structure of the odontocete lower jaw and the oily tissue between it and the ear as evidence that sound is collected by the jaw and passed from it to the ear via this 'acoustic tissue'. Whichever theory is correct, there can be no doubt that the sense of hearing, at least in the toothed whales and dolphins, is the primary source of information these animals receive from their surroundings.

### Echolocation

All the dolphins, porpoises and toothed whales augment the amount of sound they would normally receive from their environment by using a system of sonar in the same way as bats. There is some evidence that the same ability may be present in baleen whales, but it has not been proven and, if it is present, it must be much less well developed than in odontocetes.

The principle of the sonar system is that 'clicks' of sound produced by the animal are reflected off any object in their path and received back as echoes. The form of the echoes, including their loudness, can inform the whale or dolphin of the size, shape, surface characteristics and movement of the object. The time lapse between emitting the signal and receiving its echo indicates how far away the object is. With this extraordinary sensory mechanism, the animal is able to search for, chase and catch fast-swimming prey in total darkness. In captivity, a blindfolded dolphin can not only swim around a pool without ever hitting the walls, but also can be trained to demonstrate its ability to distinguish, for example, between balls of slightly different sizes or between a hollow and a solid ball of the same size at distances of many metres. The same principle applies in the sonar equipment used by naval vessels to detect submarines and by hospitals to examine unborn babies with an ultrasound scan.

Echolocation 'clicks' of dolphins are different from the whistles, groans and other sounds that they use to communicate with one another (see page 30). The clicks are typically very short (less than one millisecond in duration) and repeated many times a second, with the effect of sometimes sounding like a door creaking to the human ear. In larger species, such as the sperm whale (which also uses sequences of clicks as a means of communication), the clicks are longer and repeated less often, resembling the ticking of a grandfather clock. The sound energy is typically spread over a broad spectrum of frequency, much of it well above the human range of hearing, but often a component of the clicks can be clearly heard by the human ear.

In much the same way that we might point the beam of a hand-held torch or flashlight towards an object we wish to see at night, the clicks of cetaceans can be focused to some extent by the animal and aimed at the object, perhaps a fish, which it wants to examine. This provides a stronger signal that is effective at a greater distance. This much is agreed by

**How dolphins may send and receive sounds**

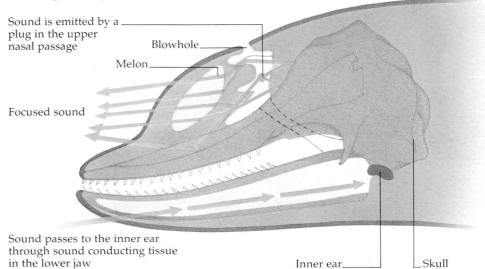

Sound is emitted by a plug in the upper nasal passage

Blowhole

Melon

Focused sound

Sound passes to the inner ear through sound conducting tissue in the lower jaw

Inner ear

Skull

cetologists, but arguments continue over how the sounds are made and how they are focused. Some say they are produced by the nasal plugs, in the air passage to the blowhole, while others argue that they emanate from the larynx. Proponents of the nasal plug theory believe that focusing is achieved by the 'melon', a structure of fatty tissue that lies under the blubber on the forehead of toothed whales, dolphins and porpoises (but not in baleen whales). They suggest that the shape of the melon can be altered by muscles in the head to change its focal length, so sound passing through it can be focused at a given point in front of the animal. Supporters of the idea of sound propagation by the larynx argue that focusing is achieved by 'bouncing' sound off parts of the skull. Recent work on acoustics, showing that some species can simultaneously produce two sounds of very different frequencies and type, suggests that both theories may be correct!

## Magnetic sense

Many organisms, from the smallest bacteria to the largest vertebrates, are known to be able to detect the earth's magnetic field and change their behaviour accordingly. Birds can navigate to some extent using this sense, and even we retain, especially in our youth, a 'sense of direction' which has been experimentally proved to rely on a magnetic sense.

Behavioural and anatomical evidence now suggests that a similar and well-developed sense is present in cetaceans. Behavioural work has focused on exam-

ination of the location of whales and dolphins at sea in relation to particular features of the earth's magnetic field. Migrating fin whales off the northeastern United States, for example, were found to regularly follow magnetic contours rather than cross a geomagnetic gradient. Most convincing of all was the discovery that strandings of live whales and dolphins were closely linked to local magnetic, rather than physical, character-

istics of the coastline (see page 40). At the same time, very careful and painstaking work by anatomists demonstrated that tiny quantities of magnetic material could be found in and around the brains of several cetacean species. So, although direct proof is lacking as yet, there seems to be very strong circumstantial evidence that cetaceans have the physical capability to sense geomagnetism and use it to navigate through the oceans.

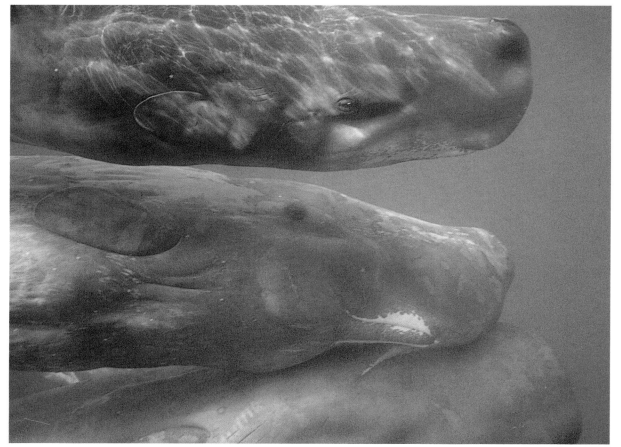

*Above: A beluga whale appears to 'kiss' a visitor at Sea World, Florida. Captive animals often solicit human contact and easily learn behaviours that may have a special significance for our species, but do not necessarily mean the same to them.*

*Left: Cetaceans, especially the group-living species, represented by these sperm whales, are very tactile in their social relationships. Touching and rubbing are common activities in both captive and wild whale populations.*

*Right: The famous ice-entrapped gray whales near Barrow, Alaska in late 1988. Does the normally fatal mistake made by these whales on this occasion tell us anything about their level of intelligence?*

## Touch

The tactile sense appears to be an important one in cetaceans, most obviously shown by the way in which captive animals frequently rub their skin against each other, sometimes swimming slowly with a fin in constant contact with the adjacent animal, or against a projection in the pool. The gentleness with which this touching is carried out suggests great sensitivity in the skin covering at least some parts of the body. Two important functions of skin sensitivity have been identified: the ability to detect when the blowhole is above the surface so it is opened at exactly the right moment, and the ability to sense the first signs of turbulence of water flow anywhere on the body so that the skin can counteract it (see page 15).

Tactile hairs on the rostrum of some dolphins persist for some time after birth and, even when they are lost, the pits from which they grow remain open, indicating that they remain functional even in the adult animal.

## Taste and smell

Both these senses involve the reception of chemical stimuli (chemoreception). For terrestrial animals, smell normally provides information about distant objects, while taste comes into play at a much closer range – in the mouth of air-living animals.

The anatomy of the brain indicates that the sense of smell has probably been lost altogether in toothed whales and dolphins and almost lost in baleen whales. Behavioural observations seem to con-

firm this. The region of the brain associated with taste is quite well developed, however, and pits on the tongues of many species are linked with this sense. It is not entirely clear what a sense of taste might be used for but, given that the receptors would be likely to pick up waterborne chemicals from both inside and outside the mouth, taste may actually perform the normal function of smell to some extent too. One example of the demonstration of taste in dolphins is of particular irritation to trainers of captive animals; dolphins have sometimes shown changing preferences for particular types of fish, even when cut up to disguise them, and refuse anything but their 'flavour of the month'.

## How intelligent are whales?

Newspaper, television and radio reports about whales or dolphins invariably contain the word 'intelligent'. Heard often enough, it is hardly surprising that many people unquestioningly accept this description of cetaceans, even when the news reports themselves reflect what appears to be the actions of unintelligent creatures. Any other animals consigning themselves to an untimely and traumatic death by swimming onto a beach, or finding themselves trapped in a tiny hole in sea ice, kept alive only by humans, because they started migrating too late in the season, would probably not be considered particularly clever.

Perhaps the first question to be asked is not how intelligent whales and dolphins are, but exactly what do we mean by in-

telligence? The term is commonly applied in a human context. We are probably justified in saying, for example, that Einstein was more intelligent than the average specimen of our species. But what do we mean when we say that a monkey is more intelligent than a donkey, or a dolphin more so than a rat? Often without realizing it, we impose a very egocentric set of values and rules on other animals when we come to judge them. We even anthropomorphize behaviour and facial features to the extent that the most familiar captive dolphin species, the bottlenose, is often said to be smiling, although its expression cannot be changed and it therefore continues to 'smile' even when in intense pain and after death.

## The concept of intelligence

The world in which cetaceans live is so very different to ours that it may well demand a different type of mental ability or agility for success. If so, it may be that our own ideas of what constitutes intelligence are inappropriate and that we are trying to evaluate the wrong factors. Hence, although we currently have little evidence of high intelligence in cetaceans as we define it, we may yet be looking for it in entirely the wrong direction.

The concept of intelligence is normally associated with thought. In man, thought is used, for example, in problem solving, predicting consequences of our actions, planning for the future and engaging in philosophical discussions about the 'meaning of life'. We know Einstein was a brilliant man because he was able to communicate his thoughts to others of his own species and we were, and are, able to evaluate those thoughts. Unfortunately, despite a great deal of dedicated and intensive research, our species has not yet been able to establish similar communication with any other species of animal, including whales or dolphins, so we must use other means of finding out about their thought processes. Two types of study have been used in this respect for cetaceans; the study of behaviour and the study of the cetacean brain.

## Insights into cetacean behaviour

Cetacean behaviour can be observed to some extent at sea, and has given us a good idea of the way in which cetaceans live. However, the study of particular behaviour likely to be a guide to higher thinking, such as problem solving and language abilities, has only recently been examined in captive animals.

At sea, the power of thought is likely to be involved in two particularly observable behaviours: foraging for food and escape from predators, including man. In the days of open-boat whaling, sperm whales were often said to move upwind of the pursuing vessel more often than chance would predict and, more re-

cently, this seemed to happen during research from a sailing boat around the Azores Islands in the Atlantic. In contrast, the same species was often harpooned while simply lolling at the surface, apparently unaware of any danger, by the gunner on a modern, noisy, 500-tonne diesel-powered catcher boat.

Dolphins in the eastern tropical Pacific have demonstrated clear learning ability by avoiding entanglement in the nets of tuna fishermen. Schools in areas where fishing is comparatively recent tend to panic when finding themselves surrounded by the net and consequently suffer a high rate of entanglement and drowning. Experienced schools in well-fished areas often quietly await release near the escape panels in the net (see page 50).

The best examples of innovative foraging are undoubtedly displayed by the killer whale. Family groups of this species around the world have developed their own specialized strategies to take

*Right: Around the world, particular pods of killer whales have developed specialized behaviours – a form of problem solving – that allow them to take advantage of local food resources. These photographs were taken at Peninsula Valdés in southern Argentina, where one group of killer whales has learned that seals and sea lions can be taken with a 'rush and grab' technique.*

advantage of locally available prey. A group off southern Argentina, for example, uses deeper channels leading up to the beach to rush and grab unsuspecting seals out of the surf, often beaching themselves temporarily in the

process. Antarctic killer whales knock or wash penguins and seals off ice floes. The frequency of whale attacks on yachts in some oceans may even indicate that they have learned that a seal-sized meal can be knocked off a different type of floating object entering their territory!

In captivity, dolphins have demonstrated an ability to learn a sequence of physical procedures quickly and carry them out on command. Their understanding of complex commands and questions has been studied using dolphins trained in a language of many hundreds of different sequences of gestures or acoustic signals. Researchers have found that dolphins are able to communicate details of their surroundings, including, for example, whether a named object such as a ball is present or absent. Sentences of up to five 'words' could be comprehended and the dolphins took account of the semantics and syntax of the sentences (i.e. the meaning and grammatical arrangement of the words), both of which are considered the essential elements of any human language. Thus, at least some cetaceans can grasp a basic language framework as we know it. As yet, however, communication between humans and dolphins has been limited to very simple messages about physical objects or attributes. Studies of both wild and captive populations have, until now, similarly found only very simple and stereotyped vocal communication between animals. Nevertheless, until we have a much better understanding of the whale and dolphin mind and the meaning of their gestures and vocalizations, we are unable to say whether communication between man and cetaceans will ever reach a higher level.

## The cetacean brain

In general structure, cetacean brains have been considered to be similar to those of primates, including man. In 1671, a gentleman named John Ray, having dissected a dolphin or porpoise, noted that 'this largeness of the brain and correspondence of it to that of man, argue this creature to be of more than ordinary wit

and capacity'. The most obvious differences are the larger cetacean cerebellum (the control centre for muscular coordination) and the more complex folding on the outside of the two main hemispheres (the seat of 'learning'). Adult male sperm whales have the largest brains of any animal on earth, typically 7-8kg in weight but reaching up to 9.2kg. The largest baleen whales have an average brain weight of just less than this, and bottlenose dolphin brains are normally about 2kg in large adults. One of the smallest cetaceans, the harbour porpoise, has a brain of about 0.5kg. In comparison, the human brain weighs about 1.5kg.

The fact that large whales have large brains is perhaps not surprising. Much of the brain is taken up in controlling non-intellectual functions such as muscular activity and responses to nerve cells in the skin, so larger bodies require, on average, a larger brain. A better indication, than relative size, of the degree of intellect is probably the size and development of the cerebral cortex, the region associated specifically with thought.

Corresponding with our view of ourselves as having the highest intellect, the cerebral cortex in man is relatively large and folded. In cetaceans part of it is small, but the neocortex – the folded 'grey matter' on the surface – is large in many species and this is considered by the Swiss cetologist and brain anatomist, Giorgio Pilleri, to 'explain the highly developed learning capacity and intelligence of these animals'. This is one of a variety of expert opinions on the interpretation of brain morphology and whether the cetacean cortex is well developed or primitive. Much more research is needed on the function of the cetacean brain to resolve the issue.

### The unanswered questions

As with so much research on whales and dolphins, the answers that we have to questions concerning their intelligence are incomplete and beg yet more questions. Since we cannot ask the study animals what they are thinking, we must resort to other ways of seeing inside their

*Far left: For years, scientists have tried to establish a means of communicating with dolphins, using such behavioural language.*

*Above: Cetaceans have proved fast learners. Does this reflect their level of intelligence? How are we to define such intelligence?*

minds. Anatomical studies of the brain are inconclusive and most behavioural and cognitive projects have been abandoned without finding evidence of an advanced intellect. Some of those that continue have been much better planned and are beginning to produce good evidence of basic skills in languages as we know them, but we cannot say how this might relate to the dolphins' ability to communicate between themselves.

On current evidence, the popular belief of high intelligence in whales and dolphins looks to be misplaced. Almost all studies of captive cetaceans reveal a capacity for learning and mimicry, but sea lions, dogs, pigeons and rats have all been trained to carry out similar tricks without being hailed as near to ourselves in intellect. Even the impressive ability of killer whales to 'work out' a new method of obtaining food involving a preparatory task is no more clever than the use of tools by some birds and primates to seize inaccessible prey.

The results of new and more sophisticated fields of study into animal thought may confirm what is for many this disappointing verdict, or it may reveal that our bench marks of intelligence are inappropriate for creatures living in such a different environment to our own.

# FOOD AND FEEDING

Animals use or lose energy in many different ways, but gain it from only one source – food. The quantity of food an animal takes each day depends on its size, its rate of growth and level of activity, its reproductive status, the time of year, the energy value of the food and the ambient temperature.

In a perfectly stable situation, daily energy intake equals energy outflow. In whales, the demands of reproduction, seasonal water temperature changes and even foraging in a patchy environment ensure that daily requirements vary. As a result – and in order to avoid the risk of death due to starvation if food cannot be found for days or weeks – cetaceans have developed an ability to store energy in the form of fat or oil for use in times of dearth. Most of this energy store is held in the blubber layer, but it can also be laid down in the abdominal cavity, in the muscle and within the bones.

Most toothed whales remain within food-bearing waters throughout the year, so fluctuations in their rate of feeding are relatively small and short term. In contrast, most of the baleen whales migrate annually between rich feeding grounds and impoverished breeding areas where little, if any, food is available. In the most extreme cases, it is likely that most of the year's energy requirements must be consumed and stored within a four- or five-month period, at the end of which the whale may be 40 percent heavier than when it arrived on the feeding grounds. This explains the single-minded obsession with which baleen whales pursue their feeding during the summer months.

All other things being equal, smaller whales and dolphins need to consume a greater proportion of their body weight than larger animals, in order to compensate for factors such as their higher ratio of surface body area to body weight, which means that they lose heat more quickly. The range of prey consumption among cetaceans is thought to average about 1.5-14 percent of body weight per day, although actual consumption will vary considerably, even between individuals of the same species.

A 50kg porpoise might ordinarily take about 4.5kg of fish per day, although it would require a much greater weight than this if the food consisted of squid. It has been estimated that a large blue whale weighing 100 tonnes would require up to four tonnes of euphausiids (krill) every day during the feeding season, representing perhaps four fills of the enormous fore-stomach (one of three stomach chambers). Over the year as a whole, the daily consumption of a large whale probably averages 1.5 to 2 percent of its body weight.

## Toothed whales (odontocetes)

Unlike most mammals, the toothed whales and dolphins retain their first teeth – the milk dentition – throughout their lives. With a few exceptions, they also differ from other flesh-eaters in that all the teeth in the mouth are uniformly shaped, although there is considerable variation in the shape, size and number of teeth between species.

The difference between species reflects their adaptation to specialized methods of feeding and to different prey groups. Most cetacean teeth are conical and provide a means of grasping prey, which is normally swallowed whole. Porpoise teeth are spade-shaped for slicing food

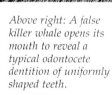

*Above right: A false killer whale opens its mouth to reveal a typical odontocete dentition of uniformly shaped teeth.*

*Above: A close view of the mat of hairs on the inside surface of fin whale baleen. They effectively strain the food out of the water.*

*Left: A blue whale feeding off southern California. Like other rorquals, blue whales are equipped with elastic tissue on the throat and chest, with pleats called 'ventral grooves'. These allow the whale to engulf huge quantities of food-laden sea water and filter this through the baleen to extract the food, before expelling the water from the sides of the mouth.*

too large to be eaten in one piece, and some river dolphins have flattened teeth with which they can crush invertebrates, such as crabs. The rough-toothed dolphin is aptly named, being uniquely adapted for holding and, perhaps, tearing its prey, whereas the killer whale has oval-section teeth for tearing prey by twisting or shaking it in the mouth. Some species, particularly the beaked whale group, retain few, if any, functional teeth. This is normally associated with a diet of squid.

**The odontocete diet** Squid and their allies (octopus and cuttlefish) and fish form the basis of most odontocete diets throughout the world. Some whales and dolphins eat only one or the other, but most will eat a mixture that reflects the relative abundance of prey in the vicinity. The killer, false killer and pygmy killer whales are the only species to consume warm-blooded prey. Packs of killer whales can tackle anything from herring to blue whales, and their diet is known to include a great variety of cetaceans, seals, penguins, turtles and many other marine creatures. To date, no humans are known to have been eaten by killer whales, but the human perception of its own species as somehow different from all others is unlikely to be shared by a hungry family of whales searching for prey.

**Locating and trapping prey** The sounds produced by dolphins to determine the direction and distance of objects nearby – their 'sonar' – can reach a deafening crescendo when they are feeding. The squeals, whistles and groans that fill the water at such times may help to confuse prey. Some scientists have suggested that odontocetes can use focused sound to stun their prey. An occasional 'crack' of intense sound energy is indeed emit-

ted by some toothed whales, but experiments in aquariums have so far failed to demonstrate that a sound within the capability of dolphins could have a crippling effect on fish or squid. However, an animal the size of a sperm whale could possibly produce sufficient sound energy to stun, if not kill, its prey. It has been proposed that a major function of the huge wax-filled 'case' that forms such a conspicuous part of the sperm whale's head is to focus sound at prey located by the animal's sonar. The theory seems plausible, because sperm whales are able to alter the shape of their case by means of muscles and tendons running the length of the head, and could thus change the 'focal length' of the case in much the same way that muscles change the focus of the eye lens. Furthermore, the wax itself has been found to exhibit properties that make it a good medium through which to pass sound and, since most odontocetes have evolved a 'case' or 'melon' containing this wax, it seems reasonable to assume that this organ must have a useful function. Why not as an aid to feeding?

A further mystery, perhaps linked to the last, is how the deep-diving odontocetes, especially the larger and slower species, manage to get close enough to their prey to swallow it in the pitch darkness of deep water or nearer the surface at night. Some, but by no means all, of the oceanic squid are luminous and so give themselves away to predators. Those that are not may be detectable by echolocation, but would have to be extremely unwary to allow an enormous and much slower-swimming odontocete, pulsing the water with sound, to come close enough to grab them. Equally puzzling is that live squid are taken by adult, male straptoothed whales that can only open their mouths a little way. Stranger

still, sperm whales have been captured with no lower jaw whatever, having lost it many months or years earlier, yet their stomachs still contain fresh, large squid. Clearly, we still have much to learn about odontocete feeding behaviour.

The ability of many odontocetes to swallow their prey whole is one of the most striking and intriguing characteristics of their feeding biology. An examination of the stomach contents of, for example, sperm whales killed by whalers at sites in the North Atlantic usually reveals a number of fresh and apparently untouched squid and fish. Rarely, such squid can measure as much as 10.5m in total length and weigh 184kg, and many will be so large that they could have put up quite a fight before being overwhelmed. This begs the question as to how sperm whales manage to catch and swallow such large prey with apparent ease, without first being forced to subdue them by tearing them apart. The answer is simply that no-one knows for certain, and this remains one of the great mysteries of cetology.

Direct observation of wild animals has demonstrated that speed and agility in the chase is sufficient for some dolphins to catch and subsequently swallow relatively small fish. Occasionally, groups of oceanic dolphins, such as *Stenella* or *Delphinus*, will surround and trap a shoal of fish against the sea surface. The dolphins then take turns to swim into the dense fish pack and gorge themselves by grabbing a few bewildered fish. Such deft skills are aided by the long, thin 'beak' characteristic of most open-ocean dolphins. In contrast, slower swimming species, such as the beluga and porpoises, have little or no beak and adopt other feeding techniques more suited to their habitat. In the beluga and Irrawaddy dolphin, which are able to 'pout' their lips, these may even include dislodging bottom-living molluscs and fish by directing a jet of water against them and sucking the prey into their mouths.

**Baleen whales (mysticetes)**
This group consists of just 11 species of whale, all relatively large. Their characteristic feature is a row of closely packed, triangular baleen plates hanging from each side of the roof of the mouth. These plates, numbering up to 400 on each side, are made of keratin (the same material as fingernails in man) and have a hairy fringe on their inner edge. The individual plates hang from their shortest edge across the mouth and are so arranged that the inner fringes overlap, effectively

forming a porous mat of fibres. This mat filters the water forced through it from inside the mouth and thus strains from it the small organisms that form the diet of baleen whales. The plates are springy and constantly growing, again much like fingernails. They wear away on the inner surface at the same rate as new growth is formed, the wear probably being caused mainly by the rasping tongue which, at least in rorqual whales, is used to sweep food into the throat before swallowing.

The filter-feeding whales are in three groups, each with its own mechanism and technique for gathering food-rich water into the mouth and extracting the edible organisms from it. With the exception of the gray whale, the usual food of the baleen, or 'whalebone', whales is a variety of zooplankton known as krill. Shoaling fish are also taken in some areas, particularly by fin, blue and humpback whales.

**Family Balaenidae** The right whales have long baleen plates suspended from arched jaws, providing a very large surface area through which water can pass. The fibres that form the filtering mechanism are very fine, thus allowing the whale to capture tiny plankton, often copepods or euphausiids only 2.5mm long, that would normally pass through the baleen of other species.

Right whales usually employ a technique known as 'skim feeding', whereby the animal swims slowly forward with its mouth open 10-15°, allowing water to flow continuously into the mouth at the front and out through the baleen plates at the sides. Any crustaceans trapped on the inner surface of the baleen are periodically swept off with the tongue, or possibly manoeuvred into the throat by means of a flow of water to 'wash' the hairs clean. Right whales often 'skim' at the surface of the sea, revealing only the tip of the upper jaw, but are known to feed at or near the seabed in depths of many tens of metres and also in mid water. The food and feeding behaviour of the pygmy right whale (*Caperea marginata*) of the Southern Hemisphere is almost unknown, but the little evidence available suggests that it has a similar diet to the other right whales.

**Family Eschrichtiidae** The only member of this family, now restricted to the North Pacific, is the gray whale, which has a unique method of gathering food. This species has quite short, coarse baleen, usually more worn on the right side than on the left, and it gathers almost all its prey from within, or just above, the layer of mud on the ocean floor. The asymmetric baleen wear is thought to be evidence that this species carries out at least part of its foraging on its right side. Observers have noticed troughs in the sediment and plumes of mud trailing behind gray whales, and these observations, to-

*Above: A lunge-feeding humpback whale. The animal's mouth is wide open and we are looking at the palate, with the inner, hairy fringe of the two baleen rows clearly visible.*

*Right: An aerial shot of a foraging gray whale, disturbing the mud in shallow water.*

*Far right: Freshly taken shrimplike euphausiids, otherwise universally known as krill.*

*Below right: Humpback whales have evolved effective group-feeding behaviours.*

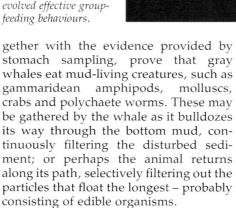

gether with the evidence provided by stomach sampling, prove that gray whales eat mud-living creatures, such as gammaridean amphipods, molluscs, crabs and polychaete worms. These may be gathered by the whale as it bulldozes its way through the bottom mud, continuously filtering the disturbed sediment; or perhaps the animal returns along its path, selectively filtering out the particles that float the longest – probably consisting of edible organisms.

Fascinating clues to the feeding mechanisms employed by gray whales were provided by a young animal held in captivity for several months in 1971. This whale took food from the bottom of the pool with a type of suction process, apparently using its tongue to depress the bottom of the mouth and thus draw in water between its lips, which could be moved independently. This indicates that a pistonlike mechanism is the most likely means by which gray whales draw water into their mouths and force it back out again through the baleen.

**Family Balaenopteridae** All members of the third baleen whale group – the rorquals, or balaenopterids – possess pleated and very elastic tissues that cover the entire underside from the tip of the lower jaw to around the umbilicus. This feature, not found in the right and gray whales, is a vital part of the rorqual feeding apparatus, allowing the animal to engulf an enormous quantity of water, then close the mouth and expel the water through the baleen – a technique known as 'gulp' feeding. Food trapped on the inner baleen surface can then be swept into the throat by the tongue and swallowed, but exactly how this is achieved is unknown. The balaenopterid tongue is enormous, and completely covers the floor of the mouth. It has a rough surface, well suited to brushing food off the matted fibres that line the sides of the mouth, but it is a very flaccid organ and perhaps 'ripples' rather than licks the baleen clean.

When a rorqual is feeding, the forward part of its underside expands to an extent that is hard to believe, making the animal resemble a gigantic tadpole in shape. To allow water to enter the mouth very quickly, thus forcing the pleated tissue to expand, the animal normally lunges forward, its lower jaw open by as much as 90°. Special pads of elastic tissue at the joints of the lower jaw permit this unusual articulation to occur. The animal then closes its mouth and contracts the muscles in the ventral tissue, forcing the water out between the baleen plates and through a gap left open between the sides of the lower and upper jaws. The lunge may be made horizontally, at or near the water surface, or sometimes vertically upwards. Vertical lunges often thrust the feeding animal partly into the air, with water and food organisms cascading out of the mouth as it is forced closed.

The one species of rorqual known to skim feed regularly is the sei whale, *Balaenoptera borealis*; indeed, some authorities

claim that it uses this technique predominantly. Sei whales have the finest baleen fibres of the family and are able to exploit tiny prey, in much the same way as the right whales. The reason why sei whales adopt the same feeding technique as right whales may simply be that skimming is more effective than gulp feeding on microplankton.

Fin, blue and humpback whales are gulp feeders with coarse baleen fibres, specializing in the larger swarming crustaceans and shoaling fish. In the Southern Hemisphere, these large whales are chiefly dependent on one species of prey, the shrimplike *Euphausia superba*, the archetypal 'krill'. *E. superba* forms the basis of all vertebrate food chains in the Antarctic Ocean, being taken by fish and squid, penguins, flighted seabirds (such as albatrosses), seals and whales. In winter, the krill sink to warmer water at depths greater than 250m, but in summer they rise to within 100m of the surface, in order to feed on smaller zooplankton as well as on plantlike phytoplankton, which derives energy from the sun. In these few summer months, the krill grow and reproduce rapidly, but are simultaneously exposed to predation from above and below. Whales feed particularly at dusk, when krill rises nearest to the surface.

As with closely related species in the Northern Hemisphere, *E. superba* occurs in enormous swarms, which can cover an area of many square kilometres. The larger rorquals have learned that their feeding can be more effective if the krill are 'herded' into tighter concentrations before being engulfed. Fin whales do this by swimming in a gentle circle on their sides, probably using the whiteness on the right side of their heads to scare the plankton or fish into a small area, before

lunging through the concentration with mouth open. Usually, all that can be seen above the surface of a feeding fin whale is one half of the tail fluke and perhaps the flipper on the same side.

Humpback whales have evolved a whole range of complex behaviours to increase their feeding efficiency. Probably the best known involves the controlled release of air under water, perhaps in one burst (producing a bubble 'cloud'), as the animal swims in a straight line (a 'curtain') or in a circle (a 'net'). In each case, the idea is to use the rising air as a physical barrier through which the prey are unwilling to pass. Having released the air, the whale usually begins its foraging run. With mouth open, the animal will swim along a 'curtain', or vertically up through the centre of a 'net'. In the latter case, the first indication that a catch is about to be made is a few bubbles hitting the surface. Gradually the circular pattern of these bubbles is revealed, and shortly after, the prey – either fish or krill – begin to jump within the circle with increasing intensity until the water appears to be boiling. Finally, the orchestrator of this panic bursts through the surface with a roar of noise, mouth closing and throat grotesquely distended, before subsiding back into the water to sieve its catch and swallow the spoil.

Humpbacks can feed individually, in pairs or in groups of up to 24 animals, the membership of which can be constant between years. Such cooperative feeding is unusual in cetaceans and is better developed in humpbacks than in any other baleen whale. The activity of a circle of humpback whales is reminiscent of a group of pelicans using the physical presence of others in the group to increase their individual catch.

# SOCIAL BEHAVIOUR

All whales, dolphins and porpoises are social animals to some extent, although the degree of sociability varies greatly from one species to another. At one extreme are species such as the river dolphins, which seem to have a relatively simple social system, forming small groups of just a few animals – rarely more than 10 in one aggregation. On the other hand, many of the oceanic dolphins almost never occur in small groups and may roam the seas in company with literally thousands of others. There can even be differences within a species; in the sperm whale, for example, females and juveniles are group forming and adult males are often solitary.

## The advantages of group living
Differences in behaviour have not evolved by chance. Living in close proximity to other animals has certain costs and benefits, so we can expect the group size adopted by a species to be the most appropriate for its environment and lifestyle. Possible reasons for living in groups include increased efficiency in searching for and capturing food, and benefits for reproduction, learning, defence and sensory integration.

Sensory integration is a term for the way in which each animal within a group contributes to the sensory information gained by the group as a whole. This attribute plays a significant part in defence and the search for food. For example, a group of hundreds or thousands of dolphins may be spread over many hectares of sea. If one animal discovers a shoal of fish or a predatory shark, it can immediately pass this information to the others in the group, so that all may benefit. A single animal or a small group may remain unaware of the food or a predator and thus miss a meal or, perhaps, suffer a surprise attack.

The size and distribution of prey probably has a powerful influence on the formation of groups. One reason for the relatively small groupings adopted by baleen whales may be that most swarms of krill, their main prey, are not large enough to support more than a few animals. Larger groups would increase the competition for food and few animals would benefit from each discovery.

## Social units
In all species, the tightest social bonding is in the mother-calf pair. Long-term father-offspring relationships are currently unproven in any species and probably rare or non-existent. Calves are dependent on their mothers for at least four months, and in some odontocetes they may continue suckling for years.

Long-term studies of individually recognizable animals have revealed varying levels of group stability between species. Killer whales and sperm whales often remain in particular groups for many years and we know that calves of these species enjoy a long period of maternal care. Adult male killer whales remain with one group, whereas mature male sperm whales seem to move between groups, remaining with each for only a few days. Recent genetic analysis of long-finned pilot whale schools around the Faeroe Islands indicates that the sexually active males spend no more than a few months in any particular group. The strong mother-offspring association has led to groups that are effectively matrilines, with daughters tending to remain in their mothers' group and sons moving away at maturity.

This same matrilineal social structure appears in another species, the humpback whale, but in a quite different type of group, namely the 'stock' of animals that uses a particular feeding ground. The reasons for this are simple and can best be explained using a particular North Atlantic stock as an example. In the summer months, a small number of shallow-water banks off West Greenland currently support a few hundred humpback whales that feed intensively during their stay. In winter, the whales from this area migrate to the West Indies, where females mate with animals from any of the North Atlantic feeding grounds and, a year later in the same area, give birth. Calves then follow their mothers north to Greenland, where they are weaned and, with insignificant exceptions, will subsequently return (but independently of the mother). Since male humpbacks summering off West Greenland mostly mate with females from other, much larger feeding stocks, their offspring rarely appear in West Greenland. In contrast, the young of West Greenland females *always* go to West Greenland in the summer. As a result, the female genetic line, or matriline, is dominant although, in contrast to the group-living sperm and pilot whales, mothers and daughters need not necessarily meet again.

## What is a group?
This raises the question of what exactly is the definition of a group. Some scientists have proposed that all animals in acoustic contact with one another should be considered a group but, given the extraordinary distances that cetacean sound is capable of travelling, this could lead to the conclusion that all animals in a huge expanse of ocean should be considered as a group. In practical terms, it is perhaps better to recognize an assembly of animals that coordinate their activity. A group may be stable over months or years, as in killer whales, or change frequently in size and membership, as in spinner dolphins. With few exceptions, including the mother/calf bond and some humpback feeding groups, associations between baleen whales are thought not to be long lived.

## Mating systems
A major influence on group size and behaviour is the mating system of the species. None are considered to be monogamous (one male mating exclusively with one female), but some are polygynous (one male mating with many females) and most are probably promiscuous (multiple mating by males and females). Polygynous species are often characterized by a high degree of sexual dimorphism, whereby adult males are much larger than females. Since few males gain access to receptive females, competition between them can be intense. Fighting, with the teeth being used as weapons, is the cause of the extensive scarring seen on, for example, male sperm and beaked whales.

Promiscuous mating seems to be the commonest strategy in cetaceans, but it may take one of two forms. In one, exemplified by humpback whales, males

compete for exclusive mating access to females and try to prevent other males from gaining subsequent access by remaining as 'escort'. In the other form, adopted by right whales, males attempt repeated copulations with as many females as possible and rely on their sperm to 'out-compete' the sperm of other males within the females' reproductive tracts. In right whales, this has led to the evolution of an extraordinary capability for producing sperm in large quantities and a combined weight for the testes of adult males of a tonne or more.

### Individual social behaviour
Animals living in large groups show a variety of behaviours that serve to strengthen bonds between individuals. Whales and dolphins are very tactile animals and body contact is important. Nudging, caressing and swimming in bodily contact are common. Youngsters of some species are often given a ride on their mother's back; there is an area of rough skin on the back of finless porpoises that may be used for just this purpose.

The sensual nature of captive dolphins is apparent from the frequent involvement of the genital region in touching or being touched. The wild but sociable male bottlenose dolphins recently occurring off Ireland, the UK and northern France also seem to use the penis as a tactile organ. Observations of cetacean groups in the wild are scanty or lacking entirely in all but a few species, but it seems likely that the day-to-day interactions of group-forming odontocetes include sexual or pseudosexual behaviour. In captivity, this behaviour can be seen even in single-sex groups and is clearly not necessarily related to courtship or mating. It may form part of the repertoire of behaviours necessary to maintain a dominance hierarchy, or 'pecking order'.

### Asserting dominance
A 'pecking order' clearly occurs in captive small cetaceans, in much the same way that it occurs in primates, birds and most other group-living higher animals. Observations of wild bottlenose dolphins indicate that the same mechanisms are at work outside the constraints of captivity.

Dominance is shown by jaw claps, chasing, biting, ramming and tail slaps against subordinates. In general, dominance rank decreases with relative body size, but the hierarchy is fluid and will alter in the face of events such as illness, disappearance of a group member and change of reproductive status.

### The role of play
Play is important, especially in young animals, and no doubt forms part of the learning process. It can involve bursts of erratic swimming around the mother, breaching, head slaps and a whole range of other antics. It can involve the use of an object, such as seaweed or a dead fish, which is perhaps thrown or carried on the jaw or flipper. In adults, breaching may sometimes be no more than play, and it is difficult to imagine that bow riding the bow wave of a boat and surfing on nearshore breakers, a speciality of Californian bottlenose dolphins, can be anything but exuberant play.

### Care-giving behaviour
Care giving may take several forms, all of which somehow benefit other animals in the group. It is assumed that such behaviour, which may involve some 'cost' to the care giver, has evolved mostly in group-living species because it eventually benefits the giver. This benefit may be direct, if, for example, the animal receiving care is related to, and carries some of the same genes as, the giver. It may be indirect, in that the apparently selfless act will subsequently, on average, be given in return. In either case,

care giving can be interpreted as being in the long-term interest of the giver. Typical examples are defence against predators, the assistance of 'midwives' at births and the way in which injured or ill animals are supported at the surface to prevent drowning.

The latter behaviour is particularly intriguing and has been interpreted by observers and scientists in many ways. It may have its origins in the way a mother helps her newborn baby to the surface and supports it on her upper jaw during its first few breaths. Similar support is also given to adults of the same species, as well as to adults of other species and even, on occasion, to humans. Many people have pointed to this as an example of the great friendship and selfless devotion shown by dolphins towards humans, but such an interpretation is probably just wishful thinking – a case of attributing human emotions to another species. Exactly the same behaviour has been directed towards animals in a way that clearly demonstrates that the care giver is unselective about what it supports. An example here is the female dolphin that killed a leopard shark in captivity and spent the next five days supporting it at the surface. There is considerable evidence that this supportive behaviour is a deeply embedded instinct, clearly triggered by the proximity of a dolphin-sized animal in obvious distress. Normally, of course, the troubled animal will be a dolphin, so the instinct is vindicated. On extremely rare occasions, however, the distressed 'trigger' is a human swimmer or diver.

### Communicating with sound
Communication using sound falls into two categories: non-vocal and vocal.

### Non-vocal signalling
Non-vocal signalling includes slapping the water surface with parts of the body – full and partial breaches, tail slaps, flipper slaps – and subsurface sounds, such as bubbling and jaw clapping (the forceful closing of the jaws under water). Most species of large whales have been seen to breach at some time, and right, gray and humpback whales do so commonly. Breaching is often 'infectious' between animals in an area and may often have no communication purpose at all. It might just be a sign of play or excitement.

Many dolphins frequently jump clear of the surface. They usually do so gracefully, without making much sound, but sometimes they deliberately land on their backs or sides, making a noise that can be heard up to a kilometre away under water. The larger species of whale make such a splash that they can be heard at a distance of several kilometres.

Humpbacks breach more frequently in rough seas, a tactic that has been interpreted as a means of being heard when normal vocalizations are obliterated by water noise. Humpbacks also use their long flippers and tails to make a sharp report by slapping them on the sea surface. Clearly, such a signal can only have a simple message. It may be 'I am here' or 'keep away'. In toothed whales and dolphins, tail slaps and jaw claps often have an aggressive purpose.

### Vocal communication
In an environment where the ability to sense sound provides more information than vision, it is not surprising that cetaceans have developed a means of communication using underwater vocalizations. Without it, animals more than 100m away from one another would be 'out of touch' even in the clearest water, and in some circumstances animals only a few metres apart would be lost.

### Producing sound
Making a noise under water is not as simple as it might seem. Terrestrial mammals, such as ourselves, force air through the vocal cords in the larynx, and these vibrate to make a sound. Once the air has passed out through the mouth or nose, it is lost and must be replaced by inhalation. In contrast, consider the humpback whale, singer of the well-known haunting whale 'songs'. It can remain below the surface, singing continuously for 30 minutes or more, yet humpbacks do not have particularly large lungs for their body size and can only sustain such singing bouts because no air is lost when they vocalize. The sounds may still emanate from the larynx, but the air that provides the energy to drive the mechanics of sound production is saved and recycled.

We do not know exactly where sound is produced in the odontocete head. Recordings reveal that some species of dolphin simultaneously produce two quite different sounds at different frequencies, which indicates that two separate sites of sound production exist. The nares (the air channel leading to the blowhole) and the larynx are the most likely sources. Baleen whales almost certainly produce sound from the larynx only.

### The function of vocalization
Cetacean vocalizations have two main functions. One is the echolocation 'sonar' of toothed whales and dolphins. The other function is communication, used by both toothed and baleen whales.

Current evidence indicates that vocal communication is simple in content and does not involve a 'language' as we know it. An animal can communicate distress and excitement, perhaps its identity and, indirectly, its location, but probably cannot, for example, complain about the poor size of fish available this season compared to last. The main function of 'social' sound production may be simply to inform other animals who and where you are, to maintain contact and spacing in a group and, perhaps, to indicate your activity and emotional state. Even humpback song, as complex as it may seem, appears to function simply as a sexual or territorial advertisement, in much the same way as birdsong.

Nevertheless, experiments on captive dolphins have demonstrated their ability to communicate more complex information. A well-known example is that of a male who was able to gain food by pressing the correct one of two paddles by listening to a female in whose pen were two lights, one of which would be illuminated. The two dolphins were visually screened from each other yet, invariably, the male pressed the left paddle when the left light was illuminated in the female's pen, and vice versa. The information

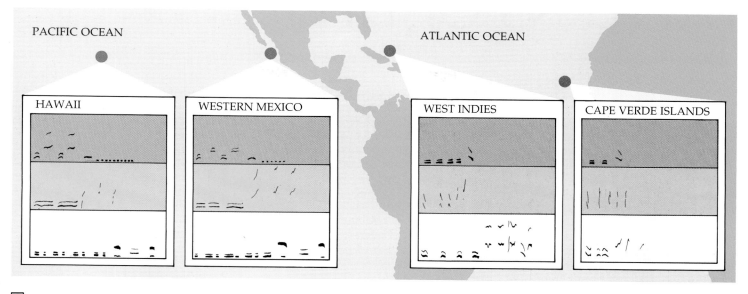

PACIFIC OCEAN

ATLANTIC OCEAN

HAWAII

WESTERN MEXICO

WEST INDIES

CAPE VERDE ISLANDS

■ Theme 1
▨ Theme 2
□ Theme 3

*Above: Tracings of humpback whale songs from four sites in 1979. Note the similarity between the themes*

*from sites within each ocean, and the dissimilarity between the oceans. Despite the great distance between sites within the same ocean (4-5,000km), there is clearly some 'cultural' interchange.*

must have been passed in vocalizations by the female who, incidentally, continued to make the sounds after the screen – and the male – were removed.

In many species, individuals make sounds that are uniquely identifiable. If humans can detect a difference between these animals, it seems reasonable to assume that the animals can, too.

Apart from these individual differences, evidence is accumulating of 'dialects' common to schools of dolphins or animals in a given geographical area. Killer whales in the Vancouver Island area possess calls that identify them as belonging to a particular pod or community, and a dolphin whistle can apparently mean something to its own group but not to another of the same species. Perhaps the best-known dialect is that of humpback whale songs. These differ not only between breeding areas, but also from one year to the next.

## Vocalization in toothed whales

The toothed whales, dolphins and porpoises can be divided into two groups – the whistlers and the non-whistlers. Whistling is generally restricted to those species of dolphin and small whale that occur in large social groups. A group of wild dolphins can whistle continuously, particularly at times of excitement or stress, such as when bow riding, feeding or being chased by a predator. In contrast, they can be silent to avoid detection.

The non-whistlers, including the river dolphins, porpoises and the largest toothed whale, the sperm, communicate with pulsed vocalizations, much like the sounds used for echolocation. Whistlers also use burst-pulse sounds as part of their repertoire. Sperm whales produce patterns of broad-spectrum sound pulses or 'clicks' known as codas. It is assumed that these codas allow sperm whales to know where each animal in their group is located, since they are likely to be out of visual contact most of the time. Other information may also be transmitted vocally, such as 'I've found a concentration of squid', but as yet we are unable to find out if this is indeed the case. Using hydrophones, the 'clicks' of sperm whales can be heard more than 10km from the animal producing them and it is

likely that other sperm whales can hear the sounds at least this far away. If clicks are made in the SOFAR (sound fixing and ranging) channel – a deep layer of water with characteristics that allow unusually good sound propagation – they could be heard perhaps hundreds or even thousands of kilometres away.

## Vocalization in baleen whales

The baleen whales have a very different sound repertoire from that of the toothed whales and dolphins – on the whole, they neither whistle nor click. Their vocalizations are generally of low frequency, mostly below 3kHz and all below 35kHz, whereas some toothed whale signals register 200kHz or more. In comparison, humans can hear sounds up to about 15kHz and bats up to about 200kHz.

Baleen whale calls have been given a wonderful variety of names, including bellows, moans, belches, rumbles, grunts, rasps, chirps and bongs. Each individual component of sound may last less than half a second or, in a blue whale 'moan', for example, it may continue for 30 seconds or more. Moans, a common type of vocalization, are typically of 12-500Hz and may be of pure tone or have a strong harmonic structure. Fin whales have a particularly common subsonic call of about 20Hz which, being of such low frequency, could theoretically carry for hundreds of kilometres in a quiet sea.

The best-known baleen whale sounds are those of the male humpback 'song'. They are quite unlike any other type of cetacean vocalization and consist of sequences of repeated noises of great variety in the range 40Hz-5kHz. The sounds form an ordered sequence of themes, which can be repeated many times in an identical pattern, for periods of many hours. Perhaps most fascinating of all was the discovery that each song can be identified with an individual singer, a geographical area and the year in which it was sung (also see page 47).

*Left: A sequence of three photographs, taken at half-second intervals, showing a humpback whale breaching off West Greenland. Here the sea is smooth, but humpbacks breach more often in windy conditions than on a calm day, perhaps because the sound they make on re-entering the water overcomes turbulent water noise more effectively than vocal communication.*

# PATTERNS OF LIFE

The basic life cycle in whales, dolphins and porpoises is the same as in all other mammals, whether they are land-dwelling, amphibious or purely aquatic. They are born alive (i.e. not from an egg, as in most fish), take milk from their mothers, go through a period of immaturity, reach puberty, reproduce and subsequently die. A few species resemble man in that they survive beyond the end of the reproductive phase, but essentially the pattern is similar no matter how large or small the animal. As we shall see, there is sometimes considerable variation in life histories between individuals in a population and between populations as a whole. Furthermore, the characteristics of individuals and populations can change in response to external factors, such as food availability and disease, so that the overall picture is constantly changing. The name given to the whole area of population life history characteristics – population dynamics – reflects this continuous state of change and by studying it we can begin to understand the way in which a population 'works'.

## The sexual cycle

Both sexes have clearly defined sexual cycles. In males it is a simple cycle that repeats itself after one year, while in females it is complex and takes between two and about eight years to complete. Males cycle annually because, although females that conceive one year will not normally be receptive the next, a new 'batch' will be ovulating after having just weaned their last calf.

The male cycle is determined by one overriding factor: the drive to fertilize females when they are in oestrus. The male cycle is therefore closely linked to the female cycle and usually involves behavioural and physical changes that bring the male to a peak of readiness when oestrus reaches a peak in females. Behavioural changes can include greater aggression towards other males, a desire to 'escort' suitable females and, in humpback whales and perhaps other species, the production of a series of vocalizations known as 'song'. The main physical change is the enlargement of the testes and epididymis, which enable the male to produce and store enough semen to fertilize the requisite number of females. In the unusually sexually active right whales, in which paternity depends on sperm quantity, the testes of a large male can weigh more than 500kg each.

The female cycle consists of ovulation, conception, pregnancy, parturition (birth) and lactation. A period of rest usually occurs between the end of lactation and the next ovulation, but this is not always the case and females of some species can become pregnant again while still suckling the previous calf. The normal time required to complete a cycle ranges from about two years in some species to three or four years in others, but in a few species (killer whales, for example), this period can exceptionally stretch to eight or even ten years. Alternatively, if two cycles can continue simultaneously, as in the case of females that are both pregnant and lactating, the interval between births can be reduced to little more than the gestation period, i.e. 11-18 months according to species.

## Ovulation and conception

Once they reach puberty, females periodically come into oestrus and become receptive to potential mates. Oestrus occurs when one or more eggs are released from ripe follicles in the ovaries and pass into the uterus, where they will be fertilized if successful mating takes place. Ovulation does not occur at regular intervals throughout the year; in most cetacean species (particularly those living at least part of the time in high latitudes, where the seasons are more apparent) it is seasonal to some extent. In migratory species, such as most baleen whales, ovulations are synchronized within the population, so that subsequent births occur at a particular stage in the migrational cycle, typically in the warmer waters of the wintering grounds. Non-migrants may still have some seasonality of ovulations – and therefore births – but the peak of activity is usually less marked and in some species ovulations may occur at almost any time of year.

Whether or not a particular female ovulates in any year is determined by the stage she has reached in the sexual cycle – her 'reproductive status'. Pregnant females cannot ovulate and those in lactation normally do not, although in some species an ovulation soon after giving birth is not unusual. If lactation is prolonged, as in many toothed whales, an ovulation towards the end of lactation often occurs.

Other than this, ovulation only occurs in females that are 'resting', having completed their previous cycle or, perhaps, having lost a foetus or calf due to illness or disease. If ovulation occurs but the egg is not fertilized for some reason, the ovaries will release an egg some weeks later and this process continues until either fertilization occurs or the mating season ends. In this case, a further period of re-

**The reproductive cycle in migratory baleen whales**

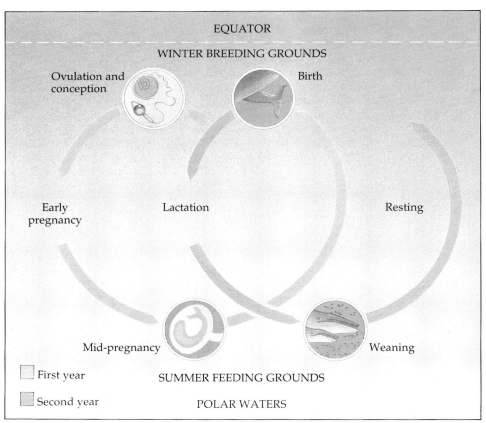

EQUATOR

WINTER BREEDING GROUNDS

Ovulation and conception

Birth

Early pregnancy

Lactation

Resting

Mid-pregnancy

Weaning

☐ First year

☐ Second year

SUMMER FEEDING GROUNDS

POLAR WATERS

productive inactivity must occur before the next season. Multiple ovulations are not the rule, and females are normally successfully mated during the first oestrus of the cycle.

Mating occurs in the usual mammalian way, with the male's penis inserted into the vagina of the female to enable the semen carrying millions of sperm to be safely delivered within access of the single egg. Mating is probably repeated on several occasions. In some, possibly most, species males will mate with more than one female, and females with more than one male (see page 28).

(see page 28)

## Pregnancy

Following successful fertilization, the egg is implanted in the wall of one of the two uterine horns, depending on which ovary released the egg. On rare occasions, two eggs are fertilized at the same time, in which case twins will start to develop, either both in the same horn or one on each side. Multiple foetuses (multiplets) are quite rare and almost all die before birth. Multiplets represent less than one percent of pregnancies in most baleen whales. There is one record of six, and one of five foetuses in fin whales. Sadly, even if more than one calf were to be born, it is unlikely that the mother would be able to provide sufficient milk for more than one to survive, although there is at least one record of successful twin killer whales.

Once implanted in the uterus, the fertilized egg, or blastocyst, begins to increase in size by a process of cell division. Thereafter, growth and development closely follow the pattern in man, except that the duration of pregnancy is longer in most cetaceans, each stage taking proportionately more time to complete. Foetal growth is continuous, but the rate varies during pregnancy. The length of pregnancy – the gestation period – varies between about 10 and 16 months according to species. Perhaps unexpectedly, the gestation period does not depend on body size. For example, the largest animal ever to have lived on earth, the blue whale, has a gestation period of 12 months or rather less, while the relatively tiny beluga and narwhal are born 14-15 months after conception.

## Foetal development

At first, most of our information about foetal development in whales came from the whaling industry, where the total body length of a foetus was the easiest measurement to take. Now it is clear that foetal growth can be conveniently con-

sidered in two parts. In the first phase, the body length increases slowly, but at an ever increasing rate. In the second phase, which takes up the greater part of pregnancy and continues until birth, the length increases at a steady daily rate (although the rate of weight gain increases each day).

The daily increase in weight towards the end of gestation is amazing, particularly in the largest baleen whales. Blue whale calves are 7m long and weigh 2.5 tonnes at birth. Using whaling data, Richard Laws showed that the near-term foetus puts on 35kg of body weight every single day. Of course, this weight has to be provided by the mother, who is probably not feeding at all; by this time she is on her wintering grounds and so her own body weight is rapidly diminishing while that of her youngster increases.

## The birth

As birth approaches, the foetus may have attained a third of the length of its mother and has been fully formed for several months. It is about to experience the greatest physical shock of its life: exchanging the warmth and protection of its parent's body at 37°C for water that, in the case of narwhal and beluga whales, may be near freezing point. Once initiated, birth is thought to occur quite rapidly, though it has rarely been witnessed in the wild. Most small toothed whales and dolphins are born tail-first, but the few observations of birth in baleen whales suggest that head-first may be the more common presentation.

## Post-natal development

The young calf continues to grow very rapidly, fuelled now by its mother's milk. This has an extremely high energy content in the form of fat, typically 16-46 percent, compared to 3-5 percent in man and cows. As a result, the calf's growth rate is proportionately higher than that of most mammals, although it doesn't approach the initial growth rate of some seals, one

*Above: Photographs of whale births are rare. Here, the head of a gray whale calf emerges after 13.5 months of gestation.*

of which – the hooded seal – doubles its body weight in under four days from birth. Body changes in the first few days after birth include the gradual stiffening of the dorsal fin (in those species that have one) and of the tail flukes. These are very rubbery in the newborn calf in order not to inhibit the birth itself. Most species also lose the body hair that is particularly evident on the rostrum or upper jaw of the foetus. Otherwise, young cetaceans differ externally from adults only in size, perhaps in colour and, to a limited extent, in body proportions.

Mothers nurse their young for at least four months and may continue to do so for years in those species with very tight family groups. Calves in such species may take milk from several females, who are probably all relatives, such as aunts or grandmothers, and may be 'looked after' by these nurses while their mother is diving for food. Calves of species that do not form such tight-knit groups tend to stay very close to their mothers throughout the suckling period and these females probably do not dive very deeply in the early stages of calf dependency.

The mechanism by which milk is transferred to the calf without wastage is rather unusual. Few cetaceans can manipulate their lips, so the calf cannot grip the nipple and suck in the same way as a human child. The propulsion of the milk is provided by the mother, who uses muscles around the mammary gland to squirt it into the mouth of the youngster, which often holds the nipple in the corner of its mouth. Daily quantities of milk vary according to the size of animal, but can amount to more than 100 litres in the largest species of baleen whale.

Weaning is a gradual process and the calf normally takes solid food long before its mother has supplied the last meal of milk. Towards the end of lactation, the

milk supply becomes poorer, both in quantity and energy value. In those species where suckling is prolonged, such as in pilot and sperm whales, the young may take squid and milk simultaneously for many months or years. For example, a 13-year-old sperm whale captured off South Africa had traces of milk in its stomach, even though it had probably started taking squid before its first birthday. In the migratory baleen whales, however, calves are no doubt urged to become independent of milk as soon as possible after arrival on the summer feeding grounds, since the mother must conserve her energy and rapidly build up her body stores before the next pregnancy starts, often only six months later.

Calves are born without teeth or baleen, but the tips of teeth or soft rows of rubbery baleen plates normally begin to erupt in the first months of life. An exception to this pattern is the sperm whale, which can take nine years to erupt its teeth and which may still have fully developed teeth below the gumline at 30 years of age. In this species, dependency on solid food starts well before the teeth erupt, demonstrating that a sperm whale can catch its prey without teeth at all.

The young whale continues to grow steadily during and after the weaning period and then – at least in some toothed whales – there is a growth 'spurt' as puberty approaches. In species with a high degree of sexual dimorphism in body length, i.e. where one sex is consistently larger than the other at the same age, the difference becomes increasingly apparent, even in the first years of life.

## The reproductive phase

Sexual maturity – the stage at which an animal is physically able to reproduce – is attained between the ages of about 2 and 20 years, depending on the species and sex. For example, both male and female franciscanas (*Pontoporia blainvillei*) can be sexually mature at 2 years old, but neither are thought to live more than 20 years. In contrast, sperm whales can live more than 50 years, so may still have a long reproductively active period, even if this does not begin until about the age of 9 years in females and 20 years in males. Even on reaching sexual maturity, a male sperm whale may still be 'socially' immature and have to wait a further five years before gaining access to receptive females and becoming a 'harem bull'.

Not all the individuals in a single population will attain sexual maturity at the same age. Female short-finned pilot whales in the North Pacific, for example, can begin to ovulate at any time between 7 and 12 years, while males become mature between 15 and 20 years. Furthermore, there is evidence that the age of sexual maturity can change in a population over a period of years, perhaps in response to a decrease in the number of animals as a result of whaling. In the Antarctic, female baleen whales were found to become sexually mature at a much younger age after whalers had devastated the stocks than before. In sei whales, the age of sexual maturity decreased typically from about 12 to 9 years over a 40-year period, but in minke whales the change may have been as much as from 14 to 5 years over a similar

period. Interestingly, the body length at sexual maturity did not alter over that time, fuelling the hypothesis that whales were growing much faster in later years as a result of the superabundance of food 'liberated' by the killing of most of the large whales.

Once sexually mature, females of most species (though not all) remain reproductively active for the rest of their lives. The rate of reproduction, i.e. the frequency with which a calf is produced, tends to diminish slowly as the mother ages. Nevertheless, from the first conception, a female is almost never without either a calf at her side or a foetus growing within her. In some species, such as the beluga, she permanently has both.

## Mortality

In a stable population, one animal dies for every one that is born. If the death rate exceeds the birth rate, the population will fall. Similarly, if births occur at a faster rate than deaths, the population will increase. We have already looked at cetacean reproduction, the way in which life begins; it is equally important to understand something of why and when those same lives come to an end.

In a group of animals like whales, dolphins and porpoises, where man has – and does – cause the direct or indirect death of a significant proportion of a population, it is normal to consider total mortality as the sum of natural and man-induced mortality. Natural mortality falls mainly into one of two categories: predation and disease. 'Unnatural', or man-induced, mortality can be obvious, such as whaling, or less obvious, such as that caused by pollution, collision with ships or entanglement with debris.

## Natural mortality

Other than man, the only significant predators of cetaceans are sharks and a few of their own number – the killer, false killer and pygmy killer whales. It is difficult to quantify predator pressure on any species, but it is generally thought to be low on adults and only of real significance on youngsters of a few species. Perhaps the best indication of the prevalence of attacks is that of tooth scars on the skin of animals that have escaped. The fact that a third of the humpback whales in one Canadian stock bore scars of killer whale teeth suggests that attacks may be common in certain localities.

Another cause of death in small cetaceans is that of a prey animal 'fighting back'. For example, bottlenose dolphins in Portugal have been observed frantically trying to dislodge an octopus that has covered the blowhole, and at least one freshly dead specimen has been found showing marks and symptoms of being suffocated in this way. Similarly, barbs from stingrays, a fish sometimes

eaten or played with, have caused death in a number of dolphins, puncturing the lungs and other internal organs.

Relatively little is known of the state of health of wild cetaceans, and estimates of mortality due to disease are unreliable. Nevertheless, the list of known cetacean diseases, compiled from examinations of animals in captivity, stranded or killed, is a long one. It includes many types of disease that also afflict humans, such as cancers, stomach ulcers, heart disease, pneumonia, jaundice and osteoarthritis. In addition, wild cetaceans are afflicted with a wide range of internal parasites that, in some severe infestations, can cause weakness and susceptibility to other diseases, or even death. Importantly, the list of diseases includes many that are symptomatic of old age or, as in the case of parasitic infestation, may become more serious with age. It is likely to be one or more of these factors that eventually result in 'death from natural causes'. We still do not know the natural lifespans of many cetaceans but, of those that have been studied, specimens of the common porpoise and franciscana are old at 10-15 years, while sperm whales, Baird's beaked whales and killer whales

may, on occasion, reach the biblical three-score years and ten. Most dolphins seem to have maximum lifespans of between 20 and 40 years, and even the enormous blue and fin whales rarely live much longer than this.

## Man-induced mortality

Until just after the middle of the twentieth century, by far the greatest threat to cetaceans from our species was that of directed catches of whales or dolphins. The impact of this was such that it sometimes swamped mortality from other causes and brought about a swift fall in the size of the exploited population.

The worst hit species were initially the slower, larger whales which had a high oil yield and so floated when dead, i.e. the right whales (including the bowhead) and the sperm whale. The gray whale became a target in the early nineteenth century, but the faster rorquals were immune from whaling until the late nineteenth century. Thereafter, blue, humpback, fin and sei whales were killed in their tens or hundreds of thousands worldwide, but especially in the rich waters of the Antarctic. The smaller minke whale only became a worthwhile quarry after these large species could no longer support the industry.

Some smaller toothed whales, particularly bottlenose and pilot whales, narwhal and beluga, have been taken for varying periods of time. Relatively few small cetaceans have sustained large-scale directed catches, but there are exceptions; 45,000 Dall's porpoises were killed in 1988 alone, for example.

There is some evidence that the birth rate of cetacean populations that have been reduced in size, usually by whaling, may subsequently increase. If so, a population may reach an equilibrium where births again equal deaths, but at a lower population size than the original, when births had only to equal deaths due to natural causes. Unfortunately, the intensity of whaling on so many species, over decades or centuries, has far outstripped the capacity of some populations to replace such losses. With a few exceptions, notably some stocks of gray and southern right whales, any excess of births over deaths is taking a long time to become apparent, even with the current total protection that exists for most species.

Probably the greatest current threat to cetaceans from man – and one which is responsible for more deaths per year than whaling at its peak – is that of entrapment in fishing gear. There are two categories here: accidental entrapment, when the animals enter nets or take baited hooks without anyone knowing, and directed entrapment, when fishermen deliberately set their nets to catch the animals. On the whole, entrapment is killing smaller species than were affected by whaling, but mortality rates may be just

*Above left: A newborn humpback whale swims beside its mother.*

*Right: Parasites, such as this barnacle and some whale lice on the skin of a gray whale, are common in and on cetaceans. External parasites are rarely a threat, but internal parasites can weaken or even kill the host.*

*Below: Nothing is too large for a pack of hungry killer whales to tackle. Here they are shown attacking a solitary blue whale.*

as high in some stocks and the actual number of deaths far higher.

Man is also responsible for another major cause of death, namely environmental degradation. In most species with a wide geographical range this may not be critical, but those with a localized distribution may be very vulnerable. The river dolphins are a case in point, with populations of the Indus River dolphin and baiji (Chinese river dolphin) pushed to the edge of extinction by a combination of man-induced factors such as pollution, disturbance, damming, etc. In this category we must also include deaths due to swallowing man-made objects, including balls, nets, pieces of plastic, etc. We know that many stranded animals have perished when the gastro-intestinal tract became blocked by such items.

### Patterns of distribution
It is fascinating to examine the current global picture of where cetaceans occur – their geographical distribution – and to see how the present-day situation has developed. Over millions of years, continental drift, global climatic changes and the evolution of both the animals themselves and their prey have all exerted an influence. During this time, species have colonized – and departed from – whole oceans. Some have been split by physical or oceanographic barriers and become two or more distinct species or subspecies. Others have become so specialized in their adaptations that, in the face of environmental change, they either died out altogether or were reduced to isolated pockets.

### Understanding distribution patterns
The greatest influence on the distribution and movements of cetaceans is their adaptation to a particular habitat and life style. This has a bearing on, for example, the type of food they are able to catch, their ability to carry out their complete

*Above: Entrapments in fishing gear cause suffering and death in even the largest cetaceans, like this entangled gray whale.*

*Above right: Species at high latitudes are forced to migrate. The summering grounds of these belugas is ice-covered in winter.*

life cycle in one area rather than have to move on a seasonal basis, the types of echolocation sounds they produce and their tendency to mass strand.

In some species, the distribution is simple and the interpretation relatively easy. Sperm whales, for example, have a global distribution that includes all but the very coldest parts of all oceans, and animals in one area look much the same as those from any other, probably because of sufficient movements of animals between such areas. In contrast, the short-finned pilot whale is confined to the warmer waters of the three major ocean basins; those in the Indian and Pacific Oceans are linked by passages between Australia and Southeast Asia, those in the Atlantic are apparently landlocked by the Americas and Africa. This raises a number of questions: whether any interchange occurs, around Cape Horn, say, by individuals able to withstand colder water; whether the species originated in the Atlantic or the Pacific/Indian Ocean complex; and whether the two groups have evolved into different races by virtue of being separated.

The whole picture was made even more interesting and complex when, in the 1980s, Japanese scientists published startling evidence that short-finned pilot whales captured in northern Japan were very different in size and reproductive characteristics from those taken in southern Japan. The geographical separation between the two groups was only a few hundred kilometres, with no physical boundary other than an oceanographic front yet, judging by their differences, genetic segregation must be virtually complete. In such circumstances, where

no obvious recent barrier exists to explain the separation of genetically discrete stocks, it may be that historical events, such as the opening of a channel to allow a passage between isolated areas, have had an influence.

The geographical distribution of the short-finned pilot whale is called pantropical because it extends to warm waters on both sides of the equator and around the globe. Its closest relative, the long-finned pilot whale, has an anti-tropical distribution that excludes the tropics but involves both hemispheres. As a result, these two small whales between them cover almost the entire globe, with little overlap. In the long-finned pilot whale, the barrier of the tropics, across which the ancestors of the North Atlantic population must once have passed (probably during a period of global cooling), has resulted in isolated groups that look quite different from one another. Taxonomists therefore question whether they should be recognized as subspecies. If the segregation of the long-finned pilot whale populations had occurred earlier, by now the differences between them might have been sufficient to allow recognition of two different species. Such has been the case in several other 'pairs' of cetacean species, including the northern and southern bottlenose whales, Baird's and Arnoux's beaked whales, and the northern and southern right whale dolphins.

One other type of distribution – circumpolar – is worth mentioning. It applies to species, such as the hourglass dolphin, that have a continuous distribution around the world at high latitudes of one or both hemispheres, and is loosely used for those, like the beluga, in which the distribution is not quite unbroken.

Many of the smaller toothed whales, dolphins and porpoises occur in relatively small areas. Most of them have closely related species, occupying a similar habitat and ecological niche elsewhere. The mostly coastal porpoise family Phocoenidae (six species) and the *Lagenorhynchus* genus of oceanic dolphins (six species) are good examples of this.

The type of habitat preferred by a species has an important influence on other aspects of its life and geographical distribution. Generally speaking, individuals of coastal species are less likely to undertake long seasonal movements and are more likely to evolve into recognizably different forms than are oceanic species. Coastal and riverine animals tend to have a small 'home range' that they get to know well, allowing them to exploit its predictable food concentrations efficiently. Offshore species have larger home ranges, move greater distances on a daily basis (average 55km, maximum 165km in *Stenella* dolphins of the eastern tropical Pacific) and forage on a more opportunistic basis.

## Migration in baleen whales

The most marked and rigid migrations of all cetaceans are those of the baleen whales. They represent a compromise between the requirements of reproduction and feeding and are as much a product of the evolutionary process as are the geographical distributions of the species. In most baleen whales, the year is split between high-latitude, coldwater feeding grounds, and low-latitude, warmwater breeding grounds, plus the long swim between the two. The need to migrate is brought about by the inability of newborn calves to survive in the cold water of the feeding grounds. Males must travel, too, because the gestation period lasts about one year, so mating and calving occur in the same general area. Feeding is concentrated into a period of a few months, so it is essential that the whales find reliable sources of zooplankton (krill) or shoaling fish (or mud-living prey in the case of the gray whale) on which to build up their energy reserves. During the migrations and the period on the breeding grounds – a total of six to nine months – little or no food is taken, so the species that make such journeys have evolved adaptations for energy storage. Oil is stored in fibrous blubber that increases dramatically in thickness, and fat is laid down around the abdominal organs. It was these characteristics that gave whalers such a high oil yield from their catches of right, gray, blue and fin whales.

Although the urge to migrate is very powerful, and probably triggered by daylength, a whole population of whales does not leave an area as one body. Different reproductive and age classes tend to leave and arrive at different times, with the result that a population may at times be strung out in a thin column thousands of kilometres long. The gray whale is a good example. First to leave the Arctic feeding grounds for the southward migration are females in the last stages of pregnancy followed, in order, by other adult females, immature females, adult males and immature males. The return journey from the Mexican calving lagoons is led by pregnant females, followed by adult males and resting females, immatures and lastly the nursing females with their young calves.

Some whales do not complete the journey. Gray whales occur off the coast of Oregon in high summer when most individuals are 3,000km away to the north west. Whalers reported humpbacks off northern Norway in winter when almost all other North Atlantic humpbacks would have been basking in the Caribbean sun. The sei whale is renowned for its variable migration behaviour. In the northeast Atlantic, most of the population apparently reaches the Denmark Strait off western Iceland in some summers, while in other years only adult

females – or no whales at all – are seen in the area. In these poor years, we must assume that the missing multitudes find adequate food stocks without having to swim so far, perhaps off the Faeroe Islands or west of the UK and Ireland.

The 'odd ones out' of the baleen whales are the Bryde's, minke and pygmy right whales. Bryde's whales never penetrate high latitudes and seem to find enough food in tropical and subtropical waters at temperatures of 15-30°C. Pygmy right whales prefer cooler waters, and Minke whales may make latitudinal movements but seem tolerant of non-extreme temperatures all year round. Large-scale migrations of the type seen in other baleen whales have not been established in these species.

Although all rorqual species (the balaenopterids) except the Bryde's whale have a continuous distribution from the equator to cold temperate waters of both hemispheres, there is a significant difference in body size between animals in the north and south, which indicates that little movement of individuals occurs across the equator. This is because the migrations in the hemispheres are six months out of phase, with the northern summer occurring simultaneously with the southern winter. The summer distribution of northern animals is thus away from the equator at the time that winter in the Southern Hemisphere is drawing whales to warmer waters near the equator, and vice versa.

## Migration in toothed whales

In no species of toothed whale, dolphin or porpoise are migrations of the whole population known to occur on the same scale as in the baleen whales. Smaller latitudinal movements are undertaken by some, and Arctic-dwelling species are forced to move because of the encroachment of ice onto their preferred feeding areas, but most species make relatively limited seasonal movements.

The sperm whale, having been exploited in so many places, is perhaps the best-known larger toothed cetacean in this respect, and also the most intriguing. Female and immature sperm whales remain in tropical, subtropical and warm temperate waters of about 14°C or more all year round. For most of the year, mature males separate from these groups and are seen as 'bachelor schools' or singly. During the spring and summer, many of these males are thought to move polewards to high-latitude waters, where they are assumed to find food in better quantities, although recent comparison of males in Icelandic and Azorean waters seems not to confirm this.

While many – perhaps most – mature males make the long journey to colder seas, some remain in the same areas as the females and immatures. We do not know what proportion choose to remain or on what basis the decision to stay or leave is made. The evidence we have of individual movements begs more questions than it answers. One male was struck by a hand harpoon in the Azores at latitude 39°N in August one year, escaped, and had the misfortune to be harpooned again exactly one year later, but this time off the west coast of Iceland at latitude 66°N, some 3,200km further north. Another was marked off eastern Canada and taken off the coast of Spain seven years later, a movement right across the Atlantic, that illustrates the probable lack of discrete sperm whale stocks in this ocean at least.

Other known seasonal movements of toothed whales are often onshore-offshore rather than north-south ones and likely to be driven by the availability of food rather than the demands of reproduction. Some *Lagenorhynchus* dolphins probably move in this way, and killer whales off Iceland and long-finned pilot whales off eastern Canada certainly do.

# STRANDINGS

In many parts of the world, the only first-hand experience of cetaceans that local people are likely to have is finding a dead animal, one of the thousands that are washed up every year along the coastline of each ocean basin. Strandings, as they are commonly known, are perfectly natural phenomena and have undoubtedly occurred ever since the ancestors of modern whales and dolphins first took to the sea. Man has probably taken an interest in strandings for countless thousands of years, but only very recently has sheer curiosity outweighed the more practical considerations of having a huge quantity of food and fuel-oil suddenly delivered to the doorstep!

Although grouped together under one general heading, it is possible to identify several different types of stranding. The most obvious distinctions are between single and multiple events, i.e. those involving one or more than one animal, and between strandings of carcasses and those of live animals.

## Single strandings
Clearly, every cetacean is destined to die somewhere at some time and, eventually, the body is likely to float to the surface for a period of weeks or even months. During this time, currents or winds may carry it towards a coastline, where it may be washed ashore. Given that thousands of cetaceans around the world must die of natural causes every day, it is hardly surprising that strandings are quite common in some areas. Most cetacean deaths attributable to natural causes occur singly and result in the stranding of only one animal at one site, if stranding occurs at all. However, most carcasses never reach a coastline. They are probably eaten by scavengers at the water surface or decompose to such an extent that they fall apart and sink.

Single live strandings are mostly the result of illness or injury. Unless its health problem is reversible and it happens to be spotted quickly by a competent passer-by who knows how to react, the animal invariably perishes where it strands.

## Multiple strandings
Multiple strandings (mass strandings) of dead animals in one locality are very rare. They may be caused by poisoning, as happened in 1987-88 to bottlenose dolphins off the northeastern coast of the United States, or by some other harmful nearshore agent capable of killing many animals in a short period of time. Multiple offshore deaths are unlikely to produce multiple strandings because the vagaries of wind and current usually scatter the animals over a wide area.

Multiple live strandings are relatively rare events but, by their very nature, they are always the subject of disproportionate interest and media coverage. The haunting spectacle of tens or hundreds of thrashing, squealing cetaceans floundering helplessly together on a beach prompts every onlooker to ask the inevitable question – why? Very occasionally, some beached whales may refloat at the next high tide but, even then, most will perish on another beach a short distance away. Few animals cast ashore in a multiple live stranding will normally survive the ordeal, even if they are otherwise fit and healthy.

## Which species strand and where?
Each year, there are a number of strandings of live animals around the world, but these rarely involve more than a total of one or two thousand animals. This may seem a lot, but actually represents only a tiny fraction of the populations to which the stranded whales belong. Although the consequences are normally fatal for the individual animals on the beach, mass strandings do not generally pose a threat to the species as a whole. This appraisal may sound cold-blooded, but it is important to understand the actual impact of what may, at first sight, seem a catastrophic blow to a population of whales and dolphins.

Of the 78 species of whales, dolphins and porpoises, only 10 are frequently involved in mass strandings and a further 10 are rarely or occasionally mass stranded. The species concerned share certain characteristics, and this in itself provides some clues to the causes of the events. Interestingly, none of the baleen whales has ever been recorded in a live mass stranding. In the toothed species, body size does not seem to be an important factor, but both the animal's normal habitat and its social organization do appear to influence the chances of it coming ashore in large numbers. Odontocetes that normally inhabit deep oceanic waters and that live in large, tightly knit groups are the most susceptible but, for some reason, only a small number of species that fit this description do mass strand. They include the sperm whale, a number of species in the pilot and killer whale family, a few beaked whales and about 10 species of oceanic dolphins. Solitary species, or those found in small groups, are naturally excluded from mass strandings, but in any case they rarely seem to come ashore alive. Cetaceans that normally venture into, or spend most of their time in, shallower coastal waters are almost never mass stranded. All porpoises are essentially immune.

Mass strandings can occur on any beach with suitable access for the whales, but most tend to take place at a relatively small number of sites. The substrate, be it sand, gravel or rock, seems to matter less than the shape of the coastline. In general, bays and estuaries are more likely to produce mass strandings than a straight coastline, but there are exceptions; during a spate of live strandings of the long-finned pilot whale in the UK in the early 1980s, no two sites were topographically similar. In eastern England, some animals even followed rivers considerable distances inland before dying. They were part of a pod that perished

*Below left: The largest species of whale likely to be mass stranded is the sperm whale, here on the coast of Oregon in the United States.*

*Above: This stranding of pilot whales in the Shetland Isles was one of several such events that occurred around the UK in the 1980s.*

over a period of several days and an area of tens of kilometres, with some whales becoming stranded and refloated on several successive tides.

### Why do cetaceans come ashore alive?

Most whales, dolphins and porpoises remain at sea for their entire lives, never actually touching land. A minority of species exist in shallow coastal water, in rivers or in estuaries. Only the killer whale, beluga and bottlenose dolphin are known, on occasion, to venture deliberately into areas of so little water that their weight is taken by the beach and not the water itself. Even then, these animals move back into deeper water after a few seconds or minutes, although a few belugas perish when left behind by a falling tide while they are scratching in estuarine gravel. Therefore, it is extremely rare for cetaceans to beach themselves. When they do so, the results are normally fatal, so why and how does it happen?

Over the years, both scientists and philosophers have put forward many explanations. Some suggest that it is a deliberate act, but most believe it is accidental. If deliberate, could it be because the animals are suicidal, or want to rest, need to rub their skin in the substrate or are seeking safety on land? If accidental, could the cause be disorientation, confusion of sonar signals in shallow water or attempts to use an old migration route now closed by geological change? Other suggestions include the effects of parasitic infestation of the inner ear, popula-

tion pressure, noise and disturbance from shipping, pollution, earthquakes, storms and phases of the moon. Some of these hypotheses cannot be put to the test, while others can be seen to be operating to various degrees in a proportion of mass strandings. Many can be rejected after closely examining the characteristic features of a large number of strandings around the world. Most informed opinion accepts that several factors are usually involved simultaneously, otherwise mass strandings would surely be a much more common phenomenon.

Nevertheless, in recent years, one particulary compelling hypothesis has emerged, which could possibly account for the otherwise apparently inexplicable characteristics of strandings. The suggestion is that most live strandings, especially those involving more than one healthy animal, are at least partly due to errors of navigation. More specifically, it is now thought that cetaceans are using the earth's magnetic field in order to navigate and, in doing so, may sometimes be led into coastal 'traps' from which oceanic species may not have the experience to escape.

Recent anatomical studies have shown that tiny crystals of magnetite, a substance capable of sensing a magnetic field, occur in the brain and skull of at least some cetacean species. Therefore, it is at least feasible that cetaceans can sense the earth's magnetic field and use it for navigation, as can insects, birds and, indeed, man. This ability would be extremely useful for a marine animal, since variations in the intensity of the magnetic field across the oceans would theoretically permit it to find its way around without requiring any degree of skills in celestial navigation or any other form of position-finding or piloting techniques.

Although the concept of magnetic-field navigation in cetaceans had been proposed earlier, the idea of testing the hypothesis with respect to strandings is attributed to Dr. Margaret Klinowska of Cambridge University. She examined the local magnetic characteristics of the known sites of cetacean live strandings around the UK coast. The locations of dead strandings showed no pattern, but live animals were found to come ashore only where lines of equal magnetic force crossed the coastline perpendicularly. The implication is that the animals were following these lines of force, in the same way that we can follow the height contours of a hill while walking, and simply blundered into the coastline where it intercepted the magnetic contour. This reliance on an unseen 'map' may seem far-fetched, but it would normally work very well for a species familiar only with the deep ocean and unaccustomed to physical barriers.

The magnetic-navigation theory explains why offshore species strand alive more often than coastal species. It also explains why many whales, even groups of whales refloated by local people, repeatedly restrand in the same locality; they are simply putting their trust once more in an ability to find their way around that had, until then, always served them well. Overall, it seems to many cetologists that this is the single most likely cause of live strandings. The theory has gained credence as studies on the eastern seaboard of the United States have confirmed the correlation between certain magnetic characteristics of the coastline and the sites of repeated live strandings.

Other factors are also undoubtedly important. A pod of, say, pilot whales finding themselves in unexpectedly shallow water may escape offshore if the coastline is straight, but are less likely to do so if they are enclosed in a bay. Increased water noise and suspended sediment resulting from bad weather are likely to confuse their echolocation abilities and increase the likelihood of stranding once a pod has already reached the coast, but a storm in itself is extremely unlikely to cause whales to go aground.

Tight social cohesion of the pods is a characteristic of all the species that most commonly mass strand, and this often seems to be the reason why an entire group, rather than just a few animals, should come ashore. Even though some, or even most, of a group have the opportunity to escape, the presence of just one individual in the shallows seems enough

**How geomagnetic fields seem to influence live strandings**

*Above: This map of an area in the Moray Firth, Scotland shows white contours of geomagnetic field and black symbols for sites of live cetacean strandings. Note how strandings occur where the magnetic contours cross the coast nearly at right angles.*

to keep all the others in the vicinity, and all may then perish.

In parts of New Zealand and Australia, this phenomenon has been skilfully overcome by rescuers, who have realized the futility of refloating and releasing one animal at a time. By holding the whales in shallow water until all the live animals have been refloated, and then releasing them in one group back to the open sea, there is a much greater chance that none will return to the site and restrand.

Not all multiple standings result in the death of every pod member, even when the animals are left to their fate. Sometimes one or two whales will be beached, but the others will turn back. It may be that the stranded individuals were sick or injured and their relatives – for that is probably what they are – were reluctant to leave them until their calls were no longer heard.

Observations of near strandings are also well documented. Pods of obviously distressed and confused whales may be sighted in the shallows, or may be partly stranded on one day, only to recover and swim away 24 hours later. This is where the topography becomes important, either facilitating or hampering escape.

To sum up, mass strandings of live animals are not preventable, almost certainly accidental and not brought about by any one factor. However, navigational error is thought to be involved in most if not all cases. Animals stranding alive normally perish, but on rare occasions may be re-floated on the next tide.

## Finding a stranded cetacean

If you are a regular beach walker, or even if you just like to take your summer holidays on the coast, sooner or later you may well come across a beached whale or dolphin. In almost all cases, the animal will already be dead, often decomposed beyond recognition, and there is nothing to be done except report your finding to an appropriate scientific organization and, perhaps, to the local civic authority. If the stranding involves just one or two small dolphins or porpoises, the animals are often merely left to decompose naturally and normally cause little or no problem. However, a multiple stranding or the stranding of a large whale can become a health hazard, especially if it occurs near human habitation. In this case, the local authority normally finds a way of disposing of the carcasses, either by removal or by burial in situ. Burial must be deep, or animals can float to the surface at subsequent high tides.

If the animal(s) are still alive, however, you may be the first person to see them and could help to relieve their suffering and perhaps rescue them by taking swift and appropriate action. You will certainly need assistance and should realize from the outset that, except in circumstances where expert help and equipment can be obtained quickly, the most humane course of action will be euthanasia carried out by a veterinary practitioner or other qualified person. Nevertheless, live animals can sometimes be saved. In some countries, particularly where live strandings are quite frequent, there are stranding 'networks' or other organizations, such as marine aquariums, that can respond quickly and either take an ill animal into captivity for treatment or help to refloat a pod of whales. In early

1989, Sea World of Florida even managed to rehabilitate a young Bryde's whale, 7m long, by taking it into care and later releasing it back to sea, so almost anything may be possible.

Success depends on swift, cool-headed action and access to appropriate expertise. The following guidance is designed to help you assess a cetacean stranding and to initiate the appropriate steps.

## Practical steps to take

First check to see if the animal(s) are alive or dead. This is usually obvious but, if in doubt, look and listen for breathing through the blowhole on top of the head. If nothing is seen or heard for 15 minutes – don't forget that cetaceans can hold their breath for a long time – the animal is dead. Take care not to approach too closely, especially near the tail, unless you are certain that the animal is not alive; a sudden movement of the tail can cause a bystander serious injury.

## Coping with live animals

If the animal is alive, get help as quickly as possible; a beached animal is dying from physiological stress by the minute. Inform the nearest authority that can contact any local stranding network and a veterinarian. The police or coastguard service will normally be able and willing to provide assistance. They will also know if a captive marine mammal facility is within reach and could help with advice or practical support. If no help is available, or it is insufficient for any reason, there is no option but to let nature take its course and allow the animals to die peacefully. Try to keep people away from the scene, since the proximity of humans only adds to the stress of the unfortunate whales.

While waiting for help to arrive, and throughout the operation, keep the animals moist and cool. If four or more people are present, it is often possible to hold a single small cetacean in a makeshift sling in shallow water. If the animals cannot be moved, splash sea water over them or, better still, drape their upper surface with a cloth soaked in sea water. Always keep the blowhole clear of water, sand and the covering cloth.

When help arrives, there must be a decision on how to proceed. Whether to attempt a rescue or humanely destroy the animals will rest on many factors, including their number, state of health, size, the presence of a local marine mammal facility and whether or not heavy lifting gear can be brought to the site. It is important to realize that attempts to rescue stranded animals can cause them considerable stress and very often result in their death. Similarly, the refloating of only a small part of a large pod – usually the smallest and, therefore, youngest animals – is likely to result in terrible trauma and a possible lingering death for dependent whales suddenly torn away from their mothers. Do not be surprised, therefore, if a veterinarian or some other trained professional takes the decision that a rapid painless death is more humane than attempted rescue. Try to accept that such a decision is often inevitable and never taken lightly. Never, under any circumstances, attempt to destroy the animals yourself. Apart from probably causing unnecessary suffering to the cetacean, you can risk the safety of onlookers and others who will come later to see the animals.

If a rescue is attempted, you can best help by simply following the requests of the person who has made the decision and who should have based that decision on a knowledge of what to do. It is beyond the scope of this book to give detailed instructions on how to proceed, since every stranding event will demand its own solution. Bear in mind that it is always better to release all animals together if possible.

Animals should be moved by first manoeuvring them onto a tarpaulin or stretcher. Never pull animals by the flipper – it can be broken or dislocated – and never tow animals in water by the tail; they will drown or probably later suffer from a respiratory infection if the blowhole is below water level.

Once a rescue is underway, or even if any such operation is abandoned and/or the animals have been humanely destroyed, try to find time to make notes and take photographs of the stranding for scientific purposes. Examination of each new stranding helps to establish the cause and can, in the case of live strandings, allow better preparations to be made for rescuing cetaceans subsequently washed ashore.

### If the animals are dead

Even if it is too late to help the beached cetaceans, there is always someone somewhere who would like to know about the event and who would be grateful if you can take a few minutes to gather the necessary information to put together a complete and accurate record.

Many countries have a central organization, usually based at a national museum or research institution, that documents and collates information on strandings. Most coastal museums, police or coastguards will advise on where to send data on strandings.

The information needed, in approximate order of priority, is as follows:
- The species involved.
- The number of animals stranded (and their body length and sex if possible).
- Date and location of stranding, preferably including a map grid reference or latitude and longitude.
- Whether the animals stranded alive or dead.
- Any obvious reasons for the stranding – entrapment in fishing gear, for example.
- Details of other animals seen at the time of stranding.
- The number of animals that were refloated and left the site.

A few photographs of individual animals are always particularly welcome and help to corroborate their identification and sex. All strandings coordinators have wonderful stories of midsized whales being identified on the beach as either dolphins or blue whales!

*Above: Live strandings of small cetaceans, such as this common dolphin, can result in a successful rescue and rehabilitation if competent help is speedily available and there is a captive facility nearby that will tend the animal.*

*Right: The death of a pod of whales on a beach, resulting in the rapid accumulation of many tonnes of rotting tissue, can pose a significant threat to health. Local authorities usually try to remove or bury the animals as soon as possible. Here, pilot whales stranded in Australia are being buried on site with all possible speed.*

# WATCHING WHALES

Public demand to see cetaceans at first hand has increased dramatically in recent years. There are essentially two ways in which this can be achieved. One, a trip to an oceanarium or leisure park where captive animals are kept and displayed, is relatively simple in most developed countries and provides the security of guaranteeing close and comfortable access to the animals. The second way is to look for cetaceans in the wild. This requires travelling to a suitable coast and then, usually, finding a boat that will take you out to a promising area. This option is less available to most people, less comfortable and certainly less predictable in its success. It is, though, the only way to see a large whale and can provide an experience that will remain in the memory forever. The chance to catch that first glimpse of a truly wild cetacean has already persuaded millions of people to part with their money to risk sea-sickness, stormy weather and, worst of all, the disappointment of failing to see a single animal.

In this section, we look in more detail at where, how and which wild cetaceans can be seen, and how captive facilities go about obtaining and maintaining their popular display animals.

## Watching wild cetaceans

The chances of seeing a cetacean, either from the shore or from a boat, depend very much on where you are in the world and the time of year. Southern Californians with a home overlooking the sea are quite accustomed to watching gray whales from their living room in spring, and residents of the Western Isles of Scotland are familiar with minke whales and several species of small cetaceans within a stone's throw of the beach, but these places are exceptional. In contrast, coastal watchers in many parts of continental Europe would grow old without ever catching sight of a whale.

Few coastal areas of the world are totally devoid of all cetaceans, but the frequency with which they are seen varies considerably. Coastal dolphins often learn where food is most likely to be had at particular times of day, and become regular in their habits. The time taken to make enquiries about where cetaceans are most likely to be seen will not be wasted; local fishermen are often the best people to ask.

Bottlenose dolphins are the most widespread and most commonly encountered coastal dolphins. Resident groups can be seen routinely by land-based observers in, for example, the Sado estuary south of Lisbon, Portugal, the Moray Firth in eastern Scotland and almost anywhere in the Gulf of Mexico and Florida.

Perhaps the best-known – and most unusual – group of dolphins in this category are the 'Monkey Mia' bottlenose dolphins of Shark Bay, Western Australia. Each day, a pod of up to 10 dolphins ventures into very shallow water, where they have become totally accustomed to people walking and swimming among them. Tens of thousands of tourists now visit the site every year, offering fish to the dolphins, which are free to come and go as they please. Crowd pressure has increased on the site since the 1970s, when stories of the dolphins' friendliness spread outside Australia, and a wardening system has been introduced in the hope of ensuring the continuity of this re-

markable phenomenon, which has now stretched to a third generation of habituated animals.

The emergence of 'wild but sociable' dolphins has allowed visitors to western Ireland, Wales, southwestern England and northwestern France to enjoy a dolphin's company in recent years. For periods of months, or even years, a series of eccentric and solitary bottlenose dolphins that apparently prefer human company to that of their own species have appeared off the coast in these areas. The dolphins become local celebrities, are given names, and usually permit swimmers and divers in the water with them.

### Whale-watching trips

In a few parts of the world, particularly in the United States and Canada, whale watching has been turned into a lucrative business. Several times each day, special boats head out for a few hours to sites just offshore, where large whales can, fairly predictably, be located and closely approached. The species most likely to be seen in this way are gray, humpback, fin and right whales, but the lucky tourist may glimpse blue, sei, sperm or killer whales, depending on the place and the season. No commercial whale-watching on this scale is currently available in Europe, although it is now possible to pay to watch sperm whales off Norway and the Azores Islands, where attempts are being made to initiate an industry in the wake of whaling. Several large cetacean species venture close inshore at many sites in Australia and New Zealand, but these countries are poorly

served with commercial whale-watching trips. Nevertheless, local yachts or fishing boats are often available for hire in ports near to known whale or dolphin concentrations in this region and also elsewhere.

An increasingly popular means of watching whales in some of the more remote locations of the world is by luxury liner or on some other type of residential trip aboard ship. For many years, visitors from southern California have travelled to the gray whale calving lagoons of Baja California in Mexico, where the whales come close enough to touch. Today, in the safety and comfort of a purpose-built liner, it is possible to join an expedition to other renowned whale-rich areas, including Greenland, Alaska, southern Argentina and parts of the Antarctic Ocean.

### Watching captive cetaceans

Every year, millions of visitors are thrilled by the sight of dolphins and small whales going through their paces in elaborate displays. The phenomenon is a recent one, and still increasing in popularity. Its impact on the public perception and awareness of cetaceans in a broader sense has been dramatic.

Although dolphins had been held for short periods in Europe as long ago as 1860, the first long-term display of captive dolphins was not set up until 1938, at St Augustine, Florida. Bottlenose dolphins were chosen for the experiment because of their appropriate size, behaviour and local availability. Elsewhere, the idea was not taken up until the 1950s, when more facilities were developed in the USA and

the first European site opened to the public at Harderwijk in the Netherlands.

By 1965, Japan, West Germany and Spain's first captive cetaceans were on display, and in 1968 Belgium's Royal Zoological Society exhibited two species, including the tucuxi of South American origin. The following year saw the first display in the UK, and during the 1970s the number of captive facilities for small cetaceans increased dramatically throughout Europe, North America and Japan.

Generally speaking, only developed countries have undertaken to build expensive facilities for public display, but a few centres in Southeast Asia have acquired expertise with local species.

Currently, many captive facilities exist worldwide, with more than a hundred in North America alone. By far the majority of these facilities are maintained for financial profit, displaying animals to the fee-paying public, but a few exist purely for research purposes, for rehabilitation or for military use.

The most common species represented in captivity is certainly the bottlenose dolphin, which has proved itself amenable to conditions very different to those it experiences in the wild, and has been bred around the world for several decades. Next in popularity come killer whales, or orcas, and Pacific white-sided dolphins, followed by *Stenella* dolphins and the beluga (also called the 'white whale').

The largest animal regularly kept in captivity is the killer whale which, despite its common name, is in fact just a large dolphin. Young individuals of a few larger species, such as gray, sperm, and

Bryde's whales, have been kept alive for periods of a few weeks or months and then released after a period of recuperation, but these animals are usually opportunistically encountered sick or, perhaps, orphaned individuals. No existing captive facilities are large enough to accommodate them long-term in a healthy condition.

### Capture, transport and acclimatization
In the case of a few commonly kept species, breeding programmes now provide display animals, but most of the cetaceans held over the last 50 years have been taken directly from the wild. Sometimes they have been stranded, but usually they were free-ranging animals. They are normally captured by net, either individually in a hoop net from the bow of a pursuing vessel, or as a group in a seine-type fishing net.

Once captured, the animals are normally given a veterinary inspection to ensure that they are in good health, before being gently lifted into a container or sling for the journey to the facility or holding pen. During transit, usually by air and road, it is vital that the animal is kept cool and calm, its skin frequently wetted or covered in a soaked cloth to avoid any cracking or drying out. Having arrived at the facility, the cetacean is allowed to acclimatize slowly, away from the public gaze, and is given a thorough health inspection. Courses of antibiotics and other medicines may be administered during this period to counteract any health problems.

Unfortunately, the stress of capture, transport and initial captivity often result in the death of an animal during the first days and weeks, so this is a very critical period. If all goes well and the animal does begin to acclimatize to its strange new environment and to a diet of dead prey, it must be introduced slowly to the presence of human observers before facing the experience of initial training and open-air contact with the general public in a display facility.

### Survival in captivity
Maintaining any wild animal in captivity can be a constant battle against ill-health and disease, especially if its natural environment is very different from the new conditions provided for it. Early attempts to keep dolphins resulted in high mortality rates, principally because pools were too small and equipped with insufficient filtration, and because health requirements were poorly understood. With experience, all these aspects of care improved and animals are now kept alive for longer periods.

### Water quality
Modern facilities are based on one of two systems. In an 'open' system, fresh supplies of sea water are constantly pumped through the tank, whereas a 'closed' system relies on sophisticated recycling of the same water. Open systems require careful monitoring of the water supply and carry a risk that undetected pollutants may kill or harm the animals. Closed systems necessitate large and expensive filtering mechanisms and close attention to changes in salinity and pH (balance of acidity and alkalinity) that could cause health problems. A bottlenose dolphin can produce 1.4kg of faeces and 4 litres of urine per day, and the filtration system must also remove other wastes, including moulted skin and food remains, as well as organic debris such as blown leaves, or accidentally introduced inorganic items, such as wrapping paper and polystyrene cups.

*Above left: This young gray whale calf, called Gigi, was maintained in California for a year before being successfully released back into the wild.*

*Left: Despite their common name, killer whales are actually large dolphins, and have proved to be as adaptable as any of the smaller species in captive conditions.*

*Above right: Captive displays provide opportunities for close contact between cetaceans and the public and have hugely increased awareness of these animals.*

In a captive environment, animals face very different health risks from those encountered in the wild. Deaths and injuries caused by predatory attacks are obviously reduced, but infections and changes to body chemistry resulting from incorrect or inadequate feeding are more likely. Regular and thorough veterinary checks are routine at all good facilities and health problems can be treated by injections, food supplements, or altering the water quality in some way.

### Feeding captive cetaceans

Controlled feeding plays an important part in maintaining a healthy animal. Body weight can be manipulated by altering both the quantity and the type of fish given. Newly caught dolphins must learn to recognize and accept dead rather than live fish, but this takes a surprisingly short time. Food supplies are bought in bulk after thorough inspection and testing for pollutants, etc., and then frozen and fed in batches, thawed daily.

### Behavioural disorders

One group of illnesses that cannot be easily combated are the psychological disorders seen in captive cetaceans as much as in other zoo animals. The problem usually shows itself as a behavioural abnormality, such as repeated (stereotyped) actions, aggression, self-inflicted injury or cessation of vocalizations. 'Prison neurosis', as it has been called, may sometimes be cured by engaging the animal in more trainer-led activities or providing more company in the pool, but often the dolphin simply wastes away and dies of an infection. Loss of appetite and subsequent weight loss may occur in any captive species, leading to weakness and an increased susceptibility to disease. In general, a captive cetacean will live for a much shorter time than a wild individual of the same species.

### The controversy

There can be little doubt that much of the new-found desire of the general public to promote cetacean conservation as a whole stems from the close contact made possible at dolphinariums and leisure parks. Public awareness and sympathy have arguably been a powerful force in bringing about the virtual cessation of whaling and in the struggle to ameliorate man's impact on cetaceans in general. Ironically, this increased awareness and concern for whales and dolphins has led to calls for the closing down of captive facilities on the grounds of cruelty and inadequate housing conditions.

The anti-captivity lobby point at incontrovertible evidence of high death rates – sometimes as high as 100 percent – during all stages of the process from initial capture to public display. They argue that even the most expensive and sophisticated facilities provide an environment

so different to the natural one that captive cetaceans always suffer sensory deprivation and stress, which manifests itself in behavioural disorders, such as those described above.

People who support the idea of keeping cetaceans in captivity do so for a variety of reasons. They may have a financial stake or a career in a facility and would lose their profits or job if it closed down; cetacean displays are big business employing thousands. They may be scientists whose work would come to a halt if they were unable to study dolphins in controlled captive conditions. They may even be conservationists, many of whom realize that without continuing contact between cetaceans and the public, the task of gaining popular support for the conservation measures

needed to protect these animals and their natural environment would be a much greater one. Most are members of the public who, together with their children, value the opportunity to see, hear and touch these fascinating creatures at close quarters, and would otherwise encounter them only on television.

There is no right or wrong answer to the dilemma. In the end, public opinion will either force the closure of marine display parks or it will continue to support them, overriding the anti-captivity lobby. The crux is really whether the stress and possible early death of a few hundred animals each year can be justified by the benefits to be gained by the captives' wild counterparts, investors and employees, the public and our increased knowledge of the animals. You decide.

# CETACEAN SCIENCE

Although we know a great deal about some species of cetaceans, our knowledge is patchy for many and almost non-existent for a few. There is no doubt that the study of cetaceans, or cetology, is lagging far behind that of birds and land mammals.

The major reasons for our lack of knowledge are not hard to find. They are, quite simply, that the habitat and behaviour of cetaceans allow relatively little contact with man. Most occur away from land and all spend a lot of their time under water. It is no coincidence that the species we are most familiar with, such as the humpback, right and killer whales and the bottlenose dolphin, occur in nearshore waters in some part of their range. Purely deepsea species, such as the beaked whales, have remained enigmatic and the subjects of great speculation. Even now, late in the twentieth century, there is a high probability that new species of living cetaceans remain to be discovered and described.

## Studying cetaceans in captivity

Many fields of research have benefited from work on captive animals, the most obvious being studies of behaviour, health and medicine, communication, physiology, reproduction and 'intelligence'. Although captivity obviously affects cetacean behaviour in many ways, we have learned a great deal from captive animals that otherwise could not have been explored at all. Social interactions are much easier to watch through the windows of an aquarium than through a diving mask at sea and, of course, the length of observations is unlimited. Scientists have been able to investigate the nature of relationships between animals living in a group. They have watched aggression, appeasement, responses to sickness and death in the group, sexual courtship, play, curiosity, fear, frustration and all the other normal day-to-day behaviours which had previously been out of reach of land- and boat-bound investigators. In some dolphins, of which the bottlenose dolphin (*Tursiops truncatus*) is the best known, the animals in many facilities have adapted to their captivity to the extent that mating, pregnancy, birth and lactation have been followed by thrilled scientists and public alike.

Until cetaceans began to appear in captivity, the little that was known of their health and disease came from examining dead animals, either stranded or killed. The pressure to radically improve this situation came from the need to keep expensive animals alive once they had been taken into captivity. Initially, dolphins rarely lived more than a few months after capture and many died from shock in the first few hours and days. Now, species from the size of Commerson's dolphin (up to 1.75m) to that of killer whales (up to 9.75m) are routinely kept for many years, and it has been the improved understanding of general physiology, blood chemistry, nutrition, shock, infections and diseases, etc., that has been primarily responsible.

Two further, related, topics of study should be mentioned here: the physiology of locomotion and the energy budget of cetaceans. Only in the controlled conditions of a swim-tank is it possible to closely examine the mechanics of swimming and diving and record the relative energetic costs of various types of activity. Animals have been trained to swim at various speeds in such tanks and to exhale into funnels, thereby allowing researchers to chemically analyze their breath and determine how fast they are using energy. The heart-rate and blood chemistry of exercising and resting animals can also be monitored, showing how their bodies cope with long periods of activity without an exchange of air in the lungs.

Two other areas of interest suited to research on captive cetaceans are those of intelligence and the senses. The difficulties of trying to assess the level of intelligence and understanding in cetaceans have been discussed on page 21. Some have sought to address this dilemma by posing practical problems that require different levels of thought, skill or learning to solve. Others have tried to assess the degree of intellect shown by the activity and communication within social groups of dolphins in a pool. Some of the most advanced work, often lasting years, has been in trying to establish the level of language complexity that dolphins can learn.

Studying the senses has been a little easier. Sensitivity to sound of different frequencies and intensity has been measured for many species, and sight is similarly fairly simple to assess. Touch sensitivity can often be judged by watching everyday behaviour or by setting tests for a dolphin with suction cups over its eyes to eliminate the sense of sight. This technique is also widely used to examine a sense of which man is totally bereft, that of echolocation. The careful and painstaking training of various small cetaceans has demonstrated that they are able to discriminate, for example, between a hollow and a solid sphere, between a large ball and a small ball, and even between fish of different types, without the aid of eyesight and at a range of many metres. Only now, after many years of research on captive cetaceans, are we coming to appreciate their ability to obtain a high-resolution sound picture of the environment in which they live.

*Below: The whole world is a laboratory for cetology. Here a researcher records the vocalizations of killer whales in a crack in sea ice off Antarctica.*

*Above right: While one scientist photographs the tail fluke pattern of a humpback, another readies a crossbow to take a skin sample for genetic analysis.*

## Studying live animals in the wild

Despite the undoubted value of behavioural work on captive animals, there is no doubt that much of the behaviour of smaller cetaceans, and all the behaviour of larger ones, can only be satisfactorily followed in the wild, if at all. Feeding in the wild, for example, very often occurs at water depths greater than those provided in dolphinariums and, of course, on live prey. The study of feeding techniques has involved observers in the water, on boats and in aircraft, and tying in their work with examinations of the stomach contents of stranded and captured animals. As a result, we have a reasonable picture of what most species eat, and where and how they catch it.

Until the 1970s, observations of behaviour in the wild usually relied on chance encounters with an unknown animal or group of animals that might have been followed for a few minutes or hours before being lost to sight and never knowingly seen again. This decade saw a major step in cetacean research; the realization that by recording their external markings and coloration, wild animals of some species could be recognized as individuals over long periods of time. This has revolutionized the study of wild cetaceans and already produced results of great value and interest in many fields of research. In terms of behaviour, we are learning, for example, about group stability, length of natural life, calving intervals, which age and sex classes leave and join which groups, foraging differences between groups, home range size and utilization. Most of this information is patiently gathered over periods of

years by researchers working from small boats, who gradually piece together an intimate knowledge of their animals.

Although many animals can be recognized by eye, particularly those with a very obvious mark such as a prominent scar, most of the characteristics used to discriminate between individuals are quite subtle. Researchers have found that a photograph of the animal or, more precisely, a particular part of the animal, is essential to confirm its identity. A photograph not only allows one worker to check if he or she has seen the animal before, but also permits any number of other people to see if 'their' animals have been recorded elsewhere. Photographic catalogues of several species have already been established, and each season's new crop of identifications are carefully compared with the existing set. This new research technique is becoming known simply as 'photo-ID'.

One of the first 'at sea' studies to earn recognition outside the community of cetacean enthusiasts was that of Roger and Katherine Payne, who pioneered work on humpback whale song. Intrigued by the length and complexity of the songs, the Paynes set out to discover if they contained any recognizable structure or pattern. By gathering recordings from several breeding sites over many years, and by carefully analyzing the sounds on sonograph machines that provide a visual representation of each type of vocalization, the researchers were excited to find that patterns did exist and that they were much more complex than had ever been guessed. Their work, and the parallel work on humpback whale photo-ID, has led to an unrivalled knowledge of this animal's behaviour and social structure.

## How many whales are there?

This question has been baffling whalers and scientists alike for centuries. Consider the task. The animals you want to count spend most of their time out of sight of land and most of it below the surface of the sea. They may move around considerably from season to season and from year to year, perhaps occurring in huge numbers at a site during one year and being almost absent there the next. Components of the stock may be separated from one another by thousands of kilometres at times (as in gray whales), may never be in the same area at the same time (as in sperm whales) and the stock may cover millions of square kilometres (most oceanic species).

Various ways have been tried to come

up with answers. A few species, such as gray whales and bowhead whales, conveniently pass close to land or sea ice at particular times and can be visually or acoustically counted. The number seen always has to be corrected for those missed at night, those passing under water or too far out to be counted, etc., but it is possible to gain reasonable estimates with care. Other species have relatively sedentary or predictable habits whereby the same animals return to the same nearshore areas year after year for considerable periods of time, or are resident there, and can be counted from boats or from land. On the whole, though, cetaceans do not lend themselves to being counted in such relatively convenient ways. While careful consideration of their behaviour, migrations and seasonal distribution is essential to reduce the area to be surveyed and increase the accuracy of the estimate, the best to hope for is that the animals you are interested in are all within one well-defined, albeit huge, expanse of ocean.

The difference between a 'count', when all animals are seen, and an 'estimate', when the total is derived from seeing a sample of the whole stock or population, is important. Counts of whale stocks are impossible to carry out, for many reasons. The best that can ever be achieved is an estimate, which is usually given as a range within which the true figure is thought to lie, e.g. 10,000 plus or minus 4,000. Essentially, there are two ways to estimate the size of a stock once the area within which it occurs has been defined. One is to use mark-recapture methods, the other is to survey the area visually or acoustically to detect the animals. Here we consider both techniques of estimating whale stocks.

**Mark-recapture** The idea here is to mark a sample of animals from a given population in such a way that they can be recognized again in the future. If certain assumptions hold, the proportion of marked animals in a subsequent sample will reflect the population size and provide the information necessary to allow its estimation. Thus, in a very simple example, if 100 whales are marked on one day and, a month later, 10 of these marked animals occur in a further random sample of 200, the estimate is of $(200 \div 10) \times 100 = 2,000$ whales in that particular population.

Marking can be carried out in several ways, but such marks need to be long lasting, and only fully implanted tags like those first used in the 'Discovery' investigations during the 1920s are likely to fulfil

*Right: All humpback whales can be uniquely identified by a combination of the black-and-white pattern on the underside of the tail flukes and the irregular outline of their trailing margin. These photographs, all taken of humpbacks off West Greenland, are some of several thousand now held in the North Atlantic catalogue. Recognizing individuals throughout their range enables cetacean scientists to investigate migration, stock size, longevity, reproduction and many aspects of behaviour.*

this requirement. 'Discovery' marks, uniquely numbered metal tubes fired into the whale from a shotgun, probably never came out of the animal if they were placed correctly, but they had the disadvantages of not being visible on the surface of the whale and only providing information once – if and when the whale was subsequently taken by whalers. Luckily, photo-ID overcomes these problems, allowing an animal to be 'recaptured' any number of times from a distance without causing it any harm.

**Visual and acoustic surveys** These surveys are designed to locate and record the number of, and distance from, animals within range of the observer (visual) or hydrophone (acoustic). The information gained is then used to derive an estimate of the total number of animals in a given area, using mathematical corrections to allow for those, the majority, not recorded. Visual surveys are normally carried out from a moving platform, usually a boat or aircraft, but can be conducted from land if the animals are known to pass the observation point. In each case, animals are recorded only while they are at the surface, so corrections have to be made by finding out what proportion of their time is spent at and below the water surface. This varies from species to species. Acoustic surveys rely on the ability to detect, and determine the distance from, cetaceans based solely on their vocalizations. The surveys use 'passive' hydrophones, which can either be towed behind a vessel or anchored, depending on the situation. All survey results have to be corrected for the fact that the ability to detect animals diminishes as distance to them increases. In many cases, the result gives an estimate of density, that is the number of animals per unit area, rather than an absolute number. The final figure can then be gained by multiplying this density estimate by the total area within which the stock is thought to occur. For example:

    0.1 (density estimate of 1 animal per $10km^2$) $\times$ 5,000 (number of square km in stock area) = 500 animals estimated.

**Migrations and local movements**
We have already seen that some species migrate close to land, so their path is fairly easy to follow. Unfortunately, most do not make things quite so simple, so we must use other techniques to monitor them. Opportunistic observations from boats and, to a lesser extent, from aircraft have helped to complete the picture in many cases. Aerial or ship surveys can then be used to confirm if a concentration of animals has been located. To prove that animals have moved we often need evidence that one or more particular individuals have made the journey.

Photo-ID has already been shown to provide evidence of individual movements, and now another modern research technique, radio telemetry, is beginning to prove its worth in this respect. The term 'radio telemetry' is used here in preference to the more familiar 'radio tracking' because radio signals are now used for more than just following the path of cetaceans, although this is still its major function. As implemented on marine animals, radio telemetry involves the use of radio transmitters to send signals from the animals to one or more remote receivers. The signals are normally pulsed, i.e. not continuous, and are transmitted in the frequency range 30-401MHz. Receivers can be on boats, on aircraft, on land or, more recently, on satellites. The idea is to be able to receive information from the animal in the wild that would otherwise not be obtainable at all or would necessitate following the animal within visual range for long periods of time. The information obtained normally includes the animal's position, but may also give details of behaviour, physiology and environmental factors.

Radio transmitters were first attached to free-living cetaceans in the 1960s. At that time, such transmitters were large and heavy, and designed to send signals over relatively short distances. By triangulating the signals, it was possible to find the animal's position at regular intervals, thus giving a timed series of locations – in effect, a track.

With advances in microelectronics, the size of transmitters rapidly diminished and, in the mid-1970s, William Watkins of the Woods Hole Oceanographic Institute in Massachusetts successfully tried out a tubular design that was fired by a modified gun directly into the whale's blubber, leaving the radio antenna protruding. This was a great leap forward, since there was no longer a requirement to capture the animal for attachment. Watkins

achieved tracks of up to 28 days on humpback and fin whales, but then encountered the same problem experienced by everyone else; the transmitters were rejected by the tissue, and fell off.

At about this time the first steps were being taken in another revolutionary branch of radio telemetry. In this, the intention was to transmit signals to passing satellites that would then beam the information down to land stations and, from there, to the researcher by telephone line. The first applications of satellite-linked telemetry were beset with problems but satellites are now used to receive signals from animals ranging in size from bottlenose dolphins to sperm, right and humpback whales.

During the relatively short period that radio telemetry has been applied to cetaceans, the size of transmitters has shrunk dramatically, to the extent that 'conventional' telemetry (the sending of signals directly to a receiver rather than via a satellite) has been carried out on even the smallest porpoises. Its use as a research tool is now widespread and has produced a great deal of valuable information. It does have limitations, however, and can prove very costly if boats or aircraft are needed to follow or locate the target animals. Satellite-linked telemetry avoids many of these disadvantages; the animals cannot 'escape' since the satellites scan the whole earth's surface, and following by boat or air is unnecessary (and unwise). Thus, day-to-day costs are low. Nevertheless, despite overcoming most technical difficulties, one major problem still remains and it is common to all types of telemetry. Until someone finds a way of preventing tissue rejection of implants, or a reliable long-term alternative means of fixing transmitters to slippery, wet animals, the useful life of each transmitter will always be cut short by it falling off the animal.

**Studying stranded and caught cetaceans**
Work on dead animals from strandings and catches is divided into two parts. The first is the examination, measurement and sampling of the animals on site and the second, usually taking much longer, is the subsequent laboratory analysis of the samples and measurements.

Depending on the circumstances, the first phase can be very smelly and uncomfortable work. Conditions at whaling

factories or at whale drives, where the animals are killed on the beach, are usually better for working than at an isolated stranding, but less time is available within which to measure and sample the catch. 'Working up' a typical carcass can take between 20 minutes and several hours, depending on the size of the animal and the equipment available. A porpoise can be managed by a team of two, but a large whale can require 10 people and heavy machinery, such as winches, to remove the blubber. Such work normally yields a series of external body measurements, internal measurements (such as the thickness of the blubber), the sex and reproductive status (whether it is pregnant or lactating, for example), notes on parasites, health and disease etc., and a whole series of specimens that need to be deep frozen or preserved in some other way.

Then the real work begins. Teeth, or in the case of the baleen whales, earplugs, have to be sectioned and examined under a microscope to read the number of layers within. This tells us the age of the animal – in a very similar way to reading tree rings. Blubber, muscle, liver and other tissue samples are chemically analyzed to provide information on the amount of pollutants, heavy metals and organochlorines, that have accumulated in them. High concentrations might help to explain any health problems noted.

Skin, liver or other tissue is used to gain a genetic characterization of the animal. A variety of new techniques permit analysis of the individual's DNA, the carrier of its unique genetic identity. Enzymes are used to 'cut' the DNA chain at every point where it recognizes a particular pattern, revealing a genetic 'code'. This code can be then used to investigate the relationship between animals in a group, between groups within a population and between populations within a species. Perhaps the best-known study technique in this field is 'DNA fingerprinting', which provides a unique genetic characterization for each animal and permits the identification of parents and offspring, grandmothers, uncles, etc., in family groups of cetaceans.

Examining the sexual organs can tell us a surprising amount about the reproductive history of the whale. Ovaries contain a permanent record of the number of ovulations during the entire lifetime of

the female and, indirectly, how many calves she has produced. When combined with an examination of the uterus and the mammary glands, ovarian characteristics also reveal the reproductive state of the animal at death. This information for all females in the sample, together with their age, provides an estimate of such important population parameters as average age of sexual maturity, inter-birth interval, length of gestation and lactation, and the overall reproductive rate. Microscopic examination of testis tissue from males allows us to assess their reproductive status, indirectly to estimate their age at reproductive maturity and to determine the timing and degree of seasonality of mating.

The stomach contents can reveal vital information about the type and size of

prey taken. Conveniently for research purposes, fish and squid have very hard bones in their heads, called otoliths and statoliths, that resist digestion and are different in each species. Squid and octopus mouthparts, called beaks, are similar in this respect. Thus, when the stomach is empty of everything except a pile of bones, as is often the case, there can still be good evidence of the composition of the last few meals, the remains of perhaps hundreds of animals, waiting to be sorted through.

Assembling such evidence from large numbers of animals can provide an accurate and detailed picture of many aspects of the population from which the animals came. Collecting and analyzing the samples is often unpleasant and always time consuming. Few scientists would even contemplate killing animals for research purposes, and very few support so-called 'scientific whaling', but nothing is to be gained by ignoring the wealth of information available from stranded or captured cetaceans. Lack of knowledge about cetaceans has too often led to their abuse in the past. Only by developing a greater understanding of them can we learn to anticipate and overcome the many problems caused by their only serious threat – man.

**Tracking a beluga whale using satellite-linked telemetry**

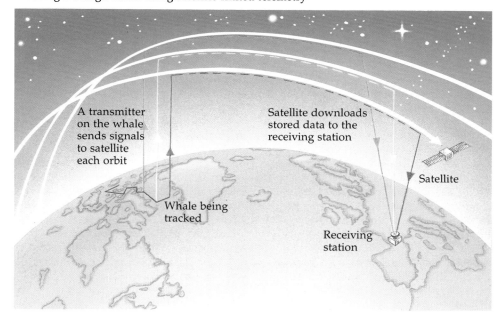

A transmitter on the whale sends signals to satellite each orbit

Satellite downloads stored data to the receiving station

Satellite

Whale being tracked

Receiving station

*The illustration above reflects an innovative technique in cetacean research – tracking animals using satellite telemetry. In this investigation, a beluga equipped with a radio transmitter (shown at right) was tracked for nearly 500km (to within 2km) in the Canadian Arctic before the transmitter fell off.*

# FISHERIES AND POLLUTION

Modern man is a very efficient exploiter of marine resources. With his sophisticated gear and huge ocean-going ships that can remain at sea for months, freezing each day's catch, no part of the globe is out of reach. Since some whales, dolphins and porpoises eat the same prey species as are targeted by human fishermen, it is not surprising that the two predatory groups often compete and otherwise interact with one another in areas where they coincide. Such interactions fall into one of two broad groups: 'predatory' and 'operational'.

### Predatory interactions with fisheries
These are the least obvious interactions and are also the hardest to prove or quantify. They are caused by cetaceans and fishermen consuming the same target species, or one taking the food or natural predators of the other's target species. If predators are removed, the interaction is beneficial, but otherwise one or both suffer to some extent. This illustrates the interdependence of components in an ecosystem, where the actions of one have repercussions on all the others.

One example is the way in which humpback whales were forced to forage in nearshore waters off Newfoundland, Canada (and subsequently often became entangled in cod traps) when the offshore stocks of their prey, capelin, failed in the 1970s, probably as a result of overfishing. Another example, and one that is causing concern because its potential effect is so great, is the developing fishery for Antarctic krill (*Euphausia superba*). Cetaceans, seals and seabirds in the Antarctic region rely, directly or indirectly, on this one species of zooplankton for food. Thus, an expanding fishery is likely, at some stage, to start adversely affecting these natural predators.

### Operational interactions with fisheries
Under this heading come interactions directly or indirectly related to the fishing operations employed by man. Such interactions are usually detrimental to both fishermen and cetaceans. In some cases they may be of considerable benefit to man, but in almost none do they benefit the whales, dolphins or porpoises involved. We can include here the deliberate or accidental entrapment of cetaceans in fishing gear and the killing or scaring of cetaceans to diminish a real or perceived threat to the livelihood of fishermen. Conversely, the cetaceans may cause damage to gear, take fish from hooks or nets, and scare away fish.

The direct killing of cetaceans often attracts widespread media attention and international condemnation, but it is a simple fact that in the past 30 years the number of cetacean lives lost to deliberate killing for food or other products is almost insignificant compared to the number drowned or suffocated in fishing nets around the world. Estimates of the magnitude of this wasteful carnage are inevitably poor, because many of the industries responsible are secretive about their activities. However, the number of animals involved can be counted in millions, perhaps 5-10 million over 30 years, and nearly all are simply thrown back into the sea after disentanglement.

Nearly all large-scale fisheries, whether they use gillnets, trawls, purse-seines, longlines or fish traps, catch and kill cetaceans to some degree. Until the advent of modern synthetic materials, accidental entrapments were probably of little threat to most cetacean populations, but with the introduction of nylon lines and nets, and larger nets hauled by hydraulic winches, the situation took a dramatic turn for the worse. Even now, the incidental cetacean kill caused by most fisheries can probably be sustained by the population, but the use of nylon driftnets worldwide and the move to the purse-seining of tuna swimming in association with dolphins in the eastern tropical Pacific has caused deaths at such a rate that some stocks of small cetaceans have been very markedly reduced.

Driftnetting is now commonplace, both in nearshore and offshore waters, and is used for many species of fish and squid. The nets form a vertical wall of mesh, into which swim the target species plus, of course, many other types of animal. The catch of fish, turtles, seabirds, seals or cetaceans quickly becomes entangled, drowns and is extracted when the fishing boat next comes by. The sheer scale of driftnetting is breathtaking. In the Pacific Ocean, on a single night, tens of thousands of kilometres of netting are set. Most nets are recovered and any unwanted corpses thrown overboard, but some, known as ghost nets, become lost and continue catching for weeks or months until the weight of animals entrapped overcomes the buoyancy of the floats. The whole grisly package then sinks slowly to the seabed, where it continues to entrap bottom-dwelling species of fish and invertebrates.

**Tuna purse-seining** For some reason that is not yet understood, perhaps linked to food searching, yellowfin tuna in an enormous area of ocean west of central America spend much of their time swimming directly underneath schools of dolphins. Fishermen have known this for decades and have taken advantage of it to locate the fish. In 1959, the fishery underwent a radical change, when synthetic materials and hydraulic machinery permitted the use of much bigger purse-seine nets. These are set by paying out a wall of mesh in a circle around the target fish, then pulling on the cable that runs through rings at the bottom of the net to draw it closed like a purse, hence the name. The new nets were sufficiently large to encompass dolphin schools, so the ships could increase their efficiency by locating a group of dolphins, setting the net on them and winching in net, fish and dolphins. Sometimes, attempts were made to release the dolphins, and a procedure called 'backdown' was later developed to pull the net out from under them but, inevitably, many were drowned or suffocated. As profits grew, larger ships were added to the fleet and began operating further offshore.

The effect on the dolphins during the first decade of the modernized fishery was devastating. Hundreds of thousands, perhaps millions, of dolphins were entangled and died, many crushed to death as they were winched over pulleys in the net. At that time, most of the fleet sailed under the flag of the United States, so the US National Marine Fisheries Service drew up regulations to cut down on the dolphin mortality. These included practical measures to ensure that nets were modified to allow dolphins to escape more easily and that the backdown procedure was carried out correctly. An observer scheme was also introduced, to provide a form of policing and an estimate of dolphin losses. The Inter-American Tropical Tuna Commission also operates an independent observer programme through which it monitors the mortality inflicted by the international fleet.

The dolphins involved in this slaughter are all oceanic species and occur in large schools. The primary targets are various races of spinner dolphin, the pantropical spotted dolphin and the common dolphin. As the fishery expanded geographically, the whitebelly spinner dolphin replaced its cousin, the eastern spinner, as a major target. The eastern spinner was so depleted that US regulations now specifically prohibit setting nets around schools of this dolphin.

In the four years between 1985 and 1988, total mortality in this fishery was estimated at 60-130,000 dolphins per

Above: Many millions of dolphins have died as a result of being deliberately captured with tuna shoals in purse-seine nets.

year. Approximately 50-60 percent were spotted dolphins, 15-30 percent spinner dolphins, 10-25 percent common dolphins and less than 5 percent other species. Despite the very high mortality over the past three decades, none of the dolphin populations involved is considered to be in immediate danger. The hardest hit, the eastern spinner dolphin, is probably at about 20 percent of its original level and currently numbers approximately 600-800,000 animals.

### Accidental entrapment
When even a small cetacean becomes caught in fishing gear, the gear itself is often damaged or has to be cut to release the unfortunate animal. When a large whale is entrapped, the gear is usually destroyed and may become so twisted around the animal that, even if it escapes, the line or net remains attached. Eventually, the gear usually kills the whale, either directly or indirectly – if it is unable to feed and starves – but occasionally a lightly hindered animal survives and can carry the gear around for years. Such has been the case with a well-known right whale, affectionately nicknamed 'Stars', that is regularly seen off Cape Cod, Massachusetts, with a rope tied tightly around her rostrum and through the baleen, but who seems, nevertheless, to be able to feed adequately.

During the 1970s, humpback whales suffered numerous entrapments in cod traps off Newfoundland, eastern Canada. They had been forced to forage near-shore after the offshore stock of capelin, their main prey fish, collapsed. During this period of a few years, fishermen lost hundreds of thousands of dollars in wrecked gear and many humpbacks died. Other recent examples of cetacean entanglement in fishing gear are harbour porpoises caught in salmon driftnets off west Greenland (estimated at 1,500 a year), several species of dolphin in nets off Sri Lanka (one estimate suggests 42,000 a year) and 2,000 dolphins killed by the Italian swordfish industry. The two most endangered cetaceans have also suffered heavy losses in fishing operations; both are now reduced to fewer than 500 animals. The vaquita, or Gulf of California porpoise, was severely affected by gillnetting, which left the species in real danger of extinction, even though the practice virtually ceased more than a decade ago. The baiji, or Chinese river dolphin, has fallen foul of several types of fishing gear, including the multiple hooks on longlines.

When gear damage becomes intense, or fishermen believe that cetaceans are responsible for declining catches, they sometimes take direct corrective action. This can be benign – the salmon fishermen of Bristol Bay, Alaska used sonic devices to scare beluga whales away from sockeye salmon runs, for example. Sometimes it is brutal, as was demonstrated by the hook-and-line fishermen of Iki Island, western Japan, in the late 1970s and early 1980s. They believed, perhaps understandably, that the abundant schools of dolphins and small whales around Iki were sometimes responsible for scaring away the yellowtail fish on which the fishery relied. Their solution was to drive cetaceans ashore and kill them. In 1976, the total destroyed was 55. In 1977, it reached 934, and in 1980, the catch rose to a peak of 1,819. The animals – bottlenose, Risso's and Pacific white-sided dolphins and false killer whales – were mostly buried, dumped at sea or shredded. The largest single kill was of over 1,000 dolphins. As has happened elsewhere, the decline in the fishery catch is now seen to be a result of over-exploitation by man, so the ineffective killing of dolphins has stopped.

### The effects of pollution
The rapid increase in levels of manmade pollution in marine organisms during the latter half of the twentieth century has prompted recent concern over the possible repercussions for cetaceans. The pollutants of most interest in this respect are organochlorines (e.g. PCBs, DDT and DDE) and heavy metals, such as lead, zinc and cadmium. Usually, they are either dumped directly into the sea or fed into it via rivers, which carry effluent from farmland, human habitation and industry. Pollutants are initially picked up by organisms at the very bottom of the food chain, such as algae, and become increasingly concentrated in the tissues of invertebrates and animals higher up the food chain as each predator in turn falls prey to a larger predator. The animals at the top of the chain, including cetaceans and seals, carry the highest concentrations and are thus potentially the most vulnerable to harmful effects.

Environmental levels of pollution vary globally and reflect the distribution of sources. The Arctic, Antarctic and Pacific Oceans are generally lightly polluted, whereas semi-enclosed seas near to industrial nations, such as the North Sea and the Baltic, show very heavy levels in the water, sediment and in most organisms. Cetaceans necessarily reflect the pollutant levels of the areas where they feed and are thus good environmental indicators. Unfortunately, the process of contamination and the effects of pollutants at the level of both the individual and the population are as yet poorly understood. At present, there is no evidence that heavy metals are causing health problems in any cetacean population. However, organochlorines, particularly polychlorinated biphenyls (PCBs), can suppress the immune system and have been linked with the poor reproduction and high rate of disease in belugas of the St Lawrence Estuary in eastern Canada. They may also be causing hormonal abnormalities in some other small cetaceans, such as Dall's porpoises. We must hope that the growing awareness of organochlorine contamination – and moves to reduce it – act quickly to lessen the resultant known and unknown hazards to marine mammals.

# PART TWO

This part of the book consists of a species-by-species account of all 78 currently recognized cetaceans. 'Recognition' is used here in the taxonomic sense, whereby a two-part scientific name has been suggested and accepted for a particular type of animal. It is important to remember that taxonomic classification is merely a guide, and one that is constantly changing as new information and new interpretations of old material are published. For convenience, the 78 species have been divided into 10 natural groups, which contain between one and 26 species each. These groups represent taxonomic families, or sometimes two or more families within a superfamily. Following convention, the 11 baleen, or 'whalebone', whales of the sub-order Mysticeti have been discussed before the 67 toothed whales, dolphins and porpoises of the sub-order Odontoceti.

The treatment of each species follows a set pattern, with the text presented under self-explanatory headings. The length of the text reflects the amount known for each species. Those that have been subject to intensive exploitation within the past 60 years or so, or are commonly mass-stranded in countries where cetacean research is carried out, are the ones about which most information is available. In addition, much behavioural and acoustic information has been gained from animals, necessarily the smaller species, held in captivity. If any of the text headings are omitted in a species account, it is because there is little or no information available about that topic.

As will be clear, some species are found in only a very small area, while others can be encountered almost anywhere in the world. Some are resident year-round, while others spend part of the year in one area, part in another, and the remainder migrating between the two. To complicate matters, our knowledge of any particular species' range can vary from fairly comprehensive to almost non-existent. The degree of certainty about the distribution of each species is reflected in the map, the map legend and usually in the text. Most maps reflect a mixture of confirmed records and informed guesswork, based on knowledge of habitat preference.

An outline drawing is shown for each species, with a human diver at the same scale for comparison. Individual animals usually change their shape to some extent as they grow older, and there will always be fatter and thinner, longer and shorter individuals within a population, but the outline shows a 'typical' adult. Differences in length between the sexes are referred to in the text.

One or more photographs, or an illustration, is provided for all species except Longman's beaked whale, which has never been seen. Preference has been given to full-length photographs of live animals, but these have simply not been taken for a great number of species. As a rule, those species for which a photograph is not shown have either only been photographed as a decomposing carcass on a beach or unrecognizably at sea. For these, illustrations are based on published observations of live and stranded animals.

*Right: The large and the small. This rare photograph, taken by a researcher in the clear waters off Hawaii, shows a group of bottlenose dolphins dwarfed by a humpback whale mother and her calf.*

# RIGHT WHALES

## BALAENIDAE · NEOBALAENIDAE

There are three genera in this group: *Balaena*, *Eubalaena* and *Caperea*. Of these, *Balaena* (represented by one species, *B. mysticetus*, the bowhead whale) and *Eubalaena* (represented by two species of black right whales – see page 58) are placed in the family Balaenidae. The third genus, *Caperea* (represented by one living species, *C. marginata*, the pygmy right whale), was also considered to be a balaenid, but some taxonomists now favour placing it in its own family, Neobalaenidae. *Balaena* is confined to the Northern Hemisphere and *Caperea* to the Southern Hemisphere, while *Eubalaena* is found in both hemispheres.

All the right whales share the following features: a smooth belly and chin with no ventral grooves; distinctive head shape with a strongly arched, narrow rostrum and bowed lower jaw; lower lips that enfold the sides and front of the rostrum; long, narrow, elastic baleen plates (up to nine times longer than they are wide) with fine baleen fringes – consequently all three feed mainly on copepods and euphausiids; the fusion of all the cervical vertebrae and other skeletal characteristics; a slow swimming speed. There are gradations in some of these characters between the three genera. In *Balaena*, for example, the head comprises about one-third of body length; in *Eubalaena*, about one-quarter of the body length; while in *Caperea*, it is less than one-quarter.

The two most similar genera are *Balaena* and *Eubalaena*. Indeed, at several times in the history of cetacean classification, they have been considered to be one genus. Both comprise large, stocky species, up to 20m or so in length and with no dorsal fin. Both exhibit a characteristic V-shaped blow on non-windy days. The large size (and hence high oil yield), long baleen, slow swimming speed and the fact that they float when killed, led both genera to suffer the same tragic story of overexploitation, with one stock after another being depleted between the fifteenth and early twentieth centuries. Apart from one stock of *Balaena* of about 8,000 whales, the remaining *Balaena* stocks and all the *Eubalaena* stocks number less than 1,000, even after over 50 years of protection from commercial whaling. While some are showing signs of recovery, it is feared that others may never recover.

In contrast, *Caperea* is a small cetacean less than 7m in length, relatively streamlined and possessing a dorsal fin. It has never been commercially exploited.

*A group of bowhead whales skim-feeding in krill. As with all balaenids, this species has an arched upper jaw to accommodate the long baleen plates.*

# BOWHEAD WHALE

## BALAENA MYSTICETUS

■ Maximum range

**Classification** The bowhead whale was classified by Linnaeus in 1758 and the name he chose, *Balaena mysticetus*, literally means 'moustached sea monster'. No subspecies are recognized.

**Local names** The common name 'bowhead' derives from the extreme arching of the upper jaw. It is sometimes known as the 'Greenland right whale' or 'Greenland whale', a legacy of its former abundance in Greenlandic waters, where whalers virtually hunted it to extinction.

**Description** The bowhead is a large stocky whale with a massive head and no dorsal fin. The average adult body length is about 14-15m, with mature females about 0.6m longer than males. Individuals up to 19m long have reputedly been captured in the past.

Records of body weights are mostly of dubious accuracy. By analogy with the closely related right whales, an average of 50-60 tonnes seems likely for adult bowheads, but an 11m male recently weighed in pieces was only 14.8 tonnes, so current length/weight calculations may overestimate the true weight.

Calves are born blue-black, but adults are predominantly black with a white or creamy 'chin' on the forward part of the lower jaw. This light patch may have black spots within it. Many individuals have a light area on the tail stock.

The baleen of this species is the longest of any whale, typically reaching 4.3m in the middle of the 350 plates on each side of the jaw. The baleen plates are dark and the hairs, particularly fine in this species, are lighter. The eye is small and set at the angle of the jaw. The flippers are relatively small and rounded. There are no throat grooves, and no known geographical variation.

**Recognition at sea** A large whale with no dorsal fin can only be a bowhead or a right whale and they can be distinguished by the presence or absence of callosities on the head (bowheads have

none) and a white chin patch (bowheads only). The blow is bushy, being ejected from the two nostrils in diverging clouds up to 6m high.

**Habitat** This is the largest of the three cetaceans that live wholly in Arctic or sub-arctic waters, and all have adapted to spending much of their lives close to the edge of the ice. (The narwhal and beluga are the other two.) Bowheads often occur in shallow water close to land, but will swim in whatever depth is necessary to follow cracks in the sea ice.

**Distribution and migration** Bowheads are restricted to the colder waters of the Northern Hemisphere, rarely far from ice. Historically, they were circumpolar, but intensive whaling has largely removed them from the North Atlantic, where recent sightings are sporadic and usually in the area of Svalbard. Their current distribution is essentially the Davis Strait, Canadian waters north and west of Labrador, the northern and western seaboards of Alaska, and the Bering, Chukchi and Okhotsk Seas.

Migrations occur northwards in spring, following leads or cracks in the retreating ice, and southwards in the autumn as the sea freezes over. The best-known movement is that of the stock wintering in the Bering Sea. The whales, often segregated by age or sexual class, move northwards and eastwards along the Alaskan coast to rich summer feeding grounds in the Beaufort Sea area. In autumn, the return passage is made in a hurry to avoid being cut off by drifting pack ice or new sea ice. Most whales are thought to travel within a few kilometres of the edge of the land-fast ice on the northward journey, thus helping scientists to count them using land-based observers and aircraft to spot the animals or hydrophones to hear their calls. Bowheads swim steadily at speeds of 2-7 kph when migrating.

**Food and feeding** Bowheads were once thought to be almost exclusively skimmers, taking food at the surface by swimming slowly along with the mouth open, straining the water through the baleen until sufficient plankton had accumulated to justify them swallowing. However, recent research has shown that this species often feeds in midwater and, in depths of 30m or less, whales have been observed bottom feeding and coming to the surface with mud spilling out of the mouth. Benthic prey has been seen in the stomachs of harvested whales in spring.

With such fine baleen hairs, bowheads are able to exploit extremely small organisms, including copepods, steropods and mysids, but they seem to take larger euphausiids most commonly. Underwater feeding seems to be an individual pursuit, but surface skimmers sometimes coordinate their activity; up to 14 have been seen in echelon formation.

**Behaviour** Small groups of three or less bowheads are common in spring, but larger aggregations of up to 50 may occasionally occur in the autumn on passage. Although an entire population of bowhead whales may follow the same migrational path and animals are often necessarily close together, this is not a particularly social or demonstrative species. Aerial activity, such as breaching and tail and flipper slaps, are not frequent, but one whale was seen to breach 57 times in 96 minutes. There appears to be a continuous decrease in the degree of socializing from spring to autumn on the northern grounds.

Dive times are normally between 4 and about 15 minutes, but dives lasting longer than 30 minutes have been recorded. Calves dive less frequently and for shorter periods.

Bowhead whales are vocal on migration, at least, and produce a variety of frequency-modulated calls, mainly at 50-300 Hz. Sounds up to 3,500Hz have been recorded, and an intensity of 156db was noted when one whale was 100-150m from a hydrophone.

Bowheads are renowned for their ability to break holes through sea ice less than 0.3m thick in order to breathe. Sometimes their passage can be seen by a line of raised mounds on otherwise flat ice. There is some evidence that whales can use sound to investigate the thickness and nature of ice in their path. They sometimes make mistakes, however, and animals can be trapped for days or weeks near small ice-free areas in otherwise impenetrable ice fields. Strandings are uncommon and mass strandings unknown. Probably only very ill or dead animals come ashore.

**Life history** Relatively little is known about this animal, partly because its harsh environment is not conducive to the type of studies normally carried out on large whales. Most evidence comes from the recent spate of work carried out by American biologists on the Alaskan Eskimo hunt, when it was thought that the species may have been in danger of extinction, but sample sizes are very

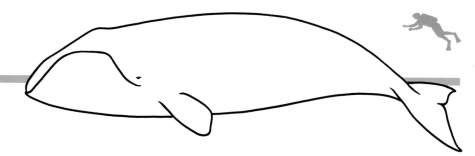

small and uncertainty still exists with regard to most parameters. A particular drawback is that no reliable method has been found of determining the age of bowhead whales, so estimates of reproductive rate have to be made indirectly, and mortality rates are totally unknown.

Little is known of the social system of bowheads but, in common with their close relatives, the right whales, they are probably promiscuous breeders. Conceptions probably peak in March, calves being born at a length of about 4m after a gestation period estimated at 12-16 months. Until recently, it was thought that bowheads bear only a single calf, but two observations by hunters of a mother with two calves suggests that twins are a possibility. Calving occurs in midwinter at the southern edge of the bowhead's range, so young animals are able to take advantage of the dense swarms of crustacean zooplankton (krill) on the feeding grounds at six months of age. Lactation probably lasts about a year, by which time the calves have grown to a length of about 7m. Mature females are thought to give birth every 2-7 years, so they may undergo a long period of rest between ending lactation and becoming pregnant again. Sexual maturity is thought to be reached at about 11.5m in males and 13-14m in females.

**World population** A decade ago, this species was thought to be perhaps the most endangered large whale in the world, having been hunted to the point of extinction in many parts of its range. The previously strong Spitzbergen to eastern Greenland stock is indeed at a very low level, but bowheads are regularly seen in the Davis Strait and Hudson Bay area, and recent estimates, which increase as methods of counting are improved, put the Bering Sea to Beaufort Sea stock at around 8,000 animals. The total world population is probably in the region of 9,000-12,000 whales and there is increasing optimism that the species is not in immediate danger.

**Man's influence** Bowhead whales have suffered considerably at the hand of man for many centuries, mostly because they are relatively slow swimmers and yield good quantities of oil and baleen.

Current levels of catch are small, but tens of thousands were taken in the nineteenth century and populations were quickly destroyed because of the species' predictability and ease of capture. Bowheads are now protected everywhere except in Alaska, where an ice-based Eskimo hunt of less than 50 animals killed per year has continued for the whole of this century. Classed as aboriginal hunters, the Inuit Eskimos are exempt from the restrictions normally imposed under the US Marine Mammal Protection Act and Endangered Species Act. There is still concern about the number of whales 'struck and lost', but the quota set by the International Whaling Commission is now for whales struck, not killed. As hunting methods improve, the proportion of wounded whales that escape and subsequently die is reduced. None has ever been kept in captivity.

*Left: An adult bowhead whale resting at the surface. The harshness of this whale's Arctic environment is shown by the thin layer of ice forming on its back. These stately creatures migrate northwards at a steady pace during spring, following cracks in the ice.*

# RIGHT WHALES

*EUBALAENA* SPP.

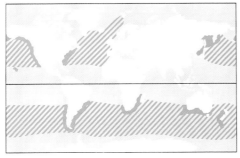

■ Known range     ⁄ Possible range

**Classification** The genus name *Eubalaena* literally translates into 'right whale'; *Eu* meaning 'true' or 'right', and *Balaena* meaning 'whale'. There is some debate as to whether there are one, two or three species of the genus *Eubalaena*. Two species are recognized by most biologists: the northern right whale, *Eubalaena glacialis* (*glacialis* meaning 'icy') and the southern right whale, *E. australis* (*australis* meaning 'southern'). It has been suggested by some that the name *E. glacialis* should be confined to the North Atlantic right whales and that North Pacific right whales should be considered a third species, *E. japonica*, but neither this, nor the view that they are all one species, *E. glacialis*, is generally accepted.

**Local names** The term 'right whale' originates from the early European whalers – they were simply the 'right' whales to catch, being slow-swimming whales that floated when dead and provided a good return in terms of both oil and whalebone (baleen). Other common names include the black right whale (both species) and the Biscayan right whale (the northern right whale only), which reflects European whaling operations in the Bay of Biscay from the eleventh century.

**Description** Right whales are large stocky whales, similar in shape to the bowhead, but generally slightly smaller. The head is large, comprising up to one-quarter of the animal's length. Like the bowhead, they have no dorsal fin or ventral grooves. The flippers of right whales are broad and spatulate.

Adults range in length from 13.5 to 17m, although larger animals have occasionally been recorded. Females are slightly longer than males of the same age (about 0.2m in mature animals), and right whales from the North Pacific are larger than those from other areas. As for all large whales, weighing whole animals is difficult. Estimated body weights for fully grown whales range from about 40 to 80 tonnes based on a small sample of

whales caught in the North Pacific and weighed in parts.

The head has a narrow, arched rostrum and a markedly bowed lower jaw. Its most noticeable feature is the presence of a series of horny growths called 'callosities'. The largest of these, on the rostrum, is called the 'bonnet', due to its resemblance to a lady's hat. Callosities are also found behind the blowholes, on the chin, above the eyes and on the lower lips. The pattern of callosities is different for each individual and this fact has enabled a considerable amount of information to be accumulated on the lifestyle of these animals.

The function of the callosities is unclear. One theory is that they are used in aggressive interactions. Another, more unlikely, theory is that they form a 'splash guard' to stop water getting into the blowholes.

The head is relatively 'hairy', up to 300 hairs being found on the tip of the lower jaw and about 100 on the upper. Hairs are also found on the callosities.

There is considerable variation in the colour of 'black' right whales, ranging from blue-black to light brown. Most animals have at least some white markings, especially on the underside; some albinos and near-albinos have been seen.

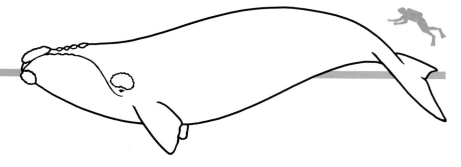

The baleen is long and narrow, the longest plates reaching almost 3m. There are 200-270 plates on each side of the jaw. Most plates are dark grey to blue-black, although some of the plates towards the front of the mouth can be much paler and even white. They may be lighter in younger animals. The fine bristles range in colour from grey to black.

While it is not possible to determine which ocean area any one animal comes from simply by examining its external appearance, a number of 'tendencies' have been noted, the most noticeable being that a far greater proportion of North Atlantic right whales have continuous callosities from the tip of the rostrum back to the blowholes. Differences in the proportions of animals showing various characters, such as lip callosities and dorsal blazes, also occur among areas of the Southern Hemisphere.

**Recognition at sea** The only species with which right whales might be confused is the bowhead, which is similar in outline and which shares the same V-shaped blow. Only right whales have callosities, however. In addition, although the ranges of the bowhead and right whales overlap in space in the North Pacific, they do not usually overlap in time; by the time the right whale has reached its most northerly latitudes, the bowhead has migrated even further north.

*Left: A southern right whale breaching. The sound of it hitting the water can be heard for many kilometres above and below water.*

*Below: An underwater shot of a right whale. Each individual whale can be recognized by its unique pattern of callosities on the head.*

**Habitat** While right whales have occasionally been seen in polar waters, in general their summer distribution is confined to temperate and subpolar waters. Although all the identified calving grounds have been near to the coast, often in shallow bays, there is insufficient information for some areas, such as the North Pacific, to state that right whales only calve in such waters.

**Distribution and migration** Right whales were once abundant in all oceans. Much of the information on their distribution comes from the records of the extensive pre-twentieth century whaling for this species. While it is generally accepted that right whales follow the usual baleen whale pattern of migration – between high-latitude feeding grounds and lower latitude breeding grounds – there is little direct evidence to confirm or deny this.

The southern right whale is circumpolar between about 20°S and 55°S. Information on stock identity is sparse, but seasonal winter concentrations are found off western and southeastern Australia, New Zealand, southwestern and southeastern South America and South Africa. Sightings have also been made around islands in temperate and subantarctic waters. There is relatively little information on the summer feeding grounds, as the early whaling vessels rarely ventured south of 50°S due to the bad weather conditions in these latitudes. Limited recent

data suggests that in summer most right whales are found north of 55°S, although some have been seen as far south as 63°S.

In the North Pacific, right whales have been caught on the eastern side as far south as central Baja California and as far north as the Gulf of Alaska and the Bering Sea. It is thought that the animals that spend the summer in the north then migrate south, but there are very few winter records. On the western side, catches have been taken off both the western and eastern coasts of Japan. These may have consisted of separate populations, both perhaps calving near the Ryukyu Islands, with the former migrating north into the Okhotsk Sea and the latter near the Kuril Islands and the Bering Sea (and possibly the Gulf of Alaska). However, no western North Pacific calving grounds have been found, either historically or in recent surveys.

In the North Atlantic, right whales have been taken on the western side as far south as the Gulf of Mexico and as far north as the coasts of Newfoundland and Labrador. Recent data shows concentrations in the Bay of Fundy and southern Nova Scotia. Spring concentrations are seen off Cape Cod, probably of animals moving north from breeding grounds near Florida, where concentrations of calves have been seen. On the eastern side of the North Atlantic, historical records show that catches were taken as far south as the Azores and northwestern Africa and as far north as southeastern Greenland, Spitsbergen and northern Norway. Calving grounds were probably near Cintra Bay in northwest Africa and the Bay of Biscay, where European whaling began. There have been very few recent sightings of right whales on this side of the North Atlantic and no known concentrations exist. Additionally, we cannot be sure if the few modern sightings were of eastern animals or of vagrants from the western North Atlantic.

**Food and feeding** Although surface feeding has been observed, right whales usually feed below the surface, sometimes at or near the seabed, on concentrations of food organisms. They are specialized feeders, preferentially taking small planktonic animals like copepods and, to a lesser extent, euphausiids, as one might expect from the fine bristles of their baleen. Some cooperative feeding has

*Right: A mother/calf pair in shallow water. Right whales migrate from colder feeding grounds to calve in warm, protected waters where their youngsters stand a better chance of survival. The calves will wean when the whales return to the feeding grounds 4-8 months later. The strange mouthline and callosities are typical of the genus. The callosities are fibrous growths of keratin on the head. They provide an ideal anchorage for the many small crustaceans, so-called 'whale lice' that infest right whales.*

been observed; in one instance, two whales were seen to maintain constant positions – one about 5m behind and to one side of the other – for six hours over a two-day period.

**Behaviour** Despite their bulky shape and slow swimming speed (maximum 9-11kph), right whales are surprisingly active, breaching, tail lobbing and flipper slapping being relatively common. Another feature, particularly observed in southern right whales, is 'head standing', where the animal hangs vertically in the water with its flukes in the air. This was once thought to be related to bottom feeding, but has since been observed in waters too deep for this to be the case.

When swimming slowly, right whales blow in a regular way, once every 1-2 minutes. As swim speed increases, dives become more irregular, lasting 0.5-5 minutes. Dives rarely exceed 15 minutes. Underwater recordings reveal that right whales make a number of sounds, the most common being a high- energy, low-frequency 'burping' sound lasting about 1.5 seconds. They also produce a simple and a frequency-modulated 'moan'.

**Life history** In both real and relative terms, right whales have the largest testes and penises of any large whale. The maximum paired testes weight is almost 14 times that for the blue whale, while the penis comprises 14.3 percent of its body length compared to 9.4 percent for the blue whale. Evolutionary theory predicts that males will compete to father the maximum number of offspring; the

size of the reproductive organs implies that in the right whale the competition will mainly be the sperm of one male competing with that of another male within a previously mated female rather than by males competing to prevent each other from mating. Behavioural observations of several males copulating with single females and relatively few observations of male-male aggression support this theoretical view. Long-term social bonding appears to be restricted to mothers and calves, which often congregate together in bays and shallow waters.

For the Southern Hemisphere, reported calving periods are late July to mid-November, with peaks in August and September. The little information for the Northern Hemisphere suggests calving between December and April. Length at birth is about 4.5-6m. The gestation period is unknown, but by analogy with other baleen whales is probably about 12 months. Information from known individuals reveals a mean calving interval of three years. Data from Argentina shows that the age at which females reach maturity ranges from 7 to 15 years, at lengths of 12.5-13.5m. Estimated mean lengths for males and females reaching sexual maturity in the North Pacific are 14-15m and 13-15m, respectively. Weaning most probably occurs when the calves reach the feeding grounds, about 4-8 months after birth.

**World population** Because almost all of the catches were taken before the twentieth century, little biological information was obtained from them. Most current

information, including population estimates, comes from a small scientific catch off Japan in the 1960s and the increasingly extensive long-term studies of individually identified living whales.

Although found in local concentrations, nowhere can right whales be considered abundant. Present stocks can be divided into three groups: 1 Those with populations of at least 400-600 (South Africa, Argentina); 2 Those with populations of 100-300 (northwestern Atlantic and Pacific, southwestern Australia, southeastern Australia/New Zealand); 3 Those thought near to extinction (northeastern Atlantic and Pacific).

Fortunately, three populations – South Africa, Argentina, and southwestern Australia – are showing signs of increasing at the rate of some 7 percent per year. However, even though direct catching is not permitted, it is most important that protection for areas of critical habitat is maintained or introduced, and that other sources of mortality, such as incidental deaths in fishing gear or collisions with ships and their propellers, are reduced to a minimum for these fragile stocks.

**Man's influence** The right whale was the first large whale to be hunted by man, beginning off the coast of Japan, possibly as early as the tenth century, and in the Bay of Biscay from the middle of the eleventh century. With the onset of pelagic whaling, they had been reduced to very low levels by the beginning of this century. Over 100,000 were killed in the nineteenth century alone. They have been completely protected since 1935.

# PYGMY RIGHT WHALE

*CAPEREA MARGINATA*

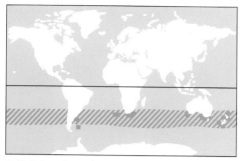

■ Sightings/strandings  ⁄⁄ Possible range

**Classification** The pygmy right whale was described and assigned to a new genus of the family Balaenidae in 1846 by John Edward Gray, Keeper of the Zoology Department of the British Museum. Recently, taxonomists have proposed that the differences between this species and the larger right whales and bowhead are sufficient to warrant it being placed in its own family – Neobalaenidae. The scientific name *Caperea marginata* (*Caperea* means to wrinkle, *marginata* means 'to enclose within a border') refers to two of its physical features: the wrinkled exterior of the ear bone and the dark marginal band on the baleen.

**Local names** The common name 'pygmy right whale' derives from its small size compared to *Eubalaena* and *Balaena*, and from the strongly arched jaw also found in the other species.

**Description** The pygmy right whale is far more streamlined than other balaenids; in this respect, as in other characteristics (such as the presence of a dorsal fin and the narrow rounded flippers), it more closely resembles the rorquals.

Most of the information on this unexploited species comes from fewer than 100 stranded specimens and a small number of sightings of live animals. The largest female recorded was 6.45m and the largest male 6.09m, suggesting that, as in the other mysticetes, there is sexual dimorphism in length. Only two animals have been weighed, in each case in pieces. A female of 6.21m was estimated to weigh about 3.5 tonnes and a male of 5.47m was estimated at 3.1 tonnes.

Like the other right whales, this species has a strongly bowed lower jaw and a narrow arched rostrum. This arching increases with age. However, the head does not constitute as large a proportion of the body as in the larger balaenids. No callosities are present.

The body is grey or black dorsally, lightening to a white or light grey belly. One albino animal has been recorded from South Africa. The flippers are dark, as is the dorsal surface of the broad flukes, which are grey on the underside.It has been suggested that younger animals are paler but, as almost all the information on coloration comes from stranded animals, post-mortem darkening may be a confounding factor.

The baleen plates, some 210-230 on each side of the jaw, are yellowish white, with a brown margin on the external edge. They are narrow with fine bristles, and the longest measures up to 70cm. These plates are said to be stronger than in any other species.

**Recognition at sea** The arched jaw (and possibly the white baleen gum) of the pygmy right whale is its major characteristic feature, so unless the head is clearly visible, it is almost impossible to tell this species from the minke whale.

**Habitat** Pygmy right whales appear to be confined to waters within 5-20°C (between about 30°S and 52°S) in all oceans of the Southern Hemisphere.

**Distribution and migration** The few strandings – and even fewer sightings at sea – make it difficult to draw many conclusions about the migrations of this species. Most strandings have occurred in the spring and summer on the southern Australian, Tasmanian and South African coasts. However, while this suggests that pygmy right whales move into inshore waters in the spring, it may merely reflect the greater likelihood of detecting a stranding during the spring and summer months.

**Food and feeding** The little information available shows that pygmy right whales feed on copepods, as one might expect from the fine bristles of the baleen.

**Behaviour** There have been few observations of living animals. One reason for this seems to be their relatively 'unspectacular' behaviour; they dive for short periods (0.6-4 minutes), and do not spend long periods at the surface. The blow is often weak and the dorsal fin is often not exposed. Despite their more rorqual-like shape, they appear to be slow swimmers, not exceeding 9kph. These whales are usually seen swimming alone or in pairs, with five to eight animals within an area of 5-8km².

**Life history** Once again, there is relatively little information for this species. By analogy with other species, and from the scant data available, it appears that length at birth is about 2m and length at weaning, when the animal is five to six months old, is about 3.5m. Calving probably occurs in the autumn-winter period, although there is some evidence of an extended breeding period.

**Man's influence** This species has not been exploited. Apart from natural causes, the only man-induced mortality is the occasional entanglement of individuals in fishing gear off South Africa.

*Below: The pygmy right whale is rarely seen, and thus very few photographs of live animals exist.*

*Most of our little knowledge of this species has come from strandings in South Africa and Australia.*

# GRAY WHALE
## ESCHRICHTIIDAE

A new taxonomic family was proposed by Ellerman and Morrison-Scott in 1951 for one existing large baleen whale species, the gray whale (*Eschrichtius robustus*). Despite sharing some characteristics with both the larger right whales (the family Balaenidae) and the rorquals (the family Balaenopteridae), this species is sufficiently different from all others that it could not reasonably be allocated to any existing family, and the new family name has become widely accepted.

The evolutionary origins of the gray whale are unknown, since fossils and sub-fossils (i.e. remains that have become calcified but not mineralized into true fossils) exist only for the last 100,000 years or so, and the oldest known gray whale ancestors were apparently no different from the modern form. This species is unique among surviving baleen whales in that it is primarily a benthic feeder, filtering small organisms from the mud of shallow seas. Unusually for the mysticetes, or baleen whales, it has a gestation period of more than a year, but like most others it is strongly migratory. There is clear evidence that gray whales occurred in the North Atlantic Ocean until the seventeenth or eighteenth centuries, but they were probably exterminated by whalers and today are found only in the North Pacific Ocean.

*Gray whales feeding in a characteristic plume of mud. This is the only cetacean to feed mainly on organisms living in the seabed.*

# GRAY WHALE

## *ESCHRICHTIUS ROBUSTUS*

■ Known range

**Classification** The earliest agreed description of this species was derived, ironically, not from a living whale in the Pacific but from a sub-fossil excavated in Sweden. Wilhelm Lilljeborg named his sub-fossil *Balaenoptera robusta* in 1861, but in the same decade John Gray of the British Museum realized the great differences between this species and the rorquals, and placed it in a new genus, *Eschrichtius*, in memory of the Danish zoologist Daniel Eschricht.

**Local names** The name gray whale reflects the animal's body colour. The North American spelling has become internationally accepted.

**Description** This is a large whale, reaching an average body length at physical maturity of 13m in males and 14.1m in females. The largest measured animal was a female of 15m. Adult body weight in the gray whale is probably in the range 14-35 tonnes.

The gray whale is more stocky than most of the rorquals, but more slender than the large right whales. It has a relatively small, narrow triangular head, pointed paddlelike flippers and, instead of a true dorsal fin, a series of bumps or crenulations along the dorsal ridge of the rearmost third of the body. The degree of arching of the upper jaw is intermediate between the rorquals and right whales. There are 2-4 short (1.5m) throat grooves and 140-180 coarse, yellowish white baleen plates hanging from each side of the palate. The tail flukes are notched and up to 3m from tip to tip.

Body colour is mottled grey, and the skin is variably encrusted with patches of barnacles and whale lice, which may be anything between yellowish white and orange. Sick animals can be almost completely covered in these parasites.

**Recognition at sea** The blow is vertical, loud, 3-4.5m high, and has been described as 'heart-shaped' when viewed from in front or behind. The head shape,

coloration, and lack of a true dorsal fin should allow discrimination between this species and other large whales.

**Habitat** This is essentially a coastal species, usually encountered over the continental shelf and often within the surf region in water less than 10m deep. At some points on the migratory pathway, nearly all animals pass within 2km of the shoreline, but occasionally animals are seen in deep water far from land. Gray whales are clearly tolerant of the great changes in surface temperature encountered during their annual migration from polar to subtropical waters.

**Distribution and migration** Although it occurred in the North Atlantic perhaps as late as the seventeenth or eighteenth centuries, the gray whale is now restricted to the North Pacific Ocean. Two stocks or populations are recognized, one along the western side from Korea in the south to the Okhotsk Sea in the north, and the other, eastern, stock from Mexico in the south to the Bering, Chukchi and Beaufort Seas in the north.

The annual migration of the gray whale is one of the best defined and longest of all whale species. Until very recently, the 12-20,000km round trip migration of the eastern Pacific, or Californian, stock was thought to be the longest of any mammal, but there is now evidence that humpback whales in the southeastern Pacific may travel even further. Most of the migration from Alaska or Siberia to Mexico takes place close to land, the main movement southward occurring in autumn and early winter and the return from spring to early summer. Not all animals journey all

*Above: A gray whale spy hops to allow it to see above the water in one of the species' calving lagoons off western Mexico.*

*Below: A mother and calf gray whale. Calves remain highly bonded to their mothers during the long northward migration to Alaska.*

the way; increasing numbers are to be found 'out of season' along the coasts of British Columbia, Washington, Oregon and California.

**Food and feeding** Uniquely among all cetaceans, the gray whale is primarily a benthic feeder, consuming a great variety of tiny bottom-dwelling organisms, which it sieves with its baleen from the top 2cm layer of mud or sand. It feeds in shallow, productive waters, usually 50m or less, but up to 120m deep.

Below: Gray whales in the breeding areas can become confiding, here toward lucky tourists.

Observations suggest that food-laden sediment may be pumped into the mouth and the filtered sediment pumped out again through the baleen, with the tongue acting rather like a piston; that much of the feeding takes place with the animal on its side, usually the right; and that whales may make two passes along a track – the first to stir up the mud and organisms with the snout, the second to filter the resultant cloud.

The most common prey on the northern feeding grounds are small shrimplike gammaridean ampiphods of many species, but they also take polychaete worms and molluscs, as well as foraging in shoals of small fish or squid when the opportunity arises. Most feeding takes place in the northern half of the range, especially in the Bering and Chukchi seas, but whales will forage on the migration route and even in the calving lagoons of Baja California. Adults probably consume 1-1.25 tonnes of food per day during the peak feeding period. This is 3-4 times the capacity of the stomach.

**Behaviour** Group size is typically small, one to three animals being usual, though up to 16 may travel together in close association. In and near the calving lagoons, mother/calf pairs and groups of two or three socially active animals are most common. On the feeding grounds, good foraging conditions may bring hundreds of animals together in an area of a few square kilometres, but these aggregations are loose and coincidental. Surfacing patterns on migration are typically of five or six blows followed by a shallow dive of 3-5 minutes. The tail flukes are usually raised before a dive.

Vocalizations are of several types, in the frequency range 15Hz-20kHz, but usually 15Hz-2kHz. Moans, whistles, chirps, rasps, growls, bongs, rumbles and clicks have all been described. Non-vocal sounds, such as underwater exhalation and breaching, may also play an important part in communication.

**Life history** Conception occurs in a three-week period in late November and early December as the whales migrate south. Two, or sometimes three, whales engage in arching out of the water, rolling and coordinated swimming. Copulation lasts 30-60 seconds, with the pair often swimming on their sides at the surface.

Gray whales are born at about 4.6m in length and with a body weight of around 500kg. Sexual maturity is reached at a mean age of 8 years (range 5-11 years) and a length of 11.1m (males) and 11.7m (females). Physical maturity, the point at which growth stops, is reached at an age of about 40 years.

The reproductive cycle is closely tied to the migratory cycle, which it drives. In the Californian stock, almost all calves are born during a brief period of five to six weeks from late December onwards in the shallow, warm and protected waters of the calving lagoons of Baja California at the southern end of the migration route. Gestation lasts about 13.5 months. Gray whales very rarely come into oestrus either soon after giving birth or when finishing lactation. With few exceptions, females complete lactation (about seven months) then 'rest' for about three and a half months, before conceiving again exactly two years after their previous pregnancy began.

**World population** Due to their coastal habit and the long series of surveys carried out on many parts of their migratory route, the population size of gray whales is among the best known for any cetacean. The western stock was thought to be at or near extinction, but recent observations suggest that it still exists at the level of high tens or low hundreds of animals. Even this may be insufficient to avoid extinction, but recovery is at least possible with complete protection. Some of these animals may be vagrants from the eastern Pacific stock, which has recovered well from heavy whaling at the rate of 2.5 percent per year and now probably numbers some 15-22,000 animals.

**Man's influence** The western stock was probably of not more than a few thousand whales when commercial exploitation began in the seventeenth century. Modern shorebased whaling in Korea took about 1500 animals from 1910 to 1933, by which time the stock was almost wiped out.

American whaling on the eastern stock of gray whales began in 1846, when the calving lagoons were discovered; thereafter, the slaughter spread to the feeding grounds. About 11,000 gray whales were killed by 1874 off California and Mexico alone. Whaling diminished as the stock was reduced, but floating factories took about 1,000 animals between 1914 and 1946, when the species gained international protection from commercial exploitation. Between then and 1989, about 5,500 gray whales were taken in aboriginal catches or by scientific permit. The catch for Siberian nationals, averaging about 170-180 annually, and that of Alaskan Inuit, of a few every year, continues.

One calf was brought into captivity in 1971 and maintained in California for a year, before being released.

# RORQUAL WHALES
## BALAENOPTERIDAE

The name 'rorqual' is derived from Norse, and refers indirectly to the many characteristic pleats, or grooves, on the ventral surface of these whales, stretching from the underside of the lower jaw to the abdomen. The grooves allow the ventral tissue to expand dramatically during the feeding process, when these whales engulf a huge quantity of food-laden water and subsequently force the water out through the baleen. All six species in the family Balaenopteridae, but no other cetaceans, share this characteristic. Additionally, they all have a dorsal fin, a broad, gently curved rostrum and short baleen plates.

The balaenopterids are all large cetaceans; even the smallest species, the minke whale (*Balaenoptera acutorostrata*) can reach a body length in excess of 10m and a weight of 13 tonnes. The largest is the blue whale (*B. musculus*), the most massive creature ever to have lived.

The family was named by John Gray in 1864 and comprises two genera. One, *Balaenoptera*, consists of five species with a great similarity in body shape: blue, fin (*B. physalus*), sei (*B. borealis*), Bryde's (*B. edeni*) and minke whale. The other genus, *Megaptera*, consists of only one species, the humpback whale (*M. novaeangliae*). The humpback is also one of the 'great'

whales, but differs from the others in the family by having a stockier build and huge pectoral fins, or flippers, that can reach 33 percent of body length.

All balaenopterids occur in all oceans, and only the distribution of Bryde's whale is severely restricted by water temperature, occurring only in tropical and subtropical regions. All six species are predominantly oceanic in habit, but they occur seasonally in coastal areas where the water depth is sufficient. In addition, some stocks of Bryde's whale (the only non-migratory species) may be resident in inshore waters, and humpback whales seek out shallow waters for calving.

*Minke whales among icebergs. Smallest of the family, this species ventures right up to the ice edge in polar seas.*

# BLUE WHALE

## *BALAENOPTERA MUSCULUS*

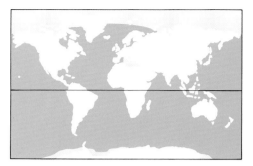

■ Known range

**Classification** The blue whale was classified by Linnaeus in 1758, using the name *Balaenoptera musculus*. A subspecies, the pygmy blue whale, *B. m. brevicauda* was recognized in 1963.

**Local names** The blue whale is also known as sulphurbottom, a descriptive name derived from the yellow-brown appearance of diatoms flourishing on the skin after the whales have been in polar waters for a while.

**Description** The blue whale is streamlined and slender in shape, with a small and variably shaped dorsal fin located about three-quarters of the way along the back. The tail flukes are large and notched. The flippers are slender and pointed, and about 14 percent of body size in length. The head is relatively broad compared with other rorquals, and the rostrum is almost flat, with only a central ridge running forward from the blowhole. The blowhole is made up of paired nostrils surrounded in front and at the sides by prominent fleshy mounds resembling a small cap, a feature common to, but not so pronounced in, other rorquals. The baleen plates, numbering between 270 and 395 on each side of the upper jaw, are broad in shape relative to their length (the longest reach 1m), and uniformly black with coarse bristles, a feature that makes their specific identification relatively easy. The throat bears 55-88 ventral grooves extending back to the umbilicus.

The coloration is darkish blue-grey, with a mottled and blotched appearance, often masked by a diatomaceous bloom that covers the skin, producing a yellowy colour in polar waters. The underside of the flippers is often pale.

The blue whale has the distinction of being the largest living animal on earth. In common with other rorquals, there is slight sexual dimorphism in the species, the female being about 5-6 percent longer than the male. Records show that a female blue whale can reach about 31m

in length and weigh more than 200 tonnes at the end of the feeding season, but the average adult length is 25m in males and 26.2m in females, with body weights of 100-120 tonnes. These sizes are primarily based on catches taken in the southern oceans; in line with the trend in rorquals, the Northern Hemisphere counterpart is slightly smaller.

As its name implies, the pygmy blue whale is smaller than the blue whale, with adult females reaching 21.6-21.9m in length, although their maximum size may exceed 24m. However, there are other size distinctions between the blue and the pygmy blue whale that only become apparent on close inspection of the carcass. The baleen plates are significantly shorter in the pygmy blue, and the head and trunk appear relatively larger in proportion to the rest of the body, with a foreshortening of the tail region. There are more caudal vertebrae in the pygmy blue, however.

**Recognition at sea** The blow rises vertically to about 9m. Blowing may occur once every one to two minutes when at rest, but increases to six blows per minute after prolonged chasing. Dives usually last about 3-10 minutes, but may last 20 minutes or more. Swimming speed while feeding may be 2-6.5kph, but reaches 5-14kph during migration, with bursts of up to 30kph when alarmed. The blue whale occasionally flukes up on diving, i.e. raises the tail flukes out of the water. Because of its position so far back, the

dorsal fin is often not immediately obvious when the whale surfaces and may not be seen until the whale dives.

Any rorqual exceeding 24m long is almost certain to be a blue whale. Discrimination between blue and pygmy blue whales may be a problem at sea in areas where the two coexist. In such areas, the blue and pygmy blue whales tend not to mingle, even though they may be feeding on the same resource.

**Habitat** The species is pelagic and thus rarely seen near the coast, except in polar regions, when they frequently follow the retreating ice-edge as summer progresses. This habit can result in the partial stranding or isolation of individuals in small sea areas entrapped by ice as the weather changes, as is frequently recorded in the Gulf of St. Lawrence in Canada. The blue whale appears very tolerant of a great temperature range.

**Distribution and migration** Blue whales are found throughout every ocean of the world, from the equator to the polar regions in both hemispheres. Marking studies have demonstrated that the whales regularly move between low and high latitudes, covering thousands of kilometres during the year. There appears to be an annual cycle of migration to polar waters in summer for feeding, with a return to low latitudes in winter for breeding. This pattern is well documented for the Southern Hemisphere, but is less clear for the North

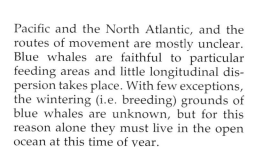

Pacific and the North Atlantic, and the routes of movement are mostly unclear. Blue whales are faithful to particular feeding areas and little longitudinal dispersion takes place. With few exceptions, the wintering (i.e. breeding) grounds of blue whales are unknown, but for this reason alone they must live in the open ocean at this time of year.

The pygmy blue whale occupies some discrete areas, mainly in the Southern Hemisphere but also probably in the northern Indian Ocean. A relatively large population is possibly resident in the subantarctic. Other groupings of the subspecies have been found off Chile and the Kerguelen Islands, but these groups do not appear to intermingle.

**Food and feeding** The blue whale appears to be more specific in its prey selection than other rorquals. Despite the coarser baleen fringe, the blue specializes in consuming swarming euphausiids in the Antarctic. The blue whale is almost certainly in direct competition with other rorquals, such as the fin, minke and sei whale, for this seasonally available food resource. The early spring migration of the blue – and its proximity to the ice-edge in order to gather the prey as soon as it is exposed by the retreating ice – underlies the importance of this food source for the species. Even when shoaling fish are available, the preferred food appears to be euphausiids in all areas in both hemispheres. Very occasionally, copepods may be taken and, off Baja California, dense swarms of a small decapod crustacean may be taken seasonally. The emphasis is thus on swarming, small planktonic crustaceans. The main stomach of an adult blue whale may hold up to a tonne of euphausiids.

**Behaviour** The blue whale is not gregarious, and is usually found as a solitary animal or in pairs, such as mother and calf associations. However, on the feeding grounds the whales may occur in some concentration, although individuals appear to be dissociated. The whales probably do not dive deeply, perhaps to a maximum of 200m, restricting their activities to the parts of the water column occupied by their prey.

There appears to be some segregation in migration, with adults leading the juveniles, but the segregation is rather loose. Pregnant females are generally the first to migrate in spring towards the food-rich polar waters, and may be among the last to leave as summer ends.

Vocalizations are mostly low-frequency moans, pulses, buzzes and rasps, but also include ultrasonic clicks that may have an echolocation function. Apart from this, breaching and tail slapping may be audible means of communication between individuals.

*Far left: Like all other rorquals, blue whales change their profile when feeding by distending the blubber on the underside of the mouth, throat and chest. In this rare photograph, a diver approaches a blue whale feeding off southern California.*

*Below: Only from the air can the immense, yet slim, streamlined shape of a blue whale be fully appreciated.*

Left: Mottled blue-grey coloration and a small, usually stubby, dorsal fin serve to distinguish blue whales from related species at sea.

Below: The blowholes of the blue whale are raised well above the level of the rostrum.

**Life history** At reproductive maturity, males are about 22.6m and females about 24m long, and body weight is approximately 70 percent of ultimate body size. The pygmy blue whale is rather smaller at reproductive maturity, about 19m, but estimates are not precise. The age at reproductive maturity for both blue and pygmy blue is probably five to six years. (This age determination has been made by a combination of baleen plate growth patterns and ear plugs, but the exact incremental rates of growth of both these tissues has not been verified for blue whales.) Maximum longevity may approach 80 years or more, but few are likely to reach this age, and physical maturity, when growth stops, is probably reached at about 25-30 years.

The mating system is not known, but temporary pairings are probable. The gestation period is about 11 months. The single blue whale calf is about 7m long and weighs about 2.5 tonnes at birth, which occurs in warmer temperate and subtropical waters in midwinter. (Pygmy blue whales are smaller at birth and similar to that of the fin whale at about 6.3m). The calf is suckled for six to seven months until it is weaned at about 12.8m long. Weaning coincides with migration into the colder more productive polar waters in spring/summer. The reproductive interval is normally two years, and is linked with the highly seasonal breeding and feeding activities. There is some indication that, unlike the blue whale, the pygmy subspecies may have two breeding seasons annually, the main one in winter and a smaller one in summer.

An estimated value of natural mortality of 5 percent has been computed for the Southern Hemisphere population. The main causes of mortality, other than illness and disease and previous exploitation by man, are attacks by sharks and killer whales on young, wounded or diseased animals.

**World population** Population sizes of blue whales (including about 10,000 pygmy blue whales) in the 1920s have been estimated at 220,000 in the Southern Hemisphere and 8,000 in the Northern Hemisphere. Mortality rates for blue whales were devastatingly high during the peak exploitation phase in the 1930s. Today, the population estimate for the Southern Hemisphere, at 10,000-12,000, may be only 5 percent of the original. Of these, perhaps more than 6,000 individuals are pygmy blues. In the Northern Hemisphere, the most recent estimate totals 3,000. However, there is evidence from sightings surveys that blue whale abundance in certain areas, notably the eastern North Atlantic, is increasing, offering some hope for possible recovery.

**Man's influence** Understandably, the unrelenting destruction of blue whale populations in this century has come to symbolize man's exploitation of whales worldwide. Once fast catcher boats and explosive harpoons became available in the late nineteenth century, all rorquals were catchable and, as the largest and therefore most profitable, blue whales were the primary target in all areas.

Catches were mostly made on the summer feeding grounds – in the cooler waters of the North Atlantic, North Pacific and, especially, the Antarctic Ocean. Nearly 30,000 were taken in the

1930/31 season alone. During the 1930s, voluntary quotas on rorqual catching in the Antarctic were introduced by whaling nations. They were set in 'blue whale units', whereby a blue whale was considered equal to two fin whales, two and a half humpbacks or six sei whales. These quotas did nothing to protect the depleted blue whale, though, and were later abandoned.

By the time restrictions on whaling became possible with the signing of the International Whaling Convention in 1946, the damage had already been done. Even then, the mounting evidence of blue whale overhunting was ignored for commercial reasons for another two decades, by which time so few remained that their exploitation ceased to be economic. By 1966, when this species finally received global protection only a century after its exploitation began, well over a third of a million blue whales had been killed and many stocks left so shattered that they may never recover.

# FIN WHALE

*BALAENOPTERA PHYSALUS*

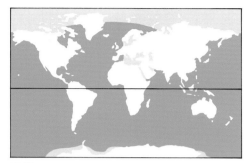

■ Known range

**Classification** The fin whale was classified as *Balaenoptera physalus* by Linnaeus in 1758. No subspecies are recognized.

**Local names** The English name derives from European names for this species, all of which use a variation of the term 'fin': finhval (Norway), finnhvaler (Iceland), Finnhval (Germany), finval (USSR) and vinvisch (Netherlands). Other local names included finn, finback, common rorqual and razorback, the last derived from the sharply ridged tail stock displayed when the whale dives.

**Description** The streamlined fin whale is second in size only to the blue whale and closely related to it. The falcate dorsal fin set about two-thirds back along the body is not as erect as in the sei and minke

whale, often sloping backwards. The broad triangular tail flukes have a median notch. The head is pointed, but not acutely so, with a flat rostrum divided by a ridge running from the blowhole forward almost to the rostral tip. As in other rorquals, the paired nostrils are made prominent by a raised crest at the leading edge. Between 55 and 100 ventral grooves run up to, and often beyond, the umbilicus. There are 260-475 baleen plates each side of the rostrum, with a finer bristle fringe than the blue whale. The maximum length of the baleen plates is about 90cm.

The body colour is mainly dark grey to brownish black, but the throat, belly and undersides of the flippers and tail flukes are all white. The head has asymmetrical pigmentation, with the white coloration extending over the right lower jaw and inside the mouth cavity. The baleen also bears this asymmetrical pigmentation, the first third of the plates on the right side being white to cream in colour. The remaining plates are dark grey with a few vertical yellow stripes. The bristles vary from cream to beige. The pale pigmentation sometimes extends to the right upper jaw. The left lower and upper jaws are quite dark by contrast. In some fin whales there is a pale chevron pattern behind the head, but this cannot be used

as a consistent diagnostic feature.

Average adult body sizes are about 21m in males and 22.3m in females in the Southern Hemisphere, females being larger than males of the same age. In the Northern Hemisphere, the adult size is slightly smaller, at 19m for males and 20.5m for females. The largest on record was a 26m female. Adult fin whales may weigh between 45 and 75 tonnes, depending on the season and their body condition.

**Recognition at sea** Its large size may help distinguish this rorqual from the sei, Bryde's and minke whales, and the dorsal fin is not as erect as that of these species. The chief distinguishing feature between the blue and fin whales at sea is the usual rapid appearance of the dorsal fin after the blow in fin whales. In blue whales, the dorsal fin is positioned so far back that it is often only visible just before the whale submerges. The sei whale surfaces at a shallow angle so that the head and dorsal fin usually appear simultaneously. The angle of surfacing is more oblique in fin whales and only the head emerges initially. At close quarters,

*Below: A fin whale almost motionless at the surface. This unusual pose reveals the whale's great length and slim form.*

the body colour (blue whales really *are* blue) and the asymmetrical head coloration of the fin whale may be visible. The blow of the fin whale is like a slim inverse cone and may be 6m in height.

Identification of stranded individuals is straightforward, because of the characteristic asymmetrical head and baleen coloration, even in young animals.

**Habitat** The fin whale is essentially an open-ocean dweller but may be seen in coastal waters in some areas. The fin whale's migrations are geared to optimize breeding and feeding conditions, so the ideal habitat changes throughout the year. Warm waters in temperate and subtropical regions are ideal for the birth of young, but the cold yet food-rich waters of high latitudes are ideal for accumulating the energy stores that will supply much of the whales' energy demands throughout the winter months.

**Distribution and migration** The fin whale is found in every ocean of the world. It ranges from the tropics to the polar regions, but the species is pelagic and rarely seen in inshore coastal waters. Being a migratory species with well-defined seasonal movements between low latitudes in winter and high latitudes in summer, the animals travel thousands of kilometres each year. The migratory movements are essentially north-south, with little longitudinal dispersion. Fin whales show some segregation by age and maturity; juveniles tend to follow the pregnant females and other adults in migration, and also tend to occupy sea areas in slightly lower latitudes than the adults. While the fin whale will readily enter polar waters, the species is not noted for its presence close to ice, unlike blue and minke whales.

**Food and feeding** The fin whale specializes in 'gulping' swarming euphausiids. In the Antarctic, the main prey is *Euphausia superba*, whereas in the North Atlantic it is *Meganyctiphanes norvegica*. Off northern Norway, Iceland and in other areas, there is some consumption of fish, including capelin (*Mallotus villosus*) and herring (*Clupea harengus*). Copepods and even squid have reportedly been taken as food. The fin whale frequently turns on its side to engulf swarming or shoaling fish and the asymmetrical pigmentation of the head may be important in this feeding manoeuvre.

Feeding is a seasonal activity. In summer it becomes vital, in order to build up energy reserves for other times when suitable prey items are not available or in short supply. During winter, daily food intake may amount to only a tenth of the summer intake. Energy reserves are stored as fat in the tail muscles, as visceral fat and as increases in blubber thickness.

**Behaviour** Fin whales are more gregarious than other rorquals, often occurring in groups of 6-10 animals, although individuals and pairs are more common. On the feeding grounds, aggregations of 100 or more may be observed. It is not known if these groups are families or just individuals travelling together with a common purpose.

The fin whale dives to a maximum of about 300m and may submerge for 10-15 minutes. The blow rate may average one to two per minute under normal circumstances, but increases to six to eight per minute when chased. Feeding fin whales are known to ignore shipping and continue with the business in hand.

Fin whales may breach clear of the water and land noisily on their sides. Whether or not this is a form of advertisement or communication to other whales is not certain. Fin whales often fluke up when diving. Vocalizations include low-frequency moans and pulses in the range 20-80Hz and grunts of 40-200Hz. High-frequency clicks of 16-28kHz have also been recorded and may be used for echolocation.

**Life history** The fin whale has a two-year reproductive cycle, with a gestation period of about 11 months resulting in a single calf, born in midwinter, measuring 6.4m long and weighing 1.75 tonnes. The calf is weaned on the summer feeding grounds at about six to seven months when it is 11.5m and about 13.25 tonnes.

The ear plug (from the external ear canal) has been used very successfully for age determination in fin whales from all parts of the world, and the age-related parameters are quite well known. Fin whales may rarely live as long as 94 years, reaching full physical maturity at around 25-30 years. The whales mature reproductively at an age of 6-12 years, depending on the stock. This is equivalent to a length of 19m in males and 20m in females in the Southern Hemisphere. The Northern Hemisphere counterparts mature at a smaller size of 17.5-18m in males and 18.3-19m in females.

There has been a decrease in the average age at maturity for most Southern Hemisphere stocks. This has been interpreted as a response to greater food abundance, made possible by the depletion caused by exploitation of blue and humpback whales, which would normally be considered to be competitors for food resources. Similar variations in the percentage of females pregnant each year have been reported for several fin whale stocks. The main explanation appears to be connected with fluctuating

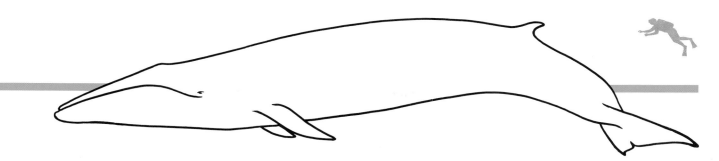

supplies of summer food resulting from both natural and man-made environmental disturbances.

Estimates of natural mortality have generally been accepted as 3.5 percent in males and 4.5 percent in females. Whaling in the Southern Hemisphere, of course, greatly increased the overall mortality, and continual over-exploitation resulted in the southern populations being virtually wiped out.

**World population** The fin whale is generally considered to be represented by three geographically separated populations: the Southern Hemisphere, North Atlantic and North Pacific. The populations do not mix across the equator. In the Southern Hemisphere, six stocks are defined for exploitation and management purposes according to geographical location, and in the Northern Hemisphere several stocks are defined, mainly according to their proximity, at certain times of year, to countries or coastal areas where whaling operations have been focused. These latter stocks are frequently quite small, numbering only a few thousands.

The current population estimate of 85,000-100,000 whales for the entire Southern Hemisphere amounts to less than one quarter of the original pre-exploitation level of 400,000-500,000. The Northern Hemisphere has fared only a little better. One source puts the Northern Hemisphere total at about 20,000 whales, (probably a conservative estimate), compared with an estimated pre-exploitation total of about 58,000. Today, we are still unable to say much about the true status of several of the fin whale stocks in the Northern Hemisphere.

**Man's influence** Fin whales have suffered greatly from exploitation in the 'modern' era of whaling; they are depleted everywhere and endangered in many regions. At their peak in the late 1950s and early 1960s, fin whale catches were in excess of 30,000 per year worldwide. By far the majority were taken in the Southern Hemisphere. The fin whales in the southern oceans were protected from further exploitation by regulations of the International Whaling Commission in 1976. The North Pacific fin whales similarly became protected. Despite the cessation of all commercial catches of the species in 1986, Iceland has continued to take up to 80 fin whales every year for research purposes under a scientific permit, until at least 1989. Although it is endangered, there are no indications that as a species the fin whale is close to extinction, but many decades or even centuries will pass before the southern ocean stocks recover to their former levels, if they ever do.

# SEI WHALE

*BALAENOPTERA BOREALIS*

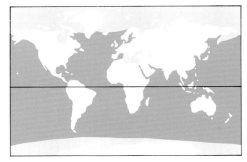

■ Known range

**Classification** The sei whale was classified by the French zoologist René Lesson in 1828 and, despite several earlier and later descriptions of this species, the name he gave it is currently accepted. The species name, *borealis*, refers to the north. There are no subspecies.

**Local names** The name 'sei' derives from the whales' habit of arriving off the north Norwegian coast with the seje (coalfish or saithe, *Pollachius virens*). Other common names include coalfish whale, pollack whale, Rudolphi's rorqual, sardine whale and Japan finner.

**Description** Although more robust than its relative the fin whale, the sei whale is typically rorqual in shape – slender with well-developed and pointed pectorals making up about 10 percent of the body size in length, a well-defined and slightly hooked dorsal fin placed about two-thirds of the way along the back (yet further forward than in other balaenopterids) and large, notched tail flukes. The

head and jaws are rather narrow and the rostrum slightly arched. The head occupies about a fifth to a quarter of the body length, depending on age. The ventral grooves are short and vary in number between 38 and 60, but average about 52. A few short sensory hairs may occur on the lower jaw and between 318 and 340 baleen plates hang down from the palate on each side of the upper jaw. The baleen has a whitish fringe of bristles, which are finer and more delicate in texture than those of other rorquals. The maximum length of the baleen plates is about 78cm.

The body is dark grey, with paler pigmentation on the ventral surface. Some mottling and pale blotches, sometimes very heavy and at least some caused by parasites and small sharks, may occur on the belly and flanks. The baleen colour is usually uniformly dark, rarely cream.

In the Southern Hemisphere, males grow to about 15m and females to 16m (maximum 18.3m). In the Northern Hemisphere, the adult size is about 10 percent smaller, with males reaching on average 13.6m and females 14.5m. Generally, females grow about 6.5 percent larger than the males. Body weight in adults may average 20-25 tonnes.

**Recognition at sea** As in other rorquals, there are two nostrils on the top of the head, but the blow appears as a moderately tall cloud, more or less vertically above the animal. The blowing rate is usually once every one to two minutes when at the surface and dives may last as long as 20 minutes. Swimming speeds

may reach 2-6.5kph when feeding and 5-14kph when migrating. When chased, sei whales can maintain a continuous speed of 20-25kph for more than an hour. The usual distinguishing feature between sei and other rorquals is the position and shape of the dorsal fin and the slightly different head shape. This is particularly important in distinguishing it from the Bryde's whale, which has additional ridges on the head but is otherwise very similar in appearance.

**Habitat** This is a pelagic species, not generally found in inshore or coastal waters. The sei whale tends to follow temperature gradients and current lines in the oceans, particularly areas of upwelling and plankton abundance, and also shelf contours. The preferred surface temperature range has been reported as 8-25°C. The Bryde's whale only overlaps in range with the sei in water temperatures of 20-25°C.

**Distribution and migration** Sei whales are found in almost every ocean and sea of the world. However, the sei shuns extreme environments and is less likely to penetrate polar waters than other rorquals. The more usual polar limit is the subarctic or subantarctic, which are favoured regions for summer feeding. Only the largest adults are encountered in true polar waters, and then mostly

*Below: A sei whale surfaces to blow. It is very similar to the* *Bryde's whale, but occurs in colder waters during the summer.*

towards the middle and end of summer. The majority of sei whales are found in temperate waters, and some in the sub-tropics, but migration into low latitudes is seasonal and associated with breeding. The Northern and Southern Hemisphere populations are quite distinct.

Mark-recapture studies show that migrations frequently take the whales several thousands of kilometres between low and high latitudes each season, with a strong tendency to return to the same area where tagging originally took place. Nevertheless, occurrence on the feeding grounds is sometimes erratic.

**Food and feeding** Observations have shown that the sei whale is quite catholic and opportunistic in feeding habits and diet. Essentially, the species will take whatever is in abundance locally, as long as the prey organism is swarming or shoaling in behaviour. The fine, dense baleen of the sei whale enables it to retain even the smallest copepods effectively, but it can also take shoaling fish up to 30cm long and squid with ease. The sei whale is able to combine the typical balae-nopterid feeding method of 'gulping' with that of 'skimming'. It frequently swims on one side through shoaling fish. The most common food in the Antarctic is the euphausiid *Euphausia superba*, where-as in high latitudes of the Northern Hemisphere, the euphausiid *Meganycti-phanes norvegica* and copepods are fre-quently predominant.

**Behaviour** In general, sei whales swim in small pods of three to five individuals. There appears to be some segregation by age, sex and reproductive status. In tem-perate waters, schools consist mainly of juveniles and lactating females, whereas adult animals predominate in high lati-tudes. The dominant sex in high latitudes varies: past catches have indicated that males frequently dominate in the South-ern Hemisphere, whereas pregnant females dominate in the North Atlantic off Ireland. The ratio of the sexes and of different reproductive status changes by the month, however, reflecting migra-tory patterns.

When diving, the sei whale usually submerges for less than 20 minutes, and probably rarely goes deeper than 300m. The flukes are not usually thrown clear of the surface. Under water, the sei whale communicates acoustically in the same way as other rorquals, using pulsed low-frequency sounds in the range 12-500Hz and of 0.4-36 seconds duration and trains of pulses of peak energy 3kHz, each

pulse lasting 4 milliseconds. Although little has been documented, surface com-munication is probably similar to the various postural displays seen in other rorquals.

The species rarely strands; reports are usually for already dead animals stranded passively by coastal currents. No records of mass strandings are known.

**Life history** Little is known about the mating system of the sei whale. In com-mon with the blue and fin whales, the sei whale has a two-year reproductive cycle. Gestation lasts about 11.5 months, result-ing in a single calf, born during mid-winter, which is suckled for about six to seven months. The calf is about 4.5m and 780kg at birth, and 8m long and 3.8 tonnes in weight at weaning, which takes place in higher latitudes in summer.

Potential longevity in the species may be as great as 70 years, but exploitation of some stocks has artificially reduced the actual longevity. Both sexes mature re-productively between 8 and 11 years, depending on the particular stock, at about 92-95 percent of full adult length and about 70-85 percent of adult body weight. Physical maturity, i.e. when further growth in length can no longer occur, takes place at about 25-30 years.

Estimates of mortality rate are very variable, in the range 6-15 percent, but are generally assumed to be higher than in fin whales. These estimates generally re-present total mortality (including exploi-tation); natural mortality may be closer to 6-8 percent. Usually the mortality rate is higher in females than in males, but we know very little about the true pattern of mortality. Apart from man, and perhaps predation by sharks and killer whales on injured, sick and newborn individuals, the only reported potential cause of fatal-ities is a type of fungal infection that rots the baleen in the mouths of animals in the eastern North Pacific, which may reduce the efficiency of feeding to the level of starvation.

**World population** The current status of several sei whale stocks, particularly in the North Atlantic, is uncertain and likely to remain so. These stocks are relatively small (in the range of perhaps 1,400-2,200 for the Canadian stocks) compared with the Southern Hemisphere stocks. The sei whale is unpredictable in appearance at certain localities, and absence has not always been consistent with depletion-

caused by exploitation. Thus, stock assessment methods using survey, catch per unit of effort (CPUE) series and even mark-recapture methods have yielded unreliable indications of stock status.

In the North Pacific, the total stock size was about 13,000 in 1974 and about 63,000 in 1963. In the Southern Hemisphere, the population has been managed assuming six stocks, historically defined in terms of the original areas of abundance of the humpback whale and subsequently adopted for all rorqual species exploited around the Antarctic. However, it is now clear that there is considerable movement between stock 'boundaries'. An estimate of total population size in the Southern Hemisphere in 1979 was 24,000, com-pared with an estimated pre-1930 level of about 100,000. Recent calculations indi-cate that the total population size for the southern oceans and the North Pacific combined in 1985 may have been about 50,000 whales, compared with a pre-ex-ploitation size of 170,000.

**Man's influence** Traditionally, the sei whale was not the prime target of whal-ing operations because blue, fin and humpback whales, which all usually occur in the same waters, were the pre-ferred quarry. In the southern oceans, sei were initially taken mostly within a few hundred kilometres of land around the South Shetlands, South Georgia and the Falkland Islands, the Ross Sea and off South Africa. A few were taken pelag-ically in the subantarctic and Antarctic. Later, sei whales were taken mainly pelagically and, around the mid-1960s, the sei was heavily exploited, coinciding with the decline and subsequent system-atic protection of blue, humpback and fin whales in the southern oceans. By the mid-l970s, the southern sei whales were all but 'fished out' and total protection was applied to all stocks there from the 1978-79 season onwards. North Pacific sei whales were also depleted to low levels. In the North Atlantic, sei have been ex-ploited by many nations, including the Faeroe Islands, Greenland, Iceland, Ire-land, Norway, Scotland and Spain. Worldwide, all sei whale stocks were given protection from exploitation in 1979, with the exception of the stock in the Denmark Strait west of Iceland, where a catch of about 85 whales was per-mitted. Between 1986 and 1988, there was a continued take of 10-40 sei off Iceland under a scientific permit.

# BRYDE'S WHALE

## *BALAENOPTERA EDENI*

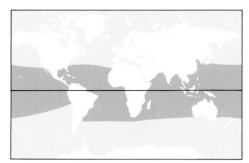

■ Probable distribution

*Right: A Bryde's whale photographed just before it surfaces. The animal has already started to exhale, so that the lungs can be almost completely emptied and refilled in the few moments of the breathing 'roll'.*

*Below right: This rare underwater shot of a Bryde's whale clearly shows the secondary ridges on the head. The ridges – one on either side of the midline – are a unique feature of this species.*

**Classification** The Bryde's whale (pronounced 'Broodahs') was described and named by Anderson in 1878. In 1912, Olsen described a species seen off the South African coast and named it *B. brydei* after the Norwegian consul to South Africa, Johan Bryde. Eventually, both descriptions were found to refer to the same species and the first description has been retained as the correct one, although the common name derives from the later specific name. No subspecies are recognized as yet, although a dwarf form is described for the Southern Hemisphere near the Solomon Islands. One type has been described as having an offshore pelagic habitat and a second is found in inshore coastal waters.

**Description** The Bryde's whale is similar in size and appearance to the sei whale, with which it has frequently been confused. However, the Bryde's whale is rather more stocky and generally shorter than the sei whale. The adult body size averages 13.7m in males and 14.5m in females, with a maximum size of 15.6m for females in the offshore form in South African waters. Adult body weight may be 16-18.5 tonnes, with a maximum of 20-25 tonnes. The smaller inshore type of Bryde's whale has an average adult size of 13m in males and 13.8m in females. The adult size of the Solomon Islands 'dwarf' form may be at least one metre less.

The well-defined, falcate dorsal fin is positioned about two-thirds back along the body. The tail flukes are broad with a median notch, and the tail stock is laterally compressed. The flippers are pointed and about 10 percent of body length in size. About 40-70 ventral grooves run aft from the lower jaw to the umbilicus. The baleen plates hanging from the upper jaw number 250-365, and are relatively short in comparison with the sei whale, reaching a maximum length of 60cm. The bristles are coarse, unlike in the sei whale.

The body colour is dark grey with some white coloration on the chin and throat. Occasionally, there is paler coloration on the back from behind the head to the dorsal fin, possibly extending down the flanks. Pock marks, caused by parasites or small sharks, frequently lend a mottled appearance to the body. The baleen is generally black or dark grey, although some front plates may be creamy coloured, at least in part. The bristles are pale in colour.

**Recognition at sea** The chief distinguishing feature of the Bryde's whale are the three ridges that run from the tip of the rostrum back to the level of the blowhole. This feature distinguishes Bryde's from all other rorquals. The blow may rise as high as 3-4m in a tall cloud. The head and blow usually appear before the dorsal fin, with a steeper angle of emergence at the surface than the sei whale. Stranded specimens are easily distinguished from other rorquals by the rostral ridges.

**Habitat** The species is found in both coastal and offshore habitats, with discrete differences between inshore resident animals and more migratory offshore ones. Bryde's whales prefer warm water, showing a preference for sea temperatures above 20°C.

**Distribution and migration** The species has a worldwide tropical to warm temperate distribution and is usually found in waters below latitude 30° in both hemispheres. (The map shows a continuous distribution between areas of known occurrence.) The species is not consis-

tently migratory; many coastal populations appear to be resident year-round, while offshore animals may migrate relatively short distances, being influenced mainly by food distribution and abundance. Migrations appear to be inshore-offshore movements rather than north-south, unlike most other rorquals.

Off South Africa, there is evidence of segregation in the population, with cow-calf pairs occurring separately.

**Food and feeding** The Bryde's whale is fairly opportunistic, readily consuming whatever shoaling prey is available. It frequently exploits the activities of other predators, swimming through and engulfing 'boils' of fish herded by them. It is therefore often found with flocks of seabirds, as well as with other cetaceans, seals and sharks in areas of high fish abundance. The coarse baleen fringe is more efficient with prey of larger size, such as fish, but the species readily takes swarming euphausiids. Feeding behaviour may involve 'gulping' or following shoaling fish in a zigzag pattern while turning on one side. Feeding is a year-round activity, and the whales appear to follow the local movements of prey. A full first stomach chamber of an adult Bryde's whale may hold 120-165kg of food, which probably represents an adequate daily supply.

**Behaviour** Bryde's whales are not gregarious, and mostly swim alone or in pairs. The largest group sizes of 10-23 are

usually loose aggregations covering a few square kilometres in area. The association of individuals may therefore be coincidental and connected by a common activity, such as feeding.

The Bryde's whale appears to be more lively than most other rorquals, and frequently breaches clear of the water. Diving behaviour is variable, depending on the prey being exploited, with dive depth varying from shallow to perhaps 300m. Dive duration is mostly 1-2 minutes, but may be up to 10 minutes. Usually 4-7 blows follow a dive of several minutes. While feeding, the swimming speed may be 2-7kph but, when cruising, Bryde's whale can attain speeds of up to 20-25kph. Vocalizations have been reported in the range 70-245Hz (with a signal length of 0.4 sec) and also in the range 3-30kHz.

**Life history** There is generally no well-defined breeding season for the Bryde's whale. Inshore coastal forms appear to breed and give birth throughout the year.

Offshore forms may have a peak in certain months, but generally the breeding and calving season is very protracted. This is consistent with an absence of migratory behaviour and with year-round feeding. The single calf is about 3.95-4.15m long at birth, after about 12 months of gestation. The calf is probably suckled for six months, but this is uncertain. The report of a two year-old animal with milk in the stomach may be unusual. At weaning, the Bryde's whale calf is usually about 7.1m in length and may weigh 2.5 tonnes.

Males mature reproductively at a length of 11.6-12.4m, depending on the locality, and at an age of 8-11 years. Females may start to reproduce at a similar age at a body size of 12-12.8m. The longevity of the species may be 50 years or more. The estimates of mortality rate vary with the stock and history of exploitation. Estimates of natural mortality have been as low as 3 percent for the Southern Hemisphere in virgin stocks, and 8.5 percent for North Pacific stocks.

**World population** The current status of Bryde's whales everywhere is in some doubt. Most stocks/populations may be close to virgin levels, but the actual size of such populations is less certain. In the Southern Hemisphere, there are an estimated 30,000 whales; in the Northern Hemisphere, 60,000. At least 17,000-24,000 whales are currently estimated in the western North Pacific alone.

Because of the coastal distribution and weak migratory habits of the species, there appear to be several fairly distinct stocks, which generally consist of resident animals. Concentrations have regularly been reported off South Africa, West Africa, Malagasy, the Seychelles, Western Australia, Solomon Islands, Fiji, Chile, Peru, Hawaii and the Bonin Islands off Japan. Actual stock boundaries have not been well defined; this is particularly true for much of the South Pacific and the North Atlantic.

**Man's influence** The longest history of exploitation for the Bryde's whale has been off Japan. Many were included in the early catches of sei whales, passing unrecognized as a distinct species. Once the species difference was appreciated, and the 1960s catches of sei whales had clearly begun to be unsustainable, a high seas pelagic whaling operation mounted from Japan became important in the western North Pacific. Japan and the Soviet Union continued these pelagic catches, along with coastal operations from Japan and Korea, until 1980. Then, with the Philippines taking coastal catches in 1984 and 1985, only the coastal fishery from Japan continued until, in 1986, the International Whaling Commission declared its moratorium on commercial whaling. South Africa, which had been taking Bryde's whales, ceased catching after 1967. Until the mid-1980s, some coastal catches in the South Pacific were taken by Peru, and Chile also took a few whales in 1983.

Bryde's whales have been systematically exploited only in the North Pacific. In comparison with other rorquals, the species has, therefore, been largely overlooked as a resource. Once its full potential was realized, measures were already in hand to stem whaling activities. Overall, Bryde's whale is considered to be neither in danger nor at depleted levels.

# MINKE WHALE

*BALAENOPTERA ACUTOROSTRATA*

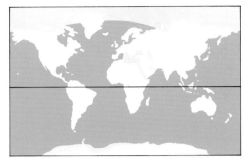

■ Known range

**Classification** The minke whale was classified by Lacépède in 1804 with the name *Balaenoptera acutorostrata*, the specific name referring to the pointed shape of the jaw. A subspecies was described by Burmeister in 1867 for the Southern Hemisphere, *B. a. bonaerensis* distinguishable chiefly by the absence of a white band on each flipper. More recently, a diminutive form of the southern minke whale has been reported from South Africa and off Australia. This form has white on the flippers, but has not been designated a subspecies.

**Local names** The common name is derived from the Norwegian 'minkehval'. Other names include little piked whale, pikehead, sharpheaded finner and lesser rorqual, the last name reflecting the small size of the minke whale in relation to other balaenopterids.

**Description** The minke whale is the smallest of the balaenopterid family. The body is relatively robust compared with the larger rorquals. The head is very acute in shape, and the rostrum is fairly flat, apart from the central ridge running from the blowhole forward. The dorsal fin is positioned approximately two-thirds of the way along the back and is relatively tall

and falcate. The tail flukes are broad, with a median notch. The flippers are pointed and about 12 percent of body size in length. The baleen varies in colour from dark grey-black at the back of the jaw to creamy yellow further forward, but always with a whitish fringe. There are 230-360 plates on each side of the rostrum, depending on geographic locality. Maximum plate length is only about 30cm. There are 50-70 ventral grooves running back from the tip of the lower jaw to just in front of the umbilicus.

The overall colour is dark slate grey, with paler grey to white on the belly and throat. There may be a pale chevron on the back behind the head resembling a small cape, with pale grey coloration extending down onto the flanks. Each flipper usually bears a discrete bright white pigmented band diagonally across its surface, although this characteristic is often absent from minke found in the Antarctic (the 'bonaerensis' type). The underside of the flippers is white.

Males grow to about 8m and females about 8.2m long in the Southern Hemisphere. The Northern Hemisphere form is slightly smaller. Adult body weight rarely exceeds 8 tonnes, although females of maximum size 10.7m may weigh in excess of 13.5 tonnes.

*Right: Most sightings of minke whales are restricted to the back and dorsal fin, here seen against an Antarctic backdrop.*

*Below: Under water, minke whales are revealed as more robust than the larger rorquals and quite similar to a dolphin in general shape.*

**Recognition at sea** The blow rises about 2-3m and is usually visible only in good weather with low wind speed. The whale does not raise its flukes when diving, although the back is well arched. The dorsal fin is usually exposed while blowing. The minke whale can swim at speeds of up to 30kph when alarmed. Unlike many rorquals, it appears to be quite inquisitive about its environment, often approaching shipping, spy hopping and lingering nearby. This behaviour and the small body size make the species easy to identify when encountered at sea.

**Distribution and migration** The minke whale is found from the polar ice-edge to the tropics. Although mainly a pelagic species, it will come quite close to the coast. The species is not known to migrate regularly between low and high latitudes, although there are definite shifts in latitudinal abundance with season. Some minke whales appear to remain in relatively small sea areas in temperate or subtropical regions for most of the year. In some areas, off Washington State and British Columbia, for example, it is possible to identify individual minke whales from dorsal fin shape, and many of these individuals do not venture far outside coastal waters. In polar waters,

the species appears to penetrate ice leads and is often found close to the ice-edge. Minke whales have sometimes been reported 'trapped' in polynyas (open water areas surrounded by ice) during winter in the Antarctic, and occasionally appear to overwinter there.

There is considerable sexual segregation by latitude, with different reproductive classes predominating at certain times of year. Changes in abundance of these classes vary seasonally according to breeding condition, with higher densities in temperate waters in winter. The adult animals tend to occupy sea areas in higher latitudes compared with juveniles. There are three distinct populations: Southern Hemisphere, North Pacific, and North Atlantic. Mixing of individuals across the equator is unlikely.

**Food and feeding** Minke whales appear to feed very little in tropical and subtropical waters. In the Southern Hemisphere, the preferred diet is euphausiids. In the Northern Hemisphere, they also take euphausiids as well as a variety of shoaling fish. Pteropods (small, free-swimming molluscs) have also been recorded as prey items.

**Behaviour** Minke whales frequently occur as solitary animals or in groups of two or three individuals. Large aggregations are mostly associated with feeding activities. The minke whale often breaches and is inquisitive. When confined in ponds in the ice, the whales may be easily approached and have even been petted by people on Antarctic expeditions. Blowing may occur in a sequence of up to eight breaths at intervals of under a minute. Dives typically last only several minutes because the whales do not need to dive deeply for food. Vocalizations, presumably linked with communication, have been described as 'grunts', 'clicks' and 'ratchet pulses' in the range 80Hz-20kHz, with some signals lasting only 30msec.

**Life history** The Southern Hemisphere minke whales mature sexually at about 7.2m long in males and 8m in females. In the Northern Hemisphere, they are smaller: males about 6.9m and females 7.3-7.45m. Body weight at sexual maturity is 4-5 tonnes. Mating patterns are not well documented for this species. The mating season is in late winter, peaking about two months later than in blue, fin and sei whales. Gestation lasts about 10 months and the single calf is born in low latitudes in winter, at a similar time of year as large rorquals. The newborn calf is 2.8m long (2.6m in the North Atlantic) and weighs about 300kg. The suckling phase lasts only about four months and the calf is about 4.5m long at this time. The young minke calf does not appear to be weaned onto taking prey for itself in the productive polar waters in summer, but in less rich areas in lower latitudes.

The ages of minke whales in the Southern Hemisphere have been interpreted from ear plugs. Since the 1940s, the age at sexual maturity has reportedly fallen gradually from 14 to about 6 or 7 years. This can be explained by faster individual growth rates made possible by reduced competition for food resources because the larger rorquals have been depleted. Age determination techniques in Northern Hemisphere populations have not been as successful. Minke whales may exceptionally live for 60 years.

Natural mortality rates for the Southern Hemisphere minke whale are estimated to be 9-10 percent. These are higher than for other rorqual species. Known enemies include the killer whale, which may attack individuals, causing permanent disfigurement or death.

**World population** In the Southern Hemisphere, the estimate of the present population, at about 380,000 whales, is higher than that of the pre-exploitation period, because the population has grown as a result of reduced interspecific competition. The current population may be higher than 440,000. The largest assessment has been in the sector 130°E-170°W.

The Northern Hemisphere populations probably total about 125,000 animals. However, great uncertainties exist for the three stocks assessed in the North Atlantic. One estimate gives an exploitable population size of 41,000.

**Man's influence** Not until the 1970s did the minke whale become a significant quarry of the whaling industry. Until that time, the species had not been considered commercially and economically worthwhile, apart from local coastal whaling operations. Large catches were taken in the Antarctic by the Japanese and Soviet pelagic fleets until 1986, when the moratorium on commercial whaling came into effect. Since then, there have been some catches under scientific permit, mainly by Japan. Historically, coastal whaling for minke whales has taken place off eastern Canada, Greenland, Iceland, Norway, Korea, China and Japan in the Northern Hemisphere, and off Brazil, South Africa, and, sporadically, off some other African nations in the Southern Hemisphere.

A minke whale has the distinction of being the first rorqual ever maintained in captivity, albeit for a very few weeks. The whale eventually escaped by breaking through the netting to the open sea.

# HUMPBACK WHALE

## *MEGAPTERA NOVAEANGLIAE*

■ Seasonally resident　　⁄ Probable range

**Classification** In many ways similar to other members of the baleen whale family Balaenopteridae, the humpback is sufficiently different from the other rorquals in form and behaviour to merit its own genus, *Megaptera*. This name means 'big wing' and clearly refers to its enormous flippers, the largest of any whale. The specific name, *novaeangliae*, (literally, 'New England'), was assigned by the German naturalist Borowski in recognition of an early description of the animal from the northeastern United States, where it was, and still is, regularly seen in nearshore waters.

**Local names** 'Humpback' clearly refers to the species' habit of raising and bending its back in preparation for a dive, accentuating the pronounced hump in front of the dorsal fin. It is known as baleine à bosse or megaptère in French, jorobada in Spanish and knølhval in Norwegian.

**Description** Average adult body length is about 12.9m in males and 13.7m in females, with an extreme record of an animal 18m in length. Body weights at a given length are variable, but an average of 25-30 tonnes in adults seems likely. The body is stouter than in other balaenopterids and the flippers are much longer, representing 23-33 percent of body length. Humpbacks have 12-36 ventral grooves, the longest running from the chin to the navel.

The upper body colour is black or blue-black. The flippers, ventral groove area, flanks and underside of the flukes can be white or black depending on geographical race and individual variation. Uniquely, the front edges of the flippers have many lumps and bumps, on which barnacles may grow. The head is rounded when seen from above, and the rostrum is flat apart from many characteristic raised lumps, called tubercles, which also occur on the lower jaws. The paired blowholes are typical of the family, raised and on the midline of the head. The dorsal fin is very variable in shape and size, and raised on a small platform of blubber. It can be anything from a long, low triangular shape to a hooked form, but is rarely very prominent. The dorsal fin can be almost white from scar tissue, especially along the ridge. This is more likely in males because they often engage in aggressive competition during the breeding season.

The tail flukes are large, notched and have an irregularly shaped trailing edge. The dorsal surface is always very dark, but the underside can be anything from all white to all black, with intricate patterns of pigmentation unique to the individual. This surface may be scarred and partially covered with yellow diatoms.

The baleen plates are dark brown or grey in colour. Each baleen row contains 270-400 plates, reaching 80-100cm in length at the deepest part. The bristles are quite coarse.

**Recognition at sea** The humpback whale is unmistakable, especially at close quarters. The combination of the dark colour, dorsal fin shape, single upright blow (sometimes bushy) and habit of raising the flukes before most deeper dives distinguishes this from any other whale of its size. When white, the flippers can often be seen as a ghostly greenish or bluish shape many metres below the water surface, even when the dark body of the whale is invisible. The dorsal fin, though variable, cannot normally be mistaken for that of any other species, and the tubercles on the head are equally characteristic. This is one of the most exuberant of all cetaceans, often breaching or slapping the water surface with the tail flukes or flippers to produce a loud 'rifle-shot' noise that can be heard many kilometres away. Humpbacks are normally relatively slow swimming, easy to approach and often inquisitive.

**Habitat** Humpbacks spend much of the year in shallower water than the other balaenopterids, usually feeding and breeding on offshore banks, but they cross thousands of kilometres of open ocean between summer and winter grounds. They occur from the tropics to polar waters.

**Distribution and migration** This is a widely distributed species, occurring seasonally in all oceans and from the Arctic to the Antarctic. With one possible exception, all populations undertake substantial migrations of many thousands of kilometres between the coldwater feeding areas occupied in summer and the tropical or subtropical breeding grounds in winter. Generally, these whales are thought not to cross the equator, so Southern and Northern Hemisphere stocks are probably discrete. Nevertheless, the humpbacks that live in the northern Indian Ocean, north of the equator, have no access to high-latitude feeding areas because of the Asian landmass. They must either migrate to the Antarctic to feed or are perhaps resident, feeding in biologically productive areas of the Indian Ocean. With this exception, it is likely that northern and southern stocks are separated by the six-month difference in the timing of their breeding

cycles, as in other migratory rorquals.

Broadly speaking, each of the major oceans has one or more warmwater breeding areas on both east and west sides, and the North Pacific has a central breeding ground (Hawaii). Generally, whales make roughly north-south or south-north migrations between these wintering places and their coldwater summer grounds in higher latitudes. The way individual whales use these areas differs between stocks. The best understood stocks in this respect are those of the North Pacific and the North Atlantic. North Pacific humpbacks use several discrete breeding grounds separated by thousands of kilometres. Individuals have been seen in Hawaii one winter and off Mexico in another – a reflection, perhaps, of what is probably the recent colonization of Hawaii as a breeding ground (less than 200 years ago). In contrast, almost all humpbacks in the North Atlantic share one wintering ground, in the West Indies, then split up to feed on one of several feeding grounds in the north to which, with insignificant exceptions, they always return. These differences are important in that they influence the level of genetic interchange within each population.

**Food and feeding** Humpback whales mostly feed within 50m of the surface. In the Antarctic, the main prey is the shrimplike *Euphausia superba* (a species of krill). Northern Hemisphere humpbacks also consume a great deal of krill, but will often take shoaling fish, including herring, sandeel, capelin and mackerel.

Like most other balaenopterids, the humpback is a 'gulper' rather than a 'skimmer', closing the mouth after engulfing a mouthful of food and water, then expelling the water through the baleen plates to leave the food on the inner surfaces and eventually swallowing it. For this method of feeding to be efficient the prey must be densely

*Bottom left: Humpbacks have an unmistakable back and dorsal fin. This individual was photographed just before a dive into rich Antarctic waters.*

*Left: The underside of humpback tail flukes can be anything between all white and all black, but is usually a combination of both.*

*Below: Humpback whales, especially immature ones, are sometimes extremely inquisitive and may even approach a quiet vessel. This animal is taking a closer look at a yacht on a calm day in the Antarctic.*

packed, albeit patchily. The feeding behaviour reflects this requirement and consists basically of the 'lunge', in which the whale swims through the prey swarm with its mouth open, often erupting at the surface with food and water pouring from the gape. The lunge may be at the surface and carried out horizontally, usually while swimming in a circle, or vertically from beneath the prey. In this last case, the whale may use bubbles to concentrate the food organisms. The

*Left: A humpback cow and calf on their wintering grounds. This association is the closest in humpback whale society (as in all cetaceans), and calves typically remain with their mothers for 10-12 months after birth.*

*Far right: A humpback blows as it approaches the camera off West Greenland. The characteristic bumps, or 'tubercles', on the head of this species are clearly visible here.*

whale produces bubbles of air from the blowhole or the mouth in any of three ways: as a single burst to produce a bubble 'cloud'; while swimming in a straight line, generating a bubble 'curtain', or while swimming in a circle or spiral to create a bubble 'net'. The rising bubbles act as a barrier to the prey, perhaps scaring them into a tighter concentration through which the whale then swims with its mouth open. Groups of up to 24 whales may synchronize their lunge feeding, the size of the group possibly being related to the horizontal spread of the prey school.

**Behaviour** Humpback whales often aggregate in large loose groups of many tens of animals for breeding or feeding, but within these groups the whales move individually or in close company with one to three others. The most stable social unit is the mother/calf pair. This association lasts for at least 10-12 months whereas most other associations, especially during the breeding season, appear to be temporary, lasting for no more than a few hours or days. The exception to this pattern is the long-term association between some animals on the feeding grounds. Scientists have shown that groups of humpbacks can retain a stable membership of recognizable animals from year to year, perhaps because they develop an efficient method of cooperative feeding.

On their breeding grounds, the social behaviour of the same whales is quite different; here, all feeding stops and the animals concentrate their activities on courtship, mating and calving. The previously gentle creatures change character, the males becoming extremely aggressive to each other in the fight to

claim stewardship of sexually receptive females. Their aim is to 'escort' the female, and they will attempt to displace an existing escort by threatening, lunging, physically displacing, charging and ultimately striking their rivals. Although wounds are caused during this activity, they are only superficial and at worst cause bleeding and subsequent scarring on the dorsal surface. The transitory nature of associations on the breeding grounds suggest that humpbacks are promiscuous, animals of both sexes pairing with several different partners during the mating period.

Another behaviour linked with breeding is what has been termed 'singing' – a complex pattern of sounds made underwater by males only. Humpback 'songs' are probably used as a means of territorial display or sexual advertisement, in much the same way as birdsong. They consist of repeated 'syllables', given such onomatopoeic names as 'chirps', 'yups' and 'whoops', that form 'phrases'. The phrases are grouped into 'themes' and the themes into songs that may last for between six and 35 minutes. The song is often repeated *identically* for hours, broken only by brief pauses for breath.

Swimming speeds vary considerably, depending on context. Migration speeds of 1.5-11kph (average 2-5kph) have been recorded, but burst speeds of up to 27kph can be attained by alarmed whales. Dive schedules reflect the near-surface location of their prey. Feeding dives of more than 15 minutes are unusual; most last 3-9 minutes, separated by breathing sequences of up to four minutes. Respiration rates are usually in the range 50-80 breaths per hour. Dives are longer, up to 30 minutes, on the wintering grounds.

**Life history** Reproduction is synchronized and seasonal, timed to coincide with the species' movement into warm waters during the winter. Mating and calving both occur on the wintering grounds, gestation lasting approximately 11-11.5 months. Newborn animals average 4.3m in body length and suckle for about 6-10 months, by which time they have grown to a length of 7.5-9m.

Sexual maturity in humpback whales is reached at four to seven years of age and a length of about 11.5m (males) and 12m (females). Calves are born every one to three years (usually two years), so an adult female may be simultaneously pregnant and suckling a young calf. Growth continues until an age of about 15 years, when males average about 12.9m and females 13.7m. Assuming two earplug growth layers per year, the oldest animal among 3,600 examined from Australian waters was 48 years, but only 5 percent of this heavily exploited stock reached 20 years. In the current climate of protection, a greater proportion can be expected to reach this age.

**World population** All populations of this species have been reduced by whaling, and most were taken to near-extinction. Some stocks have made a successful recovery, while others remain at a very low level. Before man's intervention, the majority of humpbacks lived in the Southern Hemisphere, feeding on the plentiful krill stocks of the Antarctic Ocean. At that time, there were well in excess of 100,000 animals south of the equator. Today, it is thought that fewer than 5,000 occur there, wintering off South America, southern Africa, Australia and some Pacific islands.

The original population size in the North Pacific was probably in excess of 15,000. Today about 2,000 are estimated to winter off Hawaii or western Mexico and a further 150 on the western side of the North Pacific. The North Atlantic population is currently the largest, at about 5-6,000 animals.

**Man's influence** The humpback was one of the first whale species to suffer in the modern era of whaling. Slower swimming, less easily scared and more predictable in occurrence than the other rorquals, humpback populations were quickly destroyed by whaling fleets adopting a classic 'boom-and-bust' strategy of exploitation. Humpbacks were taken on their summer feeding grounds, their winter breeding grounds and as

*Left: A lunge-feeding humpback closes its mouth, having just engulfed a huge amount of food-laden sea water. The pleats on the throat, chest and belly allow the ventral tissue to expand dramatically and accommodate the inrush of water.*

*Below: Breaching is common in humpback whales. Note the uniquely long pectoral fins, or flippers.*

they migrated between the two.

The North Atlantic saw the earliest concentrated whaling effort on this species and, by the end of the nineteenth century, catches had already dropped to a low level. Thereafter, attention switched to the North Pacific and to the rich pickings of the Southern Hemisphere, where most of the world's humpbacks lived. In the first 40 years of the twentieth century, more than 100,000 humpbacks were taken south of the equator, mainly on the almost circumpolar feeding grounds of the Antarctic Ocean. Catches fell dramatically from a peak of over 14,000 per year to less than 2,000 per year around 1920. Intermittent periods of renewed activity in the 1930s and 1950s were largely responsible for a catch as high as 50,000 between 1940 and 1963, on southern stocks struggling to recover from the earlier onslaught. Total protection from commercial hunting was afforded the species in 1956 (North Atlantic), 1963 (Southern Hemisphere) and 1966 (North Pacific).

Local subsistence hunts continued until recently off West Greenland (about 15 animals per year, ending in 1985) and Tonga (up to 10 per year, ending in 1978). Up to three humpback whales are still taken from open boats at Bequia in the West Indies, but this level of hunting does not pose a threat to the stock. Man-induced mortality other than whaling has never been at a high level, though the entrapment of humpbacks in fishery gear, particularly cod traps in Newfoundland, has caused many deaths. Here, the number of entrapped whales that drown has been dramatically reduced by a disentanglement programme organized by a local university with the fishermen.

# SPERM WHALES
## PHYSETERIDAE · KOGIIDAE

There are three existing species in this group, which has been given the taxonomic status of a superfamily, Physeteroidea. They are the sperm whale (*Physeter macrocephalus*), the pygmy sperm whale (*Kogia breviceps*) and the dwarf sperm whale (*Kogia simus*). There is a great difference in size and body form between *Physeter* and *Kogia*, which has recently led taxonomists to place the smaller *Kogia* species in a family of their own (Kogiidae), rather than in the family Physeteridae with *Physeter macrocephalus*.

All three sperm whales are oceanic in habit, rarely venturing near the coast, except where the depth increases rapidly. Live strandings are not uncommon, but only *Physeter*, because of its social structure, comes ashore in a large group. *Physeter* is truly cosmopolitan in range, appearing worldwide in all but the coldest seas. The distribution of the two smaller species is incompletely known, but they probably occur in tropical to warm temperate waters in all oceans. *Physeter* undertakes poorly defined latitudinal migrations, but nothing is known of *Kogia* movements.

The difference in size between species in this group is such that *Physeter*, which can reach 20m in length, is by far the largest of the odontocetes, or toothed whales, whereas *Kogia simus*, which is no more than 2.7m long, is the smallest species known as a whale. The three species share certain characteristics, namely a relatively large melon (or 'case') on the rostrum, narrow, underslung lower jaws, non-functional teeth in the upper jaw and a fairly simple air-sinus system. They differ in body size, relative head size (much bigger in *Physeter*) and in dorsal fin shape – upright and falcate in *Kogia*, low and stubby in *Physeter*.

*A sperm whale forages in a dense shoal of cephalopods. This is by far the largest of the toothed whales.*

# SPERM WHALE

*PHYSETER MACROCEPHALUS*

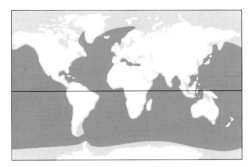

■ Maximum range

**Classification** Linnaeus established the genus *Physeter* after the Greek word *Phuseter*, meaning 'blower' or 'whirlpool', probably a reference to the single forceful blow. Currently only one species is recognized, but earlier inaccurate descriptions of specimens led taxonomists to believe that up to four species existed. There continues to be some argument as to whether the sperm whale's specific name should be *macrocephalus*, (literally 'big head'), or *catodon* ('teeth only in the lower jaw'). There is no realistic case for recognizing subspecies of sperm whales anywhere in the world.

**Local names** This species acquired its name 'sperm' whale from the milky liquid wax in its head, which whalers likened to the fluid produced by the testes to carry sperm. The name is used throughout the English-speaking world, but many other nations use a variation of cachalot (kaskelot, cachalote), from the Catalan 'quachal' for 'big teeth'.

**Description** This is the species most people probably associate with the word 'whale'. It is by far the largest of the toothed whales and the animal in which sexual dimorphism in body size is most marked. Males average about 15m in length and may reach 20.5m in extreme cases. Females, however, rarely reach 13m and average only 11m. The ratio of body weight is even bigger; adult males average about 45 tonnes and females only 20 tonnes. The largest animal reliably weighed was an 18.1m male of 57 tonnes.

Sperm whales are dark brown or dark grey in colour, sometimes looking black in poor light or in beached animals. Many have a white or light grey ventral patch or swirl, and the inside of the mouth and the lips are pink or cream coloured. Older males may have large numbers of linear scars on their heads. These derive from fights with other males and from the hooks and suckers of squid, their preferred prey in most areas. In some males, the white scar tissue covers the entire flat front to the head, and the many nicks and scratches may be infested with patches of yellow diatoms or white whale lice.

The profile of the sperm whale is unlike that of any other species. The rectangular head, already a quarter of the body length in calves, grows disproportionately until it reaches a third of total length in adult bulls. The lower jaw is roughly cylindrical for much of its length and, in adults, holds about 50 rounded conical teeth in two parallel rows. These are the largest teeth (excluding tusks) of any animal species and may weigh over a kilogram each. The upper teeth are vestigial, non-functional and, if they erupt at all, are tiny and often misshapen. The skin is hard and smooth to the touch, but the rear half of the animal usually resembles a prune, being covered in rounded irregular ridges or wrinkles. The dorsal fin or hump is usually obvious, but it is low and generally takes the form of the largest and most forward of a number of ridges leading down the dorsal surface of the tail stock.

The flippers are short and stubby, but the triangular tail flukes are large and powerful. The trailing edge may be irregular in shape due to injury. The single slitlike blowhole is positioned at the extreme front of the head, on the upper surface and on the left side.

**Recognition at sea** Sperm whales are usually first located by their single, bushy blow, which projects forward and to the left of the animal. Depending on whale size, the blow can be up to 5m high and visible as far as the horizon with binoculars. Dives are normally preceded by the

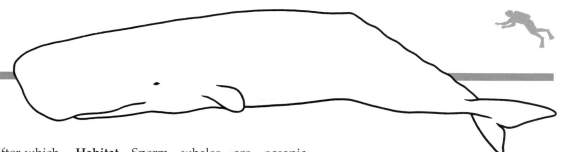

tail being raised into the air, after which the animal can remain submerged for up to 90 minutes, yet often surfaces near the same spot. Characteristically, sperm whales often remain almost motionless or swim very slowly at the surface for periods of 5-15 minutes between dives, blowing 20-60 times at regular intervals. They show little of themselves above the surface, usually no more than the dorsal surface from the blowhole to the fin.

**Habitat** Sperm whales are oceanic animals, normally venturing close to shore only when sick or where the depth of water increases rapidly away from the coast, as it often does around volcanic islands. Males can withstand a wide range of water temperatures, from the warmth of the tropics to the chill of polar regions, but females and immature animals remain in areas with a water temperature of 15°C or more at the surface.

**Distribution and migration** This species occurs in all oceans of the world, from the equator to polar waters. It rarely enters semi-enclosed areas of sea, especially if they are shallow or protected by a shallow entrance, but sperm whales are well known in the Mediterranean. A characteristic that distinguishes this from all other whales is the differential distribution of males and females, whereby only large males venture into latitudes higher than about 45° in both hemispheres. This separation is so distinct that, of the more than 2,000 sperm whales captured off Iceland (latitudes 63°-67°N) after 1948, not one was a female. Seasonal movements may occur to the extent that segments of populations move to higher latitudes of both hemispheres in summer and back again in winter. However, although individual whales have been shown to travel thousands of kilometres between locations of marking and recapture both longitudinally and latitudinally, rigid annual migrations of entire populations are not well established. In most regions of warm oceanic water, sperm whales can be found all year round. Their distribution is far from even, however, as recognized by nineteenth century whalers,

*Above: Sperm whales often raise their tail flukes before diving. Damage to the trailing edge ( here, on the left) allows researchers to identify individuals.*

*Left: A pod of sperm whales near the Azores Islands. Behavioural research on this species, patiently carried out from yachts and using hydrophones to follow study animals, is revealing details of social structure and population dynamics that could not be gained by examination of captured whales.*

*Right: A large male blows in the cold waters of the Davis Strait, west of Greenland. Only the adult males venture into high latitudes.*

*Left: A swimmer approaches a pod of sperm whales. Despite their large size and reputation for aggression when harpooned, sperm whales can sometimes be closely and safely approached by humans if they move slowly.*

*Below: A sperm whale calf. Calves are born at a body length of about 4m, after a gestation period of 14-15.5 months. They may be suckled for several years, even after they begin to take solid food (mostly squid).*

*Below right: A sperm whale breaches near the Galapagos Islands.*

who concentrated their attention on certain rich sperm whale 'grounds'.

**Food and feeding** In most areas where they occur, sperm whales feed almost exclusively on cephalopods (squid and octopi). In a few places, fish form an important part of the diet; off Alaska and Iceland, they are of greater importance than squid. Prey is taken at considerable depths, usually below about 400m and generally in midwater, although bottom feeding is indicated by the capture of fish species and octopi living exclusively on or near the seabed. Contrary to popular belief, most of the squid taken are not the giant squid of legend, but medium-sized animals with a mantle length of 0.2-1m. Nevertheless, giant squid such as *Architeuthis* are sometimes taken. Fish species eaten include rays, sharks, lanternfish, members of the cod family (Gadidae) and redfish (*Sebastes*). Larger sperm whales take larger prey, a greater proportion of fish and probably feed at greater depths. They certainly dive for longer periods.

Sperm whales feed all year round throughout the day and night and have been estimated to consume 3-3.5 percent of their body weight per day – about 1.5 tonnes in an adult male. Non-food items commonly found in stomachs include stones and floating debris.

Food searching is probably coordinated to some extent in groups of whales, recent evidence suggesting that individuals may sometimes forage in line abreast, communicating with sound to maintain their distance from neighbours.

**Life history** As one of the most heavily exploited of all whale species, the sperm whale is one of the best known in terms of basic biology, though much still remains conjecture and hypothesis. It is a long-lived species, with a low rate of reproduction and a long period of maternal care. Females bear a calf every 3-15 years, usually every 4-6 years. Older animals reproduce less frequently. Sperm whales are seasonal breeders, but mating and thus calving is not well synchronized. Mating peaks in late spring or early summer in both hemispheres and most calvings occur in summer and autumn.

Single calves are born after a gestation period of about 14-15.5 months and at about 4m in length. Lactation may last for 1.6-3.5 years, longer in older females. Calves begin to take solid food within the

first year but may sporadically take milk until they are more than 10 years old. Growth is rapid until weaning, but teeth do not erupt above the gum until several years after the young animal has become entirely reliant on squid and fish. Females become sexually mature and can reproduce at about 10 years of age (range 7-13 years) and a body length of 8.3-9.2m. Males reach puberty at 7-11 years and full sexual maturity at about 18-21 years, when 11-12m long. Nevertheless, they usually have to wait until they are 20-25 years old before being powerful enough to gain access to receptive females. This delayed 'social maturity' in males is another characteristic of polygynous animals, i.e. males mating with more than one female. Growth may continue until the age of 35-60 years in males.

**Behaviour** The basic social unit is considered to be the family group, typically consisting of 10-20 animals. These will be a number of adult females with their offspring of various ages. Females might be expected to remain in such a group throughout their lives, but males would normally leave at or near puberty and join a 'bachelor' pod of medium-sized males. As they get older, males become less social and may eventually become one of the venerable lone bulls often seen in polar and cold temperate waters. Groups of hundreds or even thousands of sperm whales are sometimes reported, covering an area of many square kilometres and obviously travelling as a unit.

The mating system is polygynous, as might be expected by analogy to other animals with such extreme sexual dimorphism in favour of large males, but little is known of the social behaviour of the males that succeed in impregnating oestrus females. Recent studies, using yachts to follow families of whales for weeks at a time, have shown that large males are rarely in attendance and then only for short periods of time, contrary to earlier theories suggesting that so-called 'harem' bulls constantly defended their group of females against all other mature males. Inter-male rivalry is certainly indicated by the high evidence of tooth rakes on the heads of older bulls, and whalers tell of great fights between animals, sometimes resulting in severe injury. However, it is likely that for much of the year sperm whale schools or pods are led by dominant matriarchs.

Vocalizations are pulsed, sounding like clicks, and are probably used both for echolocation and communication. Clicks are between 0.2 and 32kHz, mostly 10-16kHz, and 2-30msec in length. They are repeated at intervals of 0.01-10 seconds. Some repeated and stereotyped click sequences, called codas, probably convey a particular message to other whales.

This is probably the deepest and longest diving of all cetaceans. Adult males dive for longer periods than females, remaining below the surface for as long as 90 minutes (typically 20-50 minutes). The species is known to be able to dive to 1,100m, but indirect evidence indicates that it can descend to at least 3,200m. Most dives are probably to a depth of 300-600m.

**World population** Estimates of abundance are generally unreliable and the subject of much controversy. Certainly this must have been, and still is, the most abundant large whale species in the world, despite intensive worldwide whaling. One recent estimate, probably as accurate as it is possible to be, suggests a current population of about two million sperm whales, of which half are in the North Pacific Ocean. Apart from depleting the overall population size, modern whaling has also changed the age and sex structure of stocks by selectively removing large, adult males.

**Man's influence** The sperm whale has suffered one of the longest periods of sustained exploitation by man of any cetacean. The first commercial fishery for the species started in the early eighteenth century and some have been killed in every year from about 1690 until 1987. By this time, all commercial operations had stopped and only a handful of whalers from the Azores Islands ventured out to kill three whales using open boats and hand harpoons. During the total period, many hundreds of thousands have been killed in all oceans of the world, with a peak annual catch of 29,300 in 1963/64. The first restrictions were imposed by the International Whaling Commission in 1971 and commercial catches were banned after 1984. Few animals are killed accidentally by fishing operations.

Sperm whales were killed principally for oil produced mainly from the very thick blubber, and for the spermaceti wax in the head. This is the species from which ambergris comes, a waxy substance in the gut that was originally used in the perfume industry. Virtually no sperm whales have been taken for food; their black, oily meat is considered inedible by all but a few communities.

# PYGMY SPERM WHALE

*KOGIA BREVICEPS*

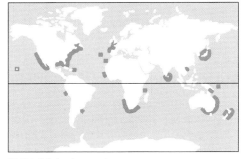

■ Established records

**Classification** *Kogia breviceps*, one of two species recognized in this genus, was named in 1838 by the Compte de Blainville. The generic name is supposed to derive from 'codger' (a miserly man), or possibly refers to Cogia Effendi, an early Turkish whalewatcher. The specific name, *breviceps*, means 'short headed'.

**Description** These small robust whales attain a maximum length of 3.3m in both sexes and weigh up to about 400kg. The head is short (15 percent or less of body length), and supports the large bulbous snout containing the spermaceti organ. In profile, the snout is pointed in young animals, becoming rectangular in adults. The short narrow mouth, so characteristic of this family, is placed under the head, and set with 12-16 curved needle-shaped teeth in each lower jaw. There are no upper teeth. The dorsal fin is small, slightly hooked and typically less than 5 percent of body length in height. The flippers have convex margins, tapering evenly to a rounded apex. The flukes are broad, tapered towards the tips and far less rigid than those of dolphins. The upper half of the head and body, the tail stock and dorsal surface of the flukes and flippers are dark bluish grey, fading to the off-white or slightly pinkish colour of the ventral surfaces of the head, body, flippers and flukes. Behind the eye, a whitish line runs downwards from the external ear to the pale throat.

**Recognition at sea** At sea, pygmy sperm whales are likely to be confused only with beaked whales (which also have small dorsal fins) and the dwarf sperm whale (*Kogia simus*). Beaked whales can be distinguished by their larger size, generally more rapid movement and, at close range, the elongate snout. The smaller dorsal fin of this species best distinguishes it from the dwarf sperm whale. The differences in fin height can be quantified accurately from photographs of slow-moving or stationary whales by recording fin height as a percentage of snout-to-fin tip length. This is 5-9 percent in pygmy sperm whales and 9-16 percent in dwarf sperm whales.

**Habitat** These are oceanic animals, possibly living over or close to the continental slope, though juveniles and females with calves appear to move onto the outer continental shelf to feed.

**Distribution and migration** These whales appear to be widely distributed in temperate, subtropical and tropical seas, with some notable gaps that could reflect the lack of observers. In the North Atlantic, records extend from Ireland and the Netherlands southward to Senegal, the Azores, Madeira and the Canary Islands, and from Nova Scotia to Cuba and the Gulf of Mexico. Southern African material includes the only South Atlantic records and several of the Indian Ocean records. The remaining few records are scattered across the Indo-Pacific.

**Food and feeding** Pygmy sperm whales prey primarily on a large variety of oceanic squids and cuttlefishes, supplemented with small numbers of fish and deepsea shrimps. Most food species are small, buoyant forms, probably not capable of sustained rapid movement, and entirely appropriate prey for a small-mouthed, slow-moving predator hunting by stealth. Over the continental slope, feeding may occur at depths of 200m or more, while the presence of cuttlefishes in females with calves suggests that prey is caught close to the bottom over the continental shelf.

**Behaviour** The few observations of pygmy sperm whales at sea suggest that they are sluggish animals, rising slowly to the surface, and blowing indistinctly. They may lie still in the water with the back and dorsal fin exposed, offering the opportunity for specific identification.

**Life history** The limited reproductive information gleaned from strandings indicates that females reach sexual maturity at lengths of 2.7-2.8m. Calves are born at about 1.2m in length after a gestation period of about 11 months. Suckling probably continues for at least a year, given that calves 2m long have stranded with lactating females. The fact that females are simultaneously lactating and pregnant suggests the potential for annual calving. Males become sexually mature at lengths of 2.7-3m.

**World population** These whales appear to be particularly common off the southeastern United States, where they are the second-most frequently stranded cetacean, and off the southern African coast, for reasons as yet unknown. There are no population estimates.

**Man's influence** Small numbers of pygmy sperm whales were killed by early whalers, and more recently by Japanese and Indonesian small whalers for food. However, these catch levels are unlikely to have influenced population levels. Of far greater concern is the current catch of these and other small cetaceans in gillnets, for example off Sri Lanka.

*Below: A pygmy sperm whale at a Florida marine park. The tiny underslung mouth, common to both Kogia species is just visible.*

# DWARF SPERM WHALE

*KOGIA SIMUS*

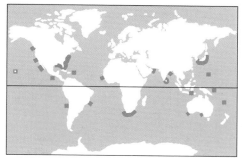

■ Strandings and sightings

**Classification** Although described by the English anatomist Owen in 1866, dwarf sperm whales were only accepted as a distinct species from *Kogia breviceps* a century later. Until then, a single variable species was recognized and consequently the identities of many early records are doubtful. The specific name, *simus*, refers to the distinctive snubbed snout of these whales.

**Description** These robust animals, the smallest of all the whales, attain a maximum length of 2.7m and a weight of about 210kg. They closely resemble pygmy sperm whales in their general form and are nearly identical in colour tones and patterns. However, in dwarf sperm whales the profile of the short snout becomes blunt and squarish in adults, and one or more short irregular grooves occur on the throat behind the tiny mouth, which is set with 7-12 teeth in each jawbone. Up to three pairs of teeth may be present at the tips of the upper jaws. The dorsal fin is tall and broad-based, with a concave trailing edge, resembling that of some dolphins.

**Recognition at sea** At sea, and at a distance, the squarish head and slow movements of dwarf sperm whales should prevent confusion with dolphins. At closer quarters, size, the form of the snout and head, and the colour pattern all distinguish this species from dolphins with elongate snouts, or blunt-headed species (such as Risso's and Irrawaddy dolphins), and pygmy killer and melon-headed whales.

Stranded dwarf sperm whales may be distinguished most readily from pygmy sperm whales on the snout-to-blowhole length (less than 10 percent of body length), as well as by differences in size and the dorsal fin.

**Habitat** As with pygmy sperm whales, stomach contents suggest that these whales inhabit the edge of the continental shelf and adjoining slope. Off South Africa, the distribution of dwarf sperm whales may be related to the mixed water region between the Agulhas and Benguela Currents, and the possible use of the Agulhas Bank as a nursery area.

**Distribution and migration** Dwarf sperm whales are widely, though sporadically, distributed through tropical and temperate seas. In the North Atlantic, there are records from Virginia to Texas, the Lesser Antilles and from Senegal. Numerous southern African records extend from the Atlantic coast to the Indian Ocean, where other records are known from Oman, Sri Lanka, India, Lomblen in Indonesia, and Western and South Australia. Similarly, Pacific specimens are limited to one or two records from Japan, Guam, New Caledonia, Canada, California, Mexico and northern Chile. These whales strand throughout the year in South Africa, suggesting that they are probably resident.

**Food and feeding** Dwarf sperm whales take prey very similar to that of pygmy sperm whales, though prey size is distinctly smaller, in keeping with the smaller mouth of this species. The depth distribution of prey suggests that foraging depths exceed 250m. Off South Africa, numerous tiny cuttlefishes are important prey for mothers with calves.

**Behaviour** The limited information available suggests that the behaviour of dwarf and pygmy sperm whales is similar. Strandings and observations suggest that groups, or pods, may include females with calves, immatures or sexually mature males and females, and usually contain fewer than 10 individuals. Japanese whalers report that these whales – and possibly pygmy sperm whales – defaecate when startled, before diving out of sight. Both species store a large volume of chocolate-brown faeces in the enlarged rectum, perhaps specifically to create a camouflage cloud when threatened. This suggestion gains credence from recent observations at sea of a mother and calf hiding themselves in a large faecal cloud when disturbed.

**Life history** Southern African animals of both sexes appear to reach sexual maturity at 2.1-2.2m in length. Calves are about 1m at birth, following a gestation period of about nine months. They are born over several months in summer and are suckled until at least 1.5m long. Nothing is known of the age at first breeding or of the interval between calves.

**World population** Information on the population size and distribution of this species is lacking, although stranding frequencies suggest that these whales are common off the southern tip of Africa. The scarcity of sightings does not necessarily infer that it is a rare species, given its apparent secretive lifestyle.

**Man's influence** Small numbers of this species were probably taken by early whalers, along with pygmy sperm whales, and a few have been killed in recent years by whalers in Japan and St. Vincent in the Caribbean. The effects of gillnet catches on populations of these whales is likely to be considerable, though very difficult to assess. Stranded animals removed to marine pools for rehabilitation have rarely survived more than a few days.

*Below: Very few dwarf sperm whales are seen at sea, partly because of their small size (smallest of all the whales) and partly because of their inconspicuous habits.*

# NARWHAL, BELUGA AND IRRAWADDY DOLPHIN

## MONODONTIDAE

John Gray of the British Museum created this family in 1821. Until recently, just two genera, each containing one living species, were considered to belong in the family. These are the narwhal (*Monodon monocerus*) and the beluga (*Delphinapterus leucas*). However, in 1973 the Japanese scientist Toshio Kasuya proposed the transfer of the genus *Orcaella*, represented by one existing species, the Irrawaddy dolphin (*O. brevirostris*), from the Delphinidae to this family. The new arrangement gained significant support, and has been adopted here.

Apart from similarities in skull structure, other more obvious characteristics are shared by two or all three of the species. The narwhal and beluga are very similar in size and shape, and lack a dorsal fin. This has been replaced by a tough, fibrous ridge just behind the midpoint of the body and is probably an adaptation to swimming under ice, as both necessarily do in their Arctic habitat. The flippers of these two species are small, rounded and

*A group of narwhals. Males of this species develop the celebrated unicorn-like tusk.*

tend to curl up at the ends in adulthood. Irrawaddy dolphins share with narwhals and belugas the ability to turn their heads in relation to the body, a rare characteristic in odontocetes and attributable to the fact that all, or almost all, the cervical vertebrae are unfused in these species. None have any throat grooves.

The beluga and Irrawaddy dolphin are the only two cetacean species that can significantly change the expression on their face. This somewhat endearing facility is probably functional in some way, perhaps in allowing them to use directed suction in feeding.

The fact that *Orcaella* is a tropical species has been used as an argument against the suggestion of recent common ancestry with the Arctic-dwelling *Delphinapterus* and *Monodon*. However, the fossil record indicates that both these genera have adapted to colder climates after originating in a more southerly region. It has been suggested that they may have become trapped during a cold period at some time within the last 12 million years and subsequently underwent rapid evolutionary changes.

# NARWHAL

*MONODON MONOCERUS*

■ Probable range

**Classification** There are close taxonomic similarities between the narwhal, the beluga (*Delphinapterus leucas*) and, to a lesser extent, the Irrawaddy dolphin (*Orcaella brevirostris*). There is some discussion about the degree of relatedness between these three species, but all workers place the narwhal in a family of its own, Monodontidae. *Monodon monoceros* means 'one tooth, one horn'.

**Local names** The Inuit peoples most familiar with this species each have their own name for it, including Kelleluak kakortok (Greenland) and quilalugaq (Canada). Countries speaking European languages use narwhal – either a derivative of the Norse for 'bloated corpse whale' (an assumed reference to the mottled coloration of both this species and a drowned man) or, possibly, from the proto-Germanic for 'whale with a narrow projection'.

**Description** The body shape is stocky, with no dorsal fin, short pectoral fins that become upturned in older animals (especially males), and tail flukes unlike those of any other species. The flukes change shape as the animal grows, with the lead-ing edge becoming increasingly concave and the trailing edge increasingly convex. The basic tail shape in adult males can be likened to a semicircle, with the curved edge rearmost.

Colour, too, changes with age. Calves are born a uniform grey or brownish grey, sometimes looking very light when viewed from the air. With increasing age, whitish patches develop on the underside, gradually increasing in size and extending onto the flanks. Meanwhile, the uniform coloration gives way to mottling of black or blackish brown on light grey. In old animals, the overall impression is often one of light grey, mottled with small dark patches, and a darker area around the face and blowhole extending in a dark line down the back. The lips protrude slightly, and the blowhole is near the centreline.

The famous tusk, responsible for the mythical stories of unicorns, is, in reality, a modified tooth. Several pairs of tooth buds are present in foetuses, but normally they all remain undeveloped except the foremost upper left tooth in males, which begins to grow forward through the upper lip. Very rarely, males may grow the righthand tooth into a tusk and females may grow one or even two tusks. Victorian museums often left visitors with entirely the wrong impression by exhibiting the two-tusked exceptions to the one-tusk rule. The tusk is always spiralled sinistrally (left-handed) when viewed from the root, but the cause of such spiralling is not yet understood. Tusks reach an average length of around 2m (maximum 3m) and weigh about 8kg (maximum 10.5kg) if unbroken.

The body length of Canadian animals is about 1.6m at birth and about 4.5-4.7m in males and 3.8-4.2m in females at physical maturity. Body weight is 80kg at birth rising to about 1.5-1.6 tonnes and 800-900kg in males and females respectively.

**Recognition at sea** Within its range, a narwhal can only really be confused with a beluga (see page 96), and then only when sighting conditions are poor. The blow is weak and usually inconspicuous. Animals in groups often surface simultaneously, breathing several times at short intervals before diving for 7-20 minutes while feeding. Migrational swimming is faster, shallower and characterized by shorter periods below the surface.

**Habitat** Narwhals occur in Arctic and subarctic waters, rarely far from ice. They may enter shallow bays and estuaries during the summer, but do so much less frequently than belugas and are more likely to be found in deep fiords.

**Distribution and migration** Narwhal distribution is discontinuous north circumpolar. They occur regularly from the central Canadian Arctic eastwards to central USSR, but are infrequent or rare in eastern Siberia, Alaska and the western Canadian Arctic. In most parts of their range, narwhals remain above the Arctic Circle all or most of the year and are rarely seen south of 60°N anywhere. Stragglers infrequently reach Europe and Newfoundland, and one recently even penetrated the eastern Mediterranean. Few are seen in winter because of the poor weather and lack of light. They must retreat in front of the advancing sea ice in October and may use areas of clear water in sea ice, called polynyas or savssats. Many probably overwinter in Davis Strait, Hudson Bay or Hudson Strait, the Greenland Sea, the Barents Sea and perhaps the Denmark Strait.

Migrations are forced on this species by the advance and retreat of sea ice in their favoured habitat. Thousands of animals are sometimes seen on the move in areas such as Lancaster Sound in Canada and Inglefield Fiord in West Greenland.

**Food and feeding** Narwhals eat mostly fish, squid and shrimps. Commonly taken fish species are Arctic cod (*Boreogadus*), Greenland halibut (*Reinhardtius*) and polar cod (*Arctogadus*). The major known squid prey is *Gonatus fabricii*. The variety of prey found in narwhal stomachs suggests diverse feeding behaviours at depths of up to hundreds of metres. The smooth tip to most tusks suggests that they are pushed inadver-

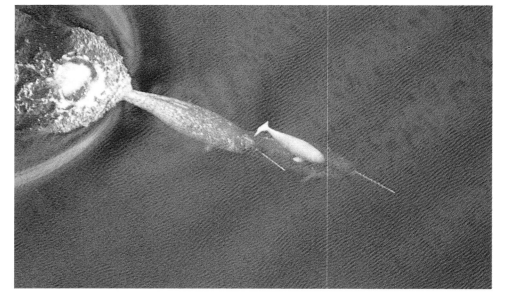

*Below left: Two adult male narwhals escort a young calf in the sheltered waters of Scoresbysund, East Greenland in August.*

*Above: A pod of male narwhals. The unique tusk is normally grown only by males and is actually an extended upper tooth.*

tently or deliberately through the bottom substrate and so could be used to 'flush' prey. However, since females and immatures have neither teeth nor tusk, feeding is clearly not dependent on them.

**Behaviour** Narwhals are usually seen in small groups of 2-10 animals, although often such groups are clearly moving as part of a much larger herd, numbering perhaps thousands of individuals, spread out over an area of many square kilometres. Mother/calf associations are very tight, and there is clear evidence of segregation by age and sex, both within the small groups and within sections of a larger herd. Narwhals and belugas often travel and feed together.

The role of the tusk in narwhal behaviour has been the subject of much conjecture and folklore. There have been suggestions that it is used for 'spearfishing', as an acoustic lance, for digging up the sea bottom and for attacking either predators or rivals. However, the evidence suggests that it is primarily used as a secondary sexual characteristic, much like the antlers of a deer. The larger body size of males suggests a polygynous mating system (i.e. each male mating with more than one female), which in turn implies rivalry between males. The tusk could be used as a visual display of rank, as a threat or, in the last resort, as a weapon. Tusk tips are sometimes found embedded in the head or even in the broken end of the tusk of captured narwhals, so duels may well take place. Males are fairly commonly seen engaging in what appears to be playful jousting, with tusks crossed at the surface. Apart from this, narwhals show very little above-water activity.

Narwhal vocalizations are, unusually, mostly narrow-band pulses from 1.5kHz to at least 24kHz. Scientists have recorded both rapidly repeated clicks of up to 300 per second (probably used for echolocation) and longer tones of up to 0.1 second duration (probably used for communication). Characteristic pulsed tones are repeated often, perhaps being used for individual recognition.

**Life history** Females become sexually mature at 5-8 years of age (at an average length of 3.4m), and males at 11-13 years (average 3.9m). Pregnancy lasts 14-15 months and lactation about 20 months. Conceptions, and thus births, are seasonal, with calving occurring in July-August at the height of summer. Most mature females produce a calf every three years, but 20 percent do so every two years. About seven calves are born annually per 100 head of population. Age determination in narwhals is difficult, because layers of dentine or cementum are not laid down regularly in the tusk or unerupted teeth. The best estimate of natural lifespan is about 50 years.

Apart from man, the only predators of narwhals are killer whales and polar bears, but such losses are probably small in relation to population size.

**World population** There are probably at least four geographically distinct stocks of narwhals, but a fairly good estimate of size exists for only one. The high-Arctic Canadian/Greenlandic stock, or stocks, summer in an area stretching from the central Canadian Arctic (around Somerset Island) to Inglefield Fiord in West Greenland. It seems likely that at least 20,000-30,000 summer in the Canadian sector and at least 4,000 in the Greenlandic sector; 1,200 animals were counted in northern Hudson Bay.

Estimates for stocks in East Greenland/ Svalbard and northwestern Europe to Siberia are inadequate, but must amount to at least several thousand.

**Man's influence** Narwhals are prized by Inuit hunters, primarily for their tusks and their skin. The tusks provide a valuable source of revenue from sales to tourists and collectors. The very thick skin, known locally as muktuk or mattak, is considered a delicacy, being traditionally eaten raw with a thin layer of adherent fat. Narwhals are hunted from ice, boats or traditional kayaks in Canada and Greenland. They are either shot and then harpooned, leading to considerable losses (as more animals are wounded than recovered), or harpooned and then shot, as in Greenland. Recent annual hunting levels have been about 300-550 in Canada, 500 in West Greenland and 60 in East Greenland. Figures for hunting elsewhere are not known. Earlier catches from the high-Arctic stock were sometimes very large and must have depleted the stock. At one time, Canadian catches alone amounted to about 3,000 animals per year, and occasionally large numbers are trapped and killed at savssats. Some 2,000 narwhals were killed in a series of savssats near Disko Bay, Greenland, in the winter of 1914/15.

Few narwhals have been kept in captivity. Seven recent examples all died within four months of capture.

# BELUGA

*DELPHINAPTERUS LEUCAS*

Known range

**Classification** The beluga was first described by the German naturalist Peter Pallas during a visit to northern Russia in the late eighteenth century. The name he gave it, *Delphinus leucas* ('white dolphin'), did not acknowledge the significant differences between this species and dolphins of the family Delphinidae, and it was later placed in a new genus, *Delphinapterus* ('dolphin without wings'), to reflect its lack of a dorsal fin. Although there is some variation in body size between stocks, no subspecies are recognized.

**Local names** Most names refer to the beluga's unique colour. 'White whale' is as common in English as beluga, the latter being a derivative of its name in Russian – belukha – again meaning 'white whale'. Old whalers used the name 'sea canary', a reference to the extraordinary vocal noise made by these animals above and below water.

**Description** This small whale has an average body length of about 4-4.5m (maximum 5.5m) in males and 3-3.5m (maximum 4.1m) in females, variable between geographically discrete populations. Body weight is normally 1-1.5 tonnes in adult males and 0.4-1 tonne in females. After the first year, males are larger than females of the same age. At most times of year, body colour is pure white in adults, becoming distinctly tinged with yellow for a period before the summer moult, when the yellow skin is sloughed off. Newborn calves are dark grey, sometimes brownish grey, but this dark coloration gradually fades during the immature years, becoming successively lighter grey until, at about four to five years, there is just a bluish tinge to the white. All animals are white by 12 years of age and some by the age of five. Females become white before males of the same age and may have their first calf before becoming totally white.

This is a stocky species, with no dorsal fin and characteristically shaped, deeply notched tail flukes. The head is small and

rounded, the lips and bulbous melon becoming more obvious with age. The neck is unfused and thus surprisingly flexible. The body is very muscular and supple, the skin rough, with ridges and scars. A dorsal ridge, accentuated in adult males, replaces the absent dorsal fin and is very tough and fibrous. In adult males, the rounded flippers become upward-curving, the shoulders are 'squarer' and the head is longer and more prominent than in the female.

There are usually nine pairs of conical teeth in the upper jaw and eight pairs in the lower. They wear fast, becoming flattened and short in older animals.

**Recognition at sea** Within its range, an immature can perhaps be mistaken for a narwhal, but then only at a distance. Normally, and especially in a group, this species can be confused with no other. Belugas are normally slow-swimming and spend a large proportion of the time at or near the water surface. Sustained speeds of up to 4.8kph have been measured over periods of many hours. The blow is low and often indistinct, but it can be heard at a range of several hundred metres on a calm day. The respiration sequence varies according to activity and water depth, but the normal 'roll' lasts two to three seconds. When pursued, belugas can exhale just underwater and inhale in a fraction of a second, so that hardly any part of the body shows above the surface.

**Habitat** With the exception of a few stragglers and one small population in the Gulf of St Lawrence, eastern Canada, this is exclusively an Arctic or subarctic species. In summer, it seeks out shallow coastal waters and estuaries, but in winter the animals are usually found offshore along the ice-edge. Belugas are essentially marine, but can withstand prolonged periods of days or weeks in fresh or brackish waters.

**Distribution and migration** The distribution is north circumpolar, occurring seasonally in most ice-free Arctic areas. Belugas are creatures of the ice-edge, patiently waiting for the sea ice to break up in July before immediately occupying their summer quarters. In autumn, forced to abandon these areas as the new ice forms, they retreat to ice-free winter quarters. As such, they are one of the few toothed whales known to follow a rigid, annual migration. An example is the stock that spends July and August in the high-Arctic region of Canada, particu-

larly Lancaster Sound and Prince Regent Inlet. When this area freezes over in autumn, the animals move eastwards, probably to winter in the ice-free parts of the Davis Strait, near the west coast of Greenland. In some years, a proportion of the stock may remain at very high lati-

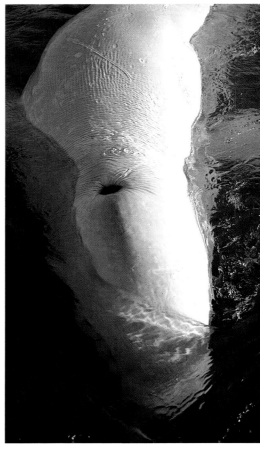

tudes all year round. There are 19 tentatively recognized stocks based on summering areas. Very little direct evidence has been gathered about migration, and much remains speculative. In reality, some 'stocks' may be part of the same genetic population.

**Food and feeding** Existing records point to a very broad variety of prey items, including fish, molluscs and other bottom-living invertebrates, and zooplankton. All the stocks examined seem to feed mainly on fish of many types and sizes, and it is likely that fish provide the staple diet in all areas. The structure of the mouth and teeth would seem best suited to this. Younger animals often take smaller prey items than adults, and it has been suggested that they may forage using suction to draw invertebrates into the mouth. The ability to change the shape of the lips, a feature shared only with the Irrawaddy dolphin, might allow this method of food gathering.

**Behaviour** Belugas are very social animals, rarely seen alone and sometimes coming together into groups of many thousands. The tightest social unit is a mother and her most recent offspring, usually one to three in number. Maternal care is prolonged over several years and mothers may aggressively defend their young against predators. Small, tight-knit groups of up to 15 animals are usual, typically consisting either of males, or mothers and their dark offspring. These associations are still recognizable when hundreds of animals are packed tightly into the mouths of rivers in summer. In Soviet waters, the all-male groups may be much larger, up to 500 animals. On migration, or when moving between estuaries in summer, belugas may travel in loose aggregations extending over 10km or more. Adults have been seen ahead of migrating groups, seemingly exploring a passage through pack ice.

Normally, belugas are not active above the water surface. In the estuaries and river mouths that they occupy in some areas in summer, however, they become very playful and noisy both above and below the surface. The movement into these areas does not appear to be associated with feeding, but may confer a temperature advantage on newborn calves. The most obvious activity linked with this movement seems to be moulting of the skin, which grows extremely quickly at this time of year. Animals swim into shallow water, sometimes stranding themselves temporarily, and begin to scratch and rub on the gravel or sand bottom. While doing so, they vocalize with a bewildering variety of squeaks, whistles and belches. They slap the water

*Above: During the summer, belugas of some stocks are attracted to estuaries and inlets, where they moult their outer layer of skin by rubbing against the substrate in shallow water. In this photograph, taken in the Canadian Arctic, an adult is vigorously rubbing and splashing in the midst of a typically large group.*

*Left: Head and foreparts of an adult beluga, clearly showing the rough skin characteristic of this extraordinary species.*

*Right: Belugas usually travel in groups, sometimes of up to several thousand animals. At times, they can be seen in great density awaiting the summer break up of the Arctic sea ice, perhaps in the company of narwhals, which share their range.*

with the tail and flippers and raise the tail and head clear of the surface. This frenzy of activity is often interrupted by 'panic flights', after which the animals slowly reassemble and start again.

Belugas have a very effective echolocation system, producing broad-band pulses in a narrow beam from the forehead. Animals may approach closely to a strange object, such as a hydrophone used for recording them, interrogating it with rapid bursts of sound.

In captivity, belugas have been trained to dive to 650m and remain submerged for 15 minutes. The only record of deep diving in a wild animal was of an adult female, equipped with a pressure-sensing device, which dived to 320m and remained there, probably feeding, for over five minutes. The swim back to the surface was at a steady rate of 2.1m/sec, and the total dive time was over 12 minutes.

**Life history** Females probably reach sexual maturity at about five years of age (range four to seven), males at eight years (range eight to nine). Females in a Canadian population are reported to cease reproduction at about 21 years, producing a maximum of six calves in their lifetime. The mating season is in late winter or spring; late February-early April off Alaska, and May in eastern Canada. Gestation lasts about 14-14.5 months, so calves are born in spring or summer (April-September in various populations). Calves are born at an average length of 1.6m and a weight of about 79kg. They grow rapidly, establishing a thick layer of blubber to protect them from an environment that may rarely be more than a few degrees above freezing all year round. Lactation is thought to last 20-24 months, but the quantity of milk produced in the second year probably declines as the youngster takes more solid food and the mother becomes physiologically prepared for the next pregnancy. The interval between births is normally three years, and every year 5-13 calves are born per 100 animals in the various stocks of animals.

Teeth begin erupting in the second year of life. It seems that belugas probably lay down two pairs of growth layers in the teeth every year, rather than the one pair that is usual in toothed whales. If so, the evidence of tooth reading suggests that they have a normal lifespan of 25-35 years. In addition to the threat from killer whales faced by most small cetaceans, belugas may be killed by polar bears or even walruses. Polar bears can stand in shallow water and attack the

*Above: Belugas have unusually soft, flexible blubber on the face and head. They are able to change their facial expression, and the forehead, overlying the melon, can visibly resonate when they are echolocating.*

whales as they swim past or, more successfully, take advantage of belugas trapped in polynyas (ice-free areas of water in sea ice) or stranded by the tide in shallow estuaries.

**World population** The accuracy of population estimates for belugas is relatively good because of their coastal and ice-edge habitat and grouping behaviour. The total world population has been estimated at 49,000-69,000. This is divided into the following regions: Bering Sea/Chukchi Sea (25,000-30,000), Hudson Bay/James Bay (9,000), High-Arctic Canada and West Greenland (10,000-19,000), Spitzbergen (5,000-10,000), and Gulf of St Lawrence (300-500).

**Man's influence** Belugas have been hunted by Arctic native peoples for more than a thousand years and the resultant mortality was probably sustainable indefinitely. Unfortunately, the arrival of large, non-native whaling expeditions in the Arctic heralded huge catches that certainly could not be sustained. Two examples serve to illustrate the seriousness of this intensive hunting. In 1871, whalers from one Norwegian town, Tromsø, took 2,167 belugas from Spitz-

bergen and Novaya Zemlya, and between 1874 and 1911, Scottish whalers took 11,000 belugas in Elwin Bay, on Somerset Island in the Canadian high Arctic. Catches in the USSR from 1900 to 1960 averaged 3,000-4,000 a year.

Current catching is at a lower level, but may still pose a significant threat to depleted stocks. The Greenlandic catch has been stable for over a century, at 400-1,000 animals per year. Canadian natives take about 600-1,000 belugas a year, Alaskans about 200-300, and USSR natives took an average of 420 in the period 1970-1980. More are killed and lost. Almost half the catches on discrete stocks of belugas may exceed the stock's ability to replace its losses.

The stock most in danger is that of the Gulf of St. Lawrence, in eastern Canada. It now numbers about 500-700 animals and is apparently suffering badly from disturbance, shipping accidents and the effects of chemical pollution, which may be causing illness and premature death. Human disturbance elsewhere is also causing concern, particularly oil exploration off Alaska and hydroelectric plants on rivers used for calving.

Belugas have been kept successfully in captivity for several decades, and appear better able to adapt to confinement than most small cetaceans. Recent moves to capture more animals from the wild off Baffin Island, Canada, have been blocked by anti-captivity campaigners.

# IRRAWADDY DOLPHIN

## ORCAELLA BREVIROSTRIS

■ Possible range

**Classification** This little-known dolphin was recognized as a distinct species by Sir Richard Owen on the basis of a skull collected from the Bay of Bengal in the 1860s and given the genus name *Orcaella* (from the Latin word for whale) by John Gray of the British Museum. Owen's specific name, *brevirostris*, from the Latin for short beak, is very appropriate for this blunt-headed animal. The species shows some characteristics of the dolphin family Delphinidae, but externally is most similar to the beluga.

**Local names** This dolphin is known as pesut, pesut mahakam or lumbalumba.

**Description** The body colour is grey, darker above and lighter below. The small, slightly falcate dorsal fin lies just behind the midpoint of the body, which narrows to a slim tail stock that bears broad, notched flukes. The flippers are relatively long and the blowhole is set to the left of the midline. The rounded, blunt head has no beak and a changeable facial expression. There are 15-18 peglike teeth on each side of the lower jaw and 17-20 on each side of the upper. Only two neck vertebrae are fused, allowing the head to move freely. Body length is about 2.15-2.75m in adults, with males probably slightly larger than females. Body weight is typically 90-150kg.

**Recognition at sea** This slow-swimming, inconspicuous dolphin is likely to be confused only with the finless porpoise or the dugong, with which it shares part of its range, but from which it can be distinguished by the presence of a dorsal fin. Typical surfacing characteristics are short dives of 30-60 seconds, followed by three respirations in quick succession. The longest dive recorded lasted 12 minutes.

**Habitat** The Irrawaddy dolphin is a warmwater species, found only in the tropics and subtropics, mostly in shallow coastal waters. Nevertheless, some animals probably live all their lives in fresh water and they occur in many major river systems, reputedly as far as 1300km from the sea.

**Distribution and migration** This species is restricted to the coasts and rivers of Southeast Asia and northern Australasia within 25° of latitude of the equator, and from about 80°E to 150°E longitude. Our poor knowledge of it is well illustrated by the fact that it was first discovered in Australia as recently as 1948, when anthropologists found it in the diet of aborigines. The range shown on the map assumes a continuity of distribution between sites of confirmed reports.

**Food and feeding** The few specimens examined to date indicate that their staple diet is fish but, in Australian coastal waters at least, cephalopods seem to be a common prey. Crustaceans and other invertebrates probably form a significant part of the diet in some areas. It seems to feed in midwater and on the bottom.

**Behaviour** Usually, Irrawaddy dolphins are seen in small groups of up to six animals, but very occasionally up to 15. In rivers, individual animals may hold mutually exclusive home ranges and can become quite tame. This species is not known for its above-water activity, but it has been seen spy hopping, tail slapping and jumping. Its preferred habitat precludes deep dives. Only one mass stranding, of three animals, has been reported.

Captive animals are apparently playful and, in common only with the beluga, can 'pucker' their lips and shoot a directed jet of water from the mouth. Recordings of vocalizations from captive animals consist of pulsed, regularly spaced sounds lasting only 25-30 microseconds at a frequency of around 60kHz.

**Life history** The mating season is probably spring and early summer and, based on very few captive records, the gestation period is probably about 14 months. Calves are born at a length of about 0.9-1m and a weight of 12.5kg. One captive youngster was weaned by two years of age. In a sample of 18 Irrawaddy dolphins from northern Australia, up to 28 pairs of layers were counted in the teeth, so the species is probably capable of living to at least 30 years. Adult body size is attained at four to six years of age.

**World population** Details are scarce. There is no indication that this species is currently under any serious threat, although its habitat is vulnerable to dams and other human disturbance.

**Man's influence** Because of their coastal and riverine habitat, Irrawaddy dolphins often come into contact with man. They seem to be killed for food in only a small part of their range, but often become entrapped in fishing nets and even in anti-shark nets in northern Australia. Fishermen in Kampuchea and Vietnam are said to regard them as sacred and use them to drive fish into nets.

These dolphins have been kept in several captive facilities in Southeast Asia, where breeding has been successful. They are said to take well to captivity and prove easy to train.

*Below: Irrawaddy dolphins adapt well to, and have bred in, captive conditions. This photo was taken at Jakarta Aquarium.*

# BEAKED AND BOTTLENOSE WHALES
## ZIPHIIDAE

This family, established by John Gray in 1865, includes 18 known living species of medium-sized toothed whales (4.5-13m in length) and probably one or two more that have yet to be described. Five genera are now recognized: *Berardius* (two species), *Tasmacetus* (one species), *Ziphius* (one species), *Hyperoodon* (two species) and *Mesoplodon* (12 species).

The family members are characterized by having a lower jaw that extends at least to the tip of the upper jaw, a shallow or non-existent notch between the tail flukes, a dorsal fin set well back on the body, three or four fused cervical vertebrae, extensive skull asymmetry and two conspicuous throat grooves forming a 'V' pattern. Additionally, all but Shepherd's and Gray's beaked whales (*Tasmacetus shepherdi* and *Mesoplodon grayi*) have only two (genus *Mesoplodon*) or four (genus *Berardius*) teeth, located in the lower jaw. The shape and position of these teeth are very diagnostic and may

be the only characteristic by which species can be positively identified, even when beached.

All 18 species are animals of the open, deep ocean, and almost nothing is known about their seasonal movements. Most are known from strandings and a very few, if any, confirmed sightings at sea. Though many beaked whales have a wide distribution, they must be thinly scattered and in very few places can any species be considered common.

The reduced number of teeth in this group is characteristic of squid-catchers, and indeed the little knowledge that we have of their diets does suggest that all species are primarily or exclusively consumers of cephalopods. Evidence from the stomachs of carcasses, and from recorded dive times and the physiology of the animals suggests that they are very deep divers, perhaps even rivalling sperm whales in this respect.

*The birth of a straptoothed beaked whale. Adult males of this little-known animal have teeth that prevent the mouth being fully opened.*

# BAIRD'S BEAKED WHALE

*BERARDIUS BAIRDII*

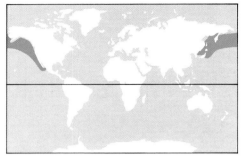

■ Probable range

**Classification** This species is named after Spencer F. Baird, a nineteenth-century American naturalist who served as Secretary of the Smithsonian Institution.

**Local names** The local name for this whale in Japan is tsuchi-kujira; tsuchi is an old-fashioned wooden hammer shaped like a bottle. The people of Chiba prefecture, where most whaling for this species has taken place, call it tsuchimbo. Whalers on the west coast of North America generally referred to it simply as the bottlenose whale.

**Description** These are the largest members of the Ziphiidae. Maximum documented length is 12.8m for females and 11.9m for males. An 11.1m female weighed slightly over 11 tonnes. The most arresting feature of this whale is its long, sturdy beak, clearly set off from a bulging forehead. The lower jaw extends appreciably farther forward than the upper, causing the front pair of erupted teeth in the lower jaw of adults to be readily visible even when the mouth is closed. The pair of throat grooves begin far forward on the beak and diverge widely behind it, extending to the angle of the mouth. There can be one or several rudimentary longitudinal furrows between the two main grooves. The centre of the rear margin of the broad flukes can have a shallow notch, a slight bulge or neither.

The flippers and dorsal fin appear proportionately small on these long-bodied animals. The low-profile dorsal fin, usually with a blunt peak, is set more than two-thirds back along the body.

The colour pattern is rather drab in comparison to those of some other ziphiids. Generally, the body is uniformly slate grey, often appearing dark brown or even black at sea. Young individuals are generally paler than adults. There are irregular spots and blotches of white on the undersides, primarily on the throat, between the flippers and at the umbilicus. Adults are always covered with long pairs of parallel scratches made

by the teeth of companions, and many have scars from bites of killer whales and cookiecutter sharks.

There are two pairs of teeth at the front of the lower jaw, the forward pair considerably larger than the hind pair. Both pairs erupt through the gums in adult males and females, although the back pair erupts only late in life. The exposed front pair of teeth can be heavily infested with whale lice (cyamid amphipods) and stalked barnacles.

**Recognition at sea** When encountered in pods, these large beaked whales can be distinguished from other ziphiids by their greater adult size, as well as by the long beak with the white teeth showing at the front of the lower jaw. Their behaviour while rafting and blowing at the surface between dives may initially call sperm whales to mind. However, the dorsal fin and rounded head, once seen, should eliminate that possibility. It is particularly important to distinguish Baird's beaked whales from the bottlenose whales, probably southern bottlenose whales, found from the equator to as far north in the western Pacific as the vicinity of Okinawa. The latter are somewhat smaller and have a less pronounced beak, a bluffer forehead and a generally taller, more pointed and more prominent dorsal fin. Also, adult southern bottlenose whales have a pale head demarcated from the body by a dark 'collar'.

**Habitat** In the western Pacific, this whale's distribution seems to be influenced by the interplay of the warm surface Kuroshio Current and the Oyashio Current. In a study off central California, sightings appeared to be related to a warmwater gyre. However, in

the Sea of Okhotsk, Baird's beaked whales are often seen in areas with very little open water between ice floes.

Sightings reported by Japanese observers in the central North Pacific are unsubstantiated, and most scientists agree that Baird's beaked whales are more or less restricted to waters of the continental slope and to areas where seamounts bring the ocean floor to within several thousand metres of the surface.

**Distribution and migration** The Baird's beaked whale is confined to the North Pacific Ocean, where it inhabits temperate and subarctic waters from about 34°N in the west and 24°N in the east to the ice-edge in the Bering and Okhotsk seas (at about 60°N). Strandings have occurred at St. Matthew Island and Pribilof Islands, and there are many records around the Aleutian and Commander Islands.

The distribution and migrations of Baird's beaked whale have only been studied closely off Japan, where a shore-based commercial fishery has operated in Chiba prefecture since 1612. It has been suggested that separate populations inhabit the Sea of Japan, the Sea of Okhotsk and the western North Pacific off Japan. The last of these populations appears to migrate along the continental slope (1,000-3,000m depths) in association with the cold subsurface Oyashio Current. Whales begin to arrive off the Boso Peninsula (at about 35°N) in early summer (May-June) and move gradually northward, reaching a peak of abundance off

*Below: Members of a pod of Baird's beaked whales often surface together. Baird's are the largest of the beaked whale family.*

*Above right: An unusual overhead view of an adult of the species, with the two lower front teeth showing prominently.*

bottom, in depths of more than 2,400m. Whales rarely spend more than five minutes at the surface before diving. Members of a pod usually surface together and raft much like sperm whales between dives. They are usually wary and difficult to approach.

An interesting feature of the catches of Baird's beaked whales in all three catching areas around Japan, as well as off British Columbia, is the predominance of males. It is unclear whether this situation is due to segregation in the population or to a characteristic of their behaviour that makes males easier to catch than females.

**Life history** Females become sexually mature, on average, at about 10.5m in length, males at 10m, when they are 8-10 years old. The peak season for calving is March-April; for pairing, October-November. Thus, the gestation period is estimated to be about 17 months. These whales are about 4.5m long at birth.

The greatest estimated ages (based on tooth growth layers) are 82 years for males and 39 years for females. The figure for males suggests this species is one of the longer-lived cetaceans.

**World population** In 1984, the population off the Pacific coast of Japan was estimated to be at least 4,220 whales. This conservative estimate applies only to a limited area. Stock units proposed for the western North Pacific (discussed under *Distribution and migration*) are based on the distribution and seasonality of catches. There is no direct evidence (e.g. tag-recapture data) about stock identity in this species.

**Man's influence** Baird's beaked whale has been exploited most intensively in Japan, where catches reached as high as 322 in 1952. The people of Chiba prefecture are particularly fond of the meat. The annual Japanese catch averaged 39 whales during 1972-81, and since 1983 the fishery has been governed by a national catch quota of 40 whales. It is generally felt that this level of catch is sustainable.

Reported catches by Soviet whalers, mainly near the Kuril Islands, totalled 176 from 1933 to 1974. The two shore stations in central California took 15 between 1956 and 1971, and the station on Vancouver Island, 24 between 1948 and 1967. Baird's beaked whales have been virtually unexploited in the eastern North Pacific since the United States and Canada ceased whaling in the late 1960s and early 1970s.

Given its wide distribution and relatively light exploitation, Baird's beaked whale is in no immediate danger.

Hokkaido (42-43°N) in October-November. Their winter (December-May) distribution is unknown. In the Sea of Japan, they have been caught mainly during the summer in Tobayama Bay (at about 37°N) and off southern Hokkaido (41-42°N); in the Sea of Okhotsk, mainly off Abashiri (at about 44°N). All three areas have deep water (deeper than 1,000m) close to shore. Baird's beaked whales are abundant in the northern Sea of Okhotsk in April-May, in water less than 500m deep.

Off central California, Baird's beaked whales are most common in midsummer (July) and autumn (September-October); off Vancouver Island, in July and August. The pattern in the eastern North Pacific suggests seasonal movements inshore and offshore rather than north-south.

Another centre of abundance is along the Emperor Seamounts which extend northwestward from the western extremity of the Hawaiian chain. Baird's beaked whale has not been reliably identified near the Hawaiian islands, however.

**Food and feeding** Baird's beaked whales feed mainly on bottom-dwelling organisms at depths of 1,000-3,000m. They eat medium-sized squid, skates, octopuses, crustaceans and deepwater fish. The frequent presence of pebbles in their stomachs, and scarring on the upper jaw and melon, have been taken as evidence that they feed on the ocean floor. Pelagic fishes, such as mackerel, sardines and sauries, also figure in their diet.

**Behaviour** This is a moderately social species. Groups of up to 50 individuals have been reported, although groups of about 5-20 are more common. The blow is low and bushy but easily detected in calm seas. The bulging melon and front part of the beak often jut above the surface as the animal blows.

These whales are deep divers, often remaining submerged for periods in excess of 20 minutes. The maximum dive time is more than an hour. Whalers report that harpooned whales dive straight to the

# ARNOUX'S BEAKED WHALE

*BERARDIUS ARNUXII*

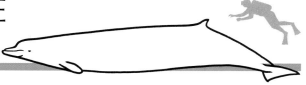

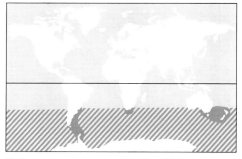

■ Known range   ⁄⁄ Possible range

**Classification** The genus *Berardius* is named after the French commander of the vessel that carried the type specimen from New Zealand to France in 1846; Arnoux was the ship's surgeon on the same vessel.

**Description** Maximum documented length is 9.75m; females are probably slightly larger than males. In appearance, Arnoux's beaked whale closely resembles Baird's beaked whale, but it is about 20 percent smaller. At sea, the body may appear light brown, with the head region noticeably lighter. Adult males can be heavily scarred on the dorsal surface, mainly with long single or paired rake marks attributed to the teeth of other Arnoux's beaked whales.

There are two pairs of teeth near the tip of the lower jaw. The front ones are noticeably larger, with triangular crowns. These four teeth erupt through the gum in both males and females, and are exposed outside the closed mouth.

**Recognition at sea** Viewed at sea, Arnoux's beaked whale is difficult to distinguish from the southern bottlenose whale (page 108). As a result, many sightings in the Antarctic are logged simply as records of 'unidentified beaked whales'.

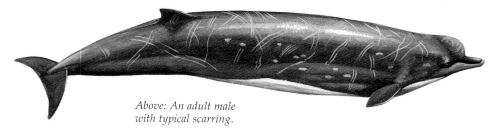

*Above: An adult male with typical scarring.*

**Distribution and migration** This species probably has a circumpolar distribution in deep offshore waters of the southern oceans south of the Tropic of Capricorn (23.5°S). Most records are from south of 40°S. Judging by the frequency of strandings, Arnoux's beaked whales are relatively abundant in the Cook Strait region of New Zealand during the summer. It has been suggested that births may occur during the summer in the Australasian region. A large proportion of sightings are from the Tasman Sea and near Albatross Cordillera in the South Pacific.

**Behaviour** Group size may average 6-10 individuals, although aggregations of as many as 80 whales have been reported.

# SHEPHERD'S BEAKED WHALE

*TASMACETUS SHEPHERDI*

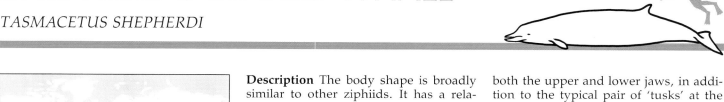

■ Strandings   ☐ Probable sighting

**Classification** The scientific names of this species refer to the Tasman Sea, the origin of the type specimen, and its collector (in 1933), Mr. G. Shepherd, a museum curator from New Zealand.

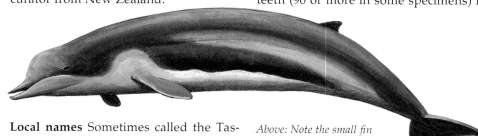

**Local names** Sometimes called the Tasman whale or Tasman beaked whale.

*Above: Note the small fin and flippers of this whale.*

**Description** The body shape is broadly similar to other ziphiids. It has a relatively steep forehead and a long, well-defined beak. The flippers are proportionately small, and the dorsal fin is small and moderately falcate. There is no notch between the flukes. Maximum recorded lengths are 6.6m (female) and 7m (male).

In general, the body is dark above and light below, with the top of the head possibly lighter than the back. The beak, flippers, dorsal fin and flukes are dark. There appears to be a lateral striping pattern, with two dark diagonal bands extending from the dark dorsal field onto the lighter flanks and belly.

Shepherd's beaked whale has many teeth (90 or more in some specimens) in both the upper and lower jaws, in addition to the typical pair of 'tusks' at the front of the lower jaw. These tusks erupt only in males. The beak is more pointed than those of other ziphiids.

**Habitat** Shepherd's beaked whale may be a deep and lengthy diver that lives well away from coasts.

**Distribution and migration** Although the distribution may be circumpolar in cold-temperate latitudes of the southern oceans, specimens have been recorded only from New Zealand, Australia, central Argentina, Tierra del Fuego and Beagle Channel, and Isla Juan Fernandez, Chile (33°S). More than half the strandings and the only (probable) sighting have occurred in New Zealand.

**Food and feeding** The stomach contents of a whale stranded in Argentina consisted mainly of fish remains, identified as *Merluccius hubbsi*, an unidentified serranid and an unidentified brotulid. It was inferred from these that the whale had fed at the bottom in fairly deep water.

# CUVIER'S BEAKED WHALE

*ZIPHIUS CAVIROSTRIS*

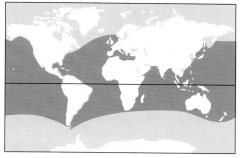

■ Maximum range

**Classification** The generic name *Ziphius* comes from the Greek *xiphos* for 'sword'. The specific name *cavirostris* is derived from the Latin *cavus* for 'hollow' and *rostrum* for 'beak' and refers to a basin on the skull just in front of the nostrils.

**Local names** An often-used alternate name for this whale is goose-beaked whale, owing to the shape of the head and mouthline in front of the eyes. In Japan, it is called akabo-kujira ('baby-face whale'), or in Chiba prefecture, kajippo.

**Description** The maximum documented length is just over 7.5m (females) and 7m (males). A female just over 6.5m long weighed close to 3 tonnes. This whale resembles other ziphiids in having a pair of throat grooves forming a forward-pointing 'V', a laterally compressed body, small flippers that fit into shallow depressions along the body and a relatively small, falcate dorsal fin. The beak is not well demarcated from the melon, and the mouthline is curved at the back to give the hint of a smile. There is sometimes a shallow notch between the flukes.

The pigmentation pattern varies. Differences may reflect an individual's sex, age or geographical race. Young are generally brown to grey, with the head and belly often paler than the rest of the body. With age, the head and nape, especially of males, become lighter and eventually mostly white. The basic body colour of adults has been described as tan, light brown, acorn brown or gunmetal blue. In bright sunlight, the skin can have a reddish cast. Swirls and brush strokes of pigmentation, as well as white linear toothrake scars and oval scars (probably from cookiecutter sharks), give each adult its own individually distinctive coloration. A common adult pattern is for the eyes to be noticeably darker, with crescent-shaped darker markings in front and behind.

The two conical teeth, situated at the front of the lower jaw, do not normally erupt in females. The more massive, erupted teeth of adult males are exposed even when the mouth is closed.

**Recognition at sea** Cuvier's beaked whales might be confused with various other beaked whales. The sloping forehead and short beak, in combination with the pale or white head and exposed tusks of adult males, should enable experienced observers to distinguish Cuvier's from similar species.

**Habitat** These are deepwater whales that are rarely seen in coastal waters, except in areas with a narrow shelf. Off the Pacific and Sea of Okhotsk coasts of Japan, catches tend to be concentrated along, or seaward of, the 1,000m contour.

**Distribution and migration** Cuvier's beaked whales are among the most wide-ranging and abundant of the ziphiids. They occur in all but the polar seas. In Japan, Hawaii and New Zealand at least, Cuvier's beaked whales are present all year round. No migrations are known.

**Food and feeding** Stomach contents suggest that these whales subsist principally on squid and deepsea fish.

**Behaviour** These whales are usually found alone (mainly adult males) or in small groups of two to seven individuals. They are said to dive for periods lasting at least 40 minutes, and their blows are low and inconspicuous. These characteristics might help to explain the infrequency of sightings. However, in Hawaiian waters at least, they sometimes approach and inspect boats, thus allowing themselves to be closely observed. At the surface, these whales appear to lurch forward, often thrusting the chin above the water. They apparently breach occasionally. The flukes are not normally lifted above the surface at the beginning of a dive. Most strandings are of single animals.

**Life history** Females can become pregnant at a body length of 5.1m or less, but the mean length at sexual maturity is probably somewhat greater. Most males 5.5m or longer are sexually mature. Length at birth is about 2.7m. The maximum documented age is about 62 years.

**Man's influence** Japan is the only area where a direct fishery has been maintained over a series of years. The annual catch from 1965 through 1970 ranged from 13 to 60 animals. There is no clear evidence that over-exploitation occurred. During recent years, the reported catch by Japan has been negligible. Cuvier's beaked whales have also been caught occasionally in other cetacean fisheries, such as that at St. Vincent, Lesser Antilles. Reports suggest that they have been shot as targets by French and Spanish military vessels in the Mediterranean.

The frequency of incidental taking is uncertain, but given its wide distribution and probable overall abundance, it seems unlikely that Cuvier's beaked whale is in any immediate danger.

*Below: Cuvier's beaked whale is one of the most widespread and abundant of all the ziphiid family. It is often stranded.*

# NORTHERN BOTTLENOSE WHALE

*HYPEROODON AMPULLATUS*

■ Probable range

**Classification** The name *Hyperoodon* is something of a misnomer, as it derives from the old Greek *hyperoe* meaning 'above' and *odontos*, 'a tooth', and refers to observations of a skull with tiny vestigial teeth in the upper jaw and no exposed teeth in the lower jaw. The specific name is more apt, as it comes from the Latin *ampulla*, meaning 'flask', and refers to the bottlelike shape of the head.

**Local names** Norwegians who hunted this species call it bottlenosen or andehval. The German or Dutch name butskopf means 'steephead'. In Greenland, the northern bottlenose whale is known as anarnaq; in Iceland, as andhvaler.

**Description** Males reach a maximum length of 9.8m, females 8.7m. Unlike most ziphiids, males are consistently larger than females.

The head shape is this whale's most distinctive external feature. Females and juveniles have a rounded forehead that is not particularly well defined from the moderately long beak. The forehead of males becomes increasingly bluff with age. In old males, the front surface of the forehead is flat and it overhangs the beak. In fact, British whalers called these old males 'flatheads' because of their squarish profile. The dorsal fin is prominent and falcate, with a pointed peak. The rear margin of the flukes has no notch, and there is the usual pair of throat grooves.

Calves appear grey to brown on the back, greyish white ventrally. Adults are darker dorsally than ventrally, brown to grey, with a blotchy or mottled appearance on some individuals. The dorsal fin is darker than the rest of the back, and the melon and face are lighter than the rest of the body. In old males particularly, the front part of the head and beak become mainly white.

There are two large conical teeth at the tip of the lower jaw. These erupt only in adult males, but they are not exposed outside the closed mouth as in *Berardius* (Baird's and Arnoux's beaked whales).

An additional pair of teeth is sometimes found behind the main pair, and there can be many toothpicklike vestigial teeth buried in the upper and lower jaws. The skull has a pair of crests, or flanges, on the upper jaw, which become larger and more prominent with age. In old males, these crests become so massive that they almost meet. In a striking example of convergent evolution, the Ganges and Indus River dolphins (*Platanista*) have very similar crests. In fact, *Hyperoodon* and *Platanista* are the only two modern cetacean genera with this feature. Scientists speculate that in both these crests play an important role in echolocation.

**Recognition at sea** Since no species of *Berardius* inhabits the North Atlantic, the male northern bottlenose is the only beaked whale with a bluff or bulging forehead. The much greater adult size and head shape of *Hyperoodon* make it reasonably easy to distinguish from other North Atlantic ziphiids at sea. However, at a distance and if only the back and dorsal fin are seen, there is a possibility of confusing females and young males with the smaller ziphiids and possibly with the minke whale.

**Habitat** Northern bottlenose whales prefer continental shelf edge and slope water in the temperature range −2°C to 17°C. They are rarely observed on the continental shelf and do not really become common until the water depth reaches 1,000m. Although whalers generally claimed that bottlenose whales remain at the edges of pack ice rather than entering the broken ice fields, these whales sometimes move a few kilometres into the ice.

**Distribution and migration** The northern bottlenose whale is found only in the northern North Atlantic. In the west, the southernmost stranding was in Rhode Island at 41°30'N. There are only two published records of strandings in the Gulf of St. Lawrence and a few records for the bays of eastern Newfoundland. There is no definite evidence for their entering Hudson Bay or Foxe Basin. In the east, bottlenose whales have been reported as far south as the Azores and Portugal. They have strayed into the Mediterranean on a number of occasions, but this sea is not considered part of their normal range. Bottlenose whales enter the North Sea regularly but the Baltic Sea only occasionally.

Bottlenose whales occur in well-known pockets of abundance on the continental slope and over deep submarine canyons.

There is no evidence of a continuous distribution across the central North Atlantic but, as with Baird's beaked whale in the North Pacific, the distribution may be essentially continuous around the northern rim of the Atlantic basin. The Gully, a canyon area northeast of Sable Island, Nova Scotia, harbours a concentration of bottlenose whales during much of the year. Other important areas in the western North Atlantic are in the Labrador Sea and Davis Strait, especially at the mouths of Hudson Strait and Frobisher Bay. Bottlenose whales are present in Denmark Strait and all round Iceland, Jan Mayen and the Faeroes. Large numbers have also been caught west and southwest of Svalbard and off the Møre and Andenes coasts of Norway.

Their migrations are not well mapped. Judging by the timing of strandings and captures, they are often considered to migrate north early in the spring, for example arriving off the Faeroes in early March and becoming extremely common between Iceland and Jan Mayen in late April, May and early June. A return southward migration supposedly has begun by early July, with the whales passing the Faeroes in August and September and arriving off British and European shores in September and October. The wintering grounds are unknown. The presence of bottlenose whales at high latitudes (e.g. 54-63°N in the Labrador Sea and Davis Strait) as early as February and March suggests that some overwinter near the edge of the pack ice.

**Food and feeding** This whale is a squid specialist. Its distribution is strongly influenced by the distribution of one species, *Gonatus fabricii*. Bottlenose stomachs have been found to contain as much as 20-25 litres of beaks and other undigested parts of squid, as well as some fish. In addition to squid, bottlenose whales eat sea cucumbers, starfishes, prawns, herring and deepsea fish. Like sperm whales, they ingest odd items such as stones, pieces of wood, fishnets and plastic paraphernalia. The presence of stones, bits of clay and shells in their stomachs suggests that they might root for food in bottom sediments.

**Behaviour** These gregarious whales are known for their habits of approaching vessels and sticking by injured companions. Both habits have made northern bottlenose whales vulnerable to whaling. Whalers sometimes managed to kill 10 or 15 individuals from an area before the survivors dispersed or fled.

The average pod size is about 4-10, but several pods can be in sight at a given time. There is some degree of segregation on the basis of age and sex. For example, males greatly outnumber females in Icelandic waters during May and June. Old males and youngsters sometimes travel alone. Mothers with calves can be found as solitary pairs or in the close company of another mother-calf pair.

Bottlenose whales are deep divers. Whalers' observations leave little doubt that these animals can remain submerged for well over an hour, perhaps for as much as two hours. One harpooned individual is said to have run out over 900m of line in 90 seconds while diving vertically. Norwegian scientists have timed dives lasting as long as 70 minutes.

**Life history** Although individual females as short as 6m and males as short as 7.3m have been found to be sexually mature, the mean lengths for reaching sexual maturity are estimated as 6.9m and 7.5m,

respectively. These mean lengths correspond to ages of 11 years (females) and 7-11 years (males). The oldest documented ages are 27 years for females and 37 years for males. Calves are born at a mean length of about 3.5m, after a gestation period of about a year. The peak calving season is April-June. Lactation probably lasts a year or more. The estimated calving interval is two years.

**World population** Nearly 30,000 bottlenose whales were caught east of Greenland between 1890 and 1900. Since one whale was shot but not secured for every three or four taken, the actual kill was in the order of 40,000. It has been reasoned that there must have been well over 40,000 bottlenose whales in the northeastern Atlantic in 1889 to have supported this level of exploitation. No information is available on current population size, but these whales are still relatively common in many of their old haunts. It is generally felt that some kind

of stock separation exists, but no direct evidence is available for defining stock boundaries.

**Man's influence** British Arctic whalers hunted bottlenose whales occasionally as early as 1850 and regularly by the late 1870s. The Norwegians developed a separate bottlenose fishery in the early 1880s and, from 1892 on, enjoyed a virtual monopoly. In 1896, 80 vessels took more than 3,300 whales. By 1927, the Norwegian fleet had declined to a single vessel, and there was little bottlenose whaling until just before the Second World War, when the Norwegian pelagic fishery for minke whales began. Bottlenose whales, along with killer and long-finned pilot whales, were taken for animal food while the minke whales were taken for human food. Nearly 6,000 bottlenose whales were taken between 1927 and 1973, all but about 800 east of Cape Farewell, the southern tip of Greenland.

During the late 1970s, there was a lively debate in the IWC Scientific Committee about the status of this species. Many feared that the duration and intensity of whaling had substantially reduced the population size. However, it was difficult to disentangle the effects of changing technology (e.g. the introduction of larger, faster whaling vessels) and relative market values of minke vs. toothed whale meat from the effects of declining availability of whales. The matter was never finally resolved before Norway stopped taking bottlenose whales, largely for economic reasons, in 1973. The IWC classified the entire population of northern bottlenose whales as a protected stock beginning in 1977, and this protection remains in force. The species has been listed as vulnerable in the IUCN Red Data Book since 1976.

*Above: Even at close quarters, bottlenose whales rarely reveal the pronounced beak from which they derive their name. The spermaceti from the male's head resembles that of sperm whales.*

*Right: Part of a pod of northern bottlenose whales photographed on the Reykjanes Ridge in the northeast Atlantic Ocean. The prominent, falcate dorsal fin is characteristic of this placid species.*

# SOUTHERN BOTTLENOSE WHALE

## HYPEROODON PLANIFRONS

■ Possible range     □ Possible sightings

**Classification** The name *planifrons*, meaning 'level browed', was given to this species because the summits of the crests, or shields, on the upper jaw are much lower than those of *H. ampullatus* (northern bottlenose whale).

**Description** The largest measured specimen was a 7.45m lactating female; the largest male was 6.94m long. In this respect, it appears that the southern bottlenose whale may differ from its North Atlantic counterpart, in which males are considerably larger than females.

The melon is bulbous and may overhang the beak. The rear half of the mouthline curves upward and there is a pair of grooves on the throat, typical of beaked whales. The dorsal fin, set well behind the middle of the back, is prominent and somewhat falcate. There may be a shallow median notch between the relatively broad flukes.

One observation, near the equator, thought to be of this species, gave the

*Below: This animal, showing the bulbous head shape reflected in the species' common name, is exhaling under water.*

adult colour as acorn brown overall, with the forehead, including the beak, much paler. Other observations give a colour of light brown or dull yellow. The ventral part of the body is much lighter than the dorsal surface. Large individuals are heavily scarred with linear scratch marks and small oval scars.

Like Cuvier's beaked whale, the southern bottlenose whale has a single pair of conical adult teeth at the front of the lower jaw. These erupt only in adult males, sloping forward and slightly outward. They do not show when the mouth is closed, as the lower jaw does not extend as far beyond the tip of the upper jaw as in *Ziphius* and *Berardius*.

**Recognition at sea** These whales are difficult to identify with certainty at sea, except when sighting conditions are extremely favourable or they are approached closely. At a distance, they might be confused with various other ziphiids, perhaps especially Arnoux's beaked whale in the Southern Hemisphere and Baird's beaked whale in the North Pacific, and with the minke whale. However, a close look at the head should reveal the bulbous melon of adults, the slight depression near the blowhole and the rather sharp demarcation between the pale head and darker body. This last feature is reminiscent of Cuvier's beaked whale, although the latter has a shorter, less well-defined beak.

**Habitat** Southern bottlenose whales are encountered frequently during summer within 110km of the ice-edge in the Antarctic. Like most ziphiids, they live along, and seaward of, the 200m contour.

**Distribution and migration** This species has a wide distribution in the southern oceans between 29°S and the Antarctic (to at least 70°S). Although there are no published records for the South Pacific north of about 33°S, sightings of whales closely resembling *H. planifrons* have been made between 20°N and 30°N near Okinawa, off the Galapagos Islands and on the equator close to the international dateline. Assuming these are *Hyperoodon*, it is not clear whether they are a northern species similar or identical to *H. ampullatus* of the North Atlantic, a disjunct tropical population of *H. planifrons*, or a part of (and continuous with) the wider Southern Hemisphere population of *H. planifrons*. Records from northern Australia and Brazil show that this species occurs in warm temperate regions. Observations by Graham Ross show that bottlenose whales occur seasonally in southern African waters. They are present there mainly in summer and are virtually absent during the winter months.

**Food and feeding** One specimen that stranded in New Zealand had 200 squid beaks in its stomach, and it is likely that squid form an important part of the southern bottlenose whale's diet.

**Behaviour** This whale is at least mildly gregarious, sometimes being found in groups of as many as 25 individuals. Pods of less than 10 are more common in the Antarctic. While being chased, they sometimes raise the head clear of the surface when breathing. Judging by their similarity to northern bottlenose whales, these animals may be deep divers and remain submerged for an hour or more.

**Life history** Very little is known about the southern bottlenose whale's reproductive biology. A 5.7m female was lactating, and a calf 2.9m long that stranded in Natal, South Africa, in early November was considered to be no more than about a month old.

**World population** In the Antarctic south of 58°S, the southern bottlenose whale is judged the most abundant ziphiid. However, no useful estimates of population size have been made, and there is no information on stock identity.

**Man's influence** A few specimens have been taken by the Soviet Antarctic whaling fleet but, otherwise, southern bottlenose whales have not been exploited anywhere. There is no reason to suppose that they face any immediate major threat.

# LONGMAN'S BEAKED WHALE

*MESOPLODON PACIFICUS*

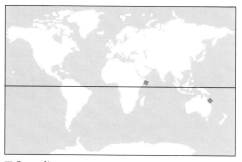

■ Strandings

**Classification** Longman considered this species to belong to the genus *Mesoplodon* and to resemble True's beaked whale, *M. mirus*. He gave it the name *pacificus* in 1926, apparently to distinguish it from *mirus*, which at the time was known from only three Atlantic specimens. Disagreement still exists as to whether this whale belongs in the genus *Mesoplodon* or in a genus of its own – *Indopacetus*. Alan N. Baker of the National Museum of New Zealand has suggested that one of the museum skulls of this species is too large for a *Mesoplodon* and that it must have come from a whale more than 6m long. He accepts *Indopacetus* as a valid genus.

**Description** Longman's beaked whale has never been identified in the flesh. The skull has two forward-pointing teeth at the tip of the lower jaw. In this feature, it resembles Cuvier's beaked whale and the northern and southern bottlenose whales. There is a distinctive lateral swelling on the rostrum, about halfway along its length.

**Distribution and migration** Two skulls found on beaches have been assigned to this species: one from Danane, Somalia, the other from Mackay, Queensland. A ziphiid observed repeatedly at sea in the eastern tropical Pacific, but as yet unidentified, may be this species. If it is, this would suggest an extensive range in the Indo-Pacific region.

**World population** It must be assumed that this species is quite rare or that it has a restricted distribution in areas rarely visited by scientists.

# HECTOR'S BEAKED WHALE

*MESOPLODON HECTORI*

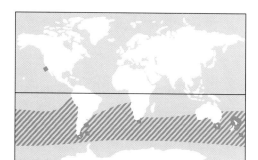

■ Sightings/strandings  ╱ Possible range

**Classification** This species was described by John Gray in 1871. Its specific name, *hectori*, is derived from J. Hector, the curator of the Museum in New Zealand that housed the type specimen.

**Local names** This species is also known as the New Zealand beaked whale.

**Description** From the few specimens available, adults appear to be a dark grey/brown above and pale grey below. Males have a white ventral surface to the flukes with dark lines radiating out from the tail stock. Scratches and scars are common on the flanks. A small triangular tooth is found on either side of the lower jaw near the tip. The longest stranded female examined was 4.43m, the longest male 4.3m and the shortest calf 2.1m.

**Habitat** From the limited data available, Hector's beaked whale appears to be confined to cool temperate waters.

**Distribution and migration** The species is known mainly from the Southern Hemisphere, with records from Chile, Argentina, the Falkland Islands, South Africa, Australia and New Zealand. In recent years, however, animals have also stranded in southern California.

**Food and feeding** Little information is available, but two lower beaks of the squid *Octopoteuthis* and a fragment of an unidentified invertebrate were reported from the stomach of an adult Hector's beaked whale that stranded in California.

*Below: Mature males have a tooth near the tip of each lower jaw, which cause these parallel body scars during fights.*

# TRUE'S BEAKED WHALE

*MESOPLODON MIRUS*

■ Confirmed records

**Classification** This species was discovered and described by the American biologist Frederick True in 1913. The specific name, *mirus*, is the Latin word for 'wonderful', and reflects his excitement at the discovery.

**Description** Northern Hemisphere animals are medium grey above and light grey below. Adults have a dark area around the eye and some areas of white, particularly around the genital region. In Southern Hemisphere adults, a white area extends back from the dorsal fin, the belly appears darker due to flecking and the beak tip becomes white. Scratches and scars are found on animals from both hemispheres, more commonly on males. A small tooth protrudes at the tip of each side of the lower jaw in males. The smallest measured calf was 2.3m long and weighed 136kg. The largest female was 5.1m long and weighed 1,394kg; the longest male measured 5.3m.

**Habitat** This species is found in temperate waters. Although its range overlaps with Gervais', in the North Atlantic it appears to prefer slightly colder waters.

The few Southern Hemisphere records are from warm temperate waters.

**Distribution and migration** In the western North Atlantic, it ranges from Nova Scotia in the north down to the Bahamas; in the east, it is found from the Hebrides (off Scotland) to southern France. In the Southern Hemisphere, strandings of True's beaked whales have been reported from South Africa and Australia.

**Food and feeding** The little information available suggests that squid are the most important prey species.

*The shape and colour of this species have been built up from stranding reports.*

# GERVAIS' BEAKED WHALE

*MESOPLODON EUROPAEUS*

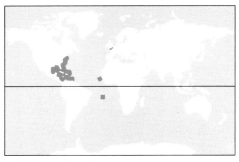

■ Sightings/strandings

**Classification** The specific name, *europaeus*, refers to the location of the first specimen, which was found floating in the English Channel. It was classified by the French biologist Gervais in 1855, hence its common name.

**Local names** Gulf Stream, Antillean or European beaked whale.

**Description** Adults are dark grey above and pale grey below (white in calves). Some females have a white patch in the genital region. The head is relatively small and sometimes white at the tip; the two small teeth are found towards the front of the mouth. Known weights range from 49kg for a 1.6m calf to 1,178kg for a 3.7m female. The longest female measured was 5.2m and the longest male 4.5m. The average length at birth is 2.1m.

**Habitat** This species inhabits tropical to warm temperate waters in the Atlantic.

**Distribution and migration** Almost all records of this species are from the western North Atlantic, and it commonly strands along the Atlantic coast of the USA from New York down to Florida and Texas. Strandings have also been recorded in the Caribbean, from Cuba, Jamaica and Trinidad. Strandings of Gervais' beaked whales have been recorded from West Africa and at Ascension Island in the South Atlantic.

**Food and feeding** Trace quantities of squid beaks were collected from three specimens, but no fish remains were found in the stomachs examined.

**Man's influence** One specimen of Gervais' was reported entangled in pound nets off New Jersey, USA.

*First described from a specimen in the English Channel, this species has not been seen in Europe again.*

# GINKGO-TOOTHED BEAKED WHALE

*MESOPLODON GINKGODENS*

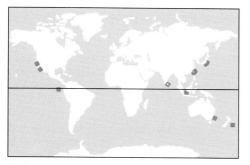

■ Strandings

**Classification** This species was discovered by two Japanese scientists, Masaharu Nishiwaki and Toshiro Kamiya, when they went to investigate a supposed sei whale found near Tokyo in 1957. The specific name is derived from the shape of its teeth, which resemble the leaves of the Japanese ginkgo tree.

**Local names** Japanese beaked whale; ichoha kujira (Japanese).

**Description** Adult males are darkly pigmented, apart from the suggestion of a faint light patch on the front half of the rostrum and lower jaw and a number of small white spots, 3-4cm in diameter, centred towards the rear of the underside. These may be parasite scars and not normal pigmentation. The characteristic teeth are found in the lower jaw, close to the middle of the beak; as in some other species, these develop only in mature males. Adult males appear to lack the linear scars of most *Mesoplodon* species. The only photographs available suggest that females are medium grey above and light grey below. The longest female measured 4.9m; the longest male 4.7m.

**Habitat** The limited data available suggest that this species lives in warm temperate to tropical waters.

**Distribution and migration** The species is only known from 13 strandings, with 10 from the North Pacific (two from the eastern side, five from Japan, three from Taiwan), two from the Indian Ocean (from Sri Lanka and Indonesia) and one from the Chatham Islands in the South Pacific.

**Man's influence** Individuals have been taken in small-scale harpoon fisheries for small cetaceans in Japan.

*This beaked whale is known only from isolated strandings around the world.*

# GRAY'S BEAKED WHALE

*MESOPLODON GRAYI*

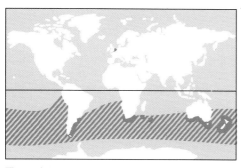

■ Confirmed records    ▨ Probable range

**Classification** The species was described by the New Zealand Museum Director Julius Von Haast in 1876. It was named after John Gray, the British biologist, who died in 1875.

**Local names** Scamperdown whale (the site in New Zealand where one specimen was found); southern beaked whale.

**Description** Adults are generally dark, although there can be several areas of lighter pigmentation on the belly, and there are white patches in the genital region. The head is small and its long narrow beak becomes white in adulthood. Two small, triangular teeth are found in the lower jaw towards the front of the beak. Until recently, they were thought to erupt only in adult males, but females with erupted teeth have now been found. There are 17-22 pairs of small teeth in the upper jaw.

Females are generally larger than males. The longest female measured 5.64m, the longest male 4.74m and the shortest calf 2.42m. Two animals have been weighed: a 4.74m male at 1,075kg and a 4.94m female at 1,100kg.

**Habitat** The available records are from cool temperate waters.

**Distribution and migration** The species appears to be circumpolar in the Southern Hemisphere, with most records from New Zealand and Australia. Other records are from South Africa, Argentina and Chile. The only Northern Hemisphere record is of a stranded animal from the Netherlands in 1927.

**Behaviour** One mass stranding (an unusual event for beaked whales) involved 28 individuals, suggesting some degree of social cohesion. Observers report that animals sometimes raise their snouts out of the water on surfacing.

*Right: The white beak of an adult Gray's beaked whale, briefly seen in 1985 off the east coast of South Island, New Zealand.*

# STEJNEGER'S BEAKED WHALE

*MESOPLODON STEJNEGERI*

■ Confirmed records

**Classification** Described by the American cetologist Frederick True in 1885, this species was named after his fellow biologist Leonard Stejneger, who found the first specimen.

**Local names** Bering Sea beaked whale; sabre-toothed beaked whale.

**Description** Few live specimens have been seen but both sexes appear to be dark above and pale below, with some white areas in the head and neck region.

The most impressive feature is the presence in adult males of two huge projecting teeth pointing forwards near the peak of the arch in the lower jaw. The longest female and male specimens measured were both 5.25m.

**Habitat** This species is distributed throughout cold temperate and subarctic waters, in deeper rather than shallower waters. Sightings made near the central Aleutian Islands were in waters between 730m and 1,560m deep.

**Distribution and migration** The species is confined to the North Pacific and most records are from Alaskan waters. Despite one of its local names being the Bering

Sea beaked whale, it more likely frequents the Aleutian Basin and Trench, rather than the shallow waters of the northern Bering Sea. On the eastern side, it ranges from St. Paul Island to southern California. In the west, it ranges from the Commander Islands to Japan.

**Food and feeding** Trace quantities of squid beaks were collected from two animals, but no fish remains were found in their stomachs.

**Behaviour** Strandings and sightings data from the Aleutian Islands suggest that the animals live in socially structured groups of 5-15 individuals, including both small and large animals.

*A typically scarred adult male specimen.*

# HUBBS' BEAKED WHALE

*MESOPLODON CARLHUBBSI*

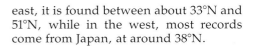

■ Confirmed records

**Classification** Described by the American biologist Moore in 1963, this species was named after the American marine biologist Carl Hubbs.

**Local names** Arch-beaked whale.

**Description** Adult males are dark grey to black, except for a white area from the tip of the rostrum and lower jaw as far as the back of the teeth, and a white 'cap' around the blowhole. This cap and the two prominent straplike teeth in the rear lower jaw are characteristic. Females and juveniles are medium grey above, lighter grey on the flanks and white on the belly.

The front half of the rostrum and lower jaws are lighter than the rest of the head, and the teeth are unerupted. In both sexes, the flukes are paler underneath and the flippers paler on top. The body has many scratches. The longest male and female measured 5.32m; average length at birth is 2.5m. The only animal weighed, a 5.3m female, was 1,432kg.

**Habitat** It is found in cold temperate waters, seemingly in association with the deep subarctic current system.

**Distribution and migration** The species is confined to the North Pacific. In the

east, it is found between about 33°N and 51°N, while in the west, most records come from Japan, at around 38°N.

**Food and feeding** Limited information from stranded animals suggests that squid and some deepwater fish are the main prey species.

**Behaviour** Most scars are probably inflicted with the mouth closed during conflicts between adult males.

**Man's influence** Individuals have been taken in small-scale harpoon fisheries for small cetaceans in Japan.

*Right: Two probable Hubbs' beaked whales, of which this is one, were live stranded in California in 1989. Both were immature and, despite dedicated and expert care, neither survived long in captivity.*

# ANDREWS' BEAKED WHALE

## MESOPLODON BOWDOINI

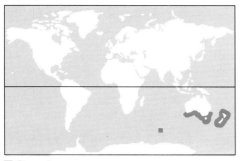

■ Strandings

**Classification** *Mesoplodon bowdoini* was named and described by the American naturalist Roy Chapman Andrews in 1908. The generic name, *Mesoplodon*, stems from three greek words, *mesos*, *hapla* and *odon*, meaning 'having a tooth in the middle of the jaw.' The specific name, *bowdoini*, derives from George Bowdoin, a trustee of the American Museum of Natural History. Some taxonomists believe that the closely related species *M. carlhubbsi* (Hubbs' beaked whale) is a subspecies of *M. bowdoini*,

based on cranial and pigmentation similarities between the two species.

**Local names** Bowdoin's beaked whale; deepcrest beaked whale.

**Description** Adult males are dark blue-black all over, with the exception of the tip of the rostrum and lower jaw, which are white as far back as the rear edge of the teeth. The two teeth in the lower jaw are set in slightly raised sockets at about the middle of the beak. Although protruding out of the mouth in adult males, they appear to be concealed in the gum of females and young animals. One 4.57m

female examined was found to be physically mature, while another measuring 4.2m was carrying a 1.57m foetus.

**Recognition at sea** It is almost impossible to distinguish this species at sea from Hubbs' and Stejneger's beaked whale.

**Habitat** The species appears to be confined to temperate waters in the southern Indian and Pacific Oceans.

**Distribution and migration** This species is known only from strandings on the southern coast of Australia, in New Zealand and Kerguelen Island.

*This species is the southern counterpart of Stejneger's and Hubbs' beaked whales.*

# STRAPTOOTHED WHALE

## MESOPLODON LAYARDII

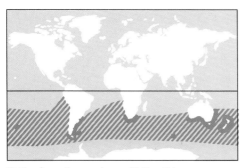

■ Confirmed records  ⧄ Possible range

**Classification** This species was described by the British biologist John Gray in 1865 from drawings made by the curator of the South African Museum, E. L. Layard, after whom it is named. The common name derives from the bizarre teeth found in adult males.

**Local names** Layard's beaked whale.

**Description** Adults are largely black apart from areas of white (yellow-grey in non-fresh specimens) and grey. The front of the upper jaw, the lower jaw and an area back to the upper chest is white. There is a white oval area in the genital

region. The remainder of the upper jaw, the melon to just in front of the blowhole and the area around the eye are black. There is a grey blaze from the melon back to almost two-thirds of the way to the dorsal fin. The leading edges of the flukes are grey. In non-adults, the pattern of light and dark areas appears to be reversed. Adult males possess two strap-like teeth that extend from the lower jaw backwards until they curl over the upper jaw, preventing it from fully opening, but not, apparently, interfering with feeding! Teeth are not visible in females or young.

The longest female measured was 6.15m, the longest male 5.84m and the shortest calf 2.8m.

**Habitat** Straptoothed whales are found in cold temperate waters.

**Distribution and migration** There are more records of this species (90) than for any other member of the genus. It is circumpolar in the Southern Hemisphere, with records from the Indian, Pacific and Atlantic between about 30°S and 55°S, notably Australia and New Zealand.

*Left: A straptoothed whale stranded at Dunedin, on the southeastern coast of South Island, New Zealand. This is a male specimen, measured at 5.4m. Of the 90 records of this extraordinary whale, by far the majority have been logged from the South Pacific coasts of Australia and New Zealand.*

# SOWERBY'S BEAKED WHALE

*MESOPLODON BIDENS*

■ Confirmed records   ⁄⁄ Probable range

**Classification** This species was named and described by the British naturalist and watercolour artist James Sowerby in 1804, from a skull collected four years earlier in the Moray Firth, Scotland, by James Brodie. The specific name, *bidens*, comes from the Latin words *bis* and *dens*, meaning 'two tooth' (see below). This species was later used by the French biologist Paul Gervais as the type species for the genus *Mesoplodon*.

**Local names** These include North Sea beaked whale; Atlanticheski remzub and remzub Sowerbi (USSR); dauphin de Dale and dauphin de Havre (France); Flosser (Germany); spidshvalen (Norway); spitsdolfijn (the Netherlands); spitssnuitdolfijn (Denmark).

**Description** Almost all the available descriptions of coloration are from dead specimens and perhaps because of this they can be somewhat contradictory, particularly regarding areas of lighter coloration, which tend to darken after death. In general, however, adults appear bluish grey or slate-coloured, with lighter flanks and belly. Greyish or whitish streaks and spots are distributed irregularly on the sides. The colour of juveniles and calves appears to be generally paler, particularly underneath, where the belly may be white. They have fewer spots and scars.

The two teeth referred to in the specific name are found in the middle of the lower jaw. In adult males, they protrude outside the mouth. Vestigial teeth may be present in both the upper and lower jaws. Some descriptions refer to a prominent bulge in front of the blowhole. This does not appear to be present in all specimens, although its presence/absence does not seem to correlate with the age or sex of the animal.

The maximum recorded lengths are 5.5m (male), 5.05m (female). The average length at birth is 2.4m. There are no recorded weights for adults, but a 2.7m calf weighed 185kg.

**Habitat** This species is known from temperate and subarctic waters.

**Distribution and migration** The species is confined to the North Atlantic, with most records coming from the eastern side. The North Sea seems to be its centre of distribution. On the east, it has been reported from northern Norway to perhaps as far south as Madeira. There are no known records from the Soviet Union. Most records come from the coasts of the United Kingdom. Those from Sweden and Denmark are confined to the open Atlantic or the shores of the Skagerrak and Kattegat. It is unlikely that the species is found in the shallow Baltic Sea. On the western side, it has been recorded from Labrador south to Florida, the latter being the only record from the Gulf of Mexico and the southernmost report of this species.

There has been a minor controversy over the presence of this species in the Mediterranean Sea; although most of the reported records have been found to be erroneous, recent work has shown that at least one record probably was of a Sowerby's beaked whale.

There does not seem to be any seasonality in the European stranding records that might provide some evidence of migration in the species. The only country for which enough records exist to make a seasonal analysis valid is the United Kingdom (41 records). Strandings have been reported in every month except February, with a tendency towards a broad peak in the summer, between July and September. However, as always, strandings data have to be interpreted with caution as numbers of reported strandings may well reflect more the migration of humans to the coast rather than an increase in the number of whales!

**Food and feeding** The limited data available from stranded animals suggest that squid and small fish are the major prey.

**Behaviour** Little is known about the behaviour of this species, as most of our information comes from stranded animals. Single animals and pairs have stranded alive and their sounds have been likened to those of cows.

**Life history** The scant information available suggests that mating and calving may occur in late winter and spring.

**Man's influence** This species used to be taken in small-scale harpoon fisheries for small cetaceans in Newfoundland. The reported take of a specimen in the village of Machico in the Madeira Islands was probably erroneous.

*Right: Centred on the North Sea, the known distribution of Sowerby's beaked whale also includes the eastern coasts of the USA and Canada.*

# BLAINVILLE'S BEAKED WHALE

## MESOPLODON DENSIROSTRIS

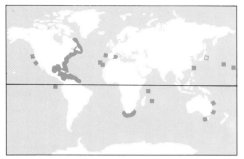

■ Sightings/strandings　□ Possible sighting

**Classification** This species was originally named by the French natural historian Henri de Blainville, based only on a small piece of the upper jaw. However, this piece of bone was extraordinarily heavy and in fact Blainville's beaked whale produces the most dense bone of any animal. This gave rise to its specific name, *densirostris*, which is derived from the Latin words *densus* and *rostrum*, meaning 'dense' and 'beak'.

**Local names** Dense beaked whale; Atlantic beaked whale.

**Description** The predominant colour pattern of this species is dark above and pale below. In calves, the back and flanks are blue-grey merging into a creamy white belly. In adults, there is a tendency for the dorsal surface to darken, as revealed by photographs of adults and young together. Adults have a dark blue-grey back and flanks. The dorsal surface of the flukes and flippers is grey-black, as is a small eye patch. From the limited number of descriptions of fresh adult females available, it appears that they develop white upper and lower jaws; there are no records of this for males. This white area merges into the white of the belly. They

also seem to aquire more white oval scars than adult males. These are found all over the belly, particularly in the genital region, but also on the flanks and back.

The most striking feature of this species is the raised arch of the lower jaw. On each side at the peak of this raised prominence is a massive tooth. In adult males, this prominence is exaggerated and the teeth erupt. These forwardly tilting teeth may protrude higher than the flattened forehead and be covered with barnacles.

Published weights range from 60kg for a 1.9m calf to 1,033kg for a 4.56m female. The longest measured male and female were almost the same lengths, 4.73m and 4.71m, respectively. The longest foetus was 1.9m and the shortest calf 2.61m.

**Habitat** This species occurs in warm temperate to tropical waters. Sightings around the Hawaiian Islands showed animals in water depths of 700-1,000m. These sightings were made on the slope of the islands, with water depths of up to 5,000m nearby. However, considerably more information is needed before we can draw any conclusions about preferred water depths.

**Distribution and migration** Blainville's beaked whale has the widest distribution of all *Mesoplodon* species, with records from all oceans. In the western North Atlantic, it is known from the Caribbean, the Gulf of Mexico and the Bahamas. There are many records of this species from the Atlantic coast of the United States and some from Nova Scotia, Newfoundland and Labrador in Canada. These Canadian records probably represent strays from the Gulf Stream waters. In the eastern North Atlantic, records of

*M. densirostris* are few. There are no records from the United Kingdom, one from Portugal, one from the Mediterranean coast of Spain and one from the island of Madeira.

Similarly, there are very few records of this species from the North Pacific. There are three specimens from Midway Island, two from Taiwan, one from Japanese waters and two from California. Small schools have been reported off the Hawaiian Islands, principally off Oahu.

In the Indian Ocean, there is one report from Australia, two from Mauritius, two from the Seychelles and 14 from South Africa. There is one record of a Blainville's beaked whale from the South Atlantic coast of South Africa and two from the South Pacific coasts of Australia.

**Food and feeding** The limited information available suggests that squid and possibly some fish are the main prey.

**Behaviour** At a live stranding of a juvenile male, some airborne sounds were recorded. The vocalizations sounded like 'whistles' or 'chirps', but when they were analyzed some of them were found to be pulsed. Pod sizes from three to seven have been reported. Dive times of 20-45 minutes and more have been recorded, with long dives being preceded by a series of blows at the surface. Scars found on some stranded animals suggest that attacks by killer whales or false killer whales may occur.

**Man's influence** In Taiwanese waters, some animals were taken in small-scale harpoon fisheries for small cetaceans. One animal was taken by fishermen in the vicinity of the Seychelles and another off the west coast of Australia.

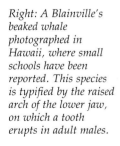

*Right: A Blainville's beaked whale photographed in Hawaii, where small schools have been reported. This species is typified by the raised arch of the lower jaw, on which a tooth erupts in adult males.*

# PILOT AND KILLER WHALES
## GLOBICEPHALIDAE

This family, closely allied to the Delphinidae and still considered by many taxonomists to be part of it, consists essentially of the pilot and killer whales. One additional species, the melon-headed whale (*Peponocephala electra*), has been included for convenience but strictly it falls somewhere between the globicephalids and the oceanic dolphins, Delphinidae (reviewed on pages 130-167).

In 1866, the British scientist John Gray, Keeper of the Zoology Department at the British Museum, proposed a new family to represent some species he considered to be significantly different from the other delphinids. These animals were generally the largest of the dolphins but, more importantly, had no 'beak' and fewer teeth. Gray's idea gained little recognition until a century later, when

Nishiwaki similarly urged a new look at the Delphinidae. He defined the new family Globicephalidae as comprising those species with blunt heads, fewer than 15 teeth on each side of both the upper and lower jaw, three or more fused neck vertebrae and more than 2.5m in body length. This would encompass the two pilot whales (*Globicephala melas* and *G. macrorhynchus*), the killer whale (*Orcinus orca*), the false killer whale (*Pseudorca crassidens*) and the pygmy killer whale (*Feresa attenuata*) – if one accepts maximum rather than average body length of this last species. The melon-headed whale also just passes the test on length, but clearly fails on tooth count, with 20-25 in each of the four tooth rows. Nevertheless, in shape and colour the melon-headed whale looks very like the other

five members of the family and is considered by some scientists to be taxonomically close enough to justify its inclusion as a globicephalid.

All six have common names that include the word 'whale', but they are generally considered taxonomically more closely allied to the true dolphins than to any of the large whale species.

Of the six species, only the killer whale can be found worldwide and only the long-finned pilot whale has a discontinuous distribution, with tropical waters separating the Southern Hemisphere population from that of the northern North Atlantic. The other species are thought to be restricted to the warmer waters of both hemispheres, though few records of positively identified live animals exist for *Feresa* and *Peponocephala*.

*A male killer whale attacks southern sea lions off Patagonia.*

117

# KILLER WHALE

*ORCINUS ORCA*

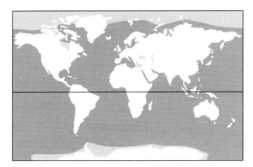

■ Probable range.

**Classification** This unmistakable species has long been known to zoologists and taxonomists, so it is not surprising that Linnaeus himself first classified it in 1758. The name he gave it, *Delphinus orca*, which literally means 'demon dolphin', was revised in 1860 when the new genus *Orcinus* was created for this animal in recognition of differences between it and the smaller dolphins. The name *Orcinus orca* is now applied to all races of the species throughout the world, between which there are a few, relatively minor, differences in shape and colour pattern. Despite its size and common name, this species is far more closely related to the dolphins of the family Delphinidae than to any of the 'great' whales.

The false killer whale, *Pseudorca crassidens*, (page 122) and the pygmy killer whale, *Feresa attenuata*, (page 124) are quite separate species.

**Local names** In recognition of the significant role of warm-blooded prey in its diet, this animal is normally called the killer whale. This may be a derivation of the name 'whale killer' once used by whalers. Alternative common names are orca, blackfish and grampus, although the last two are little used and confusing. 'Blackfish' is used in various places for several members of the family Globicephalidae, and *Grampus* is also the genus name for another large dolphin, Risso's dolphin, *Grampus griseus*.

**Description** A medium-sized cetacean, reaching an average adult body length of about 6.7-8m (maximum 9.75m) for males and 5.7-6.6m (maximum 8.53m) for females. Body weight averages 4-6.3 tonnes (maximum 10.5 tonnes) for males and 2.6-3.8 tonnes (maximum 7.4 tonnes) for females.

This is a stocky species, with a body which is almost circular in cross-section apart from some lateral compression of the tail stock. The dorsal fin is characteristic, very tall (up to 1.8m) and straight in males, about half the height and dis-

tinctly falcate in females. The head is rounded, with an indistinct beak. The flippers are very broad and paddle shaped, and the tail is distinctly notched.

In most populations, the body colour is essentially a pattern of pure white on jet black. The white occurs in three zones: a roughly elliptical or pear-shaped patch behind the eye; a continuous ventral blaze covering the entire lower jaw, lower face and throat back to the flippers, then narrowing to a wide stripe on the chest and abdomen, terminating like three prongs of a fork with the central prong covering the vent area and the outer prongs curving upwards and backwards along the lower sides of the animal; and on the underside of the tail flukes, except the outer margins. All other areas are black apart from an ill-defined saddle patch situated behind the dorsal fin, which occurs in varying shades of light or medium grey and is shaped slightly differently in every animal. At least some Southern Hemisphere killer whales are slightly different in basic body colour, the black existing only as a cape extending up and back from the upper jaw and head in a broad stripe to the dorsal fin, which is also black. All other dark areas are dark grey, not black. Areas of white are similar.

The mouth is well equipped to deal with large prey, having 10-12 pairs of large, oval-sectioned, enamelled teeth in both upper and lower jaws.

**Recognition at sea** The dorsal fin, especially on an adult male, normally allows observers to distinguish this species from all others, even at a great distance. Although they may be seen singly, killer whales are normally discovered as a pod of 3-25 animals, including at least one large male. The blow is low and bushy,

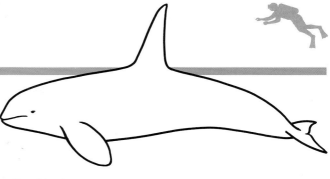

and is seen many times at short intervals between dives lasting 4-10 minutes.

**Habitat** This is a species with catholic tastes, occurring from the equator to polar regions, where it is often encountered in ice leads or among floes. Killer whales appear to be equally at home in coastal or oceanic waters and are able to adapt to almost any conditions. They may enter estuaries, for example, but then rarely occur far from the sea.

*Far left: The dorsal fin (particularly tall in adult males) is unmistakable, here off British Columbia.*

*Below: This head shot shows the strong jaws and sturdy enamelled teeth. Killer whales tear large prey into pieces by repeated biting and shaking.*

*Bottom: Breaching is a common part of surface activity. These highly social whales display an extremely wide range of individual and group behaviours.*

**Distribution and migration** Killer whales occur in all oceans and most seas, from the coast to the very deepest waters. They seem to be rather less dense in the areas furthest from land and in the less productive tropical and subtropical waters. Limits to their polar distribution are simply the degree of ice cover, although they will readily enter areas of floe ice in search of prey.

Their occurrence in higher latitudes is necessarily seasonal, as the sea ice retreats and encroaches in early and late summer. Nevertheless, north-south migrations of the type undertaken by baleen whales are not thought to exist in killer whale populations. They are able to live, reproduce and feed throughout the year in either warm or cool waters, and thus have no urge to undertake long journeys driven by the fundamental requirements of either reproduction or nutrition.

Studies of known and recognizable groups in the coastal waters of the northeastern Pacific and southwestern Atlantic have demonstrated that local whales learn how to take advantage of seasonally abundant prey in certain areas within their home range, which may cover an area of many hundreds or thousands of square kilometres.

**Food and feeding** This species probably has the most diverse diet of all cetaceans. Killer whales can tackle prey of all sizes, including blue whales, and some have devised cooperative feeding behaviours that increase the yield to each individual in the group, whether the target is a medium-sized fish, a seal or a whale. In this they are similar to terrestrial social carnivores such as lions and wolves. In some pods, such as those feeding on seals at Peninsula Valdés, Argentina, one animal takes the prey and shares it with others in the group. Known to be taken in various parts of the world are at least 24 species of cetacean, five species of pinniped (seals and their allies), the dugong, 30 species of fish, seven species of bird and two species of squid, in addition to a variety of other warm- and cold-blooded sea creatures, such as turtles. Feeding dives are normally to depths of less than 100m, and a pod may cooperate in keeping fish prey near or at the surface. There is good evidence that pods tend to specialize in taking relatively few prey

types, so no single animal is ever likely to exploit all the animals that are prey to the species as a whole.

The quantity of food in the stomachs of 41 killer whales captured off Norway was estimated to average 70 litres, with a maximum of 150 litres. Killers eat about 4 percent of their body weight daily, representing up to 250kg in an adult male.

**Behaviour** The behaviour of killer whales in the area either side of the Canada/United States west coast border has been intensively studied for many years. As a result, we know more about the lives of these coastal animals than almost any other cetacean population.

Killer whales are intensely social, living in stable pods of 3-50 members, but usually 3-25. While it is perhaps unlikely that the truly pelagic killer whales have a distinct home range, coastal animals clearly do. The size of the range varies between pods and between 'communities'. A community is a group of pods that share a range and within which pods often temporarily merge into 'super-pods'. It appears that pods from two different communities do not merge and their ranges overlap only infrequently. In the northeastern Pacific study area, home ranges of 'resident' pods are typically 600km long, while those of 'transient' pods can be many times this size.

Vocalizations are mainly of three types: short, broad-band pulses (0.8-25msecs) called clicks, or click-trains, and very probably used for echolocation; tonal signals and whistles of 1.5-18kHz (typically 6-12kHz) lasting 0.05-12secs; and intense burst-pulse or rapidly pulsed sounds described as screamlike or metallic in quality, up to 25kHz and lasting typically 0.5-1.5secs. Pods vary in their use of vocalizations, with 'resident' pods in the northeastern Pacific considered much more vocal than their 'transient' counterparts. Furthermore, 'dialects' of sounds are recognizable between pods and communities of pods, the degree of difference reflecting the degree of social interaction between the pods.

Generally, as might be expected, whales vocalize more when active, such as when hunting, than when they are inactive. When resting, whales carry out a series of long synchronous dives lasting 4-8 minutes, during which time they travel only 150m or less. Between long dives, the animals make several shallow dives and can continue this cycle of activity for up to several hours.

This species shows a lot of social and other behaviour at the surface. Breaches,

tail slaps, spy hops, etc., are commonly seen by observers, but physical aggression within a pod is rare and probably reflects the stable hierarchy thought to exist in these groups. Mass strandings of killer whales occur, but not commonly.

**Life history** Information on life history parameters is gained from both whaling records and long-term observations of live animals. Killer whale pods studied in the northeastern Pacific are thought to be extremely stable in their membership, with calves of both sexes probably remaining in their mother's pod throughout life. Outbreeding may occur when pods temporarily combine into 'super-pods', allowing adult males in one to fertilize receptive females in another. (Evidence suggests that this system works in long-finned pilot whales.) Nevertheless, recent genetical work on the coastal killer whales off Washington State indicates that breeding between closely related animals is probably common.

Calves are born at a length of 2.06-2.5m, after a gestation period estimated from whaling data to be between 12 and 16 months, but nearer 17 months in a recent pregnancy of a captive animal. Given the captive data and by analogy to related species, 16-17 months seems to be the best estimate. Breeding is diffusely seasonal in the northeastern Pacific study area; most calves are born between October and March. Sexual maturity is reached at a length of about 5.8m (males) and 4.6-4.9m (females) at ages of about 12-16 years and 6-10 years respectively in the northeastern Atlantic and 14-15 for both in the Pacific. The calving interval is very variable; reports suggest an average

of 3-8.3 years in the northeastern Atlantic, while observations in the northeastern Pacific indicate that it can be as low as 2 years in individual cows, averages 5-6 years, and can be 12 years. The normal female reproductive phase probably lasts about 21-27 years, during which time 5 or 6 calves are born. Females older than about 40 years are probably post-reproductive. Pregnancy rates (i.e. the proportion of mature females that are pregnant) of 13.7-38.8 percent have been reported for various stocks. The birth rate for the coastal northeastern Pacific stocks (i.e. the proportion of mature females giving birth in any year) averages 9.2 percent.

The studies off Washington State and British Columbia have demonstrated a net population increase of 2.9 percent between 1973 and 1987. Information of this accuracy is not available for any other species of cetacean. The figure is considered low given the significant level of recent removals (for captive display) from this stock. Annual natural mortality rates for these coastal animals are 1.8 percent for juveniles and 0.5-7.1 percent for adults, variable with age. This represents a long natural lifespan, estimated to be up to 50-60 years and 90 years in males and females respectively, but averaging 29 years in males and 50 years in females.

**World population** Estimates of abundance are available only for small areas and can do no more than give a clue as to the approximate order of magnitude of the world population size. About 300 killer whales are thought to live in coastal waters off British Columbia and Washington State, and a further 350 along the southern coast of Alaska westwards to Kodiak Island. Norwegian coastal waters probably hold at least 1500 animals, and about 7,000 were estimated in an area around Iceland from the coast to between 500 and 1,000km offshore. These estimates are all for productive waters, where the density of whales could be expected to be much higher than in tropical areas, for example. Although densities of animals vary, killer whales are clearly an abundant cetacean in world terms, and there are no current fears for the species' safety.

**Man's influence** Catches of killer whales for meat or oil have been considerable in some areas, despite this species normally being only a secondary target. American pelagic whalers of the eighteenth and nineteenth centuries would sometimes take killer whales if opportunity arose and their larger primary targets were not in the vicinity, although the level of catch was never high. Norwegian small-type whalers took 2,390 killer whales in the northeastern Atlantic and a further 45 west of Cape Farewell (the southern tip of Greenland) in the period 1938-81. Japanese whalers took 1,178 killer whales in their coastal waters between 1953 and 1977, and the USSR took 270 in the northwestern Pacific in the period 1953-1964. A further 1,654 were taken by USSR Antarctic whalers between 1953 and 1980, including 916 in the 79/80 season alone. The only other sustained postwar kill was of 2-3 per year off West Greenland.

Live captures for public display were taken mostly from the northeastern Pacific (67 between 1962 and 1973) and from Iceland (84 in the period 1975-1988, and still continuing). Killer whales have adapted relatively well to captivity and several calves have been captive-bred. The annual survivorship of animals kept in US and Canadian facilities is 91 percent.

Other pressures from man have come about principally because of the composition of the killer whale's diet. Since this includes species of fish such as salmon and herring that are of commercial importance to fishermen, this has sometimes resulted in the whales' death at the hands of either the fishermen themselves or, in the case of Icelandic whales in 1956, the US Navy, which was invited in to clear the area. Less obvious problems are the reduction in the killer whales' food supply by fishermen in overfished areas and the relatively high chemical pollutant loads in the tissues of some populations from a diet of highly contaminated animals at the top end of the food chain.

*Above left: A killer whale spy hops in order to survey the surrounding sea ice for likely prey, which could include seals and penguins on the surface of the ice. Killer whales can 'topple' an ice floe to dislodge such prey into the water.*

*Above: This dramatic photograph has recorded another hunting technique. Here, a killer whale has snatched a sea lion from the beach after rushing headlong towards the shoreline.*

*Right: Killer whales in close formation. When resting or feeding, members of such groups often synchronize their diving activities.*

# FALSE KILLER WHALE

*PSEUDORCA CRASSIDENS*

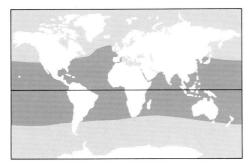

■ Probable normal range

**Classification** First known from a sub-fossil (i.e. calcified but not mineralized) skeleton from Lincolnshire, England, this species was not known to be still in existence until a mass stranding in Germany in about 1860. A Danish zoologist, Johannes Reinhardt, examined animals from this stranding and recognized their similarity to the sub-fossil skull described by Owen. With the benefit of studying freshly dead material, he amended Owen's original *Phocaena crassidens* to *Pseudorca crassidens* in recognition of its resemblance to the killer whale. *Crassidens* means 'thick-tooth', a reference to the relatively robust teeth in this species.

**Description** A medium-sized species, averaging 5.2-5.4m (maximum 5.96m) in adult males and 4.3-4.6m (maximum 5.1m) in females. Body weight is up to 2.2 tonnes and 1.1 tonnes in males and females respectively. Body shape is slim, with an upright, falcate dorsal fin about midway along the body. The head tapers to a very rounded snout that overhangs the lower jaw considerably. A crease runs from below the eye forward, above the mouthline. The flippers are unique, widening to a broad hump on the leading edge midway along their length, resembling a shoulder.

Body colour is black, apart from faint grey marks on the head, varying between races, and a chest patch similar to but less distinct than that of pilot whales. There are 8-11 pairs of thick, circular-sectioned teeth in both upper and lower jaws.

**Recognition at sea** False killer whales can be distinguished from pilot whales by the shape of the head and dorsal fin, and from other globicephalids by size and head shape. In addition, this is the only species of its size and colour to swim rapidly at the surface and bow ride.

**Habitat** Tropical, subtropical and warm temperate waters, principally in the open ocean away from land but also in semi-enclosed seas. Occasionally, false killer whales venture into colder waters as, for example, off the northern UK, Norway and Alaska.

**Distribution and migration** False killer whales are found in all the world's oceans within the right habitat, including the Red and Mediterranean Seas. Wanderers have occurred far outside the normal range. No migrations are known.

**Food and feeding** The diet consists mostly of squid and large fish, such as dolphin-fish and tuna, but this species is also reported to attack groups of small cetaceans. It has earned a bad reputation by taking bait off fishermen's lines.

**Behaviour** Group size is typically 10-50, but sometimes several hundred, in this highly social species. Animals of all ages of both sexes occur in these groups, there being no indication of any segregation. For its size, this is a fast-swimming species, often porpoising or leaping clear

of the water when excited. It readily bow rides a vessel or follows in the wake of ships that are too fast to keep up with.

It has adapted well to captivity and is easily trained, showing much less aggression than its smaller relative, the pygmy killer whale. The false killer whale often mass strands.

**Life history** Relatively little is known. Breeding occurs all year round, with no obvious seasonality. Calves are born at a length of about 1.8m (possible range 1.6-1.93m) and sexual maturity is reached at an age of 8-14 years, at body lengths of 3.96-4.57m (males) and 3.66-4.27m (females). The gestation period has been tentatively estimated at either 11-12 months or 15.5 months. Lactation may last about 18 months. A long reproductive cycle is suggested by studies of two stranded pods in which only 14 percent and 21 percent of mature females were pregnant. The sex ratio of two fairly large pods examined was 1 female to 0.85 and 0.82 males, respectively, indicating a higher death rate in males than in females, as is common in this family.

**World population** Unknown, but this is a widely distributed species that occurs quite commonly in some areas (off Japan and Hawaii, for example), and is not considered threatened.

**Man's influence** Japanese fishermen have recently killed hundreds of false killer whales by driving them ashore, not for food but in an attempt to reverse the downward slide in their catch of yellowtail, which they blame on this and other cetacean species. Some of these animals have been taken into captivity and have

proved adaptable to captive living, despite being a deepwater species.

Apart from the Japanese drives (see page 51), there are accidental kills of this species by entrapment in fishing gear, both in longlines and nets. Nevertheless, the level of catch is unlikely to have a significant impact on the stocks.

*Above left: Note the characteristic hump midway along the leading edge of the flipper.*

*Below left: This species is slimmer, with a more tapered head than the killer whale.*

*Above: In common with the killer whale, the false killer has stubby powerful teeth.*

*Below: This is one of the swiftest and most playful of the smaller species of whales.*

# PYGMY KILLER WHALE

*FERESA ATTENUATA*

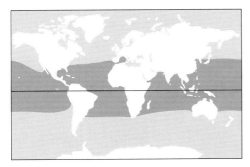

■ Possible range

**Classification** The naming of this species owes much to the work of John Gray of the British Museum. Gray examined two skulls of a then unknown species and, between 1827 and 1875, evaluated and re-evaluated them several times before deciding on the name currently used. Subsequent new material from around the world persuaded later workers that more than one species was involved, but *Feresa attenuata* is now universally accepted for all variations. There are similarities in form between this species and several other globicephalids, although the differences are sufficient to warrant the separate genus.

**Description** Smallest of the family, and similar in size to many true dolphins, pygmy killer whales average 2.1-2.3m (maximum 2.6m) in body length and 150-170kg (maximum 225kg) in weight. Males may be slightly bigger than females. Body colour is dark grey, brownish grey or blue-black, with a dark stripe from the top of the head extending and widening to and around the dorsal fin, where it becomes a saddle patch. The lips and tip of the lower jaw are white, and a light grey patch extends from the throat to the genital area, where it is at its widest, as in the melon-headed whale (see opposite).

The foreparts of the body are fairly robust and the region behind the mid-point is slimmer, with a high dorsal fin that is fairly pointed and slightly falcate. The flippers are equivalent to 18-23 percent of body length, curved on the leading edge, usually ragged on the trailing edge and rounded at the tip. The head is very rounded, and the upper jaw extends beyond the lower. There is no beak. There are 8-11 pairs of teeth in the upper jaw and 11-13 pairs in the lower. The tail flukes are faintly notched.

**Identification at sea** The pygmy killer whale is very similar to the melon-headed whale, but the head shape and, to a lesser extent, the dorsal fin shape should distinguish it at close quarters. The white 'goatee' patch and the flippers, if seen, are also distinctive.

**Habitat** Tropical and subtropical deep, oceanic waters; rarely in warm temperate areas and semi-enclosed seas.

**Distribution and migration** Assessment of strandings and sightings lead to the conclusion that this species is widely distributed in warm waters around the world. It has been recorded in the Mediterranean Sea. No migrations are known, and the species is thought to occur in at least some regions all year round (e.g. off Sri Lanka and around St. Vincent in the Lesser Antilles).

**Food and feeding** The diet consists of squid and fish of many species, including the dorado, or dolphin-fish. Observations, especially from boats involved in the tuna industry in the eastern tropical Pacific, suggest that small cetaceans may sometimes be taken. One captive animal ate 5.4kg and another 8kg of squid and fish per day.

**Behaviour** Group size is typically up to 50 animals, with a reported average of about 25 and a maximum of several hundred. Loafing pods are sometimes encountered. The species may bow ride or follow boats, but often avoids them. Leaping, spy hopping and lobtailing have all been recorded. In captivity, this can be an aggressive species, even to the extent of killing other cetaceans in the tank, and elicits fear reactions in other small cetaceans. Whistles, clicks and growls have been noted from this species, the latter being made by the blowhole rather than inside the head.

**Life history** Very little is known. Birth is thought to occur at a body length of about 80cm and sexual maturity is probably reached at a length of around 2m. One small pod of 14 animals examined in Japan had an equal sex ratio of animals, but this is unlikely to be representative of the species as a whole.

**World population** Unknown, but nowhere is this a common species.

**Man's influence** A few animals have been taken in Japanese drive fisheries and there are other small directed catches, but the level of removals is very low. Many more are killed in fishery entrapments every year, but the total number involved is unknown. It has been estimated that 300-800 are killed in this way each year off Sri Lanka. A few pygmy killer whales have been kept in captivity, but only for short periods.

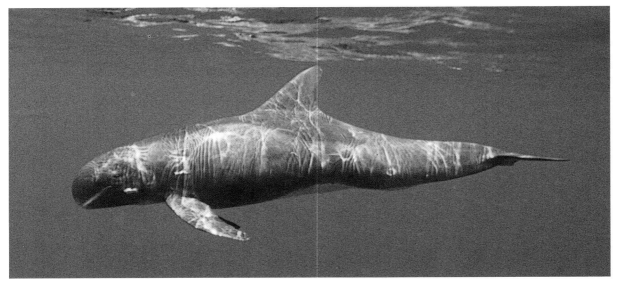

*Left: Rarely seen in the wild, pygmy killer whales share much of their warmwater range with melon-headed whales, from which they are difficult to distinguish. Despite its small size, there is evidence that the pygmy killer whale sometimes preys on other cetaceans.*

# MELON-HEADED WHALE

*PEPONOCEPHALA ELECTRA*

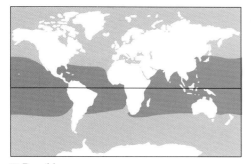

■ Possible range

**Classification** Initially considered to be a *Lagenorhynchus* dolphin, a new genus *Peponocephala* (literally 'melon-head') was created especially for this species in 1966 by Nishiwaki and Norris on the basis of new material from Japan and Hawaii. It is not closely related to any other cetacean.

**Local names** Now universally called melon-headed or melonhead whale. The names many-toothed blackfish and electra dolphin were in use before this species was reclassified.

**Description** A small species, averaging about 2.2-2.5m in body length (maximum 2.75m) and 160kg in weight (maximum about 275kg). There is no apparent difference between the sexes in size, although the sample size of measured animals is small. Body colour is dark grey, bluish black or dark brown, often with a slightly darker strip along the upper midline from the head to the dorsal fin and extending a short way down the flanks. There may also be a dark 'mask' on the face. The lips are white, and a light grey anchor pattern, reminiscent of the pilot whales, is present on the chest, continuing as a line to the navel and genital area, where it widens again. The shape of the head does

indeed resemble a melon, but is quite pointed at the tip.

Body shape is slender, with a high, falcate dorsal fin positioned midway along the body. This is often ragged, due to damage on the trailing edge. The flippers are fairly long, curved and pointed at the tip, and the tail flukes are distinctly notched. There are 20-25 pairs of small, pointed teeth in both jaws.

**Recognition at sea** Easily confused with the pygmy killer whale (*Feresa attenuata*) and, to a lesser extent, the false killer whale (*Pseudorca crassidens*), with which it shares its range, the melon-headed whale is slightly larger than the first and considerably smaller than the second. The dorsal fin is less pointed and more curved than that of *Feresa*, and the head more pointed. When frightened, *Peponocephala* pods often swim furiously at the surface, turning the water to froth. On the beach, the numerous teeth distinguish this from other globicephalids.

**Habitat** This is a species of tropical, subtropical and, rarely, warm temperate waters. It is considered to be predominantly oceanic in habit, rarely venturing close to land.

**Distribution and migration** Few records of live or freshly dead specimens came to light before the late 1950s, but since then the species has been seen in all the major oceans and is assumed to have a continuous distribution in waters of the appropriate temperature. No migrations are known, and are probably unlikely.

**Food and feeding** From the few available records, squid and a variety of small fish species are thought to be the usual prey.

**Behaviour** Little is known about behaviour, except that it is a highly gregarious species with a pod size normally in the range 100-500 and sometimes reaching at least 2,000. Melon-headed whales sometimes associate with dolphins. They are often very rapid swimmers, especially when excited. In relation to its probable scarcity, this species commonly mass strands.

**Life history** Few details are known of this animal's life history. The smallest individual in a recent mass stranding in Brazil measured 1.06m and another in Australia measured 1.12m, so the length at birth must be at or below this size. Newborn young have been reported in July and August, but no assessment of seasonality is yet possible. The adult sex ratio seems to be consistently about 2 females : 1 male, indicating a higher mortality rate in males than in females, as is found in pilot and killer whales. A tentative estimate of the age of a male of this species (47 years) would, if correct, be one of the highest for any small cetacean.

**World population** Totally unknown, but nowhere is this a common species except, apparently, around one island in the Philippines.

**Man's influence** Small numbers of melon-headed whales have been intentionally taken by Japanese fishermen in the past few decades, but otherwise this species is not subject to deliberate killing. An unknown number are drowned in seine and driftnet fisheries, especially in the Pacific. A few melon-headed whales have been kept in captivity for up to 17 months, but they can be aggressive.

*Right: This small and little-known species was considered to be a* Lagenorhynchus *dolphin until new fresh specimens collected from the North Pacific were examined in the 1960s. It is now recognized to be sufficiently different from all other species to warrant its own genus, and has tentatively been placed taxonomically nearer to the pilot and killer whales than to the oceanic dolphins.*

# LONG-FINNED PILOT WHALE

## GLOBICEPHALA MELAS

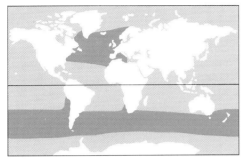

■ Probable range

**Classification** The genus *Globicephala*, meaning 'globe-head', was created in 1828 to include what we now recognize as the pilot whales, although the variety of shape, colour and size of these animals has led to confusion over how many species exist. A review of the genus in 1971 recognized just two species, reliably separated only on skull characters, but differing to some extent in the relative length of the flipper. *G. melas* (until recently, *G. melaena*) is the long-finned pilot whale, and *G. macrorhynchus* the short-finned pilot whale (see page 128). The Southern Hemisphere form of *G. melas* may merit subspecific status (*G.m. edwardii*) on the basis of morphological differences, but is not currently recognized. The word *melas* means black, so this is literally the 'black globe-head'.

**Local names** Long-finned or longfin pilot whale is usual, but 'blackfish' is used locally for this species and others in the family. 'Pothead' and 'caaing whale' (calling whale) are used in some areas, the latter by residents of the Orkney and Shetland Isles in northern UK. The name 'pilot' is said to derive from the whale's supposed piloting of fishermen towards schools of fish or from the way one whale was thought to lead the group.

**Description** A small to medium-sized whale with a high degree of sexual dimorphism, reaching 6.3m (average 5.6-5.8m) in males and 5.5m (average 4.5-4.8m) in females in the North Atlantic. Adult body weight averages 1 tonne in females and 1.75 tonnes in males. The body is grey-black or very dark brown, often depending on the light in which the whale is seen. Beached animals are very dark. Juveniles are lighter grey, with blotches and crease marks in the very young. On the throat and chest of all animals is a whitish or light grey patch in the shape of an anchor. The patch narrows and continues in a line along the belly, widening and terminating around the vent. All populations have a lighter streak behind the eye and another, called a saddle, behind the dorsal fin, but these patches vary from barely discernible to almost white.

This is a fairly stocky whale, with a bulbous head in adults (especially males) and a characteristic low, rounded dorsal fin that is set well forward, starting only a third of the body length from the front of the head. The fin is upright and triangular in juveniles, becoming longer and more bulbous with age. The flippers are pointed and long (20-23 percent of body length in adults), with an increasingly noticeable 'elbow' with age. The tail stock in front of the deeply notched flukes is deep and very flattened laterally. The small mouth has barely discernible lips and 8-13 pairs of teeth in both the upper and lower jaw. Skull characteristics distinguish this species from the short-finned pilot whale.

**Recognition at sea** Pilot whales are invariably found in groups of tens or hundreds of animals, often in association with other small cetaceans or minke whales (*Balaenoptera acutorostrata*). They are slow swimming, have almost invisible blows and rarely show much above-water behaviour except spy hopping. They often 'log' at the surface, apparently asleep. The characteristic dorsal fin of the adult makes it easy to discriminate between this and all other species, except the short-finned pilot whale with which it has a small range overlap. An underwater view of the flippers and ventral colour pattern may help to tell the difference between the long- and short-finned species, but often this is simply not possible at sea. Beached specimens can be distinguished by skull characteristics.

**Habitat** Although essentially an oceanic species, *G. melas* may enter coastal and shallower waters on a regular basis, probably in search of food. The long-finned pilot whale is one of the most commonly mass-stranded species and this tendency indicates that it is not well adapted to living in coastal areas. It prefers temperate and subpolar waters within a surface temperature range of 0-25°C.

**Distribution and migration** This species has an antitropical distribution, occurring in the North Atlantic Ocean above about 30°N and probably in a continuous belt between the Tropic of Capricorn and the Antarctic Convergence in the Southern Hemisphere, although sight records are sparse here. It is probably not a migratory whale in the normal sense, but where prey occurs in a particular place on a seasonal basis, as off Newfoundland, whales will go there in search of food and remain while stocks last. A north-south migration in British waters was postulated in the 1970s, but recent evidence does not support this.

**Food and feeding** The pilot whale is principally a squid eater in midwater, but will take fish if squid are not available in the necessary quantities. Detailed information on diet is available only from two sites in the North Atlantic; at each site, a single species of squid is the preferred food – *Illex illecebrosus* off Newfoundland and *Todarodes sagittatus* off the Faeroe Islands. *Todarodes* is probably the principal item of food throughout European waters. A considerable range of squid and fish species are eaten in smaller quantities, which suggests that this whale will exploit almost any locally abundant schooling prey. Individual prey items are fairly small. About five percent of body weight is consumed in prey every day, amounting to about 50kg in an adult female and 100kg in a male.

**Behaviour** This is an extremely social species, with most whales occurring in groups of tens or hundreds. Group size may vary seasonally, perhaps as a result of 'family' groups merging at certain times of year. The average group size captured off the Faeroe Islands over several centuries was about 100, those off Newfoundland averaged 85, but those observed or stranded off central Europe and South America averaged less than 50.

Although adult males are found in most pods, recent genetic evidence indicates that resident males may not be responsible for mating within the group, so out-breeding might occur when pods merge. The species has many characteristics typical of polygynous animals and it is likely that dominant males do fertilize many females. Fighting scars occur disproportionately on adult males, so aggressive competition is probable.

The potential depth of diving is not known, but is likely to be hundreds of metres judging by diet and by analogy to the short-finned species. Dives are normally of less than 10 minutes duration.

Vocalizations are chiefly of two types: clicks assumed to be for echolocation, and whistles, probably for communication. Whistles are of 3-5kHz average frequency, last less than a second and are repeated typically 14-41 times per minute. Some may act as 'signature-whistles', unique to individual whales.

**Life history** Most available information is from the North Atlantic. Calves are born at about 1.75-1.8m in length and a weight of 70-80kg. Males grow faster than females of the same age, but do not reach sexual maturity until 12-20 years, at a body length of about 5m. Females reach sexual maturity at an average age of 6-10 years and an average body length of 3.8m. Pregnancy lasts 14.5-15 months and lactation a further 20-22 months or so. Youngsters take solid food before the end of their first year. Calves are born to a female every 3.5 years on average, and about nine are reared in a normal lifetime. Breeding is broadly seasonal, with peak mating in April-May (probably Oct-Nov in the Southern Hemisphere) and calving July-August (January-February), but in the Faeroese stock calving can occur at almost any time of the year. On average, 10 or 11 calves are born annually per 100 long-finned pilot whales in the Faeroese population.

Recent work on age determination indicates that the normal lifetime of this species is 30-50 years. The oldest animals in a sample from Newfoundland were aged 36 (male) and 57 (female). The oldest females in the Faeroese stock cease to reproduce and may provide care for other members of the group. The sex ratio at birth is 1:1, but adult females outnumber adult males approximately 3:1, so the mortality rate in males is much higher.

**World population** The only population estimates available are for areas in the North Atlantic, and it is not clear for what geographical regions the estimates are valid. A figure of 62,000 animals in 1947 was estimated for the stock from which the 1952-68 Newfoundland catch was made. An aerial survey of a relatively small area off Newfoundland/Labrador gave an estimate of 6,700-19,600 animals in 1980. Between 6,600 and 9,700 were thought to occur in an area of ocean west of France and Ireland in the years 1981-1984. No reliable estimate has been made for pilot whales in the area from which Faeroese catches are taken, but the catch is so high, and has been sustained for so many years, that the stock must number many tens or perhaps the low hundreds of thousands.

Numbers in the Southern Hemisphere have not been estimated, but the species covers an enormous area and the density could be as high as in the North Atlantic, in which case the population would be counted in hundreds of thousands.

**Man's influence** This species has a long history of exploitation in the North Atlantic, particularly off Newfoundland and, in the east, off the Faeroe Islands, where catches have been sustained for centuries. Twentieth century coastal fisheries have existed off Orkney, Shetland, the Faeroes, Norway, Greenland and Newfoundland. The Newfoundland fishery became intense between 1951 and 1967, when the stock and fishery collapsed. Written records for the Faeroese drive fishery exist from 1584, but the catch probably predates this. The average annual kill between 1936 and 1978 was 1,552, with 4,325 taken in 1941 alone. Catches in the past three decades have been as high as in any other period since 1709, despite the removal of at least 230,000 whales from the stock since then.

Incidental catches in fishery gear have become significant in the 1980s, particularly in the Italian swordfish industry (at least eight long-finned pilot whales were captured in 1988) and in the mackerel fishery off the US East Coast, where over 100 deaths occurred in 1988 alone.

*Above: Long-finned pilot whales of both northern and southern populations have patches of lighter pigmentation behind the eye and dorsal fin, but Southern Hemisphere animals – as here – are more distinctly marked.*

*Right: A pod of pilot whales in a Shetland bay. Residents of the Shetland and Orkney Isles once drove pilot whales ashore for food, and Faeroese islanders still take an average of 1500 animals a year in a traditional hunt.*

# SHORT-FINNED PILOT WHALE

## GLOBICEPHALA MACRORHYNCHUS

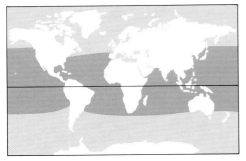

■ Probable range

**Classification** In 1846, John Gray of the British Museum named a pilot whale 'from the south seas' on the basis of skeletal material only. His educated guess that the species had a large beak was reflected in the name he gave it – *macrorhynchus*. Unfortunately, he was proved incorrect, but the name survived. Subsequently, several other forms of pilot whale in the Pacific Ocean were described, the most recent only in the 1980s, but all are considered to be variants of the same species.

**Local names** Short-finned pilot whale is the only name in common use today. One variant was previously called the Pacific pilot whale. The term 'blackfish' is sometimes used, but can refer to most of the species in this family.

**Description** The short-finned pilot whale is very similar to the long-finned species (see page 126). However, there are differences in the shape and size of the flippers – they have less of an 'elbow' and measure only 16-19 percent of body length in *G. macrorhynchus*. The number of teeth is also different, this species having seven to nine pairs in the upper and lower jaws, and there are also differences in the bone structure of the upper jaw. Even so, there is a small degree of overlap between the species in the first two of these characters, so only examination of the skull can positively discriminate between the species. Most forms of the short-finned pilot whale seem to show an obvious 'saddle' patch of grey, a darker ventral patch than in the long-finned pilot whale and a streak behind the eye of varying shades of grey.

There is an extraordinary difference in body size between races of this species, illustrated by two forms that occur off Japan but have separate ranges and are genetically distinct. Males of the southern form are on average about 1.8m shorter than the northern form in overall body length and females are about 1m shorter, representing a difference of approximately 38 percent and 28 percent

respectively. Average adult body lengths are in the range 3.64-4.67m (for females) and 4.7-6.5m (for males), with a maximum of 5.1m and 7.2m respectively. This represents a body weight of about 0.6-1.15 tonnes (max. 1.4 tonnes) in females and 1.26-3.15 tonnes (max. 3.95 tonnes) in males. Animals in the Atlantic and Indian Oceans are intermediate in length between the two stocks off Japan. The largest animals examined in mass strandings in the western North Atlantic were 3.97m (female) and 5.35m (male).

**Recognition at sea** The general characteristics are so similar to those of the long-finned pilot whale and both species are so variable that the two cannot be reliably separated at sea unless, perhaps, an underwater view is possible. Pilot whales can be distinguished from false killer whales, the only other blackish species of a similar size, by their less upright dorsal fin, more bulbous head and generally slower swimming speed.

**Habitat** Short-finned pilot whales are found in tropical, subtropical and warm temperate waters. This is typically a species of the deep ocean, but regularly occurs near land in some areas. The two stocks off Japan are separated by oceanographic boundaries. The northern one lives in waters of surface temperature 8-24°C and the southern stock in temperatures in excess of 20°C all year round.

**Distribution and migration** This species probably occurs in all oceans, and is limited only by water temperature. Records at sea are sparse, however, especially in the South Atlantic. With the exception of the northern North Pacific and polar waters, where pilot whales are absent, the short-finned species probably occupies all the non-polar areas not occupied by the long-finned pilot whale. There is a narrow band of overlap between the species, but otherwise their ranges are entirely complementary.

Seasonality of occurrence has been noted off Japan, California and in the eastern tropical Pacific, and probably reflects the relative abundance of prey. Off California, fewer pilot whales are seen in years of low squid density, while in the eastern tropical Pacific, oceanographic conditions seem to influence the distribution of this whale.

**Food and feeding** The diet consists predominantly of cephalopods (squid and octopus), but fish may be taken. The squid *Loligo opalescens* seems to be the

major prey of the short-finned pilot whale off California. Off Japan, the squids *Todarodes pacificus*, *Eucleoteuthis luminosa* and *Ommastrephes bartrami*, and the giant octopus *Octopus dofleini* are commonly taken. Off southern Africa, the squids *Loligo reynaudi* and *Oregoniateuthis* sp. have been recorded from stomachs. Off West Africa, the diet includes the squid *Illex illecebrosus coindeti*.

**Behaviour** Like the long-finned pilot whale (*G.melas*), this species is normally seen in groups, but the group size seems to be smaller, on average, than that of the long-finned species. The size range of 40 stranded pods from the Atlantic and Indian Oceans (this species is often involved in mass strandings) was 1-200 and averaged 40. Pods sighted at sea are reported to be smaller than this (average 15-43 in different areas), but visual estimates are notoriously difficult and usually under-represent the true numbers. Groups, called 'chorus lines', sometimes swim in line abreast, up to four kilometres across. *G. macrorhynchus* often associates closely with other cetaceans.

Like *G. melas*, this species is thought to be multi-male polygynous, and its social organization is probably similar to the long-finned species in most respects. Vocalizations are also similar to those of *G. melas*, varying only in the duration of whistles.

*G. macrorhynchus* is thought to be able to dive to at least 500m and for periods of up to 15 minutes, although most dives are shorter and shallower than this.

**Life history** Most information has been derived from intensive studies of the two forms occurring off Japan, which show significant differences. Figures are given first for the southern form; those for the northern form follow in brackets.

Calves are born at about 1.4m(1.85m) after a gestation period of about 15

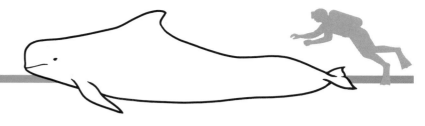

*Above: The dorsal fin of pilot whales is set characteristically far forward along the back of the animal and is very variable in shape.*

*Below right: A short-finned pilot whale approaches the camera, showing the rounded head reflected in the genus name.*

months. Females reach sexual maturity at 3.16m(3.95m) and an age of 7-12 years/ average 9 years. Males mature at about 4.2m (5.5m) and an age of 17 years. Males remain reproductively active after reaching sexual maturity, whereas females are at their most productive in the years immediately after maturity and have their last calf at an age of about 37 years. Thereafter, females may continue producing milk for a number of years and may suckle other calves in the group, which are likely to be closely related to themselves. They can survive up to 25 years after bearing their last calf.

Lactation can last between about 12 months and many years. Calves start taking solid food at about six months. Breeding is seasonal, more so in the northern form than in the southern one, and calving occurs either in spring/ autumn (southern form) or autumn/ winter (northern form). The calving interval increases as females get older, but averages 4-5.6 years.

Total adult mortality rates have been estimated at about 10 percent. The oldest females examined were aged 62 and the oldest males 45. The sex ratio of adult males:females appears to be about 1:2.2.

In a smaller study of mass-stranded animals in the western North Atlantic, sexual maturity was reached at a mean length of 3.01m (females), 4.75m (males).

**World population** The only estimates of abundance available for this species are for the two stocks recently exploited off Japan. The northern stock is thought to occur in a relatively small area of cold coastal waters off the Pacific coast of northern Japan between latitudes 35°N

and 43°N, and has been estimated at about 5,300 animals in size. The southern stock probably occurs in the Kuroshio current and countercurrent areas to 158°E and 22°N and may number about 53,000 individuals. Given the enormous geographical range of *G. macrorhynchus*, the total world population must be many times this figure.

**Man's influence** Short-finned pilot whales have a long history of exploitation, but have never suffered the intensity of catching that has been carried out on the long-finned species. American whaling crews in the nineteenth century took *G. macrorhynchus* for practice and for small quantities of high-grade oil. The total catch was probably many thousands; approximately 843 were taken by only a few ships in the period 1850-1855, and 196 were taken by one ship in 1881.

The only significant twentieth-century catches in the Atlantic have been taken off St. Vincent in the Caribbean, where whaling started in the 1930s, and off St. Lucia. Annual removals averaged 220-250 in the 1960s and early 1970s, but have subsequently declined. In the western North Pacific, catches of this species have been taken for several centuries, by driving the animals ashore in groups or harpooning them individually. In the early 1980s, Japanese catches of both forms combined averaged about 320 per year.

Incidental catches in fishing gear, particularly gillnets, may be significant, but are not adequately recorded. Off the US and Canadian west coasts, a few tens of animals may be taken annually. A few are also taken off Peru.

Short-finned pilot whales have been popular as captive exhibits for many years. At least 70 have been taken for this purpose in US waters (California and Hawaii) since 1963, and a similar number in Japan since 1974. Mortality rates in captivity are high; about half die every year.

# OCEANIC DOLPHINS
## DELPHINIDAE

This is by far the largest existing family of cetaceans, comprising 26 living species of what might be termed 'classic' dolphins. With one exception, the Risso's dolphin (*Grampus griseus*), which perhaps ought to be placed in the Globicephalidae, they are characterized by having a distinct beak (unlike the porpoises, Phocoenidae), two or more fused cervical vertebrae and 20 or more pairs of teeth in the upper jaw. None are more than 4m long.

The family name was introduced by John Gray in 1821, but he included many species that have subsequently been attributed to other families. The remaining species belong to 11 different genera: *Sousa* (three species), *Steno* (one species), *Sotalia* (one species), *Tursiops* (one species), *Stenella* (five species), *Delphinus* (one species), *Lagenorhynchus* (six species), *Lagenodelphis* (one species), *Cephalorhynchus* (four species), *Lissodelphis* (two species) and *Grampus* (one species). Of these, only *Sousa*, *Sotalia*, *Tursiops* and *Cephalorhynchus* are primarily coastal. The remaining 17 species are mainly, or exclusively, creatures of the deep, open ocean.

All but two species (the right whale dolphins, *Lissodelphis*) have a dorsal fin and, again with the exception of Risso's dolphin (which prefers squid), the primary diet of all species is fish.

Body shape is very variable within the family. At one extreme are the very slim and streamlined right whale dolphins, perfectly formed for rapid progress in water. At the other is the blunt-nosed and relatively stocky Risso's dolphin. The smallest animals in the group are the four *Cephalorhynchus* species, with a maximum length of about 1.7m. The longest is the bottlenose dolphin (*Tursiops truncatus*), which can reach 4m in length and over 650kg in weight.

*One of the largest members of the family, Risso's dolphins are group-living animals, often heavily scarred on the body.*

# HUMPBACK DOLPHINS

## SOUSA CHINENSIS; SOUSA TEUSZII; SOUSA PLUMBEA

S. teuszii    S. plumbea    S. chinensis

**Classification** Although five nominal species of humpback dolphins have been described, available information suggests that there is a single species *Sousa chinensis* consisting of three geographical groups. Until the classification has been resolved, the appropriate species names for these groups are *Sousa teuszii* (Kukenthal, 1892) in the Atlantic Ocean, *Sousa plumbea* (Cuvier, 1829) in the southern and western Indian Ocean, and *Sousa chinensis* (Osbeck, 1765) in the western Indian Ocean and eastern Pacific Oceans. The origin of the name *Sousa* is obscure; *teuszii*, *plumbea* and *chinensis* respectively honour Edward Teusz (who collected the first specimen of this group), refer to the plumbeous, or leaden, colour of the second group, and indicate the Chinese origin of Osbeck's specimens.

The description 'humpback' stems from the profile of the elongated dorsal fin base, which is suitably emphasized by the arched back before diving.

**Local names** Humpback dolphins are known by various local names, including parampuan laut in Malaya, bolla gadimi in India and darfeel in Kuwait.

**Description** Robust in form, humpback dolphins are characterized by an elongate snout, a melon with a distinct apex, broad flippers rounded at their tips, and marked keels above and below the tail stock. Set midway along the body, the triangular dorsal fin is supported on an elongate base. In Atlantic and western Indian Ocean animals, this base may be one third or more of the body length, decreasing to about one fifth in dolphins further east. The teeth are robust, up to 5mm in diameter, and vary in number from 27 to 38 in each side of each jaw, according to location. Atlantic animals have slightly fewer teeth than other populations.

Humpback dolphins reach a maximum length of 2.8m and a weight of 284kg. Off South Africa, most adults are about 2.5m long and weigh about 195kg.

Colour patterns vary considerably from area to area and with age. Atlantic animals are slate-grey on the back and sides, becoming paler grey on the belly. South African and Australian dolphins darken with age to an overall leaden grey colour, except for the off-white ventral surface. The dorsal fin tip and adjacent base may whiten with age. In the northern Indian Ocean, animals are uniformly leaden grey, although in some areas elongate bluish black flecks cover the body. Off China, the dark grey calves pale with age to become pinkish white adults with a dark eye patch, body spots and blotches.

**Recognition at sea** The distinctive dorsal fin, coastal habits and manner of surfacing (see below) will distinguish these dolphins in the field from all other species. The numbers and size of teeth are diagnostic for stranded animals.

**Habitat** These dolphins prefer shallow water less than 20m deep and frequent mangrove channels, embayments and shallow banks, such as those found in river deltas. On open coasts they stay close to the surf zone. Such waters are frequently highly turbid or muddy. Although they are marine animals, they appear to tolerate brackish water well and may swim several kilometres up large rivers.

**Distribution and migration** Humpback dolphins are widely distributed in the coastal waters of West Africa and in the Indian and western Pacific Oceans. Though essentially tropical, some populations extend into subtropical waters down the east coasts of Africa and Australia in association with warm currents. Atlantic humpback dolphins occur off Mauritania, Senegal and Cameroons. In the Indo-Pacific region, the *plumbea* form extends eastwards from the southern tip of Africa to eastern India, while the *chinensis* form occurs from Sumatra to the East China Sea and southwards to the northern and eastern coasts of Australia.

Although the northward movement of Atlantic humpback dolphins in summer has been proposed, there is no firm evidence of migration in any population. Rather, the limited information from southern Africa and China suggests residency throughout the year.

**Food and feeding** Humpback dolphins are primarily fish eaters, feeding on a variety of schooling species, including grunts, mullets, sea breams and herring-

like fishes. There is no evidence that Atlantic humpback dolphins eat vegetation, as was reported by Kukenthal in his original description. In the coastal population off South Africa, about two-thirds of the diet consists of shore or estuarine associated species, and a further quarter are typically reef inhabitants. Onshore movement and feeding in these dolphins – and those off Senegal – increases and declines with the rise and ebb of the tide, emphasizing their close association with the inshore environment.

An unusual feeding association between dolphin and man has been recorded off Mauritania, northwestern Africa, where dolphins assist fishermen to catch mullets migrating close to the shore. Summoned by sticks slapped on the water, mixed groups of bottlenose and humpback dolphins herd the fish while nets are put in place, providing a joint harvest for all the predators.

**Behaviour** Humpback dolphins in all areas typically form small schools of up to 25 animals. Most frequently, groups contain five to seven members, which may combine to form the larger schools occasionally seen. A localized population of 25 animals studied off South Africa was

*Right: Humpback dolphins are coastal in habit and occur in various forms in much of Australasia, Southeast Asia, Indian Ocean coasts and West Africa. The basic body shape is similar in all these geographic areas, but colour patterns do vary quite considerably. There is still some controversy over how many species should be given taxonomic recognition.*

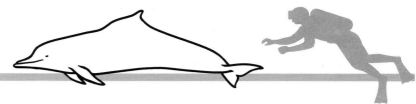

composed of five mature and nine other adults, five or six juveniles and four calves of various sizes. Adults tended to be single or in pairs, and juveniles often in groups with more than one adult.

Schools progress slowly at about 5kph, diving for comparatively long times of 40-60 seconds, interspersed with brief periods at the surface. The manner of surfacing is typical of these dolphins, where the snout and sometimes the entire head clears the surface before the body is arched tightly, humping the back and dorsal fin before submerging.

Observations of South African schools showed that dolphins used a sandy bay more frequently for resting and social interactions, such as physical contact, leaping and chasing, and fed most often along an unsheltered rocky coastline. On occasion, animals may perform complete back somersaults out of the water. Mating was observed during inverted swimming by one partner, apparently differing from the vertical surfacing behaviour of pairs in the northern Indian Ocean attributed to mating.

Humpback dolphins rarely approach boats, and can only rarely be induced to bow ride. Usually they avoid boats by diving and separating from their group, to surface some distance away in an unexpected direction.

**Life history** Information on growth and reproduction is very limited for all populations. The length at birth is probably about 1m, based on the few known newborn specimens. Observations of calves in schools indicate a protracted breeding season off Senegal, and also off South Africa, with a peak in summer. A single pregnant 2.44m dolphin and a 2.79m male from South Africa provide the only information on length at sexual maturity, while the shortest full-grown dolphins from South Africa and China were 2.54m and 2.26m respectively.

**World population** No information is available on the size of any humpback dolphin population, apart from rather crude estimates of 100 and 500 animals respectively for the Saloum Delta (Senegal) and the Indus Delta. Their small group size, long diving times and preference for turbid water hinder the design of effective censuses, other than by mark-recapture techniques based, for example, on naturally marked individuals. The difficulties of applying such techniques over most of the distribution of these dolphins make it is unlikely that estimates of population size useful for management purposes will be available in the near future.

**Man's influence** The shallow habitat favoured by humpback dolphins renders them susceptible to the effects of man's activities in this zone, particularly through fishing. Incidental catches in fishing nets are widely recorded throughout the distribution of these dolphins. Of particular concern are the effects of nets set to prevent shark attacks on human bathers off eastern Australia and Natal, South Africa. Although no catch figures are available for Australia, those off Natal appear to be high enough to make a significant impact on the local population. The continued degradation of coastal habitat by man through drainage and reclamation of, say, mangrove areas, reduces the availability of prime habitat for these dolphins and is a cause for concern.

A few humpback dolphins have been maintained in captivity during the past 25 years, including three in South Africa and a further eight in Australia. One of the latter is presently held at Sea World of Australia in Queensland.

# ROUGH-TOOTHED DOLPHIN

*STENO BREDANENSIS*

■ Strandings/sightings  ⁄ Possible range

**Classification** First described by Cuvier in 1823. The generic name, derived from the Greek word *stenos*, refers to the narrow snout, and the species was named for van Breda, an artist who first noticed the species in Cuvier's material.

**Local names** The common name originates from the fine ridges running down the enamel cap of each tooth. Local names include delfin de pico largo.

**Description** These dolphins reach a maximum of 2.8m in length, although most specimens are about 2.4m long and weigh about 150kg. The most distinctive feature is the form of the melon, which lacks an apex and slopes evenly to the tip of the snout. In profile, the conical shape of the head, together with the long gape and large eye, imparts a reptilian appearance to the species. The body is streamlined though robust, with large pointed flippers. The trailing edge of the broad-

*Below: These dolphins are distinguished by their narrow dorsal cape and conical head, which typically lacks a prominent 'melon'.*

based, tall dorsal fin is concave. There are 20-27 teeth in each side of each jaw.

Rough-toothed dolphins are predominantly dark grey or bluish grey on the back, tail stock and appendages. The paler grey of the flanks contrasts with the dark dorsal cape, particularly in the mid-chest region, where the cape is typically narrow. The lips of both jaws and the belly from chin to vent are usually pinkish white. Numbers of yellowish white blotches and spots are frequently present on the body, especially along the lower flanks and belly. These may be the scars left by bites of cookiecutter sharks.

**Recognition at sea** These dolphins could be confused with several species at a distance, particularly bottlenose, spotted and spinner dolphins, although the distinctive narrow dorsal cape and general behaviour provide useful clues to their identity. At close range, however, the conical head, white lips and blotches on the body readily distinguish this species.

Tooth counts will separate stranded dolphins from all other species, except bottlenose and some Atlantic humpback dolphins, particularly when considered together with the form of the snout and dorsal fin shape. The roughness of the teeth is not necessarily diagnostic, as it may be indistinct in some animals. Moreover, the teeth of some juvenile bottlenose dolphins show similar wrinkles.

**Habitat** Rough-toothed dolphins live over deep water beyond the continental shelf, associated with sea surface temperatures of 25°C or more, although vagrants may strand outside this range.

**Distribution and migration** Strandings and sightings suggest that this species is widespread in tropical and subtropical waters. However, the real distribution of these dolphins at sea is poorly known, other than in the eastern tropical Pacific. In the Atlantic, several strandings and other records are known from Virginia to the West Indies, off Brazil, from France to Senegal, and Tristan da Cunha. They are seen sporadically in the Mediterranean. Indo-Pacific records are known from South Africa, Aden, India and Sri Lanka, the Indonesian Archipelago and northern Australia, Japan, Polynesia and Hawaii, from northern California to Peru, and New Zealand.

**Food and feeding** The contents of the few stomachs examined included squids, free-swimming octopus and a variety of fish species.

**Behaviour** Though groups of more than 100 animals have been observed, group size is usually 50 or less and most often about 10-20. On occasion, they will associate with other cetaceans, such as bottlenose, spotted or spinner dolphins and pilot whales. They do not bow ride as readily as many other dolphins, though they are capable and powerful swimmers. Skimming behaviour has been observed recently; this involves swimming rapidly just under the surface with the dorsal fin exposed to the air and may be used for hunting surface-dwelling prey, such as flying fishes. Dolphins may also occur near floating debris, perhaps to capture prey sheltering there.

**World population** In the eastern tropical Pacific – the only region for which adequate information exists – rough-toothed dolphins are present throughout in low numbers, though no population estimates have been made. It is likely to be uncommon throughout its range.

**Man's influence** A few animals are killed by harpoon or drive fisheries for food in Japan and in the small cetacean fishery at St. Vincent, Lesser Antilles. Some dolphins are also killed in purse-seines set for tuna in the eastern tropical Pacific. The impact of these catches on local populations is unknown.

Rough-toothed dolphins have been kept successfully in captivity in Japan and Hawaii. They are good performers, capable of sustained innovative behaviour, including experimental open-ocean diving studies.

# TUCUXI

## SOTALIA FLUVIATILIS

■ Known distribution

*Left: The tucuxi is a riverine and coastal dolphin, often likened in appearance to the much larger bottlenose dolphin. It shares much of its freshwater range with the boto, or Amazon River dolphin, but is not closely related to any of the true river dolphins.*

**Classification** Although described as five different species last century, modern opinion places all populations of these dolphins in one species *Sotalia fluviatilis*, first described by Gervais in 1853. The origin of the generic name is unknown; the specific name refers to the riverine habitat of some populations. Differences in size and other features between the smaller riverine animals and those of the coastal populations may warrant recognition of subspecies.

**Local names** These dolphins are called tucuxi by the Tupi Indians of the region, who distinguish it from the boto, or Amazon River dolphin, *Inia geoffrensis* (page 184), which co-exists with the tucuxi over much of its riverine range.

**Description** This dolphin is one of the smallest of all cetaceans. Coastal populations reach a maximum length of 1.8-1.9m and weigh about 35-40kg. Animals in the Amazon River are even smaller, reaching a maximum of 1.6m. This is a robust animal, with a prominent, elongate snout demarcated from the well-formed, rounded melon, and with large, broad flippers and flukes. The dorsal fin is characteristically broad-based and nearly triangular, with a slightly concave trailing edge. Tooth counts vary from 26 to 35 in each side of each jaw.

The dorsal surfaces of the snout, head, body and the appendages are bluish or brownish grey in colour, fading on the flanks to pale grey or white on the ventral surface from the chin to the vent. The belly and throat may be pinkish. Typically, a dark stripe is present between the eye and the flipper base. At mid-chest level, a second parallel stripe extends the dark colour of the upper chest diagonally towards the vent. Colour patterns vary between populations, those in the Orinoco region being blacker dorsally and greyish below. Dolphins in all populations lighten considerably in colour with age, particularly those living in the Amazon River.

**Recognition** The darker coloration, body size and dorsal fin distinguish this species from the boto (Amazon River dolphin), which is larger, pinkish in colour and has no distinct dorsal fin. In coastal waters, the tucuxi can be set apart from the bottlenose dolphin because of the latter's greater size (adults exceed 2.4m) and larger hooked dorsal fin. In addition, in dead specimens, the tucuxi has more teeth in each side of each jaw than bottlenose dolphins of that region (19-26). In the extreme south of its range, juvenile tucuxi could be confused at sea with those of the franciscana (page 187). When dead, the larger number of teeth and the rounded flipper readily distinguish the franciscana from the tucuxi.

**Habitat** Tucuxi inhabit shallow coastal waters and turbid waters of large rivers, apparently preferring deeper channels.

**Distribution and migration** The tucuxi is restricted to northeastern South America. Coastal populations occur from Sao Paulo in Brazil to the Atlantic coast of Colombia, including Lake Maracaibo. Riverine populations extend from the river mouths about 300km up the Orinoco River and about 2,500km up the Amazon River system.

**Food and feeding** No information is available on the diet of coastal animals, although all populations are likely to take similar prey. In rivers, these dolphins feed on fish and invertebrates, including prawns and crabs. The tooth wear seen in riverine populations of dolphins of all ages may result from the hard protective armour of some prey, such as catfish, and such prey may be softened by chewing before it is swallowed. Feeding frequently occurs at the junction of tributaries and the main stream, where food may be more abundant. The well-developed echolocation system is probably vital for foraging in highly turbid conditions. Diving times are short, averaging about 30 seconds and rarely more than 80 seconds.

**Behaviour** Group size varies from approximately 1 to 25 animals, and is generally 10 or less. In the Amazon River, small cohesive groups are probably social or family units. Although dolphins are rather wary of boats, after one has passed they may leap clear of the water, falling back on their sides.

**Life history** Females in the Amazon River population are about 1.3m long when they begin breeding. Calves are born during flood periods after a gestation period of about 10 months.

**World population** No population estimates have been made for any population of the tucuxi. However, they are considered to be common along the Brazilian coast near Rio de Janeiro, the coast of Surinam, and parts of the Amazon River.

**Man's influence** An unknown number of dolphins are caught incidentally in fishermen's gillnets set in or at the mouths of rivers. Of greater concern is their capture for medicinal and ritual purposes, whereby organs of the female are dried and sold on local markets.

A few individuals have been maintained for short periods in the United States, Germany and Brazil.

# BOTTLENOSE DOLPHIN

## TURSIOPS TRUNCATUS

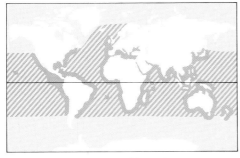

■ Primary range　　　⁄ Local or sparse

**Classification** Most cetologists classify all bottlenose dolphins as a single, highly variable species, *Tursiops truncatus*. The name is derived from the Latin and Greek words for 'porpoise' and 'face', and reflects the truncated snout of eastern Atlantic animals. Though this single-species approach may overlook the existence of other species, much of the variation between populations probably reflects differences in their respective environments. For example, the gradual southward change from the distinctive *aduncus* form to the typical *truncatus* form down the east and west coasts of Australia is correlated with decreasing water temperature.

**Local names** The resemblance of the short rounded snout to the swollen form of an old-fashioned bottle gave rise to the English name. North American alternatives are the grey or black dolphin. The alternative use of the name bottlenose porpoise has led to much confusion between dolphins and true porpoises.

**Description** Populations of these medium-sized to large dolphins vary in length between 1.9m and 4m. They are robust animals, weighing from about 90kg to over 650kg as adults.

The snout is short and slender in the smaller forms, broadening markedly with increasing body size. The well-formed melon is more rounded in some populations than others, tapering in all to a distinct apex. The broad triangular dorsal fin reaches one tenth of the body length in height, is slightly hooked and set midway along the body. The flippers are about one sixth of the body in length, broad at the base and taper to a point. The robust teeth – 5-10mm in diameter – number from 18 to 27 in each row.

Though variable, the colour pattern of most bottlenose dolphins is typically delphinid, consisting of a dark bluish or brownish grey dorsal cape and a paler grey area on the sides of the head and body, which shades gradually into an off-white ventral surface. The latter may be pinkish in life. The outer surface of the flipper and the whole of the tail flukes are dark greyish black. The tip of the snout is usually scarred white. Dark lines from the apex of the melon to the eyes and the blowhole, and a dark eye-to-flipper stripe are usually clearly visible. Some populations in the eastern tropical Pacific are very dark greyish black, obscuring this basic pattern. Coastal dolphins in the Indian Ocean and tropical western Pacific develop dark ventral spots and blotches at sexual maturity.

**Recognition at sea** Bottlenose dolphins can be distinguished from rough-toothed dolphins by the distinct apex to the melon, the short snout, the broad dorsal cape between the blowhole and the dorsal fin and the absence of white lips and blotches on the body. The more slender snout and body, paler flanks, and white dorsal spots in pantropical spotted dolphins (*Stenella attenuata*) and the body spotting of Atlantic spotted dolphins (*S. frontalis*) distinguish adults of both these species from bottlenose dolphins.

In coastal waters, the fin shape separates bottlenose dolphins from the South American tucuxi (triangular), Atlantic and Indian Ocean humpback dolphins (elongate and small fin tip), and eastern humpback dolphin populations (thickened fin base, triangular fin).

**Habitat** This is a coastal and oceanic species. Coastal populations generally occur in water less than 30m deep. They occupy diverse habitats, ranging from open coasts with strong surf to sheltered bays and waterways, lagoons, large estuaries and the lower reaches of rivers. The sea floor in such areas varies from muddy sediment to rocky reefs. In some areas – for example, off South Africa – dolphins avoid turbid water, perhaps to reduce the risk of predation by sharks.

**Distribution and migration** Bottlenose dolphins are widely distributed in cold temperate to tropical waters of all seas. Their occurrence is particularly well documented in coastal waters. They are widespread in the Mediterranean and Black Seas, and extend through the Atlantic from the North Sea and Nova Scotia to southern Argentina and South Africa. They are distributed continuously around the coasts of the Indian Ocean, through the Southeast Asian region to northern Japan and the Australian coast. They occur around New Zealand, and along the eastern Pacific coastline from California to Chile. Much less is known of this species' offshore distribution. Some populations apparently concentrate along the continental shelf edge, off southeastern Africa, for example. In the tuna fishing region of the eastern tropical Pacific, sightings decline markedly more than 800km from land. Elsewhere, records are limited largely to islands, such as St. Helena, the Seychelles and the Hawaiian Island chain.

Some populations – for example, those off North Carolina and in the Black Sea – migrate seasonally, probably in response to changing environmental conditions.

*Above: The bottlenose dolphin has the most familiar features of all cetaceans. It has adapted well to life in captivity and has been displayed in hundreds of marine facilities around the world.*

*Above right: Bottlenose dolphins, like these photographed off the Azores Islands, are natural acrobats and often leap well clear of the water surface.*

*Right: Although considered to be primarily a coastal species, bottlenose dolphins are often seen in the open ocean and may occur almost anywhere in cold temperate or warmer waters worldwide.*

**Food and feeding** Coastal dolphins eat a wide variety of fishes, squids and octopi, although four or five locally abundant prey species usually form most of the diet. They seem to prefer shoaling and bottom-dwelling species, such as grunts, croakers, snappers, mullets, mackerel, horse-mackerel and cuttlefish. Captive animals eat between 3 and 6 percent of their body mass per day.

Limited information on the diet of off-shore dolphins suggests that some are capable of diving to depths of more than 600m to catch bottom-dwelling fishes. Others eat oceanic squids or schooling fishes. A common interest in prey may also stimulate association with pilot or false killer whales.

Bottlenose dolphins are remarkably versatile in their foraging techniques. These range from group cooperation in order to surround fish shoals to sliding onto mudbanks in Louisiana to capture fishes washed up by their momentum.

There is increasing evidence that inshore dolphin groups maintain home ranges along particular stretches of coasts, although some members of a group may move intermittently.

**Behaviour** Group size is highly variable, from less than 100 animals in coastal waters to several hundred far offshore. In a resident coastal group, the size and composition of subgroups may vary sea-sonally or diurnally in response to one or more factors, including distance off-shore, prey type and availability, and protection against – or avoidance of – predators. Segregation of subadult and adult males probably reflects dominance in the social structure, while separate mother-calf subgroups may lessen aggression by adult males towards calves.

Bottlenose dolphins are powerful swimmers, as is clear when they are seen playing in the bow wave of a vessel, surfing on large waves or jumping several metres clear of the water. Foraging groups move at about 6kph, although individuals may reach speeds of 25kph. In coastal waters, dives rarely last more than three or four minutes, but may be longer in oceanic animals.

**Life history** In keeping with their lifespan of over 30 years, bottlenose dolphins have a long adolescence, and only begin breeding at 9-10 years old in females and 10-13 years old in males. The length at birth of the single calf is 1-1.3m, varying according to population. Most calves are born in spring and summer after a gestation period of 12 months. Calves suckle for up to 18 months, although they begin eating fish at about 6 months of age. Adult females calve at intervals of two to three years.

**World population** Excluding some exploited populations, this species appears to be common throughout its range.

**Man's influence** Local exploitation of coastal populations occurs in many regions, including the West Indies, West Africa, some northern Indian Ocean states and Japan, either directly for food, or by fishermen competing for fish resources. Large-scale commercial hunting in the Black Sea by Soviet fishermen until the 1960s, and subsequently by Turkey, has reduced this population to an unknown level. Worldwide, the increasing and widespread use of gillnetting in coastal fisheries is of particular concern, since the entrapment of these and other dolphins could easily exceed their replacement capacity.

Over the past 50 years, several hundred bottlenose dolphins have been kept in oceanariums and marine parks worldwide. Most of these originated in live-capture fisheries conducted in the southeastern and western United States and Mediterranean waters, South Africa, the Red Sea, Australia, Taiwan, Japan and the Philippines, amongst others.

# STRIPED DOLPHIN

## STENELLA COERULEOALBA

■ Probable range

**Classification** The striped dolphin was described by Meyen in 1833. The name *Stenella* comes from the Greek *stenos*, meaning 'narrow'; *coeruleoalba* is derived from the Latin *caeruleus*, meaning 'sky-blue', and *albus*, meaning 'white'. There are no subspecies.

**Local names** The species is known worldwide as the striped dolphin; a common name whose derivation needs little explanation. It is also sometimes known as the euphrosyne dolphin.

**Description** The shape of this dolphin is well proportioned, with no remarkable features. Its moderately falcate dorsal fin and its beak are neither long and thin nor short and wide. The basic coloration is a white ventral surface, light grey sides and a darker bluish grey dorsal surface. There are two distinctive features in the coloration: the dark stripe running from behind the eye to the anus, between the white belly and the light grey side, and the shoulder blaze, which extends from the lighter grey area on the side of the animal, curving up from above and behind the flipper towards the dorsal fin. There are between one and three additional dark bands that run from in front of the eye to the flipper, and a short stripe that starts behind the eye, running parallel to and below the eye-to-anus stripe, and stopping behind the flipper.

In the western Pacific, average length is 2.39m in males and 2.26m in females; but specimens measuring up to 2.6m have been found. Lengths are similar elsewhere in the world. Weights of stranded animals have been recorded at up to 156kg for a 2.4m animal.

There are 40-55 sharp teeth, curving slightly inwards, on each side of each jaw.

**Recognition at sea** Its dark stripes, particularly those from eye to anus and eye to flipper, distinguish this species from others of the same general size and shape.

**Habitat** The striped dolphin is primarily oceanic but also found quite close to coasts. In the eastern Pacific, the preferred habitats are areas of equatorial and subtropical waters characterized by seasonal upwelling, which causes large changes in surface temperatures and a relatively weak thermocline (the pronounced change from warm surface water to colder deeper water). The striped dolphin shares this habitat in the eastern Pacific with the common dolphin. These two species tend to occur in areas that are not a preferred habitat for spotted and spinner dolphins (see pages 140-143).

In the Indian Ocean, striped dolphins seem to prefer waters with a surface temperature of at least 22°C. Where they are found close to land, they tend to be in deep water beyond the continental shelf.

**Distribution and migration** The striped dolphin is found in warm temperate and tropical waters of all the world's oceans. In the Atlantic, it occurs from Nova Scotia to northern Argentina in the west, and from the UK to southern Africa in the east, including the Mediterranean. In the Indian Ocean, it seems to be restricted to north of approximately 35°S. In the eastern Pacific, striped dolphins are found from 35°N to 15°S off the east coast of the Americas, the distribution narrowing to a band bounded by 15°N and 5°S further west. There is a break between 5°N and the equator west of 120°W, which extends northeastwards to the coast of Mexico, suggesting two separate stocks. Animals found around Hawaii may be a local population. In the western Pacific, the species is common off Japan in winter and spring and has been found in pelagic waters as far south as the equator, suggesting that it is as widely distributed there as elsewhere.

*Above: A striped dolphin photographed in the eastern tropical Pacific, demonstrating the origin of its common name.*

*Bottom: Most striped dolphins occur in large groups, as here, showing plenty of surface activity when travelling fast.*

There is a well-documented migration off Japan associated with the warm Kuroshio Current. Schools first appear in September-October and move in a south-westerly direction along the coast. They become rare in March-April but reappear again in May, swimming northeast-wards, and are last seen in June heading towards the open sea.

**Food and feeding** The diet of the striped dolphin consists mainly of midwater fish and squid less than 30cm in length, and shrimps. Lanternfish (Myctophids) are the most common prey item, making up between one and two-thirds of the dol-

phin's diet. (The stomach of one indivi-dual from South African waters con-tained the remains of 14 species of fish and five species of squid.) The majority of the squid prey have luminous organs.

The diet suggests that coastal feeding generally occurs off the edge of the con-tinental shelf to depths of 200m. Nothing is known about pelagic feeding.

**Behaviour** School sizes range from a few tens to several thousand, but most of those encountered number between 100 and 500 animals. Studies of school com-position off Japan have shown that striped dolphins segregate into three school types, characterized by juveniles, mating adults or non-mating adults. A newborn dolphin will move from its mat-ing adult school to a juvenile school after one or two years and will rejoin an adult school after reaching sexual maturity. In years when the Kuroshio Current comes close to the coast of Japan, adult schools are more commonly seen but when the current is farther offshore, juvenile schools predominate. Schools are larger and swim closer together on the south-bound migration.

Striped dolphins are quite active and will readily leap out of the water and ride the bow wave of a boat. Known vocal-izations include whistles and clicks. There are no records of mass strandings, but individuals, often still alive, have been found on beaches in several loca-tions around the world.

**Life history** Most of what is known about reproduction in striped dolphins comes from extensive studies of animals caught off Japan. Breeding occurs twice a year: in the summer and the winter, and gesta-tion lasts 12-13 months. The average length at birth is 1m and calves are weaned at about 18 months. Sex ratios in foetuses and post-natal animals do not differ from 1:1, although there is signifi-cant variation with age in the catch data, presumably as a result of segregation in

schools of dolphins by age and sex.

Females reach sexual maturity at an average age of nine years and length of 2.16m. Fecundity decreases from the onset of sexual maturity for a few years, remains constant until about 30 years of age, and then declines rapidly. Males mature sexually at the same age as females, at an average length of 2.19m, but do not become socially mature until they are at least 16 years old. (The oldest striped dolphin on record was estimated to be 57 years old.)

Annual pregnancy rate has been esti-mated at 30 percent in the eastern Pacific and at 30-71 percent in the western Pacific. These rates correspond to calving intervals of between 3.3 and 1.4 years. Annual birth rate has been calculated to be 10.9 percent in the eastern Pacific and 10.3-11 percent in the western Pacific. Approximate annual mortality rates of 7-9 percent have been estimated from the age composition of the catch off Japan or by comparison with the spotted dolphin, but are unlikely to be reliable.

**World population** It is currently esti-mated that there are 1.6 million striped dolphins in the eastern Pacific. Rough calculations suggest that the population in the western Pacific currently numbers 100,000-200,000. (Before exploitation, this population was around 300,000-400,000.) There are no estimates from other areas.

**Man's influence** In the eastern Pacific, striped dolphins are involved to a minor extent in the purse-seine fishery for tunas, but the incidental mortality is low. In the western Pacific, a well-established drive fishery for striped dolphins took an average of 14,000 animals a year in the 1950s and 1960s. In the 1980s, the catch has fallen to between 2,000 and 4,000 per year except for a take of 16,000 in 1981. It is not known whether the catch is from a large oceanic population or a smaller local one. There is evidence that during the period of exploitation the pregnancy rate has increased, with a corresponding decrease in calving interval. In the north-eastern Atlantic, striped dolphins are harpooned from fishing boats to provide meat for the crew. No estimates are avail-able for the number of animals killed in this way but it could be tens or even hun-dreds per year.

Striped dolphins have been kept in captivity but not successfully trained.

# PANTROPICAL SPOTTED DOLPHIN

*STENELLA ATTENUATA*

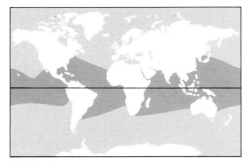

■ Probable range

**Classification** Many names have been given to the spotted dolphins of the genus *Stenella*. A recent revision of the taxonomy proposes two species, *S. attenuata*, described by Gray in 1846, and *S. frontalis* (see page 145). It is suggested that *S. attenuata* be known as the pantropical spotted dolphin because it occurs all round the world. No subspecies are recognized but three distinct forms have been described in the eastern Pacific: coastal, offshore and Hawaiian spotted.

**Local names** Except in the Atlantic, where *S. frontalis* also occurs, it is known locally simply as the spotted dolphin.

**Description** The body is slender and elongated, but the coastal form is more robust. Background coloration consists of a dark grey dorsal cape, extending from the top of the head to about halfway down the side of the animal behind the flipper, and sweeping up to end behind the dorsal fin. The ventral surface is light grey. There is a pattern of darker patches and bands around the eye, beak and flipper, but this may be indistinct. The dorsal fin is quite tall, falcate and the same colour as the cape. The beak is quite long and develops white lips in older animals.

The amount of spotting varies geographically and with age. A newborn animal is unspotted. As a juvenile, it develops spots, first ventrally then dorsally and these become bigger and more numerous as the animal grows. In mature animals, the spotting may develop to the extent that what appear to be spots are actually small remaining areas of background colour. In general, there seems to be a decrease in the amount of spotting the further the animals are from the coasts of the Americas. Coastal forms are heavily spotted, offshore forms less so. Pantropical spotted dolphins around

Hawaii in the Pacific and St. Helena in the Atlantic are hardly spotted at all.

Body size also varies geographically. Coastal forms are largest, adults averaging 2.23m (males) and 2.07m (females) in length in the eastern Pacific. Oceanic pantropical spotted dolphins from the Pacific average 2m (males) and 1.87m (females) as adults. The largest animal recorded was a 119kg, 2.57m male from the Bay of Panama. Females are smaller. There is an average of 40 teeth on each side of each jaw.

**Recognition at sea** *S. attenuata* can be identified at sea by its basic two-part coloration (but not on the tail stock), its lack of a spinal blaze and, of course, its spots.

**Habitat** The pantropical spotted dolphin is primarily an oceanic species. In the eastern Pacific, the offshore form occurs mainly in tropical waters north of the equator and in seasonal tropical waters south of the Galapagos Islands. These tropical waters are characterized by relatively constant surface temperatures greater than 25°C, low salinity and sharp thermocline (the rapid change from

Below left, left and below: Adult pantropical spotted dolphins of most stocks really are unmistakably spotted, but in the Atlantic Ocean they may be confused with the very similar Atlantic spotted dolphin. Youngsters lack spots entirely.

warm surface water to colder deeper water) well within 50m of the surface.

Pantropical spotted dolphins share this habitat with spinner dolphins and often associate with them. They also associate with flocks of feeding seabirds and yellowfin tuna. This latter association is used by fishermen to locate the tuna. Elsewhere, pantropical spotted dolphins are also found in warm waters, with a surface temperature of at least 22°C.

**Distribution and migration** In the eastern Pacific, the distribution of this oceanic species is particularly well documented. Schools occur from 25°N to 15°S near the coasts of Central and South America, their latitudinal range decreasing steadily to the west out to about 155°W. In the western Pacific, the distribution seems to be similar to that of the striped dolphin. In the Indian Ocean, schools have been seen as far south as 35°S. In the Atlantic Ocean, the latitudinal range close to the coast of the Americas is from 40°N to 40°S, narrowing to tropical waters in the east. The known oceanic distribution is limited to tropical and subtropical waters.

There are no known migrations, but recoveries of animals tagged in the northern offshore Pacific Ocean have shown substantial east-west and north-south movements of up to 2,400km.

**Food and feeding** *Stenella attenuata* feeds primarily in surface waters. The diet in the eastern Pacific consists largely of surface-dwelling squid, frigate mackerel and flying fish. Lactating females prefer flying fish, presumably because the higher calorific content of these prey helps to sustain the increased energy demands of feeding a growing calf. There is a considerable overlap in the diet with yellowfin tuna in this area, but not with the spinner dolphin. Food found in the stomachs of pantropical spotted dolphins in other areas is similar in composition. A notable exception is off Hawaii, where midwater fish and squid make up the bulk of the diet.

**Behaviour** Pantropical spotted dolphins show a wide range of school sizes, from just a few animals to several thousand in offshore regions. School size in the eastern Pacific is typically a few hundred, with coastal animals forming much smaller groups. The situation is similar in the western Pacific. Elsewhere, school sizes seem to be smaller – up to 200-300 – but this may just reflect the fewer and more opportunistic sightings in offshore areas of the Atlantic and Indian Oceans. Segregation by age, sex and reproductive status has been observed.

Pantropical spotted dolphins are active at the surface and exhibit a varied be-

haviour. They frequently jump out of the water, sometimes to great heights. Forward flips, pitch poling, tail lobbing and bow riding are included in their repertoire. Pantropical spotted dolphins produce whistles and pulses of sound less than one millisecond in length.

**Life history** Analyses of data from Pacific spotted dolphins provide almost all the available information on reproduction and population dynamics. In the northeastern Pacific, two seasonal groups are apparent, with mean calving dates in May and September. Gestation is between 11 and 12 months, so mating must occur at the same time of the year. Average length at birth is 85cm in the eastern and 89cm in the western Pacific. Average age at weaning is 20 months. The newborn sex ratio is 1:1, but females are predominant in older animals.

Sexual maturity is reached at an average length of 1.94m and an average age of 12 years in males, and at 1.82m and 9 years in females. Fecundity increases slightly with age in the western Pacific, but remains constant in the eastern Pacific after an initial decline over the two years following the onset of sexual maturity. Pantropical spotted dolphins can exceptionally live as long as 45 years.

**World population** Despite continuing and significant directed and incidental catches (see below), pantropical spotted dolphins are probably among the commonest cetaceans. Current population size in the eastern Pacific is about two million animals. There are no estimates for other areas.

**Man's influence** Pantropical spotted dolphins are the primary target of purse-seiners searching for yellowfin tuna in the eastern Pacific. Thousands of these dolphins have been killed incidentally every year for the last 30 years, reducing the population to about half its initial level. Since 1959, pantropical spotted dolphins have also been taken in the drive fishery off Japan; on average, about 1,000 animals have been killed per year. A similar drive fishery in the Solomon Islands has taken large numbers of pantropical spotted dolphins. They are also the target of many small subsistence fisheries and are taken incidentally in local fishing operations throughout the world.

*Stenella attenuata* has been successfully maintained in captivity, but it is not as hardy nor as easily trainable as some other species of dolphins.

# SPINNER DOLPHIN

## *STENELLA LONGIROSTRIS*

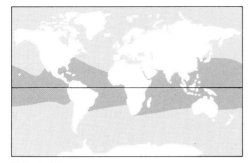

Probable range

**Classification** There are two species of spinner dolphins: one, *Stenella longirostris*, described by Gray in 1828, occurs throughout the tropics; the other, *Stenella clymene* (the clymene or short-snouted spinner dolphin, described on page 144), occurs only in the Atlantic Ocean. The name *longirostris* is derived from the Latin *longus*, meaning 'long', and *rostrum*, meaning 'beak' or 'snout'. No subspecies of *S. longirostris* are recognized, but there are four distinct forms in the eastern Pacific: Costa Rican, eastern, whitebelly and Hawaiian spinner.

**Description** The body of *Stenella longirostris* is slender, with a long, thin beak.

The dorsal fin varies substantially in shape, and the tail stock develops a keel in adult males. In the eastern Pacific, the Costa Rican spinner is the longest and slimmest form. The average adult length is about 2m, and a 2.16m male weighed in at only 57kg. The coloration of this form is a uniform slate grey and the dorsal fin is triangular or canted forward. The eastern spinner, on the other hand, is the shortest and slimmest form, the average adult length being only 1.7-1.8m. It, too, is all grey and the forward cant to the dorsal fin and ventral hump in males is often pronounced. The whitebelly spinner is more heavily built and about 5cm longer on average. It has a white belly and a grey dorsal surface. The dorsal fin may be triangular or slightly falcate. A broad grey band is visible from the eye to the flipper, and the snout has black lips and a black tip. The Hawaiian spinner is similar in shape but slightly longer than the whitebelly. Its coloration has a three-tone appearance, because a darker cape extends from the top of the head to behind the dorsal fin, which is always at least slightly falcate. Whitebelly and Hawaiian spinners are heavier than the eastern forms, reaching over 75kg.

Spinner dolphins in other areas are not well described but coloration typically includes the dark dorsal cape found in the Hawaiian form. Atlantic spinners reach a similar size to those from the Pacific Ocean, but those from northern Australia are smaller, typically being less than 1.6m in length. A very small form of *S. longirostris* has recently been found in the Gulf of Thailand. Adult length is only 1.3-1.4m and maximum known weight only 26.5kg in this form of the species.

There are 45-65 sharply pointed teeth on each side of each jaw.

**Recognition at sea** Costa Rican and eastern spinners are difficult to misidentify because of their uniform grey colour, long beaks and triangular fins. Two- or three-tone coloured spinners can be identified by the shape of the dark area on the dorsal surface, the black lips and the long black-tipped snout. Spinning in the air is diagnostic of this species and *S. clymene*.

*Below: The spinner dolphin is aptly named and among the most agile and exuberant of all the cetaceans.*

*Above right: Shape and coloration vary quite considerably between stocks. This is the Hawaiian spinner.*

**Habitat** Spinner dolphins occupy a similar habitat to spotted dolphins. For oceanic forms in the eastern Pacific, this consists of the relatively constant tropical water masses to the north and south of the equator. The spinner dolphin is also targeted by fishermen searching for yellowfin tuna in this area.

**Distribution and migration** *Stenella longirostris* is found in tropical and subtropical waters in all oceans. In the eastern Pacific, its distribution is almost the same as the spotted dolphin, being bounded roughly by a triangle with points at 25°N and 15°S near the coast and 10°N at 155°W. Costa Rican spinners are found only in a narrow band of water, less than 100km wide, off Panama, Costa Rica and Nicaragua. Eastern spinners are confined to north of the equator and east of 125°W. In the eastern Pacific Ocean, recoveries of spinner dolphins tagged offshore have shown limited movements of 300-700km, agreeing with the existence of the two offshore races.

Hawaiian spinners form a discrete population, as do animals found around the Marquesas Islands, Christmas Island and Tahiti.

Elsewhere in the world, *S. longirostris* has a similar distribution to *S. attenuata*, and is often found in the coastal waters of continents and islands.

**Food and feeding** Unlike the pantropical spotted dolphin, with which it associates closely in the eastern Pacific, *S. longirostris* feeds mainly on fish and squid found well below the water surface. The other predatory animals that share its habitat, such as the spotted dolphin, tuna and seabirds, all feed at or near the surface. There is strong evidence that spinner dolphins also differ from these other predators by feeding at night. This is certainly true off Hawaii, where schools have been observed resting inshore during the day, moving offshore to feed in deeper water at night.

**Behaviour** Spinner dolphin school sizes are similar to those for other *Stenella* species in tropical waters, ranging from a few animals to over a thousand. Very large schools of mixed spinner and spotted dolphins have been seen. Spinner dolphins have also been observed in association with other oceanic species, including pilot whales, pygmy killer whales and melon-headed whales.

Spinner dolphins are renowned for their varied and spectacular aerial displays. Their best-known activity, and the one which has earned this dolphin its common name, is the habit of jumping high out of the water and spinning round several times on its longitudinal axis.

As in other *Stenella* species, the typical vocalizations are whistles and clicks.

Both spinner and spotted dolphins can swim very quickly. For short bursts, they have been seen to match the speed of speedboats attempting to herd them as part of operations in the tuna purse-seine fishery in the eastern Pacific. Sustained speeds over periods up to an hour can be as high as 20kph.

**Life history** Information on reproduction in *S. longirostris* is based on the eastern Pacific forms. The eastern spinner breeds once a year, in late spring or early summer, but the northern whitebelly spinner has two breeding peaks, one in the spring and the other in autumn. (This pattern is similar to that of the northern offshore spotted dolphin in the same area.) Gestation is between 10 and 11 months, and average length at birth is 77cm. Average age at weaning ranges from 11 months in the eastern spinner to 19 months in the northern and 34 months in the southern whitebelly spinner. The sex ratio is approximately 1:1.

Spinners reach sexual maturity at lengths of 1.6-1.7m in offshore forms, at the age of 6-9 years in males and 4-6 years in females. Fecundity declines slowly with age in the eastern spinner, but rapidly at first in the whitebelly spinner.

Annual pregnancy rates are in the range 30-35 percent, corresponding to calving intervals of 3.3-2.9 years. Annual birth rates are 6.7-9.4 percent. There are no mortality rate estimates.

**World population** Eastern spinners currently number 600,000-800,000 animals and whitebelly spinners number about 600,000. There are no estimates from elsewhere in the world.

**Man's influence** Spinner dolphins are second in importance to pantropical spotted dolphins in their frequency of capture in the tuna purse-seine fishery in the eastern Pacific. Both eastern and whitebelly spinners can have yellowfin tuna associated with them, and thousands of animals have been killed every year since the fishery developed in 1959. Eastern spinners were the primary target of the fleet in the early years of the fishery and are believed to have been depleted to as little as 20 percent of their pre-1959 population level. Whitebelly spinner dolphins have been targeted more recently and are not as depleted.

Elsewhere in the world, spinner dolphins are commonly killed incidentally in gillnet fisheries. Off northern Australia, *S. longirostris* is the second most common cetacean captured in this way. Small numbers are also taken by harpoon in many parts of the world.

Spinner dolphins from the Indo-Pacific Oceans and around the Hawaiian Islands have been kept successfully in captivity for at least as long as 10 years.

# CLYMENE DOLPHIN

*STENELLA CLYMENE*

■ Possible range

**Classification** *Stenella clymene* was described by John Gray in 1846, almost 20 years after he described the more widely distributed spinner dolphin, *S. longirostris*. The classification was based solely on skeletal material and some cetologists doubted its existence until the external appearance was described in 1981. The specific name refers to Clymene, the daughter of Oceanus and Tethys in Greek mythology.

**Local names** This species is also known as the short-snouted spinner dolphin.

**Description** The clymene dolphin most closely resembles the Hawaiian form of *S. longirostris* in coloration and shape. It

*Below: The alternate common name of short-snouted spinner dolphin accurately reflects the major anatomical difference between this species and the closely related* Stenella longirostris.

has a three-tone colour pattern with a white belly (flecked with small spots), light grey flanks and a dark grey dorsal cape that dips low below the dorsal fin and extends to midway between the falcate dorsal fin and the tail flukes. The eye-to-flipper stripe is narrower nearer the eye and may be indistinct. The extension of the eye stripe onto the beak gives this animal a moustached appearance. The tip of the beak is black, as in *S. longirostris*, but is bordered above with a light grey blaze. The body is more robust than most spinner dolphins, and the flippers and dorsal fin are slightly smaller. The most distinctive difference is the short snout, almost stubby in comparison with the long, slender beak of *S. longirostris*. Adult clymene dolphins have been recorded at up to about 2m in length and about 80kg in weight. There are 38-49 teeth on each side of each jaw.

**Recognition at sea** The short snout of *S. clymene* and its low dipping dorsal cape are its best distinguishing features. Otherwise, it can be difficult to tell apart from *S. longirostris* at sea.

**Habitat** *S. clymene* has been observed at sea only in deep water.

**Distribution and migration** The clymene dolphin occurs only in the Atlantic Ocean in tropical and subtropical waters. To the west, there are records from the Caribbean, the Gulf of Mexico and the east coast of North America as far north as 40°N. Clymene dolphins have also been

found off the northwestern coast of Africa and in mid-Atlantic around the equator. Records of the 'Senegal dolphin', which has been described from the Cape Verde Islands to the Gulf of Guinea, are probably *S. clymene*.

**Food and feeding** Little is known about the habits of *S. clymene*, but its feeding behaviour appears to be similar to other spinner dolphins. This involves the taking of midwater fish and squid, possibly at night when they are nearer the surface of the sea.

**Behaviour** Typical school sizes are unknown but small groups of 1-10 animals have been observed in the Caribbean and about 50 animals have stranded together in the Gulf of Mexico. Data from mass strandings indicate that schools of *S. clymene* may be segregated by sex and age.

It has been seen in association with spinner and common dolphins. The clymene sometimes spins when it leaps, although not in such a dramatic way as the spinner dolphin.

**World population** There are few records of the clymene dolphin, suggesting that it is probably not very abundant.

**Man's influence** Small numbers of clymene dolphins are taken by harpoon around St. Vincent, Lesser Antilles in the Caribbean. Stranded animals brought into captivity have not survived for more than a few days.

# ATLANTIC SPOTTED DOLPHIN

## STENELLA FRONTALIS

Probable range

**Classification** *Stenella frontalis* was first described in 1829 by F. Cuvier from a specimen found off West Africa. The specific name, *frontalis*, may refer to the prominent forehead of this dolphin.

**Local names** The Atlantic spotted dolphin has been given a wide range of local names, including the spotter, spotted porpoise, bridled dolphin and the Gulf Stream dolphin.

**Description** The Atlantic spotted dolphin resembles *S. attenuata* but is heavier bodied. It is similar in colour, differing mainly in having a distinct spinal blaze that sweeps up into the dorsal cape towards the dorsal fin and a smaller area of white rather than grey colouring on the ventral surface. Spotting in adults varies markedly from very heavy to a complete absence of spots. As with *S. attenuata*, more heavily spotted animals are found closer to the continental coasts.

In external shape, the Atlantic spotted dolphin resembles the bottlenose dolphin, especially the beak, head, flippers and dorsal fin. Adult *S. frontalis* weigh about 10-30kg more than *S. attenuata* of the same length. They grow to at least 2.3m and 143kg, but offshore animals are considerably smaller than those found along the continental coasts of Central and North America. There are 30-42 teeth on each side of each jaw.

**Recognition at sea** Lightly spotted Atlantic spotted dolphins can be confused with bottlenose dolphins, which can sometimes have a few spots, but are larger. The combination of spots and spinal blaze is diagnostic for *S. frontalis*.

**Habitat** Atlantic spotted dolphins occupy both coastal and oceanic habitats. Off the southeastern coast of North America, they are found in waters less than 200m deep. They only come into nearshore waters, the habitat of coastal bottlenose dolphins, seasonally. In some parts of the Caribbean, *S. frontalis* closely resembles *S. attenuata* and may share a similar niche in this area.

**Distribution and migration** *S. frontalis* is known only from the Atlantic Ocean, where it has been recorded from as far north as 48°N to as far south as 24°S.

**Food and feeding** Atlantic spotted dolphins eat squid and a variety of fish. Around the Azores Islands, they have been seen feeding on horse mackerel, sometimes in association with shearwaters. An increase in aerial behaviour and vocalizations can accompany feeding. Coastal Atlantic spotted dolphins have wider beaks and teeth, which may indicate a preference for larger prey than those taken by oceanic animals, which have smaller mouths and teeth.

**Behaviour** School sizes are typically less than 50 animals and are smaller in coastal areas. Larger groups have been seen off northern Florida and around the Azores Islands. Atlantic spotted dolphins share a similar repertoire of surface behaviour and vocalizations with *S. attenuata*. There is some evidence of a complex social structure, and animals have been observed helping distressed individuals of their own species.

**Life history** Little is known about the reproductive habits of this species. Length at birth is in the range 76-120cm.

**World population** There are no estimates of population size, but Atlantic spotted dolphins are thought to be the commonest species in the Gulf of Mexico and off the southeastern coast of the USA.

**Man's influence** This is one of the species killed in small harpoon fisheries for cetaceans at St. Vincent, in the Caribbean and off the Azores in mid-Atlantic. It does not survive well in captivity.

*Below: S. frontalis differs from the pantropical species by having a blaze that sweeps up to the dorsal cape near the fin.*

# COMMON DOLPHIN

## DELPHINUS DELPHIS

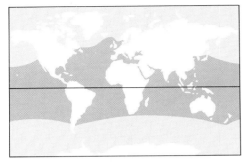

■ Probable range

**Classification** This is the species of dolphin with which the Ancients were most familiar, a fact reflected in the species' scientific name, *Delphinus delphis*, which is simply a combination of the Latin and Greek words for dolphin. There are reputed to be numerous races throughout the world, but until the taxonomy of *Delphinus* is reviewed on a worldwide basis, it is wise to avoid naming subspecies.

**Local names** Alternative names in English-speaking regions include saddleback dolphin and whitebelly porpoise. Fishermen in the various purse-seine fisheries for tuna, especially, refer to this species as the whitebelly porpoise, a name they also use sometimes for the striped dolphin, *Stenella coeruleoalba*, and Fraser's dolphin, *Lagenodelphis hosei*.

**Description** Overall, common dolphins are relatively slender and perfectly streamlined, with a body shape similar to that of *Stenella* dolphins. The maximum sizes are about 2.6m for males and 2.3m for females. Average adult sizes range from 1.7 to 2.4m for the various stocks. Most individuals weigh 75kg or less, but large males may reach close to 135kg.

The melon is set off from the long beak by a distinct crease. The flippers and flukes are recurved and pointed at the tips. The dorsal fin is tall and erect, but somewhat falcate. Some adult males have a noticeable keel on the ventral side, just behind the anus.

This is one of the most beautifully coloured dolphins. The beak, back and appendages are dark brown to black and the ventral surface is white. The front flank patches are yellow to buff and the rear flanks and sides of the tail stock are streaked light grey. These colour patterns combine to form the species' most distinctive feature: an hourglass pattern on the sides, crossing below the dorsal fin, which itself often has a lighter triangle in the middle. The eye is surrounded by black, and a narrow dark stripe runs forward to the front of the melon. Another dark stripe runs from chin to flipper and several face-to-anus stripes may also be visible. Calves generally have muted colour patterns, as is the case in many species of small cetaceans. The mouth is lined with 80-100 small pointed teeth in each of the upper and lower jaws.

Many geographical forms of *Delphinus* have been described, differing in coloration, morphology and reproductive characteristics. Separate stocks are assumed to exist in the Mediterranean, the Black Sea, the Indian Ocean, off Japan and in the eastern Atlantic Ocean. In the eastern Pacific, five stocks are currently recognized, including a long-beaked nearshore form and several short-beaked offshore forms.

**Recognition at sea** The most useful field identification features of the common dolphin are the yellowish ochre patches on the sides in front of the dorsal fin and the 'V' formed by the intersection of various colour elements just below the dorsal fin.

**Habitat** Common dolphins inhabit tropical to warm temperate waters, generally preferring surface temperatures greater than 10°C. They are found mostly in relatively deep offshore waters, but some live in shallow coastal areas.

**Distribution and migration** Common dolphins are widely distributed in warm waters. In the Pacific, they extend from central Japan and southern New Zealand in the west to central California and central Chile in the east. In the Atlantic, they occur from Newfoundland to Argentina and from southern Norway to South Africa. They are distributed throughout the Indian Ocean and are found in the Gulf of Mexico, the Mediter-

*Right: Four common dolphins off New Zealand. Although the pattern on the sides of this species varies between stocks in different geographic areas, the yellow patch above the flipper makes this dolphin easy to identify. The shape of the dorsal cape accounts for its alternative name of 'saddleback dolphin'.*

*Bottom: These adults from the tropical Pacific show a more distinct 'hourglass' pattern on their sides. Common dolphins are found in tropical, subtropical and warm temperate waters of all the oceans, both offshore and near the coast in shallow water.*

ranean, the Black Sea, the Red Sea, the Persian Gulf, the Sea of Japan, the South China Sea and Gulf of California.

Poleward distribution is apparently limited by water temperature, and common dolphins sometimes follow warm water beyond their normal range. Although present all year round throughout much of their range, they have been reported to undertake seasonal movements in certain areas. Common dolphins in several areas appear to move towards offshore banks and escarpments, where increased upwelling may provide better feeding opportunities. Apparently, herds of common dolphins sometimes move over a thousand kilometres in search of suitable prey.

**Food and feeding** Common dolphins feed on a wide variety of squids and fishes, particularly schooling fish such as sardines, anchovies, herring and pilchards. Their diet varies seasonally in some areas. The dolphins frequently adopt cooperative techniques to capture prey; for example, herds may dive below a school of fish and drive it to the surface. In the process, the fish become available to birds and other predators that flock to the area. Common dolphins have been seen to catch fish in mid-air.

Off southern California, common dolphins feed mostly at night on organisms associated with the Deep Scattering Layer (DSL), which rises towards the surface at night. Dives of up to 280m and 8 minutes have been recorded.

**Behaviour** Common dolphins live in schools, or herds, ranging from a few tens to several thousand individuals. Off California, herd sizes vary throughout the year, being larger from May until October, when schooling anchovies are the major prey item. In some areas, herds split up to feed in smaller groups at night, reassembling to rest and socialize during the day. Care-giving behaviour has been documented in this social species, which is frequently seen with other species of cetaceans. There appears to be some sexual segregation in common dolphins, with some evidence of nursery schools, consisting of large proportions of pregnant and nursing females.

Common dolphins are active and boisterous. Large travelling schools often consist of tightly packed individuals; at times, the whole school can be seen porpoising completely out of the water. At these times, or when fleeing a disturbance, schools can turn the surface of the ocean into a mass of froth with the spray from their leaps. It has been suggested that common dolphins use the sun's position to navigate.

Bow riding is a favourite activity of these dolphins, and they ride not only ships, but also the pressure waves created by large whales. Breaching, surface slaps using flippers, head or flukes and various flips or somersaults are not uncommon. It is sometimes possible to hear the squeals of these dolphins above the surface of the water while they are bow riding. Common dolphins are highly vocal, producing a wide range of whistles and pulsed sounds used in communication and echolocation.

Strandings of this species are not particularly common, but some do occur each year throughout the range. Many strandings in southern California have been linked to damage of the brain and ear cavities from parasitic worms.

**Life history** The gestation period is 10-11 months. Length at birth is 80-85cm, and the calf is nursed for 14-19 months. Estimates of the calving interval range from 1.3 to 2.6 years, and the annual pregnancy rate ranges from 38 to 75 percent.

Sexual maturity is reached at an average age and length of 6-7 years and 1.6-1.9m in females, and 5-12 years and 1.7-2m in males. Seasonal breeding peaks (in spring/autumn or summer) have been reported for some stocks, but some births probably occur all year round, especially in the tropics. It is important to note that this information is based on what is known of a few stocks. There is likely to be significant variation among the various geographical regions.

**World population** Although no reliable estimates of world population exist, the common dolphin is undoubtedly one of the most abundant of all dolphins. There are probably over one million common dolphins in the eastern North Pacific alone. Common dolphin is indeed an appropriate name.

Despite its general abundance, however, certain local stocks are in trouble, due mostly to large sustained catches in fisheries. Stocks in the Black Sea, northeastern Mediterranean and eastern tropical Pacific have apparently been depleted to levels that put them at risk.

**Man's influence** Exploitation by man occurs throughout the world. This species is one of several targets of directed fisheries in Japan, South America and the Azores. Common dolphins are taken incidentally in nets in Europe, South Africa, New Zealand, the Mediterranean region, China, and occasionally Sri Lanka. Incidental catches by tuna purse-seine vessels have been reported off West Africa and in the eastern tropical Pacific, where common dolphins are the third most frequently caught species of dolphin. Historically, the largest catches have occurred in the Black Sea, where at one time several countries combined to deliberately capture over 100,000 dolphins annually by shooting and purse-seining. Stocks there have declined and both the Russian and Turkish fisheries have ceased operation, the latter in 1988. Catches in the Black Sea were much smaller in the most recent years than previously.

Common dolphins have been kept in captivity in many different countries, but are not among the most popular species for training and display. Despite their apparent zest for life in the wild, most captive animals give the impression of being shy and easily disturbed.

# WHITE-BEAKED DOLPHIN

*LAGENORHYNCHUS ALBIROSTRIS*

■ Approximate range

**Classification** The genus was named by John Gray of the British Museum; *Lagenorhynchus* is derived from the Greek *Lagenos* for 'bottle' or 'flask' and *rhynchos* for 'beak' or 'snout'. The type specimen had a white beak and thus Gray named the species *albirostris*; *albus* is Latin for 'white' and *rostrum* means 'beak' or 'snout'.

**Local names** In English, the name white-nosed dolphin is sometimes used. Off Newfoundland and Labrador, where it is common, the species is called jumper or squidhound. White-beaked dolphins are called kvitnos ('whitenose') or springer in Norway. In Iceland, where the species is common, the local name is hnyðingur.

**Description** These dolphins grow to a maximum length of just over 3m. The short, thick beak is well demarcated from the melon. The body is robust, with a proportionately large, strongly falcate dorsal fin positioned midway along the back. The tail stock is thick, often with a dorsal and ventral keel.

Coloration is somewhat variable, but the basic pattern is dark on the back around the base of the dorsal fin, white or light grey patches on the sides extending back onto the dorsal surface of the tail stock and forward to the area between the blowhole and leading edge of the dorsal fin, and white undersides as far back as the middle of the tail stock. The entire beak is often white, but it can be mottled light grey or almost entirely dark. Light grey zones are often present in the neck region just behind the blowhole, above and in front of the base of the flipper and around the eye. The area between eye and flipper is often flecked with dark spots. There are usually 22-27 teeth in each side of each jaw, although the first three in each row may be unerupted.

**Recognition at sea** The most likely confusion is between white-beaked and Atlantic white-sided dolphins (page 150). Their appearance is broadly similar and their ranges overlap considerably. The best field mark for distinguishing the white-beaked dolphin are the white areas on the back, fore and aft of the dorsal fin; in the white-sided dolphin these areas are completely dark. When enough of the animal is seen, the brilliant white patch on the side below and slightly behind the dorsal fin, followed by a yellow or tan stripe on the flank, distinguishes the white-sided from the white-beaked dolphin. Also, the upper surface of the white-sided dolphin's beak is dark.

**Habitat** Few habitat details are known. White-beaked dolphins are scattered widely across the continental shelves, but are present in especially large numbers along the shelf edges and over the continental slopes. On the basis of UK stranding records, F.C. Fraser of the British Museum has reasoned that their distribution in the eastern North Atlantic is linked to the North Atlantic Current.

**Distribution and migration** The white-beaked dolphin is confined to the northern and subarctic North Atlantic, where they are widely distributed. In the east, a few sightings have been made as far south as Portugal, and there has been at least one stranding in France, but generally, these dolphins are rare south of the UK. In the west, the southern limit is approximately Cape Cod.

These dolphins are abundant in the Norwegian, North, southwestern Barents and Labrador Seas as well as the Denmark Strait, and possibly southern Davis Strait. They are common all round Iceland and the Faeroe Islands. Small numbers enter the Baltic Sea. There is no evidence that they enter Hudson Strait, but large numbers can be present in summer in the Gulf of St. Lawrence.

Although their migratory behaviour has not been closely studied, white-beaked dolphins are said by fishermen to approach the coast of Labrador in late June and to remain in coastal waters during the summer and autumn. They are present all year round near the UK.

**Food and feeding** White-beaked dolphins have a varied diet, dominated perhaps by clupeid and gadoid fishes. They also eat squid and crustaceans. They are often seen in the Denmark Strait feeding on capelin with fin whales.

**Behaviour** Group size varies greatly. Small groups of a few to several dozen individuals are perhaps most common, but herds of hundreds and occasionally more than a thousand are also seen at times. White-beaked dolphins can be very acrobatic, breaching high and landing on their backs or sides. They have been seen swimming among killer whales east of Greenland, with no obvious sign of predator-prey interactions. Presumably some predation by killer whales occurs.

White-beaked dolphins usually strand individually rather than in pods.

**Life history** Length at birth is probably in the range of 1.2-1.6m. Most births are thought to take place in summer and early autumn, but the evidence for this and other aspects of the reproductive cycle is very limited.

**World population** Although nothing is known about stock identity, and no estimates have been made of what can be considered an entire population, several local estimates have been attempted. A strip census of the continental shelf between St. Anthony's, Newfoundland, and Nain, Labrador, resulted in an estimate of about 3,500 white-beaked dolphins. An estimate of about 600 was made for a small area east of Cape Cod.

White-beaked dolphins are unquestionably the most abundant dolphins off southeastern Greenland, in the Denmark Strait and the seas around Iceland. Records from large-scale sightings surveys and even from catches in Greenland and the Faeroe Islands often fail to distinguish between white-beaked and Atlantic white-sided dolphins.

Impressions of trends in abundance have been noted by field researchers, but unfortunately these have proven difficult to verify. Near Cape Cod, for example, white-beaked dolphins are said to have been more common during the 1950s than they are today, while it appears that observations of Atlantic white-sided dolphins in this area have increased. Based on the frequency of strandings, white-beaked dolphins are believed to have become more common in Dutch waters since about 1960.

**Man's influence** White-beaked dolphins have long been hunted, at least opportunistically, in many parts of their range. Considerable numbers were captured formerly in the fjords of Finnmark, northern Norway. Catches of several hundred dolphins have been reported for the Faeroe Islands in the early twentieth century, but it is not certain whether these were white-beaked or white-sided dolphins, or perhaps some of each. Small catches continue there and in southern and western Greenland, but often with the species not indicated with certainty. In one recent study of cetacean exploitation off Labrador, it was estimated that, on average, 366 white-beaked dolphins were being killed a year by fishermen.

At least some incidental capture in fishing gear has been occurring for more than a century. In no area, however, has this kind of mortality been documented on a large enough scale to raise concerns about population depletion.

No significant attempt has been made to live-capture these dolphins, but five members of a group of several dozen trapped in ice off Newfoundland in March 1983 were netted and taken to the Mystic Aquarium in Connecticut.

*Below left: Light areas on the back, notably behind the dorsal fin, are useful identifiers for this dolphin.*

*Right: A single white-beaked dolphin quietly swimming among the Outer Hebrides Islands, off the coast of western Scotland.*

*Below: Although sometimes acrobatic, as here, this species is not renowned for a consistent display of aerial activity.*

# ATLANTIC WHITE-SIDED DOLPHIN

*LAGENORHYNCHUS ACUTUS*

■ Approximate range

**Classification** The species name is derived from the Latin *acutus* for 'sharp', referring to the acutely pointed dorsal fin typical of this species.

**Local names** The Norwegian name for the species is kvitskjeving, although local people on the south and west coasts of Norway refer generically to these and other small delphinids as springers. As is true of Pacific white-sided dolphins, North American whalewatchers, aquarists and researchers often just call these dolphins lags.

**Description** This fairly robust animal has a prominent dorsal fin, sharply pointed and falcate. The flippers are also pointed. The beak is short but well-defined. The maximum body length is about 2.8m for males, 2.5m for females. Males are consistently larger than females.

The colour pattern is highly distinctive. The entire dorsal surface, including the upper jaw, as well as the flippers and flukes, is black. The undersides, including the lower jaw, are white as far back as the middle of the tail stock. The sides are greyish, except for two well-defined patches. One of these is a longitudinal and slightly transverse band of white, beginning below the dorsal fin and continuing back to near the middle of the tail stock. Immediately behind this white patch, there is a narrow yellowish tan patch, also oriented longitudinally, which continues almost to the insertion of the flukes. There are 30-40 teeth in each side of each jaw.

**Recognition at sea** A useful clue to distinguishing white-beaked dolphins from Atlantic white-sided dolphins is the way the former's white or lightly pigmented zone on the flanks intrudes onto the back behind and ahead of the dorsal fin. On Atlantic white-sided dolphins, these areas are dark, as is the entire dorsal surface. Beak coloration can be misleading, since there is much variation in this feature in white-beaked dolphins.

A common error is to confuse common dolphins with Atlantic white-sided dolphins. Both are very gregarious and active at the surface, and there are superficial similarities in their pigmentation patterns. Common dolphins in the North Atlantic have a tawny yellow or brownish patch on the side, from below the dorsal fin forward. Since both species have a beak (although the common dolphin's is considerably longer), a prominent dorsal fin, a dark back and white belly and yellowish or brownish markings on the sides, brief sightings at sea can easily result in mistakes in identification.

**Habitat** In the western North Atlantic, it has been suggested that these dolphins prefer continental slope waters at a surface temperature of 9-15°C, between the warm Gulf Stream and the cold inshore waters influenced by the Labrador Current. One recent study of Atlantic white-sided dolphins sighted in shelf and slope waters off the eastern United States recorded sea surface temperatures in the range of 1-13°C (mean of 7°C, plus or minus 3°C). Also, the areas of primary occurrence had high sea floor relief. Spring aggregations of white-sided dolphins were correlated with dense concentrations of American sand lance (*Ammodytes americanus*), probably a major prey species.

Aerial surveys of the continental shelf off the northeastern United States revealed that white-sided dolphins were most abundant in water about 40-270m deep, with surface temperatures of 6-20°C. They are clearly inhabitants of the continental shelf and shelf edge regions.

**Distribution and migration** It has often been stated that in the eastern North Atlantic, white-sided dolphins have a more northerly distribution than white-beaked dolphins. This supposition, based largely on strandings in the UK and on at-sea observations off Norway, now seems to be erroneous. The white-beaked dolphin is far more common than the white-sided dolphin off Finnmark, northern Norway, and around Iceland. In the western North Atlantic, white-sided dolphins regularly move farther south than white-beaked dolphins. Nevertheless, there is much overlap in the ranges of the two species.

The normal northern limits of distribution are at about 64°N, near Nuuk in West Greenland, and Trondheim in Norway. Along the North American coast, white-sided dolphins occur at least as far north as southern Labrador at about 53°N.

Large herds enter the Gulf of St. Lawrence in summer and autumn, sometimes moving as far up the St. Lawrence estuary as the Saguenay River confluence. They are very abundant all year round in the Gulf of Maine (40-44°N) and also present, especially in spring, south along the continental slope to 37°N, east of Chesapeake Bay. Although the usual southern limit in the eastern North Atlantic is the UK, a few individual strandings have occurred in France near the southern entrance to the English Channel.

Migratory movements are not well documented for this dolphin, but seasonal changes in abundance in inshore regions have been noted.

**Food and feeding** The main prey are small schooling fishes, such as herring, sand lance and juvenile mackerel, and squid. These dolphins also eat smelt (*Osmerus mordax*) and silver hake (*Merluccius bilinearis*).

**Behaviour** Atlantic white-sided dolphins are gregarious and acrobatic. Individuals and small groups are commonly encountered, but so are herds of several hundred. These dolphins are often found in feeding areas associated with large whales, especially fin and humpback whales. The whales and dolphins appear to be attacking the same fish schools. The dolphins' behaviour near the heads of the whales appears similar to bow riding. It has been suggested that dolphins were riding and playing in the waves made by whales long before they discovered the sensations of bow riding in front of boats.

Individual and mass strandings of Atlantic white-sided dolphins are relatively common along the coasts of New England. Of the six species in the genus, *L. acutus* appears to be the most frequent mass strander. A notable mass stranding took place in September 1974 at Lingley Cove, Maine, where about 150 white-sided dolphins were left struggling on the mud flats as the tide rushed out. Many of the herd survived and returned to sea with the rising tide, but 59 carcasses of those that failed to escape were salvaged by scientists. Much of what is known about the species' natural history is based on the sample of specimens obtained from this and one other mass stranding on Cape Cod.

**Life history** Calves are 1.08-1.22m long at birth. Gestation lasts 10-12 months, lactation 18 months. Females inseminated one summer give birth the next. Some

females have been found to be simultaneously lactating and pregnant. Most males reach sexual maturity at a body length of 2.3-2.4m, females at 2-2.2m (corresponding to an age of 6-12 years). Maximum documented ages are 27 years for females and 22 years for males.

Judging by the composition of stranded groups, Atlantic white-sided dolphins are segregated by age, with young and newly maturing animals generally living apart from the mixed herds consisting of adult females, calves and a few adult males.

**World population** Although it cannot be verified in a rigorous scientific manner, many observers have the strong impression that white-sided dolphins increased in abundance and possibly expanded their range off the northeastern United States between the 1950s and 1980s. Systematic aerial surveys of the continental shelf between Nova Scotia and Cape Hatteras during the late 1970s found them to be the most abundant cetacean in the region. During June 1979, an estimated 46,000 animals were present.

**Man's influence** White-sided dolphins were once hunted along the southwestern coast of Norway. On at least two occasions in the eighteenth century, more than one thousand dolphins were taken near Bergen. In 1952, a herd of 52 animals was trapped in a harbour on Norway's west coast. Although there is some uncertainty about the species identifications, small numbers of white-sided dolphins are thought to be still taken in some years in southern and western Greenland. Tens or hundreds are currently taken annually by driving in the Faeroe Islands, where an unusually high total of more than 600 were killed for human consumption in 1988. One school alone accounted for 544 animals. They are also shot opportunistically by some fishermen in southeastern Canada.

These dolphins are taken incidentally in various kinds of fishing gear in many areas. The scale of this problem, insofar as it is documented, does not appear to be large at present.

This species has not been deliberately live-captured, although a number of individuals have been brought into captivity after stranding. Most have not lived more than a few weeks or months.

*Left: This acrobatic species can occur from the coast right out to the edge of the continental shelf.*

*Below: The dark dorsal coloration, here partly obscured by glare, separates this species from L. albirostris.*

# PACIFIC WHITE-SIDED DOLPHIN

*LAGENORHYNCHUS OBLIQUIDENS*

Probable range

**Classification** The name *obliquidens* is from the Latin *obliquus* for 'slanting' and *dens* for 'tooth'. Theodore Gill, who named the species, described the teeth as 'boldly curved' and 'directed obliquely forwards and outwards'. Basic body shape and coloration are very similar to those of the dusky dolphin of the Southern Hemisphere.

**Local names** Some older literature refers to this species as the Pacific striped dolphin, not to be confused with the striped dolphin, *Stenella coeruleoalba*. Field researchers and employees of oceanariums often call them lags (simply a shortened version of the genus name).

**Description** Males grow to a maximum length of 2.5m, females 2.4m. Average adult size may be 2.1-2.2m and 75-90kg. Individuals can weigh as much as 181kg. There is some evidence that animals from the southern part of the species range

(south of 32°N) are larger than the northern ones (north of 37°N), so there may be at least two separate stocks.

The short, dark beak is only evident when the animal is closely observed. At sea it appears absent. The tall, prominent dorsal fin is strongly recurved and wide at the base. It tends to be bicoloured – the front third dark grey or black, the rear part light grey. The flippers are similarly bicoloured but the flukes are all dark.

The overall colour pattern is greyish black on the back, paler on the sides and white underneath. A large patch of light grey to almost white dominates the thoracic region from midbody forward, narrowing as it continues onto the melon. A light grey longitudinal stripe begins on the face and forehead on either side and extends backwards through the dark cape, widening behind the dorsal fin to

become a wide lateral band on the flank. The ventral whiteness is sharply demarcated from the rest of the body by a thin black line. Details of the colour pattern vary considerably within a herd, and the intensity of the markings tends to be muted on young individuals. There are 23-36 small, pointed teeth in each side of each jaw.

**Recognition at sea** Common dolphins, which are found mainly in the southern half of the Pacific white-sided dolphin's range, have a more prominent beak and a characteristic V-shaped 'saddle' on the back and sides. The disturbance caused by a surfacing white-sided dolphin can sometimes call to mind the characteristic splash or spray made by the speedy Dall's porpoise, whose geographical range is generally similar. However, the

*Left: Part of a typically large herd of Pacific white-sided dolphins. These constantly active little dolphins are often seen leaping clear of the surface together.*

*Below: This species is very similar to the dusky dolphin of the Southern Hemisphere.*

*Above right: Bow riding is a favourite activity of these oceanic dolphins.*

Dall's porpoise has a comparatively modest, triangular dorsal fin and a sharply defined black-and-white body pattern.

**Habitat** These dolphins are found mainly on the continental shelf, continental slope and offshore. They do come into protected inshore marine waters but usually only where there is fairly deep water. Several attempts have been made to correlate sightings with water temperatures. In Monterey Bay, most sightings were made in water at 15-17°C. Few were made in water warmer than 17°C. Off British Columbia, the mean sea surface temperature for a sample of 73 sightings was 12°C, with a range of 6-17°C.

**Distribution and migration** The range is limited to the North Pacific Ocean north of 20°N. These dolphins occasionally appear in the mouth of the Gulf of California in the east and as far south as Taiwan on the western side. Their distribution appears to be continuous across the rim of the North Pacific, mainly south of the Aleutian and Commander Islands. They are common in the Gulf of Alaska (but not Prince William Sound), Sea of Okhotsk (especially the southeastern half, as well as near the Kurile Islands) and Sea of Japan, and along the Pacific coasts of Canada, the United States and Japan. There are no confirmed records in the vicinity of the Hawaiian Islands.

Migratory movements have been assumed to account for the seasonal changes in abundance of this species in a number of areas. Off southern California, for example, abundance appears to increase during winter and early spring (November-April), although the species is present there all year round. Further north, in Monterey Bay, central California, these dolphins are least abundant during late winter and spring (January-May) and most common in summer to midwinter (June-December). In inshore marine waters of Washington and British Columbia, there are records for most of the year, with peaks in January-May and November that suggest some degree of inshore-offshore movement.

**Food and feeding** These dolphins feed primarily on small schooling fishes and squid, some of which are commercially important. Among the species most frequently reported in their diet are northern anchovies, hake and the squid *Loligo opalescens*. Judging by their diet and behaviour, Pacific white-sided dolphins forage mainly in the epipelagic (0-200m) and mesopelagic (200-1,000m) zones of the sea. Research shows that they commonly feed at dusk, during the night and in the early morning hours.

**Behaviour** These gregarious dolphins are often seen in large herds, numbering in the hundreds if not thousands. The large herds may dissolve into small groups while feeding, then re-assemble during periods of rest or travel. Pacific white-sided dolphins commonly associate with other toothed whales and dolphins, particularly common dolphins, northern right whale dolphins and Risso's dolphins, and perhaps less frequently with baleen whales, fur seals and sea lions. In inshore areas of Washington and British Columbia as well as Monterey Bay in California, white-sided dolphins are generally encountered in groups of 30 or fewer.

They are demonstrative at the surface, porpoising and leaping clear of the water during high-speed runs. However, collectors working for a California oceanarium noticed that herds of Pacific white-sided dolphins were less easy to detect at a distance than were similar-sized herds of common dolphins. In fact, white-sided dolphins would often appear at the bow of the collecting vessel suddenly, without having been spotted by the crew previously. Except when busy feeding, they are enthusiastic bow riders, approaching both large and small vessels to frolic in the waves. One dolphin in a group of about 20 in Monterey Bay actually landed on the deck of a research vessel after jumping 2-3m above the water!

Efforts to catch white-sided dolphins by driving and surrounding them with nets often prove futile because they escape by swimming under the nets.

**Life history** The birth length is 80-124cm. The estimated gestation period is 10-12 months. Mating and calving take place from spring through fall. Both sexes attain sexual maturity at a length of 1.7-2.2m. These dolphins may live for as long as 46 years.

**World population** It is generally agreed that this is one of the most abundant small cetaceans in the temperate zone of the North Pacific. Aerial surveys of the continental shelf region of central and northern California (Point Conception north) in the early 1980s found the white-sided dolphin to be the most numerous cetacean. The population present in this small area alone during the autumn period was estimated to be more than 85,000 individuals.

**Man's influence** Pacific white-sided dolphins have long been important in the Japanese coastal fishery for small cetaceans. A catch of 2,385 was reported in Iwate prefecture in 1882. In some recent years, the reported catches have been high: 697 by one company in May-June 1949 and 1,605 and 2,760 by the entire fishery in 1983 and 1984, respectively. They are taken mainly by harpooning rather than by driving. The impact of the Japanese fishery on the population of white-sided dolphins in the western North Pacific has not been assessed.

In the eastern North Pacific, exploitation has been limited to occasional scientific collections and the live-capture of small numbers for oceanariums (21 in the USA during 1976-85). Incidental catches occur in various kinds of fishing gear. Off California, they have been caught incidentally in anchovy purse seines. Incidental killing in gillnets, particularly the long and highly destructive driftnets set across much of the northern North Pacific for salmon and squid, is a concern for this species as well as for the Dall's porpoise, northern right whale dolphin and northern fur seal. (See page 50 for further details on the impact of fisheries.)

Pacific white-sided dolphins have long been popular as performers in American, Canadian and Japanese oceanariums. Individuals have survived for as long as 20 years, although two-thirds of 32 animals live-captured off southern California during 1966-72 died within the first year of captivity. In Japan, 129 white-sided dolphins were live-captured for oceanariums off the Pacific coast and 130 obtained from the Sea of Japan and East China Sea between 1973 and 1982.

# DUSKY DOLPHIN
## *LAGENORHYNCHUS OBSCURUS*

■ Sightings/strandings  □ Possible sightings

**Classification** The dusky dolphin was described by Gray in 1828. No subspecies are recognized. The species name, *obscurus*, is derived from the Latin, meaning 'dark, indistinct'.

**Local names** In Spanish, this animal is known as delfin obscuro.

**Description** The dusky dolphin is a relatively small, compact species. The body coloration is complex, being dark grey to blue-black above and predominantly white below. The sides are marked with blazes and patches of light grey. The sides in front of the fin are dominated by a light grey chest patch that encompasses the face and most of the head and sides and tapers towards the belly. A crescent-shaped flank patch reaches the top of the tail stock just in front of the flukes. The front of this flank patch has two blazes: a shorter ventral and a longer dorsal one, which extends up onto the back, almost to the blowhole.

The rostrum is short but noticeably demarcated from the forehead. The dorsal fin is fairly pointed, and is moderately falcate and erect. There is a crescent of light grey of variable extent and intensity on the trailing edge of the fin; it blends into the dark grey-black of the front portion. The flippers are fairly long for the body size, with a moderate curve to the leading edge and a blunt tip. They are light grey, but darken towards the edges.

The rostrum is grey-black above and below at the tip, with the black on both jaws tapering back to include just the lips near the gape. The eye is encircled with a patch of smudgy grey-black.

The maximum recorded length is approximately 2.1m. Most adults are between 1.6 and 2m. Preliminary results show that animals in a small sample of adults from New Zealand are shorter on average – and have smaller skulls – than animals from a larger sample from Peru. Apparently healthy adults taken during fishery operations in New Zealand measured 1.6-1.8m and weighed 40-80kg.

Tooth counts carried out on animals examined in New Zealand recorded 27-36 teeth on each side of each jaw.

**Recognition at sea** At sea, dusky dolphins can be separated from the closely related but much larger and more robust Peale's dolphin by the mostly white chin and grey face of the former, and the presence of a well-developed stripe from gape to flipper and flipper to near the vent on the latter. Additionally, the dusky dolphin has two forward-pointing blazes originating from the flank patch, while the Peale's dolphin has only one. Though similar in shape to the dusky dolphin, the hourglass dolphin is strikingly black and white, with an all-black fin that may be more strongly hooked. Dusky dolphins can be readily separated from the somewhat similar common dolphin by the length of the rostrum, colour and size/shape of lateral blazes and colour patches, and by the shape and coloration of the fin of the common dolphin.

**Habitat** Throughout their range, dusky dolphins are primarily coastal and are usually found on the continental shelf out to the slope, including nearshore continental plateau regions.

**Distribution and migration** Dusky dolphins are widespread in the Southern Hemisphere. They are known to occur in the waters of New Zealand, South America and southern Africa.

In New Zealand, the dusky dolphin is normally found from about the latitude of East Cape on the North Island (37° 42'S) south through the Cook Strait to the waters of Stewart Island. There are records from the Chatham Islands, Auckland Islands and nearby waters, and Campbell Island. Local migration is known in New Zealand, as duskys leave the northern waters of Hawke's Bay in the summer when water temperatures rise and return in the autumn/winter when they drop.

In South America, duskies are found from northern central Peru (to at least 10°S) south along the coast at least as far as 33°S (Valparaiso, Chile). They may venture into southern South America only during infrequent or seasonal periods of favourable conditions, such as a rise in water temperature. On the east coast of South America, dusky dolphins probably range from southern Uruguay south to at least Peninsula Valdés.

In southern Africa, dusky dolphins are common in the cool waters of the Cape region and the southwestern coast. Their range extends from just east of the Cape of Good Hope north at least to Namibia. The northern extent of their range is unknown, but probably closely parallels the extent of cool temperate and upwelling waters of the Benguela current regime.

**Food and feeding** Dusky dolphins have been reported to take a wide variety of prey. In Argentina, at Peninsula Valdés, they feed heavily on southern anchovy (*Engraulis anchoveta*) in surface waters during the summer. While searching for anchovy, dusky herds may disperse into small subgroups, consisting typically of 8-30 animals, although larger feeding groups occur. Cooperative feeding has been observed; individual dolphins take

turns making passes through fish schools herded together by a cooperating group. In New Zealand, studies of stranded and fisheries-caught animals indicate that these dolphins prey mainly on midwater and benthic species, such as squid and lantern fishes, found in continental slope waters. They may also feed at night.

**Behaviour** Dusky dolphins are a highly social, gregarious species. They are sometimes found in large herds of over 1,000 animals, but are more likely to occur in groups of 20-500. Locality, time of day and season can greatly affect group size.

Behaviour has been studied in Argentina and New Zealand. In Argentina, dusky dolphins separate into small subgroups to feed, but after feeding may aggregate into large herds to rest, socialize and mate. It has been suggested that herds that move inshore close to breaking waves at night do so to avoid predators.

Results from radio-telemetric studies and observations of tagged animals have been particularly enlightening. In Argentina, the minimum mean daily distance travelled was 19.2km. One animal tagged

*Top left: One of the most acrobatic of dolphins, the dusky is essentially a coastal species in southern waters. It is a social animal that gathers in large groups, or herds.*

*Below: A dusky dolphin photographed in mid leap in New Zealand waters. Note the two blazes on the flank that set it apart from Peale's dolphin, which has one.*

in winter was an exception, travelling only an average of 0.7km. The minimum mean speed of two animals was calculated to be 2.28 and 3.18kph. In the summer, daytime dives were usually longer than night dives, while the opposite was usually true during the winter. Dusky dolphins generally made their longest dives at dusk. In New Zealand, radio-tagged dusky dolphins were found to move frequently in and out of an area, staying further from shore in winter and remaining relatively localized nearshore in the summer. In Argentina, two animals tagged together were resighted together almost eight years later nearly 780km from their original location!

Many species of cetaceans have been observed in association with dusky dolphins, including common dolphin, southern right whale dolphin, bottlenose dolphin, long-finned pilot whale and southern right whale. Numerous species of seabirds have been reported in association with feeding and travelling dusky schools, including several varieties of albatrosses, petrels and shearwaters, as well as gulls, terns and jaegers.

**Life history** In New Zealand, calving is believed to occur in midwinter (June-August). Gestation is estimated to last 11 months, suggesting spring mating. A 98cm male calf collected in November weighed 22kg. A 7cm male foetus was collected in December and a 66.5cm,

3.7kg female foetus was collected in late July. The mother of the latter was 1.78m long and weighed 77.5kg (with foetus) at the time of her death in a fisheries entanglement. Length at birth has been reported to be 55-70cm and lactation is estimated to last 18 months. There has not yet been any evidence of twinning. It is important to stress that these figures are based on very few specimens; so, conclusions should be taken as tentative.

**World population** Dusky dolphins are assumed to be relatively abundant throughout their range. However, very little survey work has been conducted and no estimates are available.

**Man's influence** In New Zealand, dusky dolphins are entangled in coastal gillnets; mortality at one important fishing port is estimated to be between 100 and 200 animals a year.

The situation in Peru is undoubtedly critical. It has been calculated that the fishing fleet operating from just one of a number of landings kills more than 700 dusky dolphins every year. As dolphins are sold for food, they are taken not only incidentally but also deliberately, as principal targets. Dusky dolphins have been held in captivity in New Zealand, South Africa and Australia, with low to moderate success. There have been no reports of births in captivity.

# PEALE'S DOLPHIN

## LAGENORHYNCHUS AUSTRALIS

■ Probable distribution □ Possible sighting

**Classification** Peale's dolphin was named in 1848 by the naturalist Titian R. Peale. He described and measured the first specimen, which was harpooned and brought aboard one of the ships of the United States Exploring Expedition on February 12, 1839. The specific name, *australis*, reflects the species' southern distribution. No subspecies are recognized in this dolphin.

**Local names** These include blackchin dolphin and delfin austral (Spanish).

**Description** Although few specimens have been examined, field observations indicate that Peale's dolphin is proportionately the most robust of the Southern Hemisphere dolphins of this genus. The largest specimen recorded was 2.16m long, and adults are estimated to weigh 115kg. Tooth counts for three specimens were 27 to 33 on each side of each jaw.

Peale's dolphins share coloration features with both dusky and Pacific white-sided dolphins. Peale's dolphins are greyish black above and mostly white below. They have a curved flank patch of light grey with a single dorsal spinal blaze, or 'suspender', running into the black of the back to near the blowhole. A light grey patch on the chest extends from the eye to mid-body, and is separated from the white below by a well-developed stripe of dark greyish black. There is a small loop in this stripe containing a white patch at the 'armpit', much like the one on Pacific white-sided dolphins. The face, rostrum, melon and most of the chin are dark greyish black, readily distinguishing Peale's dolphin from the dusky dolphin.

The flippers are greyish black. The fin is dark greyish black with a small crescent of light grey on the trailing margin. It is prominent, appears to be of slightly greater than average size for the genus and is pointed and moderately falcate.

**Recognition at sea** See the section on dusky dolphins (page 154).

**Habitat** Peale's dolphins are found over continental shelf and slope waters, in fjords, sounds, bays and inlets, and around islands. They are frequently sighted quite close to shore, often within and shoreward of kelp beds. The continental shelf on the east coast of Argentina extends to and beyond the Falklands, presenting a large expanse of suitable habitat.

**Distribution and migration** Peale's dolphins have a somewhat restricted distribution. They are confined to the coastal waters of southern South America from about the latitude of Valparaiso, Chile (33°S), south through the Chilean fjords, throughout the Strait of Magellan and the waters of Tierra del Fuego, and north an unknown distance along the Argentine coast. Peale's dolphins are regularly seen at the Falkland Islands and over Burdwood Bank, south of the Falklands.

A herd of dolphins tentatively identified as of this species was seen recently at Palmerston Atoll, in the South Pacific. If valid, this sighting will extend its range far to the west and into warmer waters than previously documented.

**Food and feeding** Little is known; one animal collected in the Falkland Islands had octopus remains in its stomach.

**Behaviour** Peale's dolphin has only been found in small groups, 5-30 being typical. They are frequent bow riders and will 'run' to a ship's bow, quarter or stern wakes with long, low-angle leaps. At the bow, they often speed ahead, leap high into the air and fall back into the water on their sides, producing a large splash with a loud slapping noise. Few stranded specimens have been found, and all were single strandings.

**Man's influence** Peale's dolphins are drowned at unknown levels in set nets (incidentally) and harpooned in the Strait of Magellan and around Tierra del Fuego. There is concern that the number harpooned, for use as bait in crab traps, may be sufficiently high in this dolphin's very restricted range to pose a serious conservation problem. Peale's dolphins have never been maintained in captivity.

*Below: This Peale's dolphin is in a typically energetic mood, riding a bow wave with long, low-angle leaps.*

# HOURGLASS DOLPHIN

*LAGENORHYNCHUS CRUCIGER*

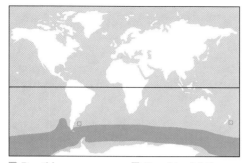

■ Possible range    □ Possible sightings

**Classification** The hourglass dolphin was described in 1824 by Quoy and Gaimard, although they originally called this species *Delphinus cruciger*. The specific name stems from the Latin *crucis* for 'cross' and *gero* for 'bear' or 'carry', and refers to the clearly visible cross pattern on the sides of the body where two regions of white intersect.

**Local names** Local names include delfin cruzado (Spanish) and, historically, Wilson's dolphin, after the celebrated Antarctic explorer Edward Wilson.

**Description** The hourglass dolphin is one of the least-known species of dolphin. What we do know from specimens, observations and, recently, some outstanding photographs is that it is strikingly marked – basically black above and white below. The black sides are interrupted by a white flank patch that fills most of the tail stock in a wedgelike shape and tapers as it rises towards the fin. Here, it gives rise to a white dorsal-spinal

*Below: An hourglass dolphin in the open sea about 1,200km south of the Kerguelen Islands.*

*The distinctive pattern that gives rise to its common name is clearly seen here.*

blaze that widens just behind the flippers, passes above the eye and covers the sides of the face, merging at the gape with the ventral white of the chest and throat. This pattern resembles an hourglass in shape and gives the dolphin its common name. The short rostrum typical of the genus is black. The eye is encircled in black, and the forehead and top of the head are also black. A white, hook-shaped pattern curves upwards and interrupts the black sides below the flank patch near the genital aperture.

The flippers, fin and flukes are all solid black. The flippers are curved and taper to a point, and are long for the body size compared to those of other small delphinids. A fairly tall dorsal fin is set about midway along the back. Recently, some individuals have been seen and photographed with a markedly hooked fin similar in appearance to that found in some Pacific white-sided dolphins, in which they are thought to develop in this way at the onset of physical maturity.

Few animals have been measured; a 1.63m male and a 1.83m female have been reported. A relatively low tooth count of approximately 28 teeth on each side of each jaw has been recorded.

**Recognition at sea** As the only truly oceanic dolphin with a dorsal fin in subantarctic and Antarctic waters, the strikingly marked hourglass dolphin is unlikely to be mistaken for another species.

**Habitat** Hourglass dolphins appear to be primarily pelagic; most sightings have been far out to sea, well away from continents and islands. In one survey, however, sightings were made near southern South America and the Antarctic Peninsula in waters of 200m or less and near

islands or banks. Studies south and east of New Zealand have revealed an association with water of 1-10°C.

**Distribution and migration** Hourglass dolphins appear to be circumpolar in higher latitudes of the southern oceans, although this distribution may, in fact, include breaks. They range up to the ice-edge in the south but the northern limits are not known. There are records of a (possible) solitary sighting off the northeastern coast of South Island, New Zealand, north of the Falklands, and as far north as 33°S off the coast of Chile. Hourglass dolphins are frequently seen in the Drake Passage between southern South America and the Antarctic Convergence.

**Food and feeding** Almost nothing is known. One of the few specimens collected where the stomach was examined contained 'a mass of more or less digested small fish, which may have been mixed with other food matter'.

**Behaviour** In recent years, reports and photographs of hourglass dolphins have increased substantially. These dolphins are well known as enthusiastic bow riders, often 'running' for the bow, stern or quarter wakes with long, low-angle leaps. They often move rapidly without leaping, usually when avoiding an approaching vessel; at such times they cause a highly visible spray.

Groups tend to be small, which is unusual for a small pelagic delphinid. Although herds of up to about 40 have been encountered, groups of 1-6 are more frequently seen. Hourglass dolphins have been sighted in association with Arnoux's beaked whales, southern bottlenose whales, long-finned pilot whales and fin whales.

Only a handful of stranded specimens have been recovered, two of which were found as beach-weathered skulls. No mass strandings have been documented.

**World population** It may be more accurate to describe this species as poorly known or uncommon rather than rare. It is likely that their numbers are at or near original population levels.

**Man's influence** With the increase in development of Antarctic and subantarctic fisheries for krill, finfish and squid, it is vital that the feeding habits of hourglass dolphins and other poorly known species be studied. Hourglass dolphins have never been kept in captivity.

# FRASER'S DOLPHIN

*LAGENODELPHIS HOSEI*

■ Probable minimum range

**Classification** The species was described by F.C. Fraser of the British Museum in 1956, based on a skull and skeleton collected in the late nineteenth century from a beach in Sarawak, Borneo. The genus is so named because the skull examined by Fraser was reminiscent of both *Lagenorhynchus* and *Delphinus delphis*. The specific name, *hosei*, honours C. Hose, the collector of the type specimen.

**Local names** For some time after Fraser's description in 1956, this species was called the Sarawak dolphin.

**Description** Fraser's dolphin grows to a maximum length of about 2.65m, but most adults are no longer than about 2.3-2.5m. Large individuals can weigh in excess of 200kg.

The external form, as well as the skull, is intermediate between *Lagenorhynchus* and *Delphinus*. The beak is very short but well defined, the body robust, the appendages proportionately small and pointed. The dorsal fin is triangular and, in some individuals, weakly recurved.

The most striking feature of the pigmentation pattern is the bold, dark grey

*Below: This striking tropical dolphin was first described as late as 1956. Its full distribution is incompletely known.*

lateral stripe, of variable width and intensity, which gives the animal a 'masked' appearance. An ill-defined cream stripe borders this dark lateral stripe above and below. The back is greyish or brownish blue, as are the fin, flippers and flukes. The ventral whiteness, often tinged with pink, is interrupted by a well-demarcated flipper stripe. Elements of this species' coloration are similar to those of both *Delphinus delphis* and *Stenella coeruleoalba*. There are 34-44 teeth in each side of each jaw.

**Recognition at sea** In the tropical regions where it is usually found, Fraser's dolphin is most likely to be confused with the striped dolphin and the common dolphin. The latter both have a longer beak and larger fin and flippers than Fraser's dolphin. In addition, the striped dolphin has a considerably narrower eye-to-anus stripe, and the common dolphin has a V-shaped cape, or saddle, which comes to a point just below the dorsal fin.

**Habitat** This is primarily an offshore species, rarely encountered in coastal waters except around oceanic islands and in areas with narrow shelves.

**Distribution and migration** Fraser's dolphin probably has a pantropical distribution between 40°N and 40°S. It is especially common in the Camotes Sea and the southern end of Bohol Strait, Philippines. Also, there is a relatively large number of sightings from the eastern tropical Pacific along the equator between 110 and 145°W.

The scarcity of sightings in the tropical Atlantic and Indian Oceans may indicate little more than a relative lack of observational effort there. It was only learned that the species is common in the Philippines because a live-capture enterprise was based there, ensuring that an intense search for dolphins took place. In the eastern tropical Pacific, a vast amount of documentation of cetacean distributions is available because of studies relating to the high-seas tuna fishery. Nothing is known about migrations.

**Food and feeding** The few stomach contents examined and reported for this species contained remains of a large variety of mesopelagic fishes, crustaceans and squid. It has been inferred from the nature of its prey that this dolphin hunts in near or total darkness, day or night, at depths greater than 250m.

**Behaviour** Little is known about behaviour. Fraser's dolphins are usually seen in herds of at least a hundred, often in the vicinity of, or even mixed with, herds of other pelagic toothed whales and dolphins, especially melon-headed whales (*Peponocephala electra*) and other globicephalids. They are very active at the surface but do not appear especially playful. It has been reported that Fraser's dolphins are extremely shy of boats. However, in the Indian Ocean and around the Philippines, this does not seem to be true. A mass stranding of at least 17 individuals occurred in Florida.

**Life history** The reproductive biology of Fraser's dolphin has not been studied and reported in any detail. The largest reported foetus was 45cm long, the smallest individual 95cm. The birth length is probably somewhat less than 1m. Females may reach sexual maturity at a body length of about 2.25-2.35m.

**World population** There are no useful estimates of population size, and nothing is known about stock separation. Judging by the frequency of reported sightings, Fraser's dolphin is much less abundant than several other tropical, oceanic dolphins. However, in some areas, such as the Philippines, it is very common.

**Man's influence** Fraser's dolphins are caught occasionally in native fisheries in the Lesser Antilles, Indonesia and Sri Lanka, and rarely in the Japanese coastal small-cetacean fishery. However, no serious impact has been documented. Sixteen of these dolphins were live-captured in the Philippines for an aquarium in Hong Kong during the mid-1970s. Of the 10 kept, only four survived more than three weeks. The last one of the group died after 100 days of captivity.

# HEAVISIDE'S DOLPHIN

## CEPHALORHYNCHUS HEAVISIDII

■ Known distribution  ☐ Possible sighting

**Classification** Heaviside's dolphin was first described by Gray from a specimen brought to London by a Captain Haviside in 1827. The extra 'e' appears to have been either a typographical error or a case of mistaken identity; Captain Heaviside was an eminent surgeon of the same period who had a large collection of non-cetacean specimens. Whatever the reason, Gray originally called the animal *Delphinus heavisidii*. The name *Cephalorhynchus* (*kephale* meaning 'head' and *rhynchus* meaning 'nose' or 'snout') was originally applied by Cuvier in 1828 as a specific, not a generic, name and refers to the clearly differentiated rostrum.

**Description** It is only recently that this species has been described from freshly recovered specimens. Heaviside's dolphin is small and stocky, similar in outline to the other members of the genus. From the small number of animals measured, it appears that adults grow to about 1.7m, but the sample is too small to determine whether there is sexual dimorphism in size. From those animals weighed, maximum weights are probably about 70-80kg. The rounded, conical-shaped head slopes smoothly from the blowholes to the tip of the snout; there is no well-defined beak. The lower jaw projects slightly beyond the upper. There are 22-28 pairs of small pointed teeth, less than 3mm in diameter, in both the upper and lower jaws.

The small flippers are characteristically blunt and swept backwards at the ends. About 60 percent of the animals examined had serrations on at least one – and usually both – flippers at the leading edge. There is insufficient information to determine whether there are differences in occurrence of these serrations related to sex and/or age, as is the case in Commerson's dolphin (see page 162).

*This sequence of views clearly shows the distinctive colour pattern becoming progressively visible.*

The dorsal fin, just behind the middle of the back, is almost triangular, with a longer, slightly convex leading edge. The broad, crescent-shaped flukes have a small median notch.

The colour pattern is striking. The dorsal and lateral surfaces are essentially dark blue-black, as far forwards as the posterior insertion of the dorsal fin where, just below the midline, it borders a grey 'cape'. The cape covers the belly, thorax and head, apart from blue-black areas around the eyes, the continuation of the dorsal blue-black region (which narrows progressively, forming a thin finger up to the blowhole, which it then encircles) and the white areas on the belly. Two thin grey blazes begin laterally just below the midpoint of the dorsal fin and extend backwards, almost meeting dorsally, about two-thirds of the way from the dorsal fin to the flukes. There are four white regions on the ventral surface. The first is a diamond-shaped area across the chest, extending backwards to end just in front of the anterior insertions of the flippers. The second and third are tear-shaped patches, one on each side, at the posterior insertion of the flippers. The fourth area is also the largest, beginning halfway between the 'tears' and extending backwards, broadening and then splitting into a trident. The central 'prong' broadens around the genital areas, finishing behind the anus in males and at the anus in females, while the laterals extend obliquely up the flanks to about as far back as the level of the anus. Within this white area there is usually a dark grey streak near the umbilicus. This pattern appears to be present from birth. White, or almost all-white, individuals have been seen occasionally.

**Recognition at sea** The combination of the characteristic dorsal fin shape and the grey cape leaves no doubt as to the identity of animals of this striking species. The white ventral markings help to distinguish beached specimens.

**Habitat** Almost all sightings of this species have been in coastal waters, mostly within 9km of the shore and in water less than 150m deep.

**Distribution and migration** The species is found along the western coast of southern Africa, from Cape Point (about 34°S, 18°30'E) in the south, to about 17°S, and possibly further north.

**Food and feeding** From the limited information available, the main food items taken by this dolphin appear to be fish and, to a lesser extent, cephalopods.

**Behaviour** This species is usually found in groups of less than ten and most commonly two, although larger short-term aggregations may occur. It is not generally 'flamboyant' but is known to approach vessels and bow ride on occasions.

**Life history** Very little is known about the life history of Heaviside's dolphins. Animals of about 1.6m or more in length are probably sexually mature.

**World population** No population estimates exist, but it is not thought to be in danger in any part of its range.

**Man's influence** This species is incidentally captured during fishing operations off South Africa and Namibia.

# CHILEAN DOLPHIN

*CEPHALORHYNCHUS EUTROPIA*

■ Known distribution

**Classification** The first published reference to this species was by Gray in 1846, who originally assigned it to the genus *Delphinus*. It was not until 1874 that it was correctly assigned to the genus *Cephalorhynchus* by Dall, although it has been classified and reclassified several times since then! The origin of the generic name is described under Heaviside's dolphin (page 159). The specific name, *eutropia*, comes from the Greek *eu* ('true', 'right') and *tropis*, *tropidos* ('head' or 'keel') and refers to its strongly keeled skull.

**Local names** The species has had a number of common names, including black dolphin (tonina negro) and white-bellied dolphin (tonina de vientre blanco), but the name currently accepted is the Chilean dolphin (delfin chileno), since the species appears to be confined to Chilean coastal waters.

**Description** The Chilean dolphin is small and stocky, similar in outline to the other members of its genus. It is known from less than 10 freshly recovered specimens, about 40 whole or part skeletons and about 80 recorded sightings. From the little material available, it seems that adults probably reach about 1.7m in length, with females being slightly larger than males, as in other species of the genus. Only two animals have been reliably weighed: a 32.5kg, 1.36m female and a 62kg, 1.52m male.

*This illustration clearly shows how an earlier common name of 'white-bellied dolphin' came to be used for this species.*

The dorsal surface curves smoothly from the forward edge of the dorsal fin to the tip of the upper jaw; there is no well-defined beak. The lower jaw projects slightly further forward than the upper. There are 29-34 pairs of small teeth, less than 4.5mm in diameter, in each of the upper and lower jaws.

The flippers are relatively short and rounded at the tips. The rounded dorsal fin is similar in shape to that of Commerson's dolphin, as are the flukes, although they are proportionately slightly larger.

Dorsally, the animal is essentially grey. On either side of the head, just behind the blowholes, is a crescent-shaped area of darker grey, wider near the blowhole and narrowing as it extends forward over the eye. A small white spot marks the ear opening. The tip of the upper jaw is also a darker grey, as is an indistinctly bordered eye-patch. The throat is white.

There is an oval white patch behind the posterior insertion of the flipper, but this is hidden when the flipper is pressed against the body. The flippers are dark grey and linked ventrally by a dark grey band that extends back to a point similar to, but not quite as large as, that in Commerson's dolphin. Behind this, the belly is white as far as the tail stock, which, like both sides of the flukes and the dorsal fin, is dark grey. There are sexually dimorphic grey genital patches.

**Recognition at sea** This species may be confused at sea with Burmeister's porpoise. However, the rounded dorsal fin of the Chilean dolphin contrasts sharply with the more triangular fin of Burmeister's porpoise, with its slightly blunt peak and convex trailing edge.

**Habitat** The Chilean dolphin is often found in shallow waters and in areas of significant tide changes, especially at entrances to fiords. It has been known to enter rivers.

**Distribution and migration** This species is found in the coastal waters of Chile, from about 33°S to 56°S. It seems likely that it may also occur in Argentinian waters off Tierra del Fuego. There is no information on seasonal migrations.

**Food and feeding** The little available information suggests that the Chilean dolphin may be an opportunistic feeder on crustaceans, cephalopods and fish.

**Behaviour** The species appears generally 'shy', only occasionally jumping or bow riding. Group size is usually small (2-15), although larger aggregations of up to 400 animals have been reported occasionally, particularly in the northern part of its range.

The only sound recordings were made using equipment unable to detect frequencies above about 30kHz – probably much too low by analogy with other members of the genus. Low-level, rapid pulses (up to 500 per second) were recorded in bursts of 0.4-2 seconds.

**Life history** Almost nothing is known about the life history of this species. 'Young' animals have been reported in sightings made in October, January, March and April.

**World population** No population estimates exist, but the species is not thought to be in danger.

**Man's influence** This species is taken for crab bait by fishermen. The extent to which this illegal practice is carried out is unknown, as is the extent of any incidental captures during fishery operations.

# HECTOR'S DOLPHIN

*CEPHALORHYNCHUS HECTORI*

■ Known distribution   □ Possible sighting

**Classification** Hector's dolphin was described and given the name *Cephalorhynchus hectori* by van Beneden in 1881. The specific name, *hectori*, comes from the New Zealand zoologist Hector, who collected the first specimen in 1869.

**Description** Like the other members of its genus, Hector's dolphin is small and stocky. Adults usually grow to 1.2m-1.5m and weigh 50-60kg; females are slightly larger than males. The longest animal measured was a female of 1.67m. The rounded, conical head slopes smoothly from the blowhole, just left of the midline, to the tip of the rostrum. The lower jaw projects slightly beyond the upper. There are 26-32 pairs of small pointed teeth in both jaws.

The small flippers are rounded at the tips. Most have serrations on the leading edge, although the level of serration can vary considerably and there is some evidence that their development may be age-related. The broad flukes have a concave trailing edge and a small median notch. The characteristic dorsal fin is broad and rounded, with its strongly convex trailing edge ending in a notch at the base. The shape of the dorsal fin – and damage to its trailing edge – allows the identification of individual animals.

The colour pattern of black, grey and white is striking. The tail, dorsal fin and tip of the lower jaw are black. The sides of the head form a continuous black area with the flippers, which are joined on the ventral surface by a black band whose rear edge forms a small 'V' pointing tailwards. In front of a thin black line that curves around the head behind the blowhole, the head is grey and finely streaked with black. The sides and back of the animal are light grey, apart from two 'fingers' of white along the lower flanks and an oval patch of white behind each flipper. There are two large areas of white on the ventral surface: one on the throat and lower jaw, and one on the belly. The latter area is (essentially) diamond-shaped, beginning between

*Left: These Hector's dolphins were photographed in relatively shallow coastal waters at Akaroa, near Christchurch in South Island, New Zealand – a typical habitat of this lively species. Note the distinctive rounded dorsal fin – an excellent identifier.*

the flippers, broadening out to the full width of the ventral surface about halfway between the flippers and the tail, and then narrowing again. Before it reaches a point, it is broken by the black end of the tail and two long fingers of black which form a 'V' stretching forwards. This creates the two white lateral fingers and a central white 'triangle' that encompasses the genital area and anus. In males, the genital slit is surrounded by a large, dark-grey patch. In females, there may be a narrow grey finger around the genital slit or no grey at all. This adult coloration is apparent at about six months; in calves, the general pattern is present, but darker and less distinct.

**Recognition at sea** The colour pattern and dorsal fin shape make identification relatively easy.

**Habitat** Hector's dolphin is a shallow-water species, usually found in depths of less than 300m and within 1km of the shoreline. It is rarely seen more than 9km offshore, and sometimes swims short distances up rivers. It was once thought to prefer muddy water near river mouths, but is found mostly in coastal habitats.

**Distribution and migration** Hector's dolphin is confined to coastal waters of New Zealand. It is most common around South Island and the western coast of North Island. There is some evidence to suggest a summer-winter, inshore-offshore migration pattern.

**Food and feeding** Hector's dolphin is an opportunistic species, feeding mainly on small fish less than 35cm long. These range from surface schooling fish, such as yellow-eyed mullet, to benthic fishes, such as red cod. It also eats squid.

**Behaviour** Hector's dolphins are usually found in small groups of 2-8 animals, which may, in turn, form loose aggregations of 50 or more. Activity, in the form of jumping, lobtailing and 'aggression', increases when small groups come together. They appear to be attracted to boats travelling at less than about 18kph and avoid those moving faster. Bow riding, spy hopping and surfing have been observed. Hector's dolphins emit low-level, high-frequency single and double pulse sounds, similar to those of Commerson's and Dall's porpoise.

**Life history** Little is known about reproduction in this species, but recent intensive studies should improve the situation. Calves, about 60-70cm long, are born during spring and early summer. Males reach sexual maturity at 1.2-1.3m; females at about 1.35m or more.

**World population** There are 3,000-4,000 Hector's dolphins around New Zealand. The species is not endangered.

**Man's influence** There is concern that incidental catches in gillnets may be a threat to local groups. Protective legislation has been introduced in New Zealand.

# COMMERSON'S DOLPHIN

*CEPHALORHYNCHUS COMMERSONII*

■ Known distribution

**Classification** When it was first classified by Lacépède in 1804, Commerson's dolphin was originally assigned to the genus *Delphinus*. It was not until 1922 that Harmer correctly assigned it to the genus *Cephalorhynchus*. The origin of that name is discussed in the section on Heaviside's dolphin (see page 159). The specific name, *commersonii*, ascribed to it by Lacépède, is still used and refers to the French physician and botanist Philibert Commerson who first observed the species in 1767 near Tierra del Fuego.

**Local names** A series of names in other languages have been applied to the dolphin (Commerson himself originally called it Le Jacobite), but the current local name in its area of occurrence in southern South America is tonina overa, which means 'black-and-white dolphin'.

**Description** Commerson's dolphin is a small stocky dolphin, similar in outline to the other members of its genus. Off South America, adult males range in length from about 1.25m to 1.40m. Males off the Kerguelen Islands grow longer – up to about 1.7m. Unusually for odontocetes, females are slightly larger, ranging from about 1.28m to 1.46m off South America and up to 1.75m off the Kerguelen Islands. Adult animals from South America weigh about 35-60kg; as one would expect, animals from the Kerguelen Islands weigh more, the heaviest to date weighing 86kg.

The rounded head slopes smoothly from the blowhole to the tip of the snout – there is no obvious beak. The blowhole is slightly left of centre. The lower jaw projects very slightly beyond the upper. There are usually 28-34 pairs of small, pointed teeth, less than 3mm in diameter, in both the upper and lower jaws.

The flippers are elliptical and slightly rounded at the ends. About half the

animals examined have a series of serrations on the leading edge of the left flipper, which appear age-related. Interestingly, their occurrence on the right flipper appears to be related to sex, being found on 80 percent of females but on less than 5 percent of males (although the sample size is small). The function of these serrations, found in some form on other members of the genus, is unknown. Theories range from their use in courtship, defence or aggression to feeding or swimming.

The dorsal fin just behind the middle of the back is characteristically rounded, with a slightly concave trailing edge. The broad flukes have a small median notch.

The most striking feature of these dolphins is their black-and-white colour pattern, which develops with age. In newborns and juveniles, the pattern is a muted grey on black or dark grey, often appearing uniform when viewed at sea. The head is black with a white chevron on the throat. The black coloration slopes downwards, approximately from the beginning of the neck to the posterior insertions of the flippers, which are themselves all black. The shape of the border between the black and white on the top of the head (the 'widow's peak') can vary considerably and is used to identify individual animals, as is the variation in the border region between the black-and-white coloration in the tail region. The flippers are connected by a black ventral band that extends back to a point along the midline. The tail is black, as is the dorsal region up to just in front of the black rounded dorsal fin. The rest of the animal is white apart from a black genital patch, the shape and position of which varies between the sexes.

**Recognition at sea** The striking colour pattern makes this a relatively easy species to identify at sea.

**Habitat** Commerson's dolphin is a coastal species, with almost all confirmed

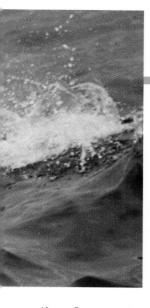

*Above: Commerson's dolphin leaping in the Strait of Magellan.*

*Below left: A diver's view highlights their bold body pattern.*

*Right: A mother and calf 'at home' in Sea World, California.*

sightings being in shallow waters less than 100m deep. They are seen off the open coast as well as in fjords, bays and river mouths. Occasionally, they even enter rivers, sometimes travelling as far as 30km upstream. They are found in calm, sheltered waters, as well as in areas of strong currents and surf, and in all parts of their range they have been observed near kelp beds. Surface water temperatures within their range can vary from 4°C to 16°C.

**Distribution and migration** Commerson's dolphin is found off the coast of southern South America – from about 53°S on the western side around Tierra del Fuego up to about 41°S on the eastern side – as well as around the Falkland and Kerguelen Islands. A published record of the species near South Georgia is no longer considered reliable. The animals around the Kerguelen Islands form a separate population. There is little information on seasonal movements from around South America; despite suggestions that they prefer coastal waters in summer, the available sightings and records of strandings reveal no such pattern. Sightings at the Kerguelen Islands are made only in summer and may indicate some degree of migration.

**Food and feeding** Commerson's dolphins are generalist feeders, foraging largely on or near the sea bottom. Mysid shrimps, fish (pejerrey, sardines and hake) and squid are the most common prey items off Tierra del Fuego.

**Behaviour** Apart from occasional, probably short-term, aggregations of large numbers (sometimes exceeding 100 animals), Commerson's dolphins are most often seen in small groups of less than 10 animals, and usually of 1-3. They are swift swimmers, often engaging in spectacular leaps and breaches, and have frequently been observed swimming on their backs. They also engage in bow riding with vessels, riding breaking waves and surfing.

Recordings of free-swimming and captive Commerson's dolphins indicate that they can produce sounds up to about 300kHz. A typical pulse lasts 350-500 microseconds, with the major frequency component at about 130kHz. Their repertoire is similar to phocoenids, particularly the' Dall's porpoise, and appears to be most useful for detecting moving objects. It has been speculated that they 'filter out' cues from stationary objects and that this makes them particularly vulnerable to entanglement in gillnets.

**Life history** Most information from South America comes from stranded animals or animals caught incidentally in fishing operations. The information from the Kerguelen Islands comes from a scientific catch of 11 animals.

The breeding season appears to be in the southern summer, i.e. November to February. Interestingly, the three live births of captive animals have also occurred in January and February, even though the animals were living in the Northern Hemisphere. The gestation

period seems to be about 11-12 months. Size at birth is about 65-75cm. South American animals of both sexes appear to attain sexual maturity at about 5-6 years and 127-131cm. Limited data from the Kerguelen Islands suggests that both sexes have reached sexual maturity by about 1.65m, corresponding to approximately 5 years in females and 8 years in males. The oldest animal examined was 18 years.

**World population** In only one part of its range has a detailed population survey been carried out – in the northern Strait of Magellan in January and February 1984, when over 3,000 animals were present. However, despite our ignorance of the total population size of this species and the sources of mortality noted below, the species does not appear to be rare or in any danger of extinction.

**Man's influence** Commerson's dolphins have been taken by fishermen for crab bait in both Chile and Argentina, but as this practice is now illegal, it is difficult to obtain accurate information regarding its current extent. They are also taken incidentally by fishermen in nets set to catch crabs and fish, such as rabalo and hake. Although some of these dolphins are donated to scientific institutions, many others are not and, once again, it is difficult to obtain detailed information on numbers killed in this manner. At least six expeditions to catch live animals for aquariums have taken place, the most recent in January 1984.

# NORTHERN RIGHT WHALE DOLPHIN *LISSODELPHIS BOREALIS*

Known or probable range

**Classification** *Lissodelphis* means 'smooth dolphin' and probably refers to the absence of a dorsal fin. The specific name, *borealis*, refers to the exclusively Northern Hemisphere distribution. No subspecies are recognized.

**Local names** Pacific right whale dolphin.

**Description** This species is probably the slenderest of all the small cetaceans, with a narrow, sometimes almost eel-like body. Males grow larger than females, maximum known lengths being 3.1m and 2.3m respectively. Maximum weight is at least 115kg.

Most of the adult's body is black (calves are greyish brown in colour), with a white lanceolate pattern of various thickness running from the throat to the flukes on the ventral surface. A white spot is present just behind the tip of the lower jaw. The rear border of the flukes is white below and light grey above.

The most conspicuous feature is the total absence of a dorsal fin. The flippers and tail flukes are small and pointed at the tips. There are 40-49 teeth in each side of the upper and lower jaws.

Geographical variation is unknown, but individuals with a more extensive white pattern are seen among schools of normally coloured animals on both sides of the Pacific.

**Recognition at sea** This is the only oceanic dolphin in its range without a dorsal fin. Its southern counterpart, the southern right whale dolphin (see opposite), has more extensive regions of white on the head, sides and belly and is found only south of the equator.

**Habitat** This generally pelagic species mostly inhabits relatively deep continental shelf and offshore waters with surface temperatures in the 8-19°C range.

**Distribution and migration** These dolphins are found only in the North Pacific Ocean, where they are normally seen between 30° and 50°N in the eastern Pacific and 35° and 51°N in the western Pacific. Movements north and south of this region probably occur during periods of unseasonable water temperatures. Large-scale migrations are not known, but seasonal inshore and southern shifts in abundance for winter and spring have been described for some parts of the range. Nothing is known of the movements of individual dolphins.

**Food and feeding** In southern California, seasonal movements seem to be linked to the life history of their major prey, market squid (*Loligo opalescens*). Lanternfish (myctophids) are also a major prey item. Other prey include various surface-swimming squids and fishes.

**Behaviour** There have been no long-term, detailed behavioural studies of this species, and nearly all that is known has been gained from occasional, brief observations. Herd sizes range up to an estimated 3,000 individuals, with 100-200 being average. Several different herd configurations have been reported for animals engaged in different activities. Northern right whale dolphins often join other species, especially Pacific white-sided and Risso's dolphins.

Travelling herds often whip the water surface with long, low-angle leaps, and breaching, belly flopping and tail slapping are often seen. These dolphins are also known to ride bow waves, especially when accompanied by other species, and are capable of high-speed swimming, possibly as fast as 35kph.

Sounds made generally resemble those of other species of social, pelagic dolphins, although right whale dolphins appear to whistle less frequently.

Single strandings are known to occur, but are not common.

**Life history** Very little is known of northern right whale dolphin reproduction. Newborns are probably about 0.8-1m long. Males become sexually mature when they reach lengths of 2.12-2.2m, females about 2m.

**World population** Population status throughout the North Pacific is unknown. There are likely to be regional stocks, but the boundaries of these are not known. About 18,000 northern right whale dolphins are estimated to be present off southern California during periods of peak density, and an additional 61,000 are estimated to be present in central and northern California.

**Man's influence** Some northern right whale dolphins are taken each year in Japanese harpoon, purse-seine and salmon gillnet fisheries, but the numbers taken do not appear to be causing serious depletion of stocks. Much more serious may be the incidental entanglement in Japanese, Taiwanese and Korean squid driftnet fisheries. Catch information from these is meagre but, based on the extent of the fishing effort, central Pacific stocks may be severely affected.

In the eastern North Pacific, small numbers have been captured alive, and animals have occasionally been killed during other fishing activities, such as driftnetting for swordfish and sharks.

# SOUTHERN RIGHT WHALE DOLPHIN  *LISSODELPHIS PERONII*

Known or probable range

**Classification** This species is named after F. Peron, an eighteenth and nineteenth century naturalist, who provided an early description of this species. No subspecies are recognized.

**Local names** Herman Melville called these animals 'mealy-mouthed porpoises' in *Moby Dick*.

**Description** Most measured adults have been between 2 and 2.5m long, but there are reasons to believe that, like their northern counterparts, they may reach lengths of 3m or more. Males appear to be slightly larger than females. Weights have rarely been reported, but they can be expected to reach at least 100kg.

Southern right whale dolphins are slender, although perhaps not quite as slim as the northern species. They have small curved flippers with pointed tips and small flukes with rounded tips. Characteristic of the genus, there is no hint of a dorsal fin. A short, but well-defined beak is present and specimens examined have had 44-49 sharp teeth in each row of the upper and lower jaws.

The dorsal surface is black, but the white below is much more extensive than on the northern species, with the white snout, melon, flippers, mid-flank, and entire ventral surface distinctly demarcated from the black above.The upper flukes grade from dark grey behind to light grey or white at the front. Many colour variations have been noted, and these appear to be useful in identifying individuals. Young calves may have a muted pattern, with a grey rather than black back and smoky rather than stark white coloration elsewhere.

*Left: The slender right whale dolphins are among the few small cetaceans without a dorsal fin. This is the northern species. Both are to be found in the open ocean, where they inhabit deep waters.*

*Right: The southern right whale dolphin shares the same body form of its northern counterpart, but is distinguished by the greater amount of white patterning on the sides and head.*

Geographical variation in this dolphin has not been systematically studied.

**Recognition at sea** The finless back and starkly contrasting black-and-white coloration serve to distinguish these dolphins during encounters at sea.

**Habitat** Like their northern counterparts, southern right whale dolphins are generally found close to shore only in deep water, and appear to prefer a pelagic, cold temperate habitat. Water temperatures at the times of sightings have ranged from 1 to 20°C.

**Distribution and migration** Southern right whale dolphins appear to be distributed throughout the temperate regions of the Southern Hemisphere. Most sightings are north of the Antarctic Convergence, the most northerly reliable sighting being at about 19°S off Chile.

Reports of southern right whale dolphins off Japan were actually abnormally coloured specimens of the northern species and reports of southern right whale dolphins at St. Helena (16°N, 5°45'W) are considered to be erroneous. Until more research has been carried out, the limits of distribution must be considered unknown. There is no information on migrations or seasonal movements.

**Food and feeding** There is little information on feeding habits but, like the northern species, it is known to feed on lanternfish (myctophids) and various species of squid.

**Behaviour** The most detailed behavioural information is from South Africa. Several different swimming modes have been described, ranging from slow rolling (with little surface disturbance) to long, low-angle leaps causing much white water at the surface. Aerial displays, such as belly, side and fluke slaps, have been observed. Dives up to 6.5 minutes long have been recorded.

Herd sizes range up to an estimated 1,000 animals, with several different configurations, similar to those of northern right whale dolphins. This species is not uncommonly seen alongside other dolphin species, especially those of the genera *Lagenorhynchus* and *Globicephala*. They are capable and willing bow riders.

Although not common, both individual and mass strandings have been reported. Live-stranded animals in New Zealand have been successfully pushed back to sea.

**Life history** Virtually nothing is known of the life history or reproduction of this species. Calves are seen most frequently in the southern summer.

**World population** There are no population estimates available. Although likely to exist, separate stocks of these dolphins have not been described.

**Man's influence** Small numbers of this species were taken for fresh meat by nineteenth century whalers, and some animals are still caught deliberately by fishermen in South America, but nowhere does there appear to be a large take of this species, and apparently none have been taken into captivity.

# RISSO'S DOLPHIN

## GRAMPUS GRISEUS

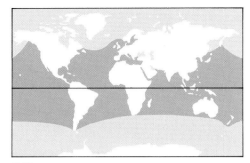

■ Known range

**Classification** *Grampus* means 'grand fish' and *griseus* refers to the grey coloration. No subspecies are recognized.

**Local names** Risso's dolphins are also called grampus or grey grampus. Confusingly, killer whales, *Orcinus orca*, and some other large globicephalids were also sometimes called grampus in older whaling literature and occasionally still are.

**Description** The average adult size is 2.8-3.3m, with males somewhat larger than females. The maximum recorded length is 3.85m. Total body weight of Risso's dolphins may reach close to 500kg.

Risso's dolphins are robust animals, with large blunt heads, a squarish profile and no beak. A unique feature of this species is a vertical groove on the front of the melon, although this is often not visible at sea. The mouthline is relatively straight and slants upwards. There are seven (or fewer) pairs of teeth at the front of the lower jaw, and none in the upper jaw. The long, sickle-shaped flippers are pointed at the tips, while the dorsal fin is tall and falcate, ranging from pointed to rounded at the tip. The tail stock is not noticeably tall, top to bottom, and the flukes have a concave trailing edge and a deep notch. Geographical variation has not been systematically studied with large samples.

**Recognition at sea** Adult Risso's dolphins are easily recognizable by their distinctive scarring. Most adults are grey above and are covered with white scratches, splotches and circular marks. They have a white anchor-shaped patch on the chest, and much of the body is also often white, although the fin and flippers are usually somewhat darker. Some (possibly older) adults are so scarred and splotched as to appear almost uniformly white. Newborn calves are light grey and unscarred, the body darkening to dark brownish grey in juveniles, before lightening again as adults. Juveniles have a muted anchor-shaped patch on the chest.

**Habitat** Risso's dolphins prefer tropical and warm temperate offshore waters and avoid very cold temperate and polar waters. For the most part, these deep-water animals are seen close to shore only where the continental shelf is narrow, such as around oceanic islands.

**Distribution and migration** The northern limit of this species is Newfoundland and Shetland (in the Atlantic), the Gulf of Alaska (in the Pacific) and the northern boundary of the Indian Ocean. They range south to Cape Horn, the Cape of Good Hope, and to Australia and New Zealand, and the species distribution is probably continuous in tropical and warm temperature regions in between. The distribution of Risso's dolphin also includes the Gulf of Mexico, the Mediterranean, the North Sea, the Baltic Sea, the Red Sea, the Persian Gulf, the Sea of

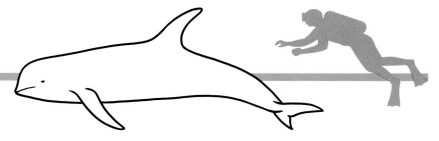

*Above: This vertical 'spy hopping' posture, with the head right out of the water, provides a clear view above the surface of the water.*

*Below left: A Risso's dolphin leaping. Note the blunt head, high falcate dorsal fin and profuse body scarring.*

*Below right: Ships do not normally hold a strong attraction for Risso's dolphins, but this animal is shown riding a bow wave in the Pacific Ocean. The overhead view clearly shows the body scars inflicted by other Risso's; they rarely cause serious harm.*

animals. However, Risso's dolphins do occasionally form large herds, the largest reportedly containing 4,000 individuals. They commonly form mixed aggregations with other dolphin species.

Often, Risso's dolphins are observed surfacing leisurely side-by-side in formations called 'chorus lines'. When moving quickly, schools sometimes porpoise out of the water. Spy hops, breaches, fluke slaps and flipper slaps are not uncommon in travelling or socializing groups.

Due to their extensive scarring and large, frequently nicked fins, Risso's dolphins are good subjects for photo-identification studies. Such a study in Monterey Bay, California, has suggested that Risso's live in somewhat stable subgroups. Work underway in other areas aims to provide information on long-distance movements of individual dolphins.

Risso's dolphins make a variety of sounds, including whistles, and it has been suggested that these may contain signature information.

Both individual and mass strandings of

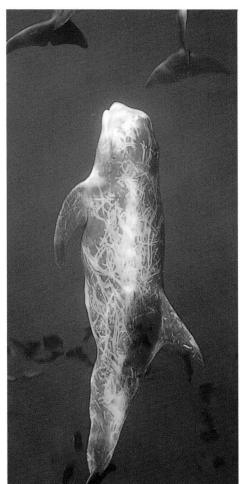

this species are not uncommon. Live mass strandings have been reported in various parts of the range, but the reasons for these remain unclear.

**Life history** The gestation period of Risso's dolphin is estimated to be 13-14 months and length at birth is thought to be about 1.2-1.5m. There is some disagreement as to the timing of the calving season, possibly because tropical populations may have a more protracted breeding season than temperate populations, and there may be some geographical variation in the season of peak births. Nevertheless, records for the North Atlantic suggest a summer calving period.

Sexual maturity seems to occur at lengths of about 2.6-2.8m in both sexes. Age at sexual maturity is not known, but Risso's dolphins apparently reach puberty sometime before the age of 13.

**World population** In the past, Risso's dolphins have been considered uncommon, but we now know that they are more widespread and abundant than previously thought. Reliable estimates of world population size are not available, but they seem to be relatively abundant in lower latitudes. Numbers in central and northern California are estimated at between 13,000 and 30,000.

**Man's influence** Risso's dolphins are taken in drive fisheries in Japan, including the controversial Iki Island conflict (see page 51). Small numbers have also been taken in various fisheries in Europe, the Black Sea, the Caribbean, Peru, the Indo-Pacific islands and North America. This is one of the major species taken by gillnet and hand harpoon in the small cetacean fishery in Sri Lanka. With the likely exception of the Sri Lankan fishery, Risso's dolphin populations are probably not affected by human exploitation.

A few animals have been captured alive in Japan and in the United States. Some have adapted well to captivity but, in general, pelagic species such as this do not do well in oceanariums.

In Ireland, three unusual dolphins stranded in 1933. The best guess as to their identity was that they were hybrids between *Grampus griseus* and *Tursiops truncatus* (the bottlenose dolphin). This seems more likely now that captive dolphins of these two species have mated and produced a viable hybrid calf.

Japan and the Gulf of California.

Large-scale migrations are not known, and Risso's dolphins are present all year round in most of their range; some individuals shift towards the poles, mainly in the warmer-water months. In the eastern North Pacific, where seasonal distribution has been detailed, movements to the northern parts of the range and inshore over the continental shelf in southern California appear to be associated with periods of warm water in the summer. Long-term changes in distribution, such as the periodic use of Monterey Bay, California, are probably related to cyclic large-scale environmental changes.

**Food and feeding** Risso's dolphins are known to take both fish and cephalopods (squid and their allies), but studies of stomach contents have shown squid to be the major prey. The low number of teeth would seem to be further evidence of this, as squid specialists among cetaceans often show a trend towards few teeth and/or tooth loss. Many of the scars on the bodies of adults are thought to be caused by confrontations with squid, but many others undoubtedly result from aggression, play, and sexual encounters between members of the same species.

**Behaviour** Most groups are quite small, consisting of a dozen or several dozen

# PORPOISES
## PHOCOENIDAE

The first use of the name Phocoenidae at the family level is attributed to Bravard in 1885, although Gray had introduced the root of the name in 1825. There are six living species, arranged in four genera, within this evolutionarily old family, and examination of living and fossil species indicates that two lineages, recognized as subfamilies, are represented. One, Phocoeninae, comprises the harbour porpoise (*Phocoena phocoena*), the vaquita (*P. sinus*), the finless porpoise (*Neophocaena*

*phocaenoides*) and Burmeister's porpoise (*Phocoena spinipinnis*). The other subfamily, Phocoenoidinae, includes only two living species – the spectacled porpoise (*Australophocaena dioptrica*) and Dall's porpoise (*Phocoenoides dalli*).

All six species are small (a maximum body length of 2.2m) with small flippers, notched tail flukes and no beak. All carry at least 11 pairs of small teeth in the upper and lower jaws and, uniquely among cetaceans, the teeth are laterally com-

pressed, providing a sharp edge with which to cut the prey – predominantly fish. All but one species, the finless porpoise, have a well-defined dorsal fin. With the exception of Dall's porpoise, all are essentially coastal, although their geographical range varies from extremely limited, as in the vaquita, to extremely wide, as in the harbour porpoise. Dall's porpoise and the spectacled porpoise differ from other members of the family in having a well-defined colour pattern.

*Harbour porpoises among kelp. This species is the most widespread of the family, occurring in the North Pacific and North Atlantic.*

# HARBOUR PORPOISE

*PHOCOENA PHOCOENA*

◼ Known distribution

**Classification** The genus and species name for the harbour porpoise, *Phocoena phocoena*, are from the Latin and Greek roots for porpoise. The species was named by Linnaeus in 1758. No sub-species are recognized.

**Local names** This species is often called the common porpoise or simply porpoise in the United Kingdom. Local names include pourcil (French Canada), marsouin commun (France), Braunfisch (Germany) and marsopa (Spain).

**Description** Harbour porpoises are small cetaceans with a rounded head and no beak. The dorsal fin is triangular with a series of small, blunt spines called tubercles on its leading edge. Some reports mention that only some porpoises have tubercles, but they have been present in most, if not all, specimens examined for this feature, except calves.

The back is dark grey fading gradually to whitish on the belly. The white area extends onto the sides of the animal in the area near the flipper and a light grey stripe extends from the flipper to the dark zone around the gape of the mouth. The fin, flippers and flukes are also dark.

Average adult sizes are 1.5-1.7m (females) and 1.4-1.5m (males); average adult weight is 40-60kg. The very largest animals may reach 2m in length and 90kg in weight. There are 22-28 pairs of spatulate teeth in the upper jaw and 21-25 pairs in the lower jaw.

**Recognition at sea** Harbour porpoises can be identified by their small size, triangular dorsal fin, greyish body and by their swimming behaviour. In most of their range, there are few other species with which they may be confused.

**Habitat** Harbour porpoises live in murky waters, such as are found in bays and

*Above: Often called common porpoises in the UK, harbour porpoises show little of themselves at the surface and can be easily overlooked.*

*Below: This porpoise has no beak, small flippers and a small, almost triangular fin.*

*Above right: Harbour porpoises are essentially coastal, although sightings are sometimes made, for example, in the middle of the North Sea. Some groups are seasonal residents of a particular area, whereas others may be present year round.*

estuaries, in areas of coastal upwelling and in tidal races. Such areas are often highly productive, but abundance of prey may be unpredictable over time.

They are thought to be restricted to shallow water, but in the Bay of Fundy (off Nova Scotia), they are regularly caught incidentally in gillnets set on the bottom at a depth of 100m. They also occur in water 300m deep away from the coast, although they may not be feeding on the bottom in these areas.

**Distribution and migration** The harbour porpoise is distributed more or less throughout the temperate and subarctic waters in the Northern Hemisphere. In the North Pacific, it ranges from Japan across the coastal and island regions of the northern Pacific and around the coast of North America to central California in the United States. Harbour porpoises have been found as far north as Point Barrow, Alaska, and Wrangel Island, USSR, and historically ranged as far south as Point Conception in California. In the eastern North Atlantic, harbour porpoises generally range from the New England coast of the USA northwards along the coastal regions and islands of Canada as far north as Baffin Island. They occur along the southern coast of Greenland, Iceland and around the Faeroe Islands. They are or have been common in the waters of northern Europe, including the North, Barents and Baltic Seas. At one time, they ranged along the European coast, throughout the Mediterranean, and along the African coast as far south as Senegal, where a small population still exists. An isolated population occurs in the Black and Azov Seas.

Little is known about the migration patterns of harbour porpoises. In some areas, they tend to be more common in summer than in winter. Year-round resident groups have also been reported. An inshore-offshore migration in the summer and winter has been suggested for some populations.

**Food and feeding** Harbour porpoises are bottom feeding, specializing on small schooling fish such as herring or anchovy. In the Bay of Fundy, calves eat euphausiid crustaceans.

**Behaviour** Harbour porpoises generally form small groups. Their swimming has been described as a slow forward roll and, although they have occasionally been seen to 'pop' out of the water showing a larger portion of their back, they do not leap out of the water as many dolphins do. They regularly nap at the surface and this behaviour was initially thought to aid the nursing of calves, but it is typical of both males and females. By remaining still, particularly at night, they may avoid detection by sharks, their main predator in some areas.

In the Bay of Fundy, radio-tracked individuals were found to occupy one small area for a long period of time, perhaps throughout a summer. This behaviour supports the theory that, at least in part of their range during part of the year, harbour porpoises show a preference for a particular site and remain there.

**Life history** After an 11-month gestation period, calves usually measure 70-90cm at birth. Harbour porpoises appear to be seasonal breeders, giving birth during the summer months. Females reach maturity at about three years of age, at a length of about 1.5-1.6m, and have a calf each year afterwards. They nurse the calf for somewhat less than a year, often becoming pregnant with the following year's calf during this time. Males mature at about 1.4-1.5m in length and at a slightly greater age than females. The oldest animal recorded was 14 years, but most die before they reach nine.

**World population** The world population is unknown but it is clear that harbour porpoises have suffered badly at the hands of man. A population in the Baltic Sea has all but disappeared because its foodbase is almost gone and water pollution levels are high. Harbour porpoises have been eliminated from the Mediterranean, and where they were once very common along the Atlantic coast of France, they are now rare. Their numbers have also been declining around Denmark and the south and east of England. Populations in the Black Sea, if they still exist, are seriously threatened, while those in the North Sea, Bay of Fundy and Gulf of Maine are also threatened. In California, the southern end of their distribution is retreating northwards.

Harbour porpoise populations seem to live on the edge of survival, because of their food and habitat preferences and their reproductive rates. When fishery mortality, overfishing of prey species, degradation of habitat, or high pollution levels further affect the populations, they seem unable to withstand the pressure.

**Man's influence** These porpoises are highly susceptible to exploitation. They are caught in many areas for human consumption. Recently, there have been directed fisheries for harbour porpoises by coastal Indians in Washington State and Maine in the USA and similar fisheries have occurred in Canadian waters in the Bay of Fundy and the Gulf of St. Lawrence. Harbour porpoises are taken in Iceland, in the Azov and Black Seas in the USSR, and in Turkey. The largest current directed fishery for harbour porpoises is in Greenland; although the total kill is not known, combining directed and incidental takes it may be 1,500 animals per year.

Incidental catches of harbour porpoises by entanglement in gillnets set for fish occur, in general, in areas where gillnets are set on the bottom in shallow coastal waters that harbour porpoises inhabit, including the United States, Canada, Europe, Greenland and Japan. They have also been taken in otter trawls, traps and on baited hooks.

A few harbour porpoises have been maintained in captivity, and have even been trained. On the whole, however, the species has not done well in captivity.

# VAQUITA

*PHOCOENA SINUS*

■ Known distribution

**Classification** *Phocoena sinus* was described by US biologists Norris and McFarland as recently as 1958. *Sinus* is Latin for 'a pocket, recess, or bay' and refers to the vaquita's localized distribution in the Gulf of California.

**Local names** Fisherman in the upper Gulf of California call this animal vaquita, meaning 'little cow'. The term cochito ('little pig') was applied to this species in the past by the International Whaling Commission, but this is a general term for dolphins used by Mexican fishermen.

**Description** The vaquita is one of the smallest, if not the smallest, species of cetacean. Although few specimens have been examined, there appears to be sexual dimorphism in body length; the average length of adult females is about 1.5m and males 1.4m. There are 20-21 pairs of spade-shaped teeth in the upper jaw, 18 pairs in the lower.

The vaquita is grey, with a darker upper surface and greyish white belly. A grey stripe runs from the flipper to the chin. Dark pigment around the mouth, similar to that seen in the spectacled porpoise, gives the appearance of 'lips'. Also, as in the spectacled porpoise, there is a dark patch around the eye. The flippers are dark, standing out against the lighter coloration of the body in that area. The snout is typically rounded.

The vaquita's triangular dorsal fin is relatively taller than that of other porpoises and has small tubercles on its upper leading edge, as in several other species. The tubercles become more developed with age; juveniles have only whitish spots where the tubercles will be.

**Recognition at sea** There is little chance for confusing this species, as it is the only porpoise, and the only small cetacean with a lower triangular fin and no beak in the upper Gulf of California. Dolphins found in the same area are bigger and tend to travel in large groups.

**Habitat** The vaquita inhabits the shallow waters of the upper Gulf of California, which has one of the world's most extreme tidal ranges. The waters are murky and productive for species able to exploit the shallow lagoons when the tide allows. Vaquitas have been seen in mangrove lagoons in water so shallow that their backs protrude above the surface.

**Distribution and migration** The vaquita has the most limited distribution of any cetacean in the world. It is endemic to the northern Gulf of California, Mexico, in the Colorado River delta. It is likely that this species does not migrate to a large degree. Seasonal movements probably occur; the waters of the northern Gulf get very warm in summer and the animals are seen less frequently.

**Food and feeding** Almost nothing is known about vaquita feeding habits. The stomach from one animal contained remains of croaker, grunt and squid.

**Behaviour** Few observations have been made of live animals; vaquitas are difficult to sight because they occur in small groups and surface with a slow, forward-rolling movement that hardly disturbs the surface of the water. Their flukes stay

*Right: At sea, the vaquita's triangular dorsal fin is a useful identifier. Combined with its retiring nature, this feature serves to distinguish it from all other cetaceans in the Gulf of California, the only area where it occurs.*

*Below: This photo, one of the first to show the appearance of a fresh specimen, reveals a darkened eye patch and dark lips, together with a dark stripe from flipper to chin.*

below the surface. Vaquitas have not been seen to leap.

**World population** Vaquitas are highly endangered; there may be fewer than 100 individuals left, although few surveys have been conducted and vaquitas are difficult to sight.

**Man's influence** Vaquitas are taken incidentally in gillnets, often those set illegally for totoaba (a protected species of fish), as well as in gillnets set for sharks and rays. The number of porpoises killed in these nets is unknown. During the early 1970s, the annual kill may have been in the tens to hundreds. Vaquitas have not been kept in captivity.

# SPECTACLED PORPOISE

## *AUSTRALOPHOCAENA DIOPTRICA*

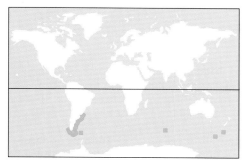

■ Sightings and strandings

**Classification** The spectacled porpoise was first described by the Argentinian naturalist Lahille in 1912 as *Phocoena dioptrica*. The root of the species name, *diopter*, is Greek for an optical instrument. The name refers to the distinctive white ring encircling a black patch around each eye. The species was reclassified in 1985 by Barnes because of its differences from other species in the genus *Phocoena*. The name, *Australophocaena*, refers to its southern ocean distribution.

**Local names** The English common name for the spectacled porpoise is a direct translation from the Spanish common name marsopa de anteojos. In references from the Atlantic coast of South America, it has also been referred to as the bicolour porpoise, but this name is not common. In Chile, the spectacled porpoise may be called marsopa anteojillo or tonina (a general term for porpoise).

**Description** The spectacled porpoise is the largest of the six species of porpoise. Although only a handful of specimens have been measured, it appears that males reach about 2.2m and females about 2m in length. Few specimens have been weighed, none of them adult.

One of the most prominent features of the spectacled porpoise is the striking contrast between the black dorsal and the white ventral surfaces. Black pigment surrounding the mouth gives the appearance of black 'lips'. Generally, the flukes are black above and white or light grey beneath.

The dorsal fin is triangular, canted towards the rear, and rounded at the tip. It is larger in adult males than in adult females. Early reports on the spectacled porpoise mentioned the existence of tubercles on the dorsal fin, but recent accounts have stated that tubercles are not present. There may be some individual variation; this will become clear after more specimens have been examined.

The flippers and flukes are small relative to the size of the body. The snout is

blunt and conical, with no pronounced beak. There are 17-23 pairs of typical spatulate teeth in the upper jaw and 16-20 pairs in the lower jaw.

**Recognition at sea** Along the Atlantic coast of South America, the spectacled porpoise overlaps in range with Burmeister's porpoise. The latter is a more or less uniform grey, however, and has a very distinctive dorsal fin. Confusion between these two species is reduced around offshore islands, where only the spectacled porpoise is known to occur.

Over at least part of its range, the spectacled porpoise occurs with dolphins of the genus *Cephalorhynchus*. These also have a black-and-white colour pattern and are similar in size, but the white usually extends along the back and is visible when the animals surface. However, one species, the Chilean dolphin (*C. eutropia*), which occurs in the channels of Tierra del Fuego, has a black dorsal surface and white ventral surface, but can be distinguished by its more falcate dorsal fin with a rounded tip.

**Habitat** Spectacled porpoises were thought to be primarily coastal due to the relatively high incidence of strandings, occasional capture in nearshore fishing nets, and the lack of sightings in pelagic waters. But it has been suggested that the main distribution is offshore, because the species is similar in body form to the pelagic Dall's porpoise.

**Distribution and migration** Stranded animals have been recorded on the Atlantic coast of South America from the southern coast of Uruguay to Tierra del Fuego in Argentina. This species has also been sighted in the eastern Strait of Magellan in Chilean waters. The few at-sea sightings and beached specimens outside that area have been from widely separate locations in the subantarctic southern oceans, including the Falkland

Islands, South Georgia, the Auckland Islands, Macquarie Island, Tasmania, Heard Island and the Kerguelen Islands, suggesting a circumpolar distribution in subantarctic latitudes. Nothing is known about migration.

**Behaviour** The few glimpses of spectacled porpoise suggest that they occur in ones or twos. The reported swimming behaviour, of a slow forward-rolling movement, makes them difficult to sight at sea. They have not been seen to leap or react to vessels.

**Life history** Nothing is known. Males 2m and 2.4m in length were thought to be sexually mature and two pregnant females were measured at 1.86m and 1.91m long. Length at birth is unknown.

**World population** The current status is unknown. For about 60 years after its discovery, this species was considered to be very rare. Since then, it has been reported as one of the most commonly stranded cetaceans along the coast of Argentina. Beached specimens are typically found in relatively uninhabited areas, which may explain the infrequent reports formerly.

**Man's influence** Some historical accounts document the occasional directed catch of spectacled porpoise for consumption by fishermen in Uruguay and Argentina. More recently, incidental catches have been a concern. In Argentina, spectacled porpoises have become caught and have drowned in tangle nets for commercial species of fish. A number of the salvaged specimens have been found on beaches near where these nets are set, although, as most are found in an advanced state of decomposition, it has been impossible to determine whether they died in the nets. The number taken in this manner is unknown. No spectacled porpoises have been kept in captivity.

*This is the largest of the porpoises and recognizable by its well-defined pattern of black and white.*

# BURMEISTER'S PORPOISE

*PHOCOENA SPINIPINNIS*

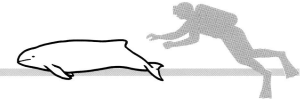

■ Known distribution

**Classification** Burmeister, a German biologist who became Director of the Natural History Museum in Buenos Aires, described this porpoise in 1865. He based the species name, *spinipinnis* ('spiny fin'), on the presence of many small, horny spines (tubercles) on the dorsal fin.

**Local names** The local name in Uruguay, Argentina, and parts of Chile is marsopa espinosa, which means 'spiny porpoise'. In Peruvian waters, fishermen refer to Burmeister's porpoise as tonino. (Throughout Latin America, the similar name 'tonina' is used as a general term for dolphins and porpoises, or to describe a particular species.)

**Description** The most distinguishing feature of Burmeister's porpoise is the dorsal fin, which is located further back on the body than in other porpoises or dolphins. It rises at a low angle relative to the back, has a long leading edge, a bluntly pointed tip, and a convex trailing edge. The numerous tubercles occur in two to four rows along the entire leading edge. In some cases, they are pro-nounced enough to be seen on a free-swimming animal.

This species is normally grey to black in coloration, but has also been described as brown. The darker dorsal surface fades gradually to a lighter colour ventrally. A white or light patch begins beneath the lower jaw and extends along the ventral surface to the anus, but there seems to be much individual variation in the extent and location of white patches and the degree of countershading. A dark grey stripe extends from the flipper along the throat to a light patch on the lower jaw.

Burmeister's porpoise has fewer teeth than other porpoises: 11-16 pairs in the upper jaw and 16-19 in the lower.

The largest specimen recorded was 1.85m in length, but there is currently insufficient information about average adult lengths or whether length is sexually dimorphic.

**Recognition at sea** The dorsal fin and the dark coloration of the back distinguish this porpoise at sea. The most likely small cetacean that may be confused with it on the Pacific coast of South America is the Chilean dolphin (*Cephalorhynchus eutropia*), which is about the same size and also has a completely black back. The fin on this dolphin, however, is placed further forward and is falcate, with a blunt, rounded tip. On the Atlantic coast, Burmeister's porpoise overlaps in distribution with the spectacled porpoise. The latter is black on the back and white on the underside, but, again, its fin is very different in shape.

**Habitat** Burmeister's porpoise is found in relatively shallow waters over the continental shelf and in estuaries. Its specific habits and use of these areas is unknown.

**Distribution and migration** Burmeister's porpoise inhabits the temperate and sub-antarctic coastal waters of South America. The northernmost record on the Pacific coast is from 5°S in the cold waters of the Humboldt Current off Peru. The northernmost record on the Atlantic coast is in southern Brazil at about 28°S. Recent records indicate that the distribution is more or less continuous around the southern tip of South America.

Little is known about seasonal movements; one population appears to spend summer in the Peninsula Valdés area of Argentina and winter elsewhere.

**Food and feeding** A large sample of stomachs were collected from Burmeister's porpoises taken by fishermen in Peru. Anchoveta were found in the majority of stomachs and made up half the diet. A variety of other fish species, such as drum, hake and sardines, as well as squid, made up the rest. Anchoveta and sardines are small schooling fish that live in shallow water. Juvenile hake form large aggregations off Peru; these generally occur in water of 100m depth or more, deeper than the expected habitat of Burmeister's porpoise.

**Behaviour** Burmeister's porpoises have been seen in groups of one to eight. They surface with little disturbance of the water, and so are difficult to sight.

**World population** It appears to be more common on the Pacific coast of South America than on the Atlantic coast, but the current status is unknown.

**Man's influence** Burmeister's porpoise has a long history of exploitation. Bones have been recovered from aboriginal middens (refuse heaps) dating back 6,500 years in Tierra del Fuega. Exploitation still occurs as a directed fishery off Peru and Chile, where the animals are used for human consumption or as bait for crab traps. In Peru alone, up to 2,000 porpoises may be taken in some years. On the Atlantic coast, they are accidentally caught in fishing gear.

One animal that stranded alive survived in captivity for nine days.

*Below: A Burmeister's porpoise captured by fishermen. Note the low-angle dorsal fin set further back than in other porpoises.*

# FINLESS PORPOISE

## NEOPHOCAENA PHOCAENOIDES

■ Probable distribution

**Classification** The finless porpoise was described by Cuvier in 1829. Its current scientific name, *Neophocaena phocoenoides*, taken from the Greek, means a new species of porpoise similar to *Phocoena*. Three geographical forms occur: one in Japanese waters, one in the Changjiang (Yangtze River) in China, and one in the coastal and estuarine waters of Asia.

**Local names** Each region in the finless porpoise range has its own common name for this species. It is called sunameri in Japan, jiang zhu (meaning 'river pig') in the Changjiang in China, shushuk in Pakistan and limbur in Java. In India, the name gaddada is given to the finless porpoise as well as to other small cetaceans taken in fishing nets.

**Description** The most distinctive feature of the finless porpoise is the absence of a dorsal fin. Along the back there is a ridge lined with tubercles, similar in form to the tubercles found along the dorsal fin in Burmeister's and the harbour porpoise. The tubercles extend from the area between the flippers to the beginning of the tail stock, but the extent of the area covered with tubercles differs in animals from different regions. It may be limited to a narrow row along the ridge or it may cover a wide area. This difference has been used to support the existence of subspecies.

As with other porpoises, the finless porpoise has a rounded head with no beak. There are 13-22 pairs of small spatulate teeth, typical of the porpoises, in the upper and lower jaws.

The finless porpoise is a fairly uniform grey in colour, being somewhat lighter on the underside than on the back. The colour seems to darken with age, and dead animals turn dark grey or black. Early descriptions and the name 'black finless porpoise' were based on dead animals that had already darkened.

Based on data from a few specimens, the finless porpoise reaches 1.8-1.9m. At birth it is thought to measure 70-75cm.

**Recognition at sea** The lack of a dorsal fin and the size and colour of the body make the finless porpoise easy to identify. There are no other species similar in appearance in its range.

**Habitat** Finless porpoises inhabit shallow, warm waters. They are found in marine and estuarine environments, as well as in rivers. In some parts of their range, particularly in the Changjiang in China, finless porpoises live in extremely murky water.

**Distribution and migration** The finless porpoise is known to occur in the waters of Japan, throughout Malaysia, China, Pakistan and India. Sightings have occurred as far west as the Persian Gulf. Unconfirmed sightings of finless porpoise have been reported along the Indian Ocean coast of Africa, as far south as South Africa. In China, finless porpoises occur far up the Changjiang, hundreds of kilometres from the ocean.

There appears to be some seasonal migration of finless porpoises. In Japan, they migrate into the Inland Sea of Japan in summer at calving time and then leave in winter. Along the coast of India, the results from a fishery for porpoise shows them to be most abundant during the winter months, although little is known about their abundance or distribution during the summer monsoon season, when fishing does not occur.

**Food and feeding** In Japan, finless porpoise are thought to eat sandlance (*Ammodytes*). Along the Asian coast, they also take shrimp, prawns and octopus. They seem to feed near sandbanks or forage at the bottom of rivers. This bottom feeding has been shown in captivity, where they ingest objects on the bottom of their tanks. Three animals in a zoo died from swallowing bottlecaps; one animal had 57 caps in its stomach.

**Behaviour** Finless porpoises seem to exhibit a behaviour unique among cetaceans: in the Changjiang at least, adult porpoises have been reported to carry young calves on their backs, the tubercles perhaps providing 'grips'.

Finless porpoises generally form small groups of 1-4 animals, although groups of 20-50 have been seen. They surface with little disturbance of the water. Normal vessel movements and other human activities not directed towards the porpoise do not seem to cause them to change their behaviour. Leaping is rarely seen, but spy hopping has been observed.

**Life history** Finless porpoises are born in early to midsummer after a gestation period of about 11 months. Calves may nurse 6-15 months. Adult females seem to calf every other year. Longevity and age at sexual maturity are unknown.

**World population** In a survey in the Inland Sea of Japan, a population size of 5,000 animals was estimated, but estimates do not exist for other areas.

**Man's influence** In Pakistan, there is a directed, but apparently small, take of finless porpoise. In Japan, they are protected and in China they are not taken commercially and have been protected since 1980, although the population is probably decreasing due to habitat destruction. Finless porpoises are incidentally caught in fishing nets in Sri Lanka and many other areas.

In Japan, small numbers of finless porpoises are captured for public display and some have survived in captivity for as long as 10 years. In 1976, one born in captivity in Japan lived only 17 days.

*Below: A small group of finless porpoises. In this species, the dorsal fin is lacking and replaced by a ridge lined with tubercles.*

# DALL'S PORPOISE

*PHOCOENOIDES DALLI*

Dalli-type          Truei & dalli-types

**Classification** The Dall's porpoise is similar to porpoises in the genus *Phocoena*, but different enough to warrant being placed in a separate genus. Its genus name, *Phocoenoides*, reflects this similarity. The porpoise was classified in 1885 by Frederick True, Head Curator at the Department of Biology of the US National Museum. He named the species *dalli* after an eminent zoologist, W.H. Dall, who brought this previously undescribed species to True's attention. No subspecies are recognized in the Dall's porpoise, although two distinct morphological forms, the oceanic dalli-type and coastal truei-type, occur.

**Description** Dall's porpoises have very striking external features. Most of the body is deep black, while a large patch of white extends along the sides and under the belly. The extent of the white patch is a characteristic that separates the dalli- and truei-types; in the truei-type animals, the patch extends just forward of the flipper, while in the dalli-type, it begins behind the flipper. In both types it expands back to just behind the anus. A few all-white, all-black, or grey individuals have been seen.

Dall's porpoise shares this contrasting black-and-white colour pattern with only one other species of porpoise, the spectacled porpoise (described on page 173), and indeed the Dall's and spectacled porpoise are more closely related to one another than to other species. Other porpoises are a more uniform colour that may lighten ventrally.

Adult body lengths are 1.8-2.1m (max. 2.2m) for males and 1.7-2m (max. 2.1m) for females in the nearshore truei-type, slightly less in the offshore dalli-type.

Another outstanding feature of Dall's porpoise is its robustness. It has a large girth for its length and this bulk is primarily due to enlarged muscles, with correspondingly enlarged dorsal processes on the vertebrae, and a prominent keel on the tail stock. The blubber layer is relatively thin for a coldwater species.

In contrast to the large body, the head, flippers and flukes are small. The head has no beak, but is not as blunt as in some other species. The teeth are extremely small, numbering 23-28 in the upper jaw and 24-28 in the lower jaw. The dorsal fin is triangular and often has a variable patch of white on the upper or trailing edge. The trailing edges of the tail flukes are white.

**Recognition at sea** The triangular shape of the dorsal fin and the 'rooster tail' splash created by this porpoise distinguish it from other species. Over part of its range, Dall's porpoise overlaps with the harbour porpoise, but the harbour porpoise lacks a white patch on the dorsal fin. The Pacific white-sided dolphin does have a patch of white on the dorsal fin similar to Dall's porpoise, but these species may be distinguished by the shape of the fin: falcate in the dolphin and triangular in the porpoise.

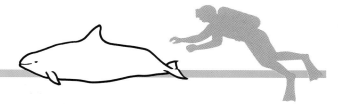

*Left: Dall's porpoises seen from above on a calm day. The typical colour pattern of the tail flukes is visible from this angle.*

*Below left: Dall's is the only pelagic porpoise and easy to distinguish at sea by its size, colour pattern, stubby body form and uniquely shaped dorsal fin. This photograph was taken through the observation bubble of a research ship.*

*Right: This action shot clearly shows the 'rooster-tail' splash created at the surface by a Dall's porpoise travelling at speed. This robust and striking species is found only in the North Pacific Ocean.*

**Habitat** Dall's porpoises are found in cold water, where the surface temperature is between 3°C and 20°C. They appear to prefer the continental shelf and slope, and when they occur close to shore are found in areas with deepwater channels.

**Distribution and migration** The Dall's porpoise is found only in the North Pacific Ocean. Its range extends from the waters around Japan, throughout the pelagic waters of the north Pacific into the Bering Sea, and along the west coast of the United States to southern California. In years when the water is particularly cold, it may occur further south. The dalli-type occurs throughout this range. The truei-type is limited to waters off the Pacific Coast of northern Japan and the Kuril Islands. In these regions, the two morphological forms occur together.

In Japanese waters, Dall's porpoises migrate seasonally. The truei-type migrates offshore in summer, while the dalli-type migrates from the Sea of Japan-Okhotsk Sea to the Pacific coast of Japan. Little is known about migration in other parts of the Dall's porpoise range, although it appears that some offshore-inshore seasonal migration may occur.

**Food and feeding** Dall's porpoises are deep divers and very fast swimmers. In the North Pacific, they take mainly surface and midwater squid and midwater lanternfish. In the coastal waters off California, they eat small schooling fish, such as hake, the juveniles of which are known to form schools in deep water.

**Behaviour** Dall's porpoises form small groups, although there are a few observations of groups as large as several thousand. They have been seen to form single-file processions of individuals, each individual separated by about 30m. They are very fast swimmers, possibly reaching speeds as high as 55kph. When they are swimming quickly, they produce a V-shaped, forwardly directed splash called a 'rooster tail'. Segregation by age, sex and reproductive status can occur.

**Life history** Animals of the dalli-type mature sexually at about 1.83m and 6 years for males, and 1.7m and 3-4 years for females. The truei-type are larger, maturing at about 1.95m and 8 years for males, and 1.87m and 6.8 years for females. Females give birth to a calf measuring 95-100cm on average at intervals of 1-3 years after a gestation period of about 11.5 months. A peak in calving occurs in summer. Although the oldest animals may live about 20 years, most animals seem to live for less than 10 years. However, this apparent age structure may represent a bias in the samples collected.

**World population** Dall's porpoise is one of the most abundant species of cetaceans in the North Pacific Ocean. Population estimates range from one to almost three million animals.

**Man's influence** There are two major sources of exploitation for Dall's porpoise. Off the coast of Japan, they have been taken for human consumption in a hand-harpoon fishery; during the 1960s and 1970s, an average of 6,000 animals was taken each year. The take has increased; in 1988, about 45,000 animals were killed. Estimates of population size in these waters suggest that the population cannot sustain such a high take.

Dall's porpoise are also taken incidentally in the international gillnet fisheries for salmon and squid, which began in 1952. Mortality from the salmon gillnets may have been as high as 10,000-20,000 animals in the 1960s, but was reduced to about 3,000 in the mid-1980s. In addition, there is mortality from Japanese salmon research vessels. The high-seas driftnet fishery for squid has not been monitored until recently and the level of kill is unknown, but could be high.

Dall's porpoises have not survived well in captivity. Although one animal was kept alive for over a year, others have died within weeks of capture and often at the time of capture.

# RIVER DOLPHINS
## PLATANISTOIDEA

Five species of dolphin are sufficiently different from all others – and sufficiently similar to each other – to have been placed in a separate taxonomic group, the superfamily Platanistoidea.

The five species are: *Platanista gangetica* (Ganges River dolphin) and *P. minor* (Indus River dolphin), from the Indian subcontinent; *Inia geoffrensis* (boto, or Amazon River dolphin) from northern South America; *Lipotes vexillifer* (baiji, or Chinese river dolphin) from eastern China; and *Pontoporia blainvillei* (franciscana) from southeastern South America.

The classification of the group is uncertain and in need of thorough review. Until quite recently, all five species were considered to be members of a single family, Platanistidae, but the consensus now is that the similarity in form and function seen within the group may well be due to the convergent evolution of species living in a similar habitat, rather than divergence from a comparatively recent common ancestry. Consequently, three or four separate families are now generally recognized within the superfamily: Platanistidae (for *Platanista gangetica* and *P. minor*), Iniidae (for *Inia geoffrensis*), Lipotidae (recognized by some taxonomists for *Lipotes vexillifer*), and Pontoporiidae (for *Pontoporia blainvillei* and perhaps also for *Lipotes vexillifer*).

All five species have adaptations to facilitate fish catching: a long, forceps-like beak with numerous small teeth in both jaws, broad flippers to allow tight turns, and unfused neck vertebrae to allow the head to move in relation to the body. All have evolved small eyes, probably because vision is impeded in turbid rivers, and only two (*Lipotes* and *Pontoporia*) have a recognizable dorsal fin; the other three species have only a fibrous dorsal ridge.

The common name given to this group – the 'river dolphins' – accurately reflects the habitat of all except the franciscana, *Pontoporia blainvillei*, which is estuarine and coastal in habit. The group name is confusing, however, in that it excludes several other cetaceans with a full or partial freshwater distribution, notably the tucuxi (*Sotalia fluviatilis*), which shares the riverine distribution of the boto, or Amazon River dolphin.

*Ganges River dolphins among mangroves. These dolphins are almost blind and use their flippers as organs of touch as they swim on their sides.*

# GANGES RIVER DOLPHIN

## PLATANISTA GANGETICA

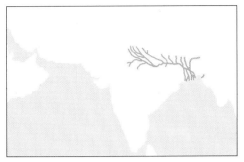

■ Approximate distribution

**Classification** The name *Platanista* was first applied to the Ganges River dolphin by the ancient Greek historian Pliny the Elder. Its literal meaning and derivation are unknown. The species name *gangetica* refers to the Ganges River, an important part of this dolphin's range.

The dolphins in the Ganges-Brahmaputra-Meghna-Karnaphuli river systems are geographically separate from those in the Indus system, and the two groups are generally regarded as separate species, *P. gangetica* and *P. minor* (=*indi*), respectively. However, the differences between them are slight, and it may be more appropriate to view them as subspecies.

**Local names** Apart from Ganges or Ganges River dolphin, the most widely used name is Ganges susu. It is also called the gangetic dolphin or blind river dolphin. There are many local names, some said to derive from the sound made by the dolphin when it breathes at the surface. The Bengali name is susuk or sishuk; the Sanskrit name is sansar or sisumar. In Assam, this dolphin is called hiho or seho; in Sylhet and Cachar, huhh. The Nepalese call it swongsu.

**Description** Females grow somewhat larger than males, reaching a maximum length of about 2.5m, compared with about 2.1m for males. The maximum weight is probably about 85kg. Females also have proportionately longer beaks, a feature that becomes noticeable after the body length reaches about 1.5m.

The prominent beak has been likened to a pair of forceps. It is long (making up to a fifth of the total body length), slender, very compressed laterally and upturned at the tip in adults. The dentition consists of 26-39 backward-curving teeth in each side of the upper jaw and 26-35 in each side of the lower jaw. The anterior upper and lower teeth, which are longer than the rear teeth, interlock and overlap the sides of the jaw, giving these diminutive dolphins an uncharacteristically wicked appearance (by dolphin standards) even when the mouth is closed. This feature shows up most strongly in juveniles; the teeth of older individuals are considerably worn and consequently less fearsome-looking.

The small head, with its rounded melon, is set off from the fat, chunky body by a constriction in the neck region. There is a pronounced ridge along the midline of the melon in front of the blowhole, which is a longitudinal slit. The tiny vestigial eye is barely visible in a deep fold just above the corner of the mouth, and the larger opening of the ear canal is above and behind the eye.

The dorsal fin is little more than a triangular ridge. The rear margin of the flukes is deeply concave and there is a small but distinct median notch. The flippers are large, broadly splayed and squared off at the ends.

The colour is uniformly greyish, but some individuals have a pinkish belly grading into the dark grey dorsal surface.

**Recognition** The only other cetacean regularly found in the same river systems is the similarly sized Irrawaddy dolphin. The latter has a dorsal fin, albeit a low one with a rounded peak and slightly concave rear margin. The most obvious difference is the Irrawaddy dolphin's lack of a beak; it has a high, bulbous forehead which overhangs the small mouth. Although it probably does not normally ascend the rivers inhabited by the Ganges River dolphin much above the limits of tidal influence, the Irrawaddy dolphin does occur in the Sundarbans and it has been sighted as far up the Pusur River as Mungla. In this region, the Irrawaddy dolphin is darker than the Ganges River dolphin.

**Habitat** Ganges River dolphins live in slow-flowing stretches of the Ganges on the plains of India, as well as some relatively clear, fast-flowing rivers in Nepal. (See also Indus River dolphin, page 182.)

**Distribution and migration** The range of Ganges River dolphins extends throughout much of modern India and Bangladesh and into parts of Nepal and Bhutan. In the Brahmaputra River system, they occur as far northeast as the Dihing, Buri Dihing and Lohit rivers in eastern Assam and as far north as the Tista River and its tributaries, which extend into Sikkim and Bhutan. They are present in Nepal as far upstream as Dioghat on the Narayani River, 250m above sea level, and in portions of the Karnali, Kosi and Mahakali (Sarda) river systems. In Bangladesh, they ascend the Meghna River system at least to Sunamganj in Sylhet district. In the Ganges system, they are present as far west as the Chambal and Yamuna (Jumna) rivers. The downstream limits are uncertain, but river dolphins are present in the Hooghly River below Calcutta, and they have been seen within 3km of the mouth of the Karnaphuli River in eastern Bangladesh. They are present in the Sundarbans.

Seasonal movements are determined in large part by the availability of water. During the dry season from October to April, many dolphins leave the tributaries and congregate in the main channels of the major rivers. Some, mainly juveniles, remain in tributary streams and become isolated in pools during the dry season. The huge Farakka Barrage, completed in 1975, has probably isolated dolphins upstream from those downstream. Other dams, such as the Kaptai Dam on the Karnaphuli River in eastern Bangladesh, have probably also contributed to the fragmentation of the population.

**Food and feeding** These dolphins eat a variety of fish, crustaceans and molluscs. They may also eat small turtles. A river dolphin which had been captured and placed in a pond attacked a domestic goose that was probing the pond bottom for food. Although the goose survived the attack, its neck and head bore rows of tooth marks on both sides. On two occasions, dolphins were observed chasing ducks on the Karnali River in Nepal. It is not clear whether waterfowl are ever actually eaten by wild river dolphins.

**Behaviour** Although side-swimming (as described in the Indus River dolphin account on page 182) is commonly observed while these dolphins are in captivity, in the wild they are also seen chasing fish in a normal upright swimming position. When a large fish is caught, the dolphin often shakes it vigorously at the surface before attempting to swallow it. These dolphins appear not to dive for longer than about three minutes. They occasionally porpoise above the water in low leaps but are generally not acrobatic at the surface. They do not bow ride.

**Life history** Little is known with certainty about the reproduction and population dynamics of these dolphins. The length at birth is usually about 90cm, although free-swimming calves as small as 67cm have been recorded. Gestation periods of eight to nine months or one year are often cited in the literature, but these estimates rest on little empirical evidence. Young

river dolphins begin taking solid food within a month or two after birth and are probably weaned before the end of their first year. Births take place during much of the year, with an apparent peak in December-January and possibly another in March-May.

**World population** Censuses have been carried out in only small portions of the Ganges River dolphin's range. For example, along a 570km stretch of the Chambal River the population was estimated as about 45 dolphins during the mid-1980s. A census of the Meghna, Brahmaputra and Jamuna rivers in Bangladesh in 1970 gave a count of a few hundred. Densities of over 180 dolphins per 100 nautical miles (185km) searched were calculated for the lower and upper Meghna and lower Jamuna rivers. The entire population of dolphins in Nepal was recently estimated as less than 100, and it is believed to be declining.

*Below: The long, forceps-like jaws of the Ganges River dolphin are superbly adapted for catching fish and other aquatic creatures in their river habitat. Note the tiny eye.*

The immense deltaic region of the Ganges, covering an area of about 20,000km², may contain a large population of dolphins that helps to repopulate upstream regions. There are probably at least several thousand Ganges River dolphins alive today.

**Man's influence** The river dolphins of the Indian subcontinent face a variety of threats. The Ganges Valley is one of the most densely populated areas of the world; nearly a tenth of the world's human population lives within the Ganges-Brahmaputra drainage area. Many rivers used by the dolphins have been or soon will be dammed for electricity and the diversion of water for irrigation. Chemical pollution, boat traffic and fishing are ever increasing.

These factors alone are serious but, in addition, the dolphins are killed purposefully and accidentally in much of their range. For example, an estimated 30-40 dolphins are killed deliberately each year by tribal peoples living along the Brahmaputra system, mainly during the dry season, October-July. They value the oil and meat for medicinal reasons and use the oil as a fish attractant. Some direct catching of dolphins also occurs in the Bhagalpur and Patna areas of the Ganges, and dolphin oil is sold commercially there and in Calcutta. In spite of official protection, dolphins are still hunted with harpoons and deliberately netted in Nepal, where there is a strong demand for their meat and oil. The latter is used as an illuminant, a folk medicine and a fish attractant.

Although some fishermen in India and Bangladesh reportedly attempt to release dolphins accidentally caught in their nets, incidental mortality is substantial, particularly in winter when water levels are low and the large pools are intensively fished.

Ganges River dolphins are present within some existing wildlife reserves, such as the Royal Chitwan National Park and the Royal Karnali-Bardia Wildlife Reserve in Nepal. However, special dolphin reserves, where rivers (or at least portions of them) are kept unspoiled and human activity is regulated, need to be created to protect this species before its conservation problems become a crisis.

# INDUS RIVER DOLPHIN

*PLATANISTA MINOR*

■ Approximate distribution

**Classification** The accepted species name for the dolphins of the Indus River system is *minor*, referring to their supposedly smaller size. The species name *indi* is used by some authors. See also Ganges River dolphin (page 180).

**Local names** This species is often called the Indus susu or the blind river dolphin. In Sind province of Pakistan, which harbours the largest surviving population, the Sindhi names bhulan and sunsar, or variants of these, are used. Most local names are supposed to imitate the sound made by the dolphins during breathing.

The name gangetic dolphin is sometimes applied generally to the dolphins in the genus *Platanista*.

**Description** There is no obvious physical difference between the Indus River dolphin and the Ganges River dolphin.

**Recognition** No other cetacean is known to occur in the Indus River system above Kotri Barrage.

**Habitat** There is no reason to believe that Indus River dolphins lived in marine waters even before Kotri Barrage was built. They are entirely confined to riverine not tidal water, and they are behaviourally adapted to live in the heavily turbid, silt-laden waters of the Indus River system in which 50 percent of the annual discharge occurs in summer (July-September) and only 15 percent in winter (October-March). Dolphins avoid the narrow, turbulent areas where a river enters foothill country or flows between shingle banks, and they also avoid irrigation canals and small by-rivers.

Dolphins are said to be most plentiful in the deep channels and at junctions where tributaries meet the main river. The substantial reduction in flow following the erection of barrages and diversion of water for irrigation has taken away much of the available habitat for dolphins. Today, the tributary rivers of the Indus, such as the Ravi and Sutlej, and even the Indus itself downstream of Kotri Barrage, virtually dry up during the winter months. The dolphins must find refuge in deep channels or isolated pools at this season.

River dolphins have been observed in water as cold as 8°C and as warm as 33°C; it appears that factors other than water temperature govern their distribution and movements. If seasonal migrations in response to any factor other than the availability of adequate water and prey took place in the past, it is likely that such migrations would have been disrupted by the barrages.

**Distribution and migration** The historic distribution was approximately between the latitudes 24°N and 34°N and the longitudes 68°E and 77°E, including the

*Exclusive to the waters of the Indus River, these constantly active and near-blind dolphins use pulsed sounds to navigate and find food near the riverbed. In form, they are identical to Ganges River dolphins.*

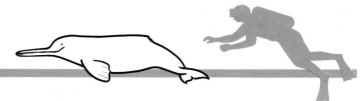

Indus River upstream to Attock as well as its major tributaries (Sutlej, Ravi, Chenab and Jhelum). This distribution has been reduced and fragmented, largely due to the construction of barrages and the withdrawal of water from the Indus River system for irrigation. There are now two dams, six barrages and ten headworks in the Indus system of Pakistan. Dolphins are confined to about 1600km of the river's length. It is occasionally claimed that dolphins pass downstream through the barrage overflows, but such movements are at best very rare.

The current distribution is centred in Sind province, between the Sukkur and Guddu barrages, a stretch of the main Indus channel about 130km long. The present upstream limit for the species is the Jinnah Barrage in northwestern Punjab. Few or no river dolphins occur downstream of Kotri Barrage. A small population remained during the early 1970s in the pondstream on the Sutlej River above the Suleimanki Barrage but was apparently exterminated in the late 1970s.

**Food and feeding** These dolphins eat mainly fish and crustaceans. Catfishes, carps, gobies, mahseers and clupeids are among the fishes eaten, and prawns apparently can be important prey at times. Adults sometimes take fish as long as 30-45cm. In captivity, they eat 500-1,500kg of fish daily. Much of their feeding activity in the wild seems to be near the bottom; they may even root in the bottom sediments for benthic prey.

**Behaviour** It is difficult to say how gregarious these dolphins are. Groups of as many as 10 are common; groups of 25-30 are exceptional. Much depends on how these groupings are defined, however. Nothing is known about the stability of groups or subgroups.

These river dolphins are essentially blind, as their eyes lack a crystalline lens. They are apparently able only to sense the intensity and perhaps the direction of light. In the almost complete absence of a visual sense, the acoustic sense is paramount. Blind river dolphins produce trains of high-frequency pulses, mainly in the range of 15-150kHz and separated by intervals of a minute or less, throughout the day and night. Their virtually constant barrage of echo-ranging sounds allows them to navigate and find food in a habitat where visibility is poor. These river dolphins not only vocalize but also swim almost constantly.

Although they surface to breathe in a normal dorso-ventral plane, these dolphins almost always swim on their sides under water. One flipper trails along or several centimetres above the bottom, with the body at an oblique angle of approximately 10° with respect to the bottom and the tail held slightly higher than the head. The head nods constantly, making a lateral sweep over the bottom. Most individuals swim mainly on their right sides. The flippers not only provide stability but also function as tactile organs, giving the dolphin important information about its position relative to the riverbed. Side-swimming river dolphins forage in water as shallow as 30cm.

It has been suggested that the gavial crocodile could have posed a threat to young river dolphins in earlier times, when both species were abundant in the Indus. However, the crocodile is now extremely rare, and humans are the dolphins' only significant predators.

**Life history** Little is known with certainty about the reproduction and population dynamics of this species. (See Ganges River dolphin, page 180).

**World population** The construction of three barrages – Sukkur in 1932, Kotri in 1955 and Guddu in 1969 – had the effect of controlling water levels so that a vast area previously almost uninhabited by man became available for agricultural and other development. The barrages also partitioned the aggregate population into small, virtually isolated groups.

Surveys have been conducted more or less regularly since the early 1970s, mainly in the Sukkur-Guddu stretch, but occasionally in other parts of the species range. The best that can be said of the results is that they provide an order-of-magnitude estimate of the population size, which is a few hundred – certainly much less than a thousand. Although repeated surveys from 1974 to 1980 indicated a steady increase in the Sukkur-to-Guddu population, this apparent increase is probably at least partly due to improved counting procedures and other factors in addition to an actual growth in the dolphin population. Nevertheless, the results do seem to show that the population in this portion of the river (Sind province) has at least been maintaining itself.

Upstream from the Guddu barrage to the Jinnah barrage (Punjab province), only about 60-70 dolphins survived in the mid-1980s.

**Man's influence** Exploitation of river dolphins in the Indus River system has been both direct and incidental. Specially trained otters were once used to help catch dolphins near Sukkur. The feeding otters apparently attracted the dolphins to an area where they were more easily netted. Other fishermen in Sind have used herons and egrets, attached to their boats by a long lead, to track dolphins. A special net, called a 'kularee', was held by a fisherman standing on a specially erected platform high on the river bank. When a dolphin approached near enough, the man would throw the kularee over it and jump into the water to secure the animal in the net. In some cases, a small live fish would be dangled on a line into the water to lure the dolphin within range.

Most Muslims traditionally shunned dolphin meat and oil, but low-caste Hindus valued both products highly in some areas. They ate the meat and used the oil for cooking. Some of the oil was sold for waterproofing boats and preserving leather, for mixing with flour to make animal food, or as a liniment. People along the Indus traditionally considered the oils of dolphins, certain turtles, crocodiles and pelicans to be capable of invigorating the back and loins and combating rheumatism. Dolphin oil was also used for lighting homes. Sansee women ate dolphin flesh in the expectation that it would enhance their fertility.

Accidental capture in fishing nets has long been responsible for a certain amount of dolphin mortality in the Indus. The fishermen have not always welcomed such a by-catch, however, since their nets are often damaged by the struggling dolphins.

The Indus River dolphin has had complete legal protection in Sind province since 1972 and in Punjab since 1973. The Sukkur-Guddu stretch of the river was declared a dolphin reserve in December 1974. Hunting continued in Sind through the 1970s, but the ban was said to have become enforced by the early 1980s.

Several dolphins captured in the Indus River during the late 1960s were flown to San Francisco, California, and kept alive for a few months at the Steinhart Aquarium. G. Pilleri and his colleagues at the Brain Anatomy Institute in Berne, Switzerland, began collecting Indus River dolphins in 1969, and they managed to keep some of their dolphins alive in captivity in Switzerland for several years. The observational and experimental work with captive specimens has provided some information on the behaviour and sensory systems of these dolphins.

# BOTO (AMAZON RIVER DOLPHIN)

## INIA GEOFFRENSIS

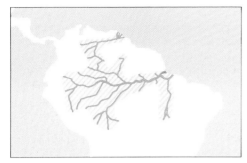

■ Main rivers          Maximum range

**Classification** *Inia* is the name used for this dolphin by the Guarayo Indians along the San Miguel River in Bolivia. Geoffroy St. Hilaire was a French naturalist who collected zoological specimens for Napoleon Bonaparte. He obtained the type specimen from Portugal after it had been collected in the upper Amazon. Two or perhaps three subspecies are recognized in this river dolphin.

**Local names** This dolphin is called boto vermelho, or just boto (sometimes incorrectly spelled bouto), in Portuguese-speaking Brazil and bufeo or tonina in Spanish-speaking Bolivia, Peru, Colombia and Venezuela. The internationally accepted common name for the species is boutu, but should be boto.

**Description** Males can be close to 2.6m long and weigh up to 160kg, while females reach 2m and 100kg. These odd-looking dolphins have a long beak lined by well over 100 teeth (23-35 per row). Unlike any other dolphin, the boto has a differentiated dentition. The front teeth are conical but, like those of most dolphins, the rear teeth are shaped more like molars. The upper surface of the beak has rows of stiff, flattened hairs that presumably serve as tactile organs. The mouthline is turned up at the corners to suggest a perpetual smile. The domelike melon is malleable and the animal inflates or deflates it at will.

Instead of a dorsal fin, there is a broad-based triangular hump about two-thirds of the way back from the tip of the snout, continuous with a prominent median ridge extending forward and backward from the hump. The broad flukes are often frayed or ragged along their concave rear margins. The long, flexible flippers are used for propulsion to some extent as well as for steering.

Although individuals, groups or populations of some other dolphin species have pinkish tones in their coloration, the Amazon River dolphin is the only species for which pinkness is a consistent feature. It is sometimes called the pink dolphin. There is much local or regional variation, but for the most part young animals are dark grey dorsally and lighter grey ventrally. They lighten with age, the snout, sides, undersides and flukes becoming pinkish. Adults, especially males, can be completely pink or blotched pink. Several captive dolphins kept in clear, shallow water became darker over time, and it was suggested that the clarity of water, and consequent exposure to sunlight, influenced the pigmentation to some degree. In the wild, dolphins living in black or turbid water are paler than those in clear water.

**Recognition** Since it never enters marine waters, the boto is only likely to be confused with cetaceans that enter its freshwater habitat in tropical eastern South America. It shares much of its range with the smaller tucuxi (*Sotalia fluviatilis*, see page 135), but the two species are readily distinguished by the latter's relatively high, falcate dorsal fin, much shorter snout and generally more dolphinlike appearance and behaviour. Bottlenose dolphins may enter the estuaries of rivers inhabited by boto but are readily distinguished from them by the same features as the tucuxi.

**Habitat** During the flood season (December-June), these dolphins readily leave the main river channels and enter the inundated forests and grasslands. They are found mainly in brownish, turbid and slow-moving water. During the dry season, some animals, especially juveniles, become trapped in stagnant ponds. As long as the ponds do not dry up entirely

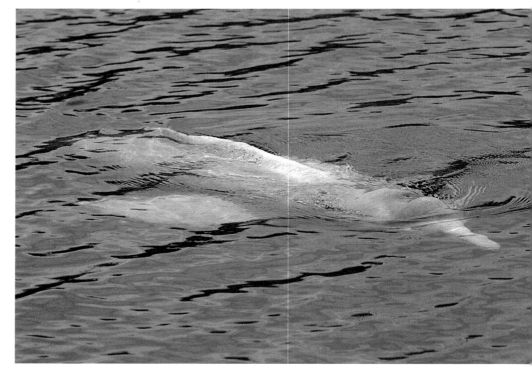

*Above right: In these silt-laden waters, the typical habitat of* Inia geoffrensis, *sighting live animals can be very difficult.*

*Left: Some botos are accidentally drowned in fishing nets; others are deliberately killed.*

*Below: During the flood season, botos leave the rivers and range far afield out into grasslands and forests in clear waters.*

and they are left undisturbed, the dolphins survive such entrapment well. Many catfishes and characids are usually trapped as well, making them easy prey for the dolphins.

**Distribution and migration** This tropical river dolphin inhabits the Amazon and Orinoco drainage basins of South America and thus occurs mainly in five countries: Brazil, Bolivia, Peru, Colombia and Venezuela. It is found along almost the entire length of the Orinoco River. In the Amazon system, it is found above Iquitos in Peru, more than 4,000km from the sea. Although the dolphins in the Beni and Guapore river systems of Bolivia are considered by some to be isolated from those in the Brazilian Amazon, the Amazon and upper Madeira (from which the Beni and Guapore branch) are connected. Seasonal migrations, if they occur, are apparently local and short range, undertaken mainly in response to changing water levels.

**Food and feeding** Most of the food remains in the stomachs of these dolphins have been from fishes and crabs. They seem to prefer solitary, bottom-dwelling fish, although they also prey regularly on schooling species. The stomach of one animal caught in a gillnet in the Japura River contained a bewildering assortment of fish parts, representing nine families and approximately 11 species. In addition, it contained a 7cm turtle. The list of fishes confirmed as prey of botos includes at least 18 families and 50 species. In most cases, large fish are torn into pieces to help swallowing. Large or hard-bodied prey are manoeuvred to the back of the mouth and crushed or chewed before being swallowed.

**Behaviour** Amazon River dolphins are essentially solitary and are rarely seen in groups larger than two in some areas, but cohesive groups of 12-15 have also been observed. Group size probably depends at least partly on water levels and the availability of prey. Since the dolphins are forced into restricted areas of adequate water depth during the dry season, the groupings may tend to appear larger at this time than during the floods.

Many observers have remarked on the way small groups of individuals tend to remain in the same area for days or weeks, in some instances even after being chased and shot at. Their degree of shyness varies from area to area, no doubt depending on the nature of their experience with people and boats. Hunting and harassment seem to suppress these dolphins' natural inquisitiveness.

In eastern Colombia at least, botos sometimes associate closely with giant river otters. The otters fish close to shore while the dolphins remain a few metres farther out, possibly catching fish that escape from the otters.

These dolphins are generally slow-moving (perhaps 3-4kph, on average). Their unfused cervical vertebrae allow the head to move in any direction. They often surface at a fairly flat angle, showing the top of the head, then the dorsal fin and a portion of back, before humping the tail and descending. They seldom show flukes, and dives rarely last longer than 90 seconds. Their exhalations can be explosive and loud at times.

Amazon River dolphins have degenerate eyes but can see reasonably well. They sometimes lift the head high enough above the surface to expose the eyes, apparently to examine their environment. Their large, bulging cheeks are thought to hamper vision below the horizontal plane of the eyes, but they seem to compensate for this by frequently swimming upside down.

**Life history** Males are sexually mature by the time they are about 2m long, and females are usually mature when somewhat less than 1.8m long. Size at birth is approximately 80cm and 7-8kg. Most calving is believed to occur during May to July, coinciding with peak water levels and the start of their seasonal decline. The estimated gestation period is 10-11 months. Females simultaneously pregnant and lactating have been reported.

Males have lived in captivity for at least 19 years; the teeth of a 2m female had 28 annual growth layers. Thus, these dolphins might live as long as 30 years.

**World population** There are no good population estimates for these dolphins. They are still abundant, however, and continue to occupy most of their extensive historic range.

**Man's influence** The escalating development of the Amazon Basin is transforming the habitat of the river dolphins. Small-scale projects impound water for irrigation, causing dolphins and other organisms to become trapped in ponds or lakes that dry up. Large-scale hydroelectric projects disrupt movements of the dolphins and their prey and create small isolated populations. Fishermen increasingly regard them as competitors and destroyers of fishing gear. The dried eyeballs and sex organs of Amazon dolphins, taken incidentally in Brazil, are sometimes sold as charms for attracting love partners. The meat and oil of dolphins caught incidentally in the Orinoco system are consumed, the latter still regarded by some local people as having medicinal properties.

Professional hunters were netting dolphins deliberately in Bolivia's Ichilo River as recently as the early 1970s. Such hunting was banned in the mid-1970s, but shooting of dolphins by members of Bolivia's many hunting and fishing clubs reportedly continued. Traditionally, river people in much of the Amazon River dolphins' range were superstitious and, whether out of reverence or dread, they did not intentionally hunt them. As the great South American river systems have been rapidly colonized and developed during the late twentieth century, the indulgent attitudes of primitive peoples toward the dolphins have been eroded or made obsolete.

As of 1988, the boto was explicitly protected in all areas of Brazil and Bolivia and implicitly or partially protected by wildlife laws established in Peru, Colombia and Venezuela.

The Amazon River dolphin has been the most popular of the river dolphins for aquarium collectors. About 100 were taken from Brazil, Colombia and Venezuela from the mid-1950s to the mid-1970s for the aquarium trade. They are hardy and tractable. The opportunity to work with captive animals has meant that Amazon River dolphins were among the first cetaceans proven to be active echolocators. Since the mid-1970s, European and South American institutions have continued to exhibit live botos. Five animals were collected in Venezuela in 1975 for the Duisberg Zoo in West Germany. Two were on display at an aquarium in Valencia, Venezuela, in 1985 and at least 12 were live-captured in Brazil in 1985.

# BAIJI (CHINESE RIVER DOLPHIN)

*LIPOTES VEXILLIFER*

■ Maximum range

**Classification** There is only one species in this genus. The genus name is from the Greek *leipo* meaning 'left behind'; it refers to the species' restricted distribution. *Vexillifer* derives from the Latin *vexillum*, 'a banner', and the suffix - *fer*, 'to bear'.

**Local names** In China, fishermen call this dolphin baiji and this is also its internationally agreed common name. It is also sometimes known in English as the Chinese river dolphin, Yangtze dolphin or Yangtze River dolphin.

**Description** The maximum length is just over 2.5m, and baiji can weigh more than 160kg. Males appear to be smaller than females, reaching 2.2m and 125kg. The baiji has a long, narrow beak, slightly upturned at the tip, with 30-35 conical teeth in each row. The forehead is steep, the eyes small, degenerate and located just above the angle of the gape. The dorsal fin is triangular with a blunt peak.

Baiji are pale bluish grey dorsally and white ventrally. The flukes and flippers are bluish grey above and white below. The lower jaw is white, as is the lower margin of the upper jaw. Broad white stripes intrude from below onto the bluish grey regions between the flipper and ear opening and in two areas on either side of the tail stock.

**Recognition** The only other cetacean commonly found in the baiji's range is the finless porpoise (see page 175). Although their body size and colour are similar and they are sometimes seen together, these two species should be easy to distinguish. The finless porpoise has no dorsal fin or hump and no beak, and it tends to be more active and less shy than the baiji, often approaching shore and tolerating vessel traffic.

**Habitat** Over the last three and a half centuries, major changes have occurred in the baiji's habitat. For example, huge amounts of sediment have been deposited in Dongting Lake, and the land around it has been diked and cultivated. In the middle and lower portions presently inhabited by baiji, the Changjiang (Yangtze River) is wide, open and slow moving, with an average current speed of 1-2m per second. It has many sandbars, and the downstream ends of well-developed sandbars tend to create zones of high productivity, where fish, fishermen and baiji become concentrated, especially during rainy seasons.

**Distribution and migration** The baiji is exclusive to China. Until recently, Western scientists believed that it lived mainly in Dongting Lake and associated rivers. However, it is now known to have inhabited a much larger area, virtually from the mouth of the Changjiang to Yichang. Much of this range is still inhabited by baiji, but in greatly reduced numbers. Seasonal migrations are apparently short and local, probably related to changes in water level and prey density.

**Food and feeding** Baiji apparently feed on a great variety of fishes, including a species of long, eel-like catfish and another large-scaled species, both of which have been found in stomachs.

**Behaviour** Group size occasionally reaches 8-10 animals, but individuals, pairs or groups of three to six are most common. Chinese scientists believe that the aggregate population consists of a number of small subpopulations whose integrity is maintained by their association with particular sandbar areas.

Normally when a baiji approaches the surface, its head region breaks the surface first, followed by the back and dorsal fin. Then the head disappears and the dorsal fin remains exposed for some time before the animal disappears. From a distance, sometimes only the dorsal fin can be seen above the surface. Generally, the flukes are not seen as the animal dives. Baiji are usually difficult to approach and wary of boats.

**Life history** The reproductive biology of this species has been little studied. Calves are born at a body length of less than 95cm and weighing less than 10kg.

**World population** The baiji is considered the most endangered cetacean. Its estimated population size is in the low to mid hundreds, and the decline in numbers is believed to be continuing.

**Man's influence** Baiji are not only in competition for food with China's human population, but they also run foul of fishing gear with alarming frequency. In fact, hooks on longlines set in prime fishing areas, mainly for sturgeon, are responsible for nearly half the documented baiji mortalities. Ship traffic on the Changjiang approximately doubles every 10 years, and collisions with vessel propellers cause some dolphin mortality. Lakes along the middle and lower reaches of the river are being intensively 'reclaimed' for farmland, and as well as reducing the water area this trend has had a severe impact on fish productivity, which in turn has probably lowered the river's carrying capacity for fish-eating dolphins.

Conservation of the baiji has become a high priority with the Chinese government. The species is explicitly protected from purposeful killing, and a plan is underway to create several reserves, where baiji will be held in semi-captive conditions.

The first baiji to be brought into captivity was a young male captured in 1980 and held at the Institute of Marine Biology in Wuhan. This animal, 'Qi Qi', was still alive in March 1987, as was a young female, 'Zhen Zhen', captured in March 1986. Maintenance and propagation of baiji in captivity are of particular importance, considering their precarious situation in the wild.

*Left: The shy baiji is difficult to photograph. This shot shows an individual just surfacing, the long beak emerging first. This fish-eating dolphin, probably the most endangered cetacean, competes for food with man in the overcrowded waters of the Changjiang (Yangtze River).*

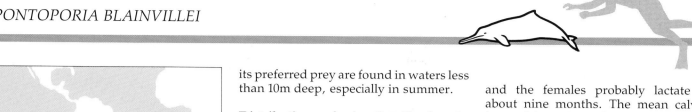

# FRANCISCANA

*PONTOPORIA BLAINVILLEI*

■ Approximate range

**Classification** The franciscana belongs to a monotypic genus and possibly to a separate family of dolphins. Its closest living relative appears to be the baiji (Chinese river dolphin, see page 186). The generic name, *Pontoporia*, is a combination of the Greek *pontos* for 'open sea' and *poros* for 'passage' or 'crossing', apparently referring to the belief, now known to be false, that this dolphin moved interchangeably between salt and fresh water. The specific name refers to Blainville, a famous French naturalist.

**Local names** This dolphin is often called the La Plata dolphin, referring to its distribution in the La Plata estuary in Uruguay. Although it is known as franciscana in Spanish-speaking Uruguay and Argentina, the Portuguese-speaking Brazilians call it toninha or cachimbo.

**Description** Females consistently grow larger than males. The longest measured female was 1.74m, and the heaviest nonpregnant female weighed more than 53kg. The longest male was 1.58m, and the heaviest male weighed 43kg.

The most obvious distinguishing feature of this dolphin is its long, narrow beak, which becomes proportionately longer with age. The dorsal fin is triangular, with a rounded peak. Colour is generally grey, with the dorsal side darker than the ventral. There are usually 51-58 teeth in each row, meaning that most individuals have a total of more than 200 teeth. The front teeth are slightly longer, although this feature is much less evident in *Pontoporia* than in *Platanista*.

**Recognition at sea** The long, narrow beak and small, triangular dorsal fin help to distinguish this species from most other small marine toothed whales and dolphins within its range.

**Habitat** Although related to the platanistoid river dolphins, the franciscana is primarily a marine species. It appears to live mainly inside the 30m contour, and its preferred prey are found in waters less than 10m deep, especially in summer.

**Distribution and migration** The franciscana's documented range is limited to coastal waters of eastern South America, from Peninsula Valdés in Argentina (42°30'S) to the Doce River mouth near Regencia, Brazil (19°37'S).

**Food and feeding** These dolphins eat fish (especially sciaenids), squid, octopus and crustaceans. Penaeid shrimps are taken especially by young franciscanas. Much of their prey is found at or near the bottom. In Brazil, franciscanas appear to prey selectively on benthic sciaenids less than 5cm long.

**Behaviour** There are few published observations of live franciscanas. They do not form large groups and generally avoid boats. Seven-gilled sharks (*Notorhynchus cepedianus*) and hammerhead sharks (*Sphyrna* spp.) prey on franciscanas caught in gillnets, but it is not known whether they attack free-swimming dolphins. Since killer whales are fairly common in parts of the franciscanas' range, they probably prey on them.

**Life history** Both sexes reach sexual maturity at two to three years of age, when males weigh 25-29kg and females 33-35kg. Females are physically mature by about four years of age. At birth, these dolphins are about 75-80cm long and weigh 7.3-8.5kg.

Gestation lasts about 10.5-11.1 months and the peak calving season is in November and December. Calves begin taking solid food at about three months of age, and the females probably lactate for about nine months. The mean calving interval is estimated as two years. Instances are known of females lactating and being pregnant simultaneously.

The oldest documented female was only 13 years old, suggesting that the life span of females is no more than about 15 years. The oldest male was 16 years old, suggesting they may live 18-20 years.

**World population** There is no information on the world population or conservation status of franciscanas.

**Man's influence** Since the 1940s, hundreds to several thousands of franciscanas have been killed annually in gillnets. There has been a large and relatively well-documented incidental catch of franciscanas in the Uruguayan shark fishery centred at Punta del Diablo. In 1969, the estimated take was 2,000 animals. The level of mortality at Punta del Diablo and elsewhere in Uruguay has declined since 1975 because of changes in the fishery. Other similar gillnet fisheries, for sharks as well as for bony fishes, exist in Argentina and Brazil, so franciscanas are incidentally exploited over a large part of their range. However, there is no known direct fishery for them.

In one area of Argentina, the back muscles of fresh franciscanas caught incidentally are salted, sun-dried and eaten by local Turks, Jews and Arabs. Franciscanas have not been held in captivity.

*One of the smallest of all cetaceans, the franciscana is restricted to coastal waters of eastern South America. Few live specimens have been seen in the wild.*

# INDEX

Page numbers in **bold** indicate major references, including accompanying photographs and illustrations. Page numbers in *italics* indicate captions to other photographs and illustrations. Less important text entries are shown in normal type.

# PICTURE CREDITS

## Artists

Copyright of the artwork illustrations on the pages following the artists' names is the property of Salamander Books Ltd., except where indicated. The artwork illustrations have been credited by page number.

Peter Bull Art Studio: 31, 40, and the distribution maps on pages 56-187

Rod Ferring: 11, 17, 19, 32, 49

Pieter Arend Folkens © Pieter Arend Folkens: 13

Bruce Pearson: Endpapers, 2-3, 54-5, 62-3, 66-7, 84-5, 92-3, 100-1, 116-7, 130-1, 168-9, 178-9

David Thompson: Species illustrations on pages 104, 109, 110, 111, 112, 113, 144, 159, 160, 173, 182, 187 and scale outline drawings on pages 56-187

## Photographers

The publishers wish to thank the following photographers and agencies who have supplied photographs for this book. The photographs have been credited by page number and position on the page: (B) Bottom, (T) Top, (C) Centre, (BL) bottom left etc.

Heather Angel: 16(T), 70(CR)

Ardea London Ltd: 21(Francois Gohier), 64(T,B, Francois Gohier), 70(T, Francois Gohier), 71(Francois Gohier), 73(Francois Gohier), 148(Liz & Tony Bomford), 149(T, Liz & Tony Bomford)

Biofoto, Denmark: 170(B, T.B. Sorensen), 171(T, T.B. Sorensen)

Bruce Coleman Ltd.: 162-3(T, Francisco Erize)

Mark D. Conlin: 68

Vera M. F. da Silva: 135, 184(C,B)

Earthviews: 10(Ken Balcomb), 14(Robert Pitman), 15(Richard Sears), 33(Ken Balcomb), 36(Bob Talbot), 38(Robert Pitman), 41(C, Robert Pitman), 43(Pieter Folkens), 57(Bruce Krogman), 60(R. Payne), 61(Bill Dawbin), 76(Robert Pitman), 77(B. Tershy & C. Strong), 78(BL, H. Suzuki), 99(S. Leatherwood), 103(K. Balcomb), 105(James D Watt), 112(B, Paul Jones), 118-119(B, K.C. Balcomb), 121(B), 124(James D Watt), 125(Howard Hall), 132-3(Bill Dawbin) 134(Robert Pitman), 139(Robert Pitman), 140(Marc Webber), 149(B, Richard Sears), 151(C, Richard Sears), 153(Robert Pitman), 156(Birgit Winning), 158(Robert Pitman), 164(Robert Pitman), 166(Robert Pitman), 167(Robert Pitman), 172(B, Robert Pitman), 174(Robert Pitman), 175(B, Ken Balcomb), 176(T, K. Balcomb)

Deborah A. Glockner-Ferrari: 29(T), 34, 52-3, 123(TR)

M. P. Harris: 127(C)

Therese L. Hoban: 35(C)

Rus Hoelzel: 8-9, 22(T), 23(TL,TR), 121(C)

Hubbs Sea World Research Institute: 35(B)

International Fund for Animal Welfare: 20(B), 86, 88(T,C), 128-129(T), 137(T)

Thomas Jefferson: 177

Joyce Photographics: 41(B)

Fujio Kasamatsu: 107(B), 111(B), 157

Frank Lane Picture Agency Ltd: 20(T, M.B. Withers), 90(Marineland of Florida), 181(Ted Stephenson)

Stephen Leatherwood: 44(B), 46, 69, 78-9(B), 120( c Evans), 154, 162(B)

Tony Martin: 16(B), 18, 23(CR), 24(CR), 25, 27(CL), 30(BL, BR), 31(B), 37, 39, 44(C), 47, 48(TC,TR), 49(TL,TC,BR), 72, 83(T), 87(C,B), 94, 95, 96-7(T), 96(B), 97(B), 119(T), 145

National Marine Fisheries Service: 26(CR, H. Braham), 152(C)

Natural History Photographic Agency: 42(Agence Nature), 65(Agence Nature)

Nature Photographers Ltd.: 81(T, Paul Sterry), 127(B, C.H. Gomersall), 170(TR, C. Mylne)

Chris Newbert: 123(TL)

Michael W. Newcomer: 28-9(B), 74, 102, 107(C), 123(B), 138-9(B), 142, 146(B), 152(B), 167(T), 176(B)

Ocean Images, Inc.: 24(B, Doc White), 27(B, Al Giddings), 83(B, Al Giddings, C, Rosemary Chastney)

Okeanos Ocean Research Foundation: 79(T)

Oxford Scientific Films: 80(Ben Osborne), 81(B, Ben Osborne), 113(B, Kim Westerskov), 136-7(B, Kim Westerskov)

Pacific Ocean Stock: Half-title(James D. Watt), 26(T, Dan McSweeney), 59(R.M. Mandojana), 129(B, James D. Watt)

W.F. Perrin: 51

Photobank Image Library: 161(S. Dawson)

Planet Earth Pictures: 89(T. Arnbom), 115(James D. Watt)

Bill Rossiter: 151(B)

Michael Scott: 58

Sea World: 163(TR, Frank S. Todd)

Gregory Silber: 172(C)

Tom Stack & Associates: 6(Jeff Foott), 22(B), 45(Dave B. Fleetham), 82(Ed Robinson), 118(T, Jeff Foott), 122(Ed Robinson), 136(C, Brian Parker), 141(T, Jack Swenson)

Survival Anglia: 19(Jeff Foott), 185(Alan Root)

B. Tershy: 91

D. Thompson: 146-7(T), 165

A.J. Ward: 108

Bernd Wursig: 143, 155, 186

Zefa: 4(Panda Photos), 98(Wisniewski), 141(C, B. Curtsinger)

# ACKNOWLEDGEMENTS

The publishers acknowledge the following sources for artwork illustrations: The sperm whale head on page 17 is based on an illustration in the Journal of The Marine Biological Association of the UK, 58:581-7 (M. R. Clarke). The sound production and reception diagram on page 19 is based on published material attributed to Ken Norris. The portions of humpback whale songs on page 31 are taken from a paper by H. E. Winn, T. J. Thompson, W. C. Cummings, J. Hain, J. Hudnall, H. Hays, and W. W. Steiner in Behav. ecol. sociobiol. Volume 8, pages 41-46. The map of magnetic contours and live strandings on page 40 is based on material supplied by the Zoology Department of the British Museum (Natural History), the British Geological Survey and Dr. Margaret Klinowska.

The publishers would like to thank the following people for their help in preparing this book: Joanne King for excellent picture research, Stuart Craik for preparing the index so efficiently and Mike Harrington of SX Composing Ltd. for his skill, dedication and patience during the typesetting process.

Tony Martin would like to thank the following people for their prompt and thorough reviews of portions of the text: Dr. Larry Barnes, Sidney Brown, Phil Clapham, Dr. Jonathan Gordon, Dr. Phil Hammond, Dr. Rus Hoelzel, Simon Northridge and Dave Rugh. Generous help in various ways was provided by Gilly Banks, Martin Knowelden, Stan Minasian and a large number of photographers around the world who provided their material for consideration.